D0699925

The Dynamic Constitution

In this book Harvard law professor Richard H. Fallon, Jr., introduces nonlawyers to the workings of American Constitutional Law. He writes with clarity and vigor about leading constitutional doctrines and issues, including the freedom of speech, the freedom of religion, the guarantee of equal protection, rights to fair procedures, and rights to privacy and sexual autonomy. Along the way, Fallon describes many of the fascinating cases and personalities that have shaped constitutional law. He shows how historical, cultural, and other factors have influenced constitutional adjudication, making clear the dynamic nature of the Constitution. For both the courts and the American people, Fallon argues, the Constitution must serve as a dynamic document that adapts to the changing conditions inherent in human affairs. Fallon goes on to defend dynamic constitutionalism by confronting head on the concerns that some critics have raised.

Richard H. Fallon, Jr., is the Ralph S. Tyler Professor of Constitutional Law at the Harvard Law School. He earned his B.A. from Yale University, matriculated as a Rhodes Scholar at Oxford University, and then took his legal education at the Yale Law School. Widely known for his expertise in constitutional law and the federal courts, Fallon has been a valuable advisor to many organizations and litigants facing constitutional issues. Professor Fallon is also an accomplished educator. He is coeditor of a leading constitutional law case book, and he was voted the most outstanding teacher on the Harvard Law School faculty by the 2000 graduating class. Born and raised in Maine, Dick Fallon now lives with his family in Belmont, Massachusetts.

THE DYNAMIC
CONSTITUTION

An Introduction to American
Constitutional Law

Richard H. Fallon, Jr.
Harvard University

CAMBRIDGE
UNIVERSITY PRESS
OCM54349624

CAMBRIDGE UNIVERSITY PRESS
Cambridge, New York, Melbourne, Madrid, Cape Town, Singapore, São Paulo

Cambridge University Press
32 Avenue of the Americas, New York, NY 10013–2473, USA

www.cambridge.org
Information on this title:www.cambridge.org/9780521840941

First published 2004
First paperback edition published 2005
Reprinted 2006

Printed in the United States of America

A catalogue record for this book is available from the British Library.

Library of Congress Cataloguing in Publication Data
Fallon, Richard H., 1952–
The dynamic Constitution: an introduction to American constitutional
law / Richard H. Fallon, Jr.
p.   cm.
Includes bibliographical references and index.
ISBN 0-521-84094-5 – ISBN 0-521-60078-2 (pbk.)
1. Constitutional law – United States.   I. Title.
KF4550.F35   2004
342.73 – dc22   2004043578

ISBN-13   978-0-521-84094-1 hardback
ISBN-10   0-521-84094-5 hardback

ISBN-13   978-0-521-60078-1 paperback
ISBN-10   0-521-60078-2 paperback

For Jenny

Contents

Preface	*page* xi
Prologue: Bush v. Gore	xv
Introduction: The Dynamic Constitution	1
History	2
Original Constitutional Design	4
The Constitution as Higher Law: Foundations of Judicial Review	9
Marbury v. Madison: An Enduring Symbol of Judicial Power	10
Politics and Judicial Review	14
A Preliminary Perspective on How the Supreme Court Interprets the Constitution	16
A Brief History of Judicial Review	19
An Outline of What Is to Come	26
Part I: Individual Rights Under the Constitution	
1 **Freedom of Speech**	31
The Foundations of Modern Doctrine	32
Proximate Origins of Modern Doctrine	34
Expressive Conduct	42
Shocking and Offensive Speech	44
Remaining Unprotected Categories, Including Obscenity	45
Commercial Speech	48
The Broadcast Media	51
Freedom to Associate and Not to Associate	53
Concluding Note	55

2　**Freedom of Religion**   57
　　Introduction to the Establishment Clause   59
　　Religion in the Public Schools   61
　　Governmental Aid to Religious Institutions   63
　　The Free Exercise Clause   67
　　Voluntary Governmental Accommodations of Religion   71
　　Tensions Between the Free Exercise and
　　　　Establishment Clauses   72

3　**Protection of Economic Liberties**   75
　　Early History   76
　　The Fourteenth Amendment   78
　　Substantive Due Process   81
　　Modern Contracts Clause Doctrine   86
　　The Takings Clause   87
　　Concluding Thoughts   89

4　**Rights to Fair Procedures**   91
　　Procedural Rights in Criminal Cases   92
　　Time, Elections, and Change   97
　　The Law on the Books versus the Law in Practice   98
　　Procedural Rights in Civil Cases   100
　　Due Process in Administrative Proceedings   101

5　**Equal Protection of the Laws**   106
　　Equal Protection and the Constitution   109
　　Rational Basis Review   111
　　Race and the Constitution: Invidious Discrimination   114
　　Race and the Constitution: Disparate Impact   122
　　Affirmative Action   123
　　Gender and the Constitution   129
　　Discrimination Against Homosexuals   133
　　Conclusion   136

6　**Fundamental Rights**   138
　　The Idea of Fundamental Rights   140
　　Sexual Privacy or Autonomy   142
　　Roe v. Wade and Abortion Rights   144
　　Gay Rights   147

Rights Involving Death and Dying 151
Fundamental Rights Involving the Family 152
Conclusion 154

Part II: The Constitutional Separation of Powers

7 **The Powers of Congress** 157
Elements of "The Original Understanding" 160
Doctrinal and Conceptual History 162
Crisis and Revision 164
The Rehnquist Court: A Shift of Direction? 166
Congressional Regulation of State and
    Local Governments 168
The Spending Power 171
Concluding Thoughts 172

8 **Executive Power** 173
The *Youngstown* Case 174
Foreign Affairs 177
Delegated Power in Domestic Affairs 178
Legislative Vetoes and Line-Item Vetoes 180
Appointments and Removals 184

9 **Judicial Power** 189
The Character of Judicial Power 191
Anxieties About Judicial Power 194
Limits on Judicial Power 200

Part III: Further Issues of Constitutional Structure and Individual Rights

10 **Elections, Political Democracy, and the Constitution** 207
Voting Rights: The "One-Person, One-Vote" Cases 210
Beyond "One-Person, One-Vote" 212
Majority–Minority Districting 214
Equality in the Counting of Votes 216
Ballot Access 218
Campaign Speech and Finance Regulation 220
Conclusion 224

11 **Structural Limits on State Power and Resulting
    Individual Rights**   225
    How Federal Power and Federal Law Can Restrict
        State Power   226
    The Privileges and Immunities Clause   227
    The "Dormant" Commerce Clause   231
    The States as "Market Participants"   234
    Conclusion   235

12 **The Constitution in War and Emergency**   237
    The Power to Initiate War   240
    Federal Powers During Wartime   242
    War and Individual Rights   243
    The Constitution and the "War" on Terrorism   247
    Some Categorical Limits on Constitutional Rights   249
    Conclusion   252

13 **The Reach of the Constitution and Congress's
    Enforcement Power**   254
    State Action Doctrine   254
    The Paucity of "Positive" Fundamental Rights   257
    Congressional Power to "Enforce" the
        Reconstruction Amendments   262

14 **Conclusion**   269

    Appendix: The Constitution of the United States   278

    Notes   299
    Index   327

Preface

This book provides an introduction to contemporary constitutional law for intelligent readers who are not, or not yet, lawyers. It is a reasonably short book, which leaves out much detail. I have also done my best to write it in plain language – or at least to explain the jargon used by courts and lawyers before employing it myself. But the book does not talk down to the reader or omit central considerations. It aspires both to inform and to challenge nonlawyers who are interested in constitutional law, as well as law students seeking an introduction to the subject and lawyers who would like a refresher.

I still remember the intellectual thrill of my own first encounter with a book about constitutional law. It came in 1971, when I was a college undergraduate. The book was Robert McCloskey's *The American Supreme Court*, written in 1960. Over the years, when people have asked me to recommend a book introducing constitutional law to nonlawyers, I have usually named McCloskey's. Increasingly, however, I have done so hesitantly. The organization of McCloskey's book is mainly historical. It discusses successive eras in the history of the Supreme Court, often brilliantly, but without attempting to provide the clear portrait of contemporary constitutional law, and of the debates surrounding it, that some readers want. In addition, *The American Supreme Court* has inevitably grown dated with the passage of time, despite able efforts by one of McCloskey's former students to summarize recent developments in additional chapters. McCloskey's book naturally reflects the political and scholarly concerns of the period in which he wrote it, now more than four decades ago. It is time for a new introduction to American constitutional law, written in the twenty-first century for a contemporary audience.

In writing a book for twenty-first-century readers, I have addressed constitutional law from several simultaneous perspectives. First, and perhaps most important, this book sketches the basic outlines of current constitutional doctrine. In chapters with headings such as "The Powers of Congress," "The Freedom of Speech," "The Equal Protection of the Laws," and "The Constitution in War and Emergency," the book discusses leading Supreme Court cases dealing with the powers of Congress and the President and with such issues as hate speech, race and gender discrimination, abortion, gay rights, and affirmative action. It explains why the Court has analyzed these issues as it has, describes debates among the Justices, and anticipates future challenges.

Second, although the book principally focuses on the present, it locates current constitutional doctrines and debates in historical context. Most chapters include a brief account of what the authors and ratifiers of a particular constitutional provision apparently had in mind. I also describe the Supreme Court's historical efforts to interpret the Constitution's language before offering more detailed discussion of contemporary law. In many cases the history is fascinating, often bound up with central currents in the nation's political, economic, and cultural life. In any event, it is often impossible to understand today's law without some awareness of the historical context from which it emerged.

Third, the book refers repeatedly to debates about the Supreme Court's proper role in American government. During the 1930s, when a conservative Supreme Court threatened to thwart President Franklin Roosevelt's New Deal efforts to revive the national economy, critics called passionately for judicial restraint. Many argued that courts should invalidate legislation only when it was clearly unconstitutional, not when there was any room for doubt. Today, another school of so-called "originalists" argues that the Supreme Court should consistently enforce the "original understanding" of individual constitutional provisions – what those provisions meant to those who wrote and ratified them. Meanwhile, various others have maintained that the Court plays a vital role in adapting vague constitutional language to the needs of changing times. In summarizing current doctrine, I talk about how these and other competing views both do and ought to affect the Court.

Fourth, this book deals openly with the now familiar insight that loosely "political" values and concerns influence Supreme Court decision-making. As any reader of newspapers knows, the Court has "liberal" and "conservative" Justices who attract those labels by reaching conclusions that can plausibly be identified as liberal or conservative most of the time. This is a phenomenon that needs to be explained, not ignored, and surely not denied. At the same time, I do not believe that judicial politics are simply a concealed form of partisan electoral politics. In this book I try to explain the ways in which Supreme Court decision-making is and is not (or at least should not be) "political."

Before concluding this Preface, I should probably say explicitly what is perhaps evident already. Constitutional law is an *argumentative* subject. There are certain facts of the matter – what the Constitution says, what the Supreme Court has held in past cases, and so forth. But lawyers, concerned citizens, and Supreme Court Justices all argue ceaselessly with each other about how the Constitution should be interpreted and applied. At some points, this book tries to stand outside of constitutional arguments and explain them dispassionately. Even then, I am probably too engaged by some issues to adopt a truly neutral perspective. At other points I join the arguments unabashedly and offer my own opinions, partly because I cannot help myself, because I cannot be indifferent, and partly because constitutional law is ultimately inseparable from constitutional argument. To a large extent, to understand constitutional law is to know how to participate in constitutional debates. There would be no better indication that this book has succeeded in introducing constitutional law successfully than if the reader, at certain points, feels both provoked and empowered to argue with my judgments.

In one sense, this book has been many years in the making. It reflects my reading and writing about constitutional law, and perhaps especially my teaching, over a period of roughly twenty years. In another sense, the book grows directly from a suggestion by Michael Aronson that I write a brief "primer" on constitutional law for non-lawyers. I am very grateful for his encouragement. Ed Parsons gave me enormously helpful editorial advice at a crucial stage in the book's gestation and has continued to provide valuable help through the end. I also owe large debts to a number of friends and colleagues who read earlier drafts. Heartfelt thanks go to David Barron, Erwin Chemerinsky, Jesse Choper, Heather Gerken, Ken Kersch, Sandy Levinson, Daniel Meltzer, Martha Minow, Fred Schauer, Margo Schlanger, and Lloyd Weinreb. Whatever the book's deficiencies, their comments, criticisms, and suggestions made it much better than it would otherwise have been, as did the labors of my extraordinary research assistants Mark Freeman and Josh Segal.

Prologue: *Bush v. Gore*

It is emphatically the province and duty of the judicial department
to say what the law is. Those who apply the rule to particular cases,
must of necessity expound and interpret that rule.

– *Marbury v. Madison* (1803)[1]

[W]hoever hath an absolute authority to interpret any written or
spoken laws, it is he who is truly the lawgiver, to all intents and
purposes, and not the person who first spoke or wrote them.

– Bishop Hoadly's Sermon, preached before King
(George I of England), March 31, 1717

On December 9, 2000, American politics slammed to a halt as the
nation awaited a Supreme Court decision likely to settle that year's
presidential election. Roughly a month earlier, the voters had gone
to the polls and produced nearly an even split between Republican
George Bush and Democrat Al Gore. Before the long election night
was over, three things became apparent. First, more Americans voted
for Gore than for Bush. Second, despite Gore's popular victory, the
presidency would go to the candidate who carried Florida. Third,
the initial Florida count had Bush winning by a narrow margin,
but the correctness of the machine-counted tally remained subject
to question.

Florida turned out to be key to the presidency because the Constitution provides for the President to be chosen by the "electoral
college" rather than the nationwide popular vote. Under the electoral college system, each state has an assigned number of presidential votes, based mostly on its population. Without Florida, neither

Gore nor Bush had the necessary electoral votes to win the election. A Florida victory would put either over the top.

Unfortunately, confusion and irregularity plagued the Florida count. Among the sources of confusion, several large counties used voting machines that required voters to punch holes in their ballots with a stylus. The hand-punched ballots were then fed into machines designed to tally the votes. But the machines were imperfect: It was known that they would fail to count a small percentage of even perfectly punched ballots, and they were especially unlikely to register votes when voters left hanging "chads" or partial but incomplete perforations. After the votes had been counted and recounted by machine, Gore wanted ballots on which the machines had registered no vote for President to be reexamined by human counters.

After complex legal struggles in the Florida courts, on Friday, December 8, the Florida Supreme Court, by a bitterly contested vote of 4–3, had sided with Gore and ordered an inspection of ballots failing to indicate a presidential vote. Gore hoped, and many expected, that this partial recount would swing Florida in his direction. The situation was endlessly complicated, however. Even if Gore had won the Florida recount, whether he would have gained Florida's electoral votes remained unclear. Article II of the Constitution provides that each state's electors, or voters in the electoral college, shall be appointed "in such Manner as the Legislature thereof may direct." The Republican Party controlled the Florida legislature. In the view of the state's Republican leaders, the recount ordered by the Florida Supreme Court reflected an effort by a Democrat-dominated tribunal to steal an election that Bush had fairly won. If a recount threatened to reverse the outcome, the Florida legislature was prepared to "appoint" its own electors to the electoral college, all pledged to Bush, and to claim that it was merely exercising its constitutional prerogative to "appoint" electors in "such Manner" as it chose. Had events unfolded in that way, it is not clear what would have happened next. There would have been two slates of Florida electors claiming a right to vote in the electoral college – one appointed at the direction of the Florida Supreme Court following a judicially ordered recount and pledged to Gore, the other appointed by the Florida legislature and pledged to Bush.

With the Florida recount about to begin on Saturday, December 9, lawyers for Bush raced to the Supreme Court of the United States. They made two main arguments. First, the Bush lawyers argued that the state court's decision to order a recount violated Florida law, because the time set for recounts by the Florida legislature had already passed. Ordinarily, the Supreme Court would leave the interpretation and enforcement of Florida law to the Florida courts and intervene only to correct violations of the *federal* Constitution. But this case was unusual, Bush argued, because the Florida Supreme Court's disobedience of Florida law was itself a violation of the federal Constitution: Article II specifically directs that presidential electors should be chosen "in such Manner as the [state] Legislature," rather than state courts, may direct. Second, Bush contended that the Florida Supreme Court had violated the Constitution's Due Process and Equal Protection Clauses by ordering a recount and giving vote counters no more direction than that they should seek to identify "the intent of the voter." If the Florida court could order a recount at all, it had to give further guidance, he said, to ensure that different vote-counting teams would not reach different conclusions based on identical facts.

On the same Saturday that Bush filed the case, the Supreme Court, by a vote of 5–4, ordered the Florida recount halted until it was able to rule on Bush's arguments – even though December 9 was just three days before what a majority of the Justices understood to be a Florida deadline of December 12 for the state's voters in the electoral college to be finally certified. At the same time, it scheduled oral arguments for Monday, December 11. With the Court's order, nonjudicial politics went temporarily into suspension.

Following arguments on Monday, the Supreme Court issued its decision in *Bush v. Gore*[2] on Tuesday, December 12, just after 10 P.M. The Court's opinion did not have an identified author, as Supreme Court rulings usually do: It was issued *per curiam*, or "by the Court." Nor did the Court's opinion say plainly which Justices were part of the majority and which dissented, either in whole or in part. But when the additional "concurring" and "dissenting" opinions are taken into account, six and possibly seven Justices had agreed that for a recount to proceed on the terms specified by the Florida Supreme Court would violate the Constitution's Equal Protection Clause, which provides that "[n]o State shall...deny to any person within its jurisdiction the equal protection of the laws." "The problem," the Court wrote, "inheres in the absence of specific standards" to ensure that the abstract "intent of the voter" test would be applied equally: "[T]he standards for accepting or rejecting contested ballots might vary not only from county to county but indeed within a single county from one recount team to another."[3]

The margin narrowed to razor closeness, with the Justices dividing 5–4 on the next point, which was equally vital to the decision: There was no time for the Florida courts to fix the equal protection problem by giving the vote counters clearer directions, because Florida law required a final certification of election results by December 12, and December 12 was already at hand. With that decision by the Supreme Court, debate and uncertainty about who would be the next President ended. Bush, the pre-recount winner, won Florida's electoral votes and with them the presidential election.

Bush v. Gore is the kind of "great case" that comes along no more than once in a generation. It would be a huge mistake to think that the Supreme Court's decision illustrates how the Court "usually" functions. Even so, *Bush v. Gore* provides an instructive prism through which to begin to examine the Constitution of the United States, some of the legal and political practices that have grown up around it, and the role of the Supreme Court. A few central points stand out:

The Constitution literally constitutes, or establishes and empowers, the United States of America. Americans are a dramatically diverse people in many ways – racially, religiously, geographically, and economically. For the most part, however, we are joined by our allegiance to the Constitution and our shared acceptance of the governmental structure that the Constitution creates. All of the legal and political debates in *Bush v. Gore* were debates under the Constitution, unimaginable in its absence.

The Constitution assigns important roles to a variety of institutions, all vital to an understanding of constitutional law. The Constitution creates the presidency that was at stake in *Bush v. Gore*. It also establishes a judicial system, headed by the Supreme Court, and a Congress. Representation in the House of Representatives is based on population, but each state, regardless of size, gets two votes in the Senate. The Constitution gives the states important roles in the structure of government, as is witnessed by the fact that voting for President occurs by state and that the procedures for counting votes in Florida were established by state law. Among the less well-known institutions created by the Constitution is the electoral college – whose role in electing the President was of course what made *Bush v. Gore* so important. (Under the electoral college system, the winning presidential candidates in 1824, 1876, 1888, and 2000 all got fewer votes than their opponents.)

The Constitution has limitations or deficiencies as well as strengths. Many people think it unfair for the President to be elected based on votes in the electoral college, rather than the popular vote, and for every state to have two Senators, regardless of size. Others disagree and believe that these provisions make good sense. Beyond these contestable points, some provisions of the Constitution seem deficient by any measure. For example, if two sets of Florida electors had cast competing votes, one for Gore and the other for Bush, some institution would have had to decide which votes to count. In providing for the counting of electoral votes, the Twelfth Amendment – which was itself written to correct a perceived defect in the original Constitution's provision for presidential elections – says that the votes of the electoral college shall be opened in the presence of both Houses of Congress and that "the votes shall then be counted." Counted by whom? Who would resolve disputes, and on what basis? The Constitution simply does not say. We have good reason to accept the Constitution as our basic framework of government, but we should not worship it or assume that it is perfect in every respect.

The courts have ultimate authority over most issues of constitutional interpretation. This is a hugely important power. Nearly two centuries ago, the French observer Alexis de Tocqueville shrewdly noted that in the American mind, most political issues have a legal or constitutional dimension. Moreover, as *Bush v. Gore* illustrates, judicial decisions can have profound political implications.

Constitutional adjudication is frequently a highly judgmental process. Some people may assume that the Supreme Court decides constitutional cases by simply taking note of the Constitution's plain language, perhaps in light of "the framers' intent," and then applying the written text rather mechanically to the problem at hand. This image is often dramatically misleading. In *Bush v. Gore,* a majority of the Justices concluded that the recount ordered by the Florida Supreme Court would have violated the Equal Protection Clause because different vote-counting teams would predictably have applied different standards in determining which ballots to count. Maybe this decision was correct, but no one suggested that the Equal Protection Clause was originally understood or intended to bar electoral recounts occurring under vague standards. That provision was ratified in the wake of the Civil War, with concerns about racial discrimination foremost in mind, in a period when there were no voting machines and nearly all ballots were hand-counted in an effort to discern the intent of the voter. The decision in *Bush v. Gore* turned not on the plain or originally understood meaning of the Equal Protection Clause, but instead reflected the current Justices' assessment of what is fair and unfair – a question on which reasonable minds might differ, as the Justices in fact did. Two Justices wrote opinions saying that they saw no constitutional defect in the Florida recount, and a third Justice joined those opinions, or said that he agreed.[4] In their view, the crucial starting point for analysis was that voting machines admittedly make mistakes – sometimes failing even to count ballots on which a hole has been indisputably punched. As Justice Ruth Ginsburg wrote, "I cannot agree that the recount ordered by the Florida court, flawed as it may be, would yield a result any less fair or precise" and thus any more in violation of the Equal Protection Clause than the mostly machine count that preceded the ordered recount.[5]

The role of "politics" in constitutional adjudication is a complex and worrisome issue. If the Supreme Court appropriately decides what is fair in some cases, rather than what those who wrote and ratified the Constitution historically thought was fair, then constitutional adjudication is inherently judgmental, and it may even be unavoidably "political" in a broad sense of that term. If so, it is natural to worry whether judgments about how it is best or fairest to read the Constitution can be kept adequately separate from more overtly "partisan" political judgments and motivations. For many Americans, *Bush v. Gore* brought this anxiety dramatically to the fore. The Supreme Court's five most conservative Justices all joined the Court's ruling stopping the Florida recount and ensuring the election of the conservative Republican presidential candidate George Bush. The four more liberal Justices, whose views probably aligned more closely with those of Al Gore, all dissented in whole or in part from the Court's ruling.

The correctness and "legitimacy" of judicial rulings can be questioned even when judicial power is not doubted. Judicial power to issue ultimate rulings on constitutional issues seems largely unchallenged, at least for the time being. But the legitimacy of particular exercises of that power is always open to question. People may agree that the Supreme Court is entitled to decide, but no one believes that the Court always decides correctly. As Supreme Court Justice Robert Jackson once quipped, "We are not final because we are infallible, but we are infallible only because we are final"[6] – which is of course to say that the Court is not really infallible at all. The Court's decision in *Bush v. Gore* did not settle whether its ruling was the right one or whether it thought about the contested issues in the proper way, even though everyone (or nearly everyone) agreed that its ruling had to be obeyed. Even after the Court speaks, constitutional debate properly goes on, as the American people judge the performance of the Supreme Court under the Constitution.

Introduction: The Dynamic Constitution

[O]ur Constitution ... is an experiment, as all life is an experiment.
— Justice Oliver Wendell Holmes, Jr.[1]

ALTHOUGH THE CONSTITUTION OF THE UNITED STATES is a single written document, American constitutional law — the subject of this book — is a complex social, cultural, and political practice that includes much more than the written Constitution. Courts, and especially the Supreme Court of the United States, interpret the Constitution. So do legislators and other governmental officials as they consider their responsibilities. Very commonly, however, "interpretation" of the Constitution depends on a variety of considerations external to the text. These include the historic practices of Congress and the President, previous judicial decisions or "precedents," public expectations, practical considerations, and moral and political values. By talking about constitutional law as a "practice," I mean to signal that factors such as these are elements of the process from which constitutional law emerges.[2]

To be sure, arguments about how to interpret the Constitution occur frequently in constitutional practice — not least among Justices of the Supreme Court. (Among the difficulties in studying constitutional law is that the rules of constitutional interpretation are nowhere written down in authoritative form.) Nonetheless, a few fixed points command nearly universal agreement. First, at the center of the frequently argumentative practice of constitutional law stands the written Constitution of the United States. Second, when the Supreme Court decides a case, it is almost universally supposed that its ruling binds public officials as well as citizens, despite their possibly contrary views. Supreme Court rulings occasionally encounter resistance, and in a few rare cases they have provoked actual or threatened defiance – matters that I discuss later in this book. Normally, however, the Court gets to say authoritatively what the Constitution means.

In subsequent chapters, I plunge directly into discussions of how particular provisions of the Constitution have been interpreted, especially but not exclusively by the Supreme Court. This chapter explores the textual and historical foundations of our constitutional practice. It first sketches the history that led to the Constitution's adoption, then briefly describes the central provisions of the Constitution itself. Today, we tend to take it for granted that the Supreme Court will interpret and enforce the Constitution. But it was once contested whether the Court should play this role at all; and *how* the Court should play it, as we saw in the Prologue, is a subject of continuing controversy. As background to current debates, the final sections of this chapter therefore outline a bit more relevant history. I discuss the case in which the Supreme Court first claimed the power of judicial review, *Marbury v. Madison*³ (1803), and then conclude with a brief survey of the Court's use of its power.

History

At the time of the American Revolution, the fledgling nation seeking independence consisted of thirteen separate colonies. Brought together by their common opposition to the taxing policies of the British Parliament, the colonies began sending delegates to a Continental Congress in 1774. This arrangement was initially quite informal. Delegates were elected by the assemblies of their respective colonies. Meeting in Congress, they could vote requests that the various colonies raise troops or furnish funds, but the Congress itself possessed no direct authority to enforce its requests.

In 1777, before the Revolutionary War concluded, the Continental Congress moved to formalize the relationship among the colonies by proposing the Articles of Confederation, which were ratified by the assemblies of all thirteen states or colonies and took effect in

1781. Like the more informal scheme that had preceded them, the Articles established a confederation of equal states, each with one vote. The national government, such as it was, still had to look to the states to enforce its directives. If it wished to lay a tax, for example, it had to request the states to assess and collect it. The Articles carefully enumerated the purposes for which the states were united; any power not specifically given to the national Congress was denied to it. The Articles of Confederation did not create an independent executive branch, and there was almost no judicial system. For the Congress to act, nine states needed to concur in ordinary decisions. More fundamental actions required unanimous consent.

As swiftly became clear, the government created by the Articles of Confederation was too weak. Although fighting with Britain stopped in 1781, and a formal peace followed in 1783, the European powers continued to pose threats that could be met only by decisive, coordinated action. At home, an economic downturn revealed the need for a national economic policy including a uniform currency and safeguards against inflation and nonpayment of debts.

To deal with these and related problems, the Continental Congress asked the colonies (or states) to send delegates to a convention in the summer of 1787 to draft proposed amendments to the Articles of Confederation. When the Convention met in Philadelphia, however, the delegates decided almost immediately to ignore their mandate and to draft an entirely new Constitution. The Convention also determined to ignore the Articles of Confederation insofar as the Articles forbade major changes in the scheme of national government without the unanimous approval of the thirteen states voting in Congress. Article VII of the new, draft Constitution provided that it would take effect on ratification by nine states and further directed that the ratifications should be by "conventions" of the people of the states, not by the state legislatures.

The decision of the Constitutional Convention to ignore or defy the Articles of Confederation – which were, after all, the then-prevailing "law" – is at least interesting in its own right and probably possesses enduring significance for American constitutional law.[4] Were the Constitution's authors (or framers as they are more commonly called) and ratifiers (or those who voted to approve it in separate state conventions) "outlaws" in their own time? Why were they not obliged to follow the Articles of Confederation in all of their written detail? How could valid law, in the form of a Constitution, emerge from actions not authorized by prior written law? It is not enough to say that the framers decided to start over; surely not every group is entitled to "start over" whenever it feels like doing so – for example, by staging a coup or pronouncing itself not bound by current constitutional law. In thinking that they were entitled to ignore the written law of their time, whereas others living under the new Constitution would be bound by it, the framers and ratifiers – followed by subsequent generations who have lionized them – appear to have assumed that unwritten principles of moral and political right preexist, and in some sense are more fundamental than, any written law. In light of the Constitution's origins, it should come as no surprise that debates about whether the Constitution presupposes background principles of moral and political right, even if it does not list them expressly, have echoed throughout American constitutional history.[5]

Original Constitutional Design

By any reasonable measure, the delegates to the Constitutional Convention were an extraordinarily able group. They pursued their work with a mixture of idealism, imagination, practicality, and self-interest. As in the Continental Congress, each state had one vote in the Convention's deliberations. Predictably, the delegations disputed whether each state should retain one vote in the new government's legislative branch or whether representation should instead reflect population. The delegates ultimately agreed to a compromise: Representation in the House of Representatives depends on population, but each state, regardless of size, gets two Senators.[6]

Throughout the Convention's deliberations, the delegates took it for granted that slavery must continue to exist under the new Constitution. Otherwise the slave states would not have participated. In at least three places the Constitution makes veiled reference to slavery but avoids the shameful term.[7] No women attended the Constitutional Convention. Not until after the Civil War could the Constitution even plausibly be viewed as a charter of equal human freedom.

From a modern perspective, it also bears note that there were no political parties at the Constitutional Convention. On the contrary, the framers disliked the very idea of parties, which they associated with "factions" hostile to the general or public interest. Nevertheless, a party system quickly grew up. For the most part, the parties have worked within a constitutional structure not designed for them.[8]

Although much of the framers' specific thinking now seems embedded in a worldview that is difficult to retrieve, on other issues their aspirations seem timeless. At the highest level of abstraction, they wanted to create a national government that was strong enough to deal effectively with genuinely national problems but would not threaten the liberties of a free people (on the uncomfortable assumption that slaves did not count). In pursuing these aims, the basic structure created by the Constitution has impressed most Americans as adequate, and even admirable, for more than 200 years.

Apart from a brief Preamble, the Constitution – which is reprinted as an appendix to this book for readers who may want to consult it – is not a rhetorical document. Working from the ground up, it literally constitutes the government of the United States. The main structural work occurs in the first three Articles.

Article I provides that "[a]ll legislative powers . . . shall be vested in a Congress of the United States, which shall consist of a Senate and House of Representatives." Following sections that deal with qualifications, apportionment, and election, Article I, Section 8 lists the powers of Congress in a series of seventeen clauses that include the "Power to lay and collect Taxes" and to "regulate Commerce." The list concludes with the so-called "Necessary and Proper Clause," authorizing Congress "to make all Laws which shall be necessary and proper for carrying into Execution the foregoing Powers, and all other Powers vested by this Constitution in the Government of the United States." The Necessary and Proper Clause has been read as mandating a broad interpretation of Congress's other powers.

Article II vests the executive power in a President of the United States. It provides for the election of the President and Vice President, then specifies the President's powers and duties in a reasonably detailed list. Among other things, the President is made the Commander-in-Chief of the armed forces and is empowered to make treaties and to appoint ambassadors, judges, and other officers of the United States "by and with the Advice and Consent of the Senate." The President also possesses a power to veto or reject legislation enacted by Congress, subject to override by two-thirds majorities of both Houses.

Article III vests "the judicial Power of the United States" in "one Supreme Court, and in such inferior Courts as the Congress may from time to time ordain and establish." Both in the Constitutional Convention and in the ratification debates, it appears to have been taken for granted that the courts, and especially the Supreme Court, would determine whether legislation enacted by Congress and the states comports with the Constitution.[9] But the text of Article III leaves the power of "judicial review," as it is called, implicit rather than explicit.

Article IV contains miscellaneous provisions. The so-called "Privileges and Immunities Clause" imposes an antidiscrimination rule: It limits the freedom of states to discriminate against citizens of other states who might travel or pursue business opportunities within their borders. Another clause of Article IV provides for the admission of new states. A third empowers Congress to legislate for the territories.

Article V establishes the process for amending the Constitution. Unlike ordinary laws, constitutional amendments require the concurrence of two-thirds of both Houses of Congress and of three-fourths of the states.

Article VI states explicitly that "[t]his Constitution, and the Laws of the United States which shall be made in Pursuance thereof . . . shall be the supreme Law of the Land." This so-called Supremacy Clause establishes that whenever state law conflicts with either the Constitution or with federal laws passed by Congress, state law must yield. Article VI also forbids the use of any religious test "as a Qualification to any Office or public Trust under the United States." Article

VII provides for the Constitution to be ratified by conventions in the several states, not by the state legislatures.

As originally written, the Constitution included only a few express guarantees of rights. To safeguard liberty, the framers relied principally on the strategy of making the federal government one of limited or "enumerated" powers. They saw no need to create an express right to freedom of speech, for example, because they thought that the delegated powers of Congress, properly construed, included no authority to enact legislation encroaching on speech rights.

During the debates about whether the Constitution should be ratified, however, the absence of a bill of rights was widely criticized, and the Constitution's main champions – the so-called Federalists – promised to remedy the perceived defect. After the Constitution's ratification, the first Congress proposed twelve amendments, ten of which were quickly approved and took effect in 1791. Known collectively as the Bill of Rights, these ten amendments are today regarded as mainstays of constitutional freedom. The First Amendment guarantees freedoms of speech and religion. The Second provides that "[a] well regulated Militia, being necessary to the security of a free State, the right of the people to keep and bear Arms, shall not be infringed." The Third Amendment forbids the quartering of troops in private homes without the owners' consent, except in time of war. The Fourth Amendment creates rights against "unreasonable" searches and seizures. The Fifth Amendment forbids deprivations of "life, liberty, or property, without due process of law." Along with the Sixth Amendment, it also provides a variety of rights to people accused of crimes. The Seventh Amendment protects rights to trial by jury. The Eighth bars "cruel and unusual punishments." The Ninth says that "[t]he enumeration in the Constitution, of certain rights, shall not be construed to deny or disparage others retained by the people." Finally, the Tenth Amendment emphasizes the continuingly important role of the states (the powers of which come from their own constitutions and not, interestingly and importantly, from the Constitution of the United States): "The powers not delegated to the United States by the Constitution, nor prohibited by it to the States, are reserved to the States respectively, or to the people."

Strikingly to modern eyes, the Bill of Rights originally applied only to the federal government and imposed no restrictions on the states.[10] In other words, it left the states free to regulate speech and religion, for example. In the context of the times, national governmental power obviously aroused more distrust than state power. But trust of the states soon eroded, especially in the long struggle over slavery that increasingly dominated American politics in the first part of the nineteenth century.

That struggle ultimately produced the Civil War, which in turn led to adoption of the Thirteenth Amendment abolishing slavery, the Fourteenth Amendment requiring the states to accord to every person "the equal protection of the laws," and the Fifteenth Amendment forbidding race-based discrimination in voting. Beginning in the twentieth century, the Supreme Court has also construed the Fourteenth Amendment as making nearly all guarantees of the Bill of Rights applicable against the states – a development specifically discussed in Chapter Five. This is a phenomenon of enormous importance, which marks a sharp divide in constitutional history. Since the "Civil War Amendments," twelve further amendments have been ratified, for a total of twenty-seven. Among the most important, the Sixteenth Amendment authorizes Congress to impose an income tax, the Nineteenth guarantees voting rights to women, and the Twenty-Second bars a President from serving more than two terms in office.

One further feature of the Constitution's design deserves emphasis. As is discussed in greater detail in Chapter Fourteen, virtually without exception the Constitution applies only to the government, not to private citizens or companies. Accordingly, if a private company fires an employee for criticizing the boss, it does not violate the constitutional right to freedom of speech – which is only a right against the government. So it also is with other constitutional provisions, including the Equal Protection Clause of the Fourteenth Amendment, which generally prohibits race-based and certain other kinds of discrimination by the government. If private citizens discriminate on the basis of race, they may be acting wrongly as a moral matter and may also violate laws enacted by Congress or state or local governments, but they do not violate the Constitution.

8

The Constitution as Higher Law: Foundations of Judicial Review

Although many changes have occurred subsequently, the ratification of the Constitution, as supplemented by the Bill of Rights, created the basic framework of federal law that persists today. On one level there is ordinary law, enacted by ordinary majorities in Congress, state legislatures, and local governments. On another level stands the Constitution, as higher law, which not only establishes and empowers the national government, but also imposes limits on what ordinary law can do.

The status of the Constitution as higher *law* is crucial to the role played by courts, and especially the Supreme Court, in the American scheme of government. In nonconstitutional cases, such as those involving questions about whether people have committed crimes or broken contracts, courts routinely interpret and enforce the law. Given the status of the Constitution as higher law, most Americans living today probably take it for granted that courts should interpret and enforce the Constitution as well. In fact, to allow the Supreme Court to interpret the Constitution, and to treat other branches of government as bound by the Court's decisions, was a choice. It was certainly not an inevitable choice in 1787, when the Constitution was written. Indeed, critics have sometimes questioned whether the Constitution authorizes courts to rule on the constitutionality of legislation at all.

Nowhere does the Constitution say expressly that the courts should have the power to review the constitutionality of legislation. Nor is "judicial review" by any means a logical necessity. In Britain, the source of many American legal principles, the courts traditionally had no role in testing the validity of legislation. The rule was "parliamentary sovereignty": Any legislation enacted by Parliament and approved by the monarch was law. To be sure, Britain did not have a written constitution. Even under a written constitution, however, it would be possible to take the same approach. It could have been left to Congress to judge the constitutionality of legislation, and the courts would simply have enforced the law as passed by Congress.

Despite the possibility of constitutionalism without judicial review, and despite the absence of any express reference in the constitutional text, the power of the courts to determine the constitutionality of legislation can fairly be viewed as implicit in Article III, which deals with the judicial power. Article III calls for the federal courts to decide cases "arising under this Constitution" – language best understood as referring to cases in which questions of constitutional law are presented for decision. In addition, Article VI says that state judges are bound by the Constitution, "any Thing in the Constitution or Laws of any State to the Contrary notwithstanding." Again, this language implies that state judges must assess the constitutional validity of state laws. If the power of judicial review is given to state judges, then surely it must exist in the Supreme Court, which the Constitution empowers to hear appeals from state court judgments.

Historical evidence supports this conclusion. Several discussions at the Constitutional Convention anticipated that the courts would exercise judicial review.[11] During the ratification debates, Alexander Hamilton plainly stated in one of the Federalist Papers that the Constitution assigned this role to the judiciary.[12] Indeed, several early decisions of the Supreme Court assumed the power of judicial review without anyone paying much attention.[13]

Marbury v. Madison: An Enduring Symbol of Judicial Power

In the early years, however, much was in flux. Government under a written constitution, enforced by an independent judiciary, was a novelty in the history of nations. Many elements of the experiment were precarious, as became plain when a crisis developed in the aftermath of the 1800 presidential election. Although the framers of the Constitution did not envision the rise of political parties, partisan divisions quickly emerged, and the election of 1800 was bitterly fought between the Federalists supporting John Adams and the Republicans backing Thomas Jefferson. The Federalists, who had dominated the national government during the presidential administrations of George Washington and his successor Adams, generally supported broad national authority, a sound currency, and domestic and foreign policies promoting commercial interests. By contrast, the Republicans were the party of states' rights and political and economic democracy.

After the Republicans won a stunning triumph at the polls, the outgoing Federalists remained in office for a brief period before the inauguration of the new administration. In that interlude, they sought means to safeguard their party and the nation against the anticipated reckless adventures of Jefferson's Republicans. Lacking other plausible options, they decided to rely on the courts. In the brief period between the election and Jefferson's inauguration, the outgoing Federalists hatched and swiftly implemented a plan to preserve Federalist values through the federal judiciary.[14] First, President Adams named his Secretary of State, John Marshall, as the new Chief Justice of the United States. The Senate then swiftly confirmed him. Second, Congress created sixteen new federal judgeships, to which Adams nominated and the Senate quickly confirmed sixteen new "midnight judges," all Federalists. Finally, in a much less significant move, the outgoing Federalist Congress authorized the President to appoint forty-two minor office-holders, called justices of the peace, for the District of Columbia. In the confusion of the Adams administration's last days, several of these commissions failed to be delivered. When William Marbury did not get his, he filed a suit in the Supreme Court, asking it to order the Secretary of State of the new Jefferson administration, James Madison, to deliver his commission.

Understandably under the circumstances, Jefferson's Republicans took office in a state of fury about the lame-duck Federalists' efforts to commandeer the federal judiciary. Without compunction, the Republicans set out to stop the Federalists from retaining through the courts the influence that they had lost at the polls. On one front, the Republican Congress abolished the new federal judgeships that its predecessor had created. On another, after William Marbury filed his suit in the Supreme Court in December of 1801, Congress enacted legislation that effectively barred the Court from meeting for more than a year, until February 1803. On a third, the Jeffersonians set out to "impeach" and remove from office Federalist judges that they believed had abused their powers.[15]

When William Marbury's suit against James Madison came before the Supreme Court in this bitter climate, the Court stood at a crossroads with disaster threatening on both sides. *Marbury v. Madison* had plain overtones of Federalists versus Republicans. If the Court ruled for the Federalist Marbury and ordered Madison to deliver his commission, it was widely expected that Madison – acting at the direction of President Jefferson – would defy the Court's order. Jefferson and Madison could surely have gotten away with defiance in the political climate of the day, and it is even likely that Marshall might have been impeached if he had ruled against the popular new administration, which had solid congressional majorities behind it. Had events developed in this way, the Supreme Court would have been diminished. If, however, the Court simply ruled against Marbury and in favor of Madison, the precedent of bowing before political threats, or even of appearing to do so, might have boded equally badly for the constitutional ideal of an independent judiciary.

With remarkable ingenuity, Marshall found a way to establish *Marbury v. Madison*[16] as an enduring symbol of judicial power, not impotence. He did so by focusing on a technicality, involving what lawyers call "jurisdiction" or the authority of a particular court to decide a particular case. In plain terms, Marbury had sued in the wrong court. By constitutional design, the Supreme Court functions almost exclusively as an "appellate" court, reviewing decisions already made by lower courts to correct errors on points of law. In only a few categories of cases will the Constitution allow someone to sue directly in the Supreme Court without going to a lower court first. Marbury's suit against Madison did not fall within any of those exceptional categories. As a result, the Supreme Court had no "jurisdiction" to rule on Marbury's suit against Madison. Although this is the conclusion to which John Marshall's opinion ultimately came, he got there by a very circuitous route, which required him to make broad rulings on the Supreme Court's power.

Marshall began his opinion by holding that William Marbury had a right to his commission. He held next that for every right the laws of the United States must furnish a remedy – including, if necessary, the remedy of a judicial order commanding action by high governmental officials such as the Secretary of State. This was an enormous claim of judicial power, which Jefferson and Madison would have denied and indeed defied if the occasion had arisen. But that occasion had not yet arrived, and within the structure of Marshall's opinion it never would, because the Chief Justice had still not reached the jurisdictional question of the Supreme Court's authority to rule on the case at all.

When Marshall finally addressed that question, he might have treated the answer as obvious: Under the Constitution, the Supreme Court is mostly supposed to hear appeals, not to act as a trial court in cases such as Marbury's. Instead, Marshall pointed to a statute authorizing the Supreme Court to issue the kind of *remedy* that Marbury sought, a "writ of mandamus" ordering government officials to perform their legal duties. By enacting that statute, Marshall's opinion reasoned, Congress had attempted to give the Supreme Court jurisdiction to act as a trial court in every case in which one party sought a writ of mandamus. In the view of most commentators, this was a clear misreading of the statute. Read in context, it authorized the Court to grant the remedy of mandamus only in cases that it otherwise had jurisdiction to decide.[17] By twisting the statutory language, however, Marshall managed to create a constitutional question about the power of the Supreme Court to engage in judicial review: A congressionally enacted statute directed the Court to act as a trial court in all cases involving claims to writs of mandamus, but the Constitution will permit the Court to exercise original or trial jurisdiction in only a narrower category of cases. So when a statute conflicts with the Constitution, by ordering what the Constitution forbids, which should a court follow, the statute or the Constitution?

With the question framed in this way, Marshall answered it easily, by giving the ruling for which *Marbury* is famous: It would defeat the purposes of a written Constitution if the courts had to enforce unconstitutional statutes. The courts must exercise judicial review because the Constitution is law, and it is the essence of the judicial function "to say what the law is."

With this conclusion, Marbury lost his case. The Supreme Court could not order Madison to give Marbury his commission as a justice of the peace because it had no jurisdiction to do so. The fact that Marbury lost and Madison won solved Marshall's immediate problem, involving the specter of the President and Secretary of State defying a Supreme Court ruling and being applauded by Congress for doing so. But the chain of reasoning that led to the case's outcome involved assertions of enormous judicial power. Madison won, and Marbury lost, only as a result of a precedent-setting ruling that the Supreme Court must review the constitutionality of acts of Congress. *Marbury's* holding on this point has endured, and has generally been honored, into the present day.

Politics and Judicial Review

Today, many lawyers regard *Marbury* as perhaps the most important case ever decided by the Supreme Court, because it was the first clearly to establish the power of judicial review. If *Marbury* is the foundation stone of judicial review, however, its status as such is partly ironic. The irony emerges from Marshall's reasoning about the purposes of a written Constitution and about the necessity of judicial review to promote them. As Marshall recognized, the Constitution aims to remove some questions from the domain of political decision-making. Without the guarantees of a written constitution, it would be open to Congress and ultimately to political majorities to decide whether to permit or deny freedom of religion, for example, and to determine whether the Supreme Court could exercise original jurisdiction in cases such as William Marbury's.

But it is one thing to say that the Constitution aims to remove certain questions from politics, another to determine which branch of government should interpret the Constitution. In suggesting that a written Constitution would be a nullity without judicial review, Marshall manifested a plain distrust of Congress and other political actors: He assumed that they could not be trusted to interpret the Constitution and the limits that it places on their power. This view is compelling, so far as it goes. Strikingly, however, Marshall stopped short of asking any searching questions about the possibility that politics, of one or another kind, might influence the exercise of judicial power. Although Congress, if left unchecked, might twist and torture the written Constitution in the service of its political goals, is there not also a risk that the Supreme Court might do the same?

In *Marbury* itself, for example, it appears that Marshall may well have concluded that Marbury had to lose in order to avoid the political consequences for the judiciary, including a continued program of impeachments of Federalist judges, if a ruling went in Marbury's favor. It also seems likely that Marshall both deliberately misconstrued a federal statute in order to frame the question whether the Constitution authorizes judicial review and that he constructed the Court's opinion to lay the broadest possible foundation for future judicial power. He presumably did so partly because, in his view, the governmental framework would be a better one if it included a central judicial role, but he may also have acted as he did partly because he wanted to save his own job and to establish its significance.

In describing *Marbury* as itself possibly influenced by political considerations, I should not put the point too strongly. The term "political" admits of varied usages. If Marshall thought that a strong judiciary would enhance the fairness or stability of government under the Constitution, that would be a political view in one sense of the term, but it would not be objectionably political in the same way, for example, as a decision motivated by a desire to promote the fortunes of a favored political party in the next election. Courts probably cannot help relying on views that are political in the first sense. The Constitution is, among other things, a practical plan of government. In interpreting it, courts necessarily take practical considerations into account. By contrast, it would be scandalous if courts behaved politically in the sense of trying to tip elections to a preferred political party. (That is part of why *Bush v. Gore*, in which some observers thought they saw partisan motivations at work, stirred so much controversy.) Sometimes, however, the line between acceptable and unacceptable judicial politics may grow blurry. *Marbury* itself may be a case in point if the Court predetermined that a way must be found to ensure that William Marbury lost his case in order to reduce political pressures on the Court and its members, or if it deliberately misread a statute in order to create an opportunity to enhance the power of the judicial branch by claiming and exercising the function of judicial review.

A Preliminary Perspective on How the Supreme Court Interprets the Constitution

As this short discussion of politics and judicial review probably suggests, *Marbury v. Madison* presented at least two important questions about judicial power under the Constitution. The first was *whether* courts have the power of judicial review. On that question the Court spoke relatively conclusively. Since *Marbury*, the power of courts to "say what the law is" in constitutional cases has largely been seen as settled, though I should probably offer a caution at this preliminary point that this is a somewhat weaker claim than it might appear to be on the surface. As will become clearer in subsequent chapters, although the Supreme Court has a central, often dominant role in our constitutional practice, the Court is by no means the only relevant actor.

The second question presented in *Marbury* was *how* courts ought to interpret the Constitution – what considerations they should take into account in giving constitutional rulings. On that question, *Marbury* said little and settled nothing. In supporting the necessity of judicial review, Chief Justice Marshall cited the possibility of statutes that plainly violated constitutional commands. For example, the Constitution says that no one may be convicted of treason except on the testimony of two witnesses in open court.[18] Surely, he argued, a court could not be required to give effect to a statute authorizing convictions of treason based on the testimony of a single witness.[19] In many cases, however, how the Constitution ought to be interpreted, and whether it permits or condemns a governmental act or policy, will not be obvious.

The question "how" the Constitution ought to be interpreted cannot be defined, much less answered, along a single dimension, and it would be a mistake to become bogged down in a lengthy discussion before the reader has encountered a broader sample of cases. Nonetheless, a bit of historical perspective may be helpful. Admittedly treading on contested ground, I would say that if any short statement of the Supreme Court's characteristic approach to constitutional adjudication will stand up, it might be this: The Court typically decides cases in light of what the Justices take to be the Constitution's largest purposes and the values that it presupposes as well as those that it more expressly embodies. If any single sentence encapsulates the Court's outlook, it is probably one written by John Marshall sixteen years after *Marbury* in *McCulloch v. Maryland*[20] (1819): "[W]e must never forget that it is a *constitution* we are expounding." A constitution, Marshall explained, does not "partake of the prolixity of a legal code" and must be construed as "adapt [able] to the various *crises* of human affairs."

McCulloch presented two questions. The first was whether the Constitution authorized Congress to create a "Bank of the United States" (with branches throughout the country) as a depository for federal funds and as a means of creating networks of commercial credit. Although all agreed that Congress possesses no powers not conferred by the Constitution, and although Article I nowhere refers expressly to a congressional power to create a national bank, Marshall had no difficulty in upholding the Bank of the United States. He reasoned that the Constitution grants Congress a number of "great powers," including those "to lay and collect taxes ...; to borrow money ...; to regulate commerce ...; to declare and carry on a war; [and] to raise and support armies."[21] All of those great powers being given, it would make no sense, he wrote, to read the Constitution as precluding the use of a means – in this case a national bank – that Congress reasonably thought necessary or appropriate in executing those powers.

With Congress's power to create the bank having been established, the next question was whether it was constitutionally permissible for Maryland to tax the bank. Marshall briskly ruled that it was not. No bit of constitutional language spoke to this issue, but Marshall again appealed to the Constitution's broadest purposes and its underlying assumptions. The power to tax the bank was the power "to destroy" it, he wrote. A Constitution that empowered Congress to create a bank thus could not sensibly be read to leave the states with a power to tax it.

To most commentators on the Constitution, the main methodological assumptions of Marshall's opinion in *McCulloch* have appeared sound. He was right that the Constitution, which does not "partake of the prolixity of a legal code," must be adaptable to "crises of human affairs." What is more, if there are two linguistically plausible interpretations of the Constitution, one of which would make it fairer or more workable than the other, or more capable of realizing its overriding purposes, he was right that courts should take this consideration into account. Good judging requires practical and occasionally moral judgment, not just beady-eyed attention to linguistic detail. This, among other reasons, is why Marshall is generally regarded as perhaps the greatest Justice in Supreme Court history.

The difficulty with Marshall's argument in *McCulloch*, which he never really confronted, is that different people will predictably, sometimes systematically, differ in their views of what would make the Constitution fairer or better or truer to its dominant purposes. Looking at the national bank at issue in *McCulloch*, Marshall emphasized the character of the Constitution in vesting Congress with "great powers," the full effectuation of which should not be frustrated. But an opponent of the bank might as easily have emphasized the plain constitutional design to give Congress only carefully limited powers, as subsequently emphasized by the Tenth Amendment: "The powers not delegated to the United States by the Constitution, nor prohibited by it to the States, are reserved to the States respectively, or to the people."

When Marshall's analysis in *McCulloch* is contrasted with that of a readily imaginable critic, the issue of politics in constitutional adjudication – to which I have alluded already – comes starkly to the fore. If Marshall's methodological assumptions are granted, it seems unavoidable that constitutional decision-making should sometimes rest on political considerations of a kind. In determining how the spare language of the Constitution is *best* interpreted, a judge's views about what is fair and sensible will often come inescapably into play.[22] And if loosely political judgments about what is fair and sensible and most in accord with the Constitution's most important purposes often underlie judgments of how *best* to interpret the Constitution, then loosely political disagreements will often drive disagreements about constitutional law. In *McCulloch*, Marshall thought it more sensible to read the Constitution as investing Congress with broad powers; those who feared federal authority would have reached the opposite conclusion.

From one perspective, it seems troubling that political judgments could influence constitutional law and that political disagreements could underlie constitutional debates. But it is worth pausing over the precise way in which practical and political considerations often enter the picture. In a dispute over whether *McCulloch v. Maryland* was correctly decided, it would not be accurate to say that those on either side had allowed their political views to contaminate a judgment that should have been based on the Constitution alone – whatever that form of words might mean. A good judge or Justice will never ignore the Constitution. It is, indeed, the Constitution that he or she is "expounding." But the meaning of words often depends on their context, and in the context of constitutional adjudication, considerations of fairness and practicality are almost always relevant to interpretive meaning, even when they are not decisive.

A Brief History of Judicial Review

A judicial power to determine how the Constitution is *best* interpreted can obviously be understood either relatively narrowly – for example, only as a tie-breaker when two interpretations of the Constitution are otherwise exactly equally plausible – or more broadly, so that judicial judgments exert a substantially greater influence. That power can also be used either for good or for ill.

History has generally smiled on the exercise of judicial review by the Supreme Court under John Marshall. In broadest terms, Marshall's Court was committed to nation building, including the establishment of federal judicial power as a tool for binding the states into a single, unified country. The Marshall Court upheld the exercise of expansive power by the federal government, but it did not hesitate to invalidate *state* legislation based on purposive, value-based interpretations of constitutional provisions (few in number, before the Civil War Amendments) conferring rights against the states. Seen in retrospect, Marshall's thirty-four-year tenure as Chief Justice – from 1801 to 1835 – was extraordinary in nearly every way. Marshall forged a remarkable unity among the Justices of his Court, including those appointed by his former political opponents. Dissenting opinions were rare as Marshall presided with casual, unpretentious charm over dinnertime conferences sometimes eased by the consumption of wine. Initially, the wine was reportedly reserved for rainy days. Later the Justices relied on the theory that it was always likely to be raining somewhere in the great territorial mass of the United States.

After Marshall had departed and as the country crept toward Civil War, the Court proceeded less steadily. It took large interpretive liberties in the infamous case of *Dred Scott v. Sandford*[23] (1857), which held that Congress lacked authority to ban the spread of slavery in the federal territories that were not yet states. At the time, questions involving slavery and its spread were literally tearing the country apart. The Court apparently thought it could help to heal the divide by taking one big part of the slavery issue – involving the permissibility of slavery in the territories – "out of politics" and making it pointless for national politicians to fight about it. But the *Dred Scott* decision was a fiasco. The Justices were probably wrong about the Constitution's originally understood meaning, to which they appealed, on at least some of the questions in issue. If driven to their position by moral and political considerations, they also took the wrong side. And they foolishly, quixotically overestimated the practical reach of judicial power: A Supreme Court ruling had no chance of defusing an issue about which the country would soon descend into war.

After *Dred Scott*, as the bonds of constitutional government frayed, judicial power went into eclipse. During the Civil War, the Supreme Court generally acquiesced in actions by Congress, the President, and the Union army that quite arguably overstepped constitutional bounds. In a relatively isolated case of judicial resistance to intrusions on civil liberties during wartime, Abraham Lincoln actually defied a ruling by the Chief Justice denying the authority of military officials to hold suspected Confederate sympathizers without bringing them into court and proving them guilty of crimes.[24] The Court thereafter shrank from the limelight. In the immediate aftermath of the Civil War, it declined to exercise powers rather plainly conferred on it by the Civil War Amendments – a matter discussed more fully in Chapter Three.

The Court emerged from its retreat by the end of the nineteenth century and began some of the protection of civil liberties for which it would later earn acclaim. At roughly the same time, however, the Court began to adopt constitutional positions that frustrated "progressive" legislative efforts to prohibit child labor, give workers the right to unionize, and establish minimum wages and maximum hours for laborers. The Court fought its constitutional battle on two fronts. First, in cases challenging federal legislation, the Court frequently held that Congress had exceeded the bounds of its power under Article I of the Constitution. Second, when it was the states that enacted "progressive" legislation, the Court's conservative majority often ruled that restrictions on "the freedom of contract" infringed on individual liberty in violation of the Due Process Clause, which says that no one may be deprived of "life, liberty, or property, without due process of law."

The so-called *Lochner* era, which took its name from a notorious case[25] and was marked by what many observers would characterize as "judicial activism" by a conservative Supreme Court, stretched into the 1930s. Controversial from the outset, the Court's antiregulatory stance increasingly triggered outrage during the Great Depression, especially as the Supreme Court invalidated central elements of President Franklin Roosevelt's New Deal and threatened to scuttle others. Following a massive triumph in the 1936 elections, and with the programs on which he had won reelection very much at risk, Roosevelt went to Congress and asked its help in checking the Court: He proposed legislation that would have expanded the Court's size and permitted him to "pack" it by appointing a number of new, pro-New Deal Justices. (Although the Supreme Court has had nine Justices since 1869, the Constitution permits Congress to fix the number by statute. At earlier points in American history, the Court had as few as six and as many as ten Justices.) Roosevelt's Court-packing proposal failed in Congress, but only after it had become unnecessary. In several cases decided during 1937, Justice Owen Roberts, who had cast the crucial fifth vote to invalidate New Deal legislation in some of the earlier cases, switched sides.

Historians continue to debate whether Roberts was affected by political currents in general or the Court-packing plan in particular.[26] Whatever the cause for his changed position, the effect proved dramatic. In the short term, the New Deal was safe. The Court also gave up closely scrutinizing state legislation under the Due Process Clause. And Roosevelt swiftly got to make a string of Supreme Court appointments as the result of retirements. In making those appointments, Roosevelt self-consciously looked for judicial "liberals" in a historical context in which "conservatives" had frustrated the enactment of progressive legislation. In the parlance of the time, judicial liberals were generally those who believed that the Supreme Court should give Congress and the state legislatures a relatively free hand in enacting legislation. In other words, New Deal liberals preached judicial deference or restraint.

As the *Lochner* era faded, however, further reflection on its lessons occurred. Virtually no one advocated a return to the kind of judicial activism that the Court had practiced in the early twentieth century. But while some Justices and commentators took the position that the Court should show "judicial restraint" (and uphold challenged legislation) in nearly all settings, others began to argue that the Court's prior error lay in its effort to protect the wrong substantive rights (such as broad rights of "freedom of contract") under the wrong provisions of the Constitution. In their view, the Court should almost never invalidate economic regulatory legislation enacted by Congress and the state legislatures, but it should not hesitate to protect other rights, including freedom of speech; and, in particular, it should give vigilant protection to the rights of racial and religious minorities.

The latter position ultimately rose to ascendancy under the Warren Court, so-called after Chief Justice Earl Warren, who was named to the bench in 1953. One of the early landmarks of his tenure came in

1954 when the Court held in *Brown v. Board of Education*[27] that the Equal Protection Clause of the Fourteenth Amendment forbade race-based discrimination in the public schools. As is discussed further in Chapter Five, this conclusion was probably contrary to the "original understanding" of the Equal Protection Clause, yet nearly everyone regards *Brown* as among the triumphant moments of Supreme Court history. It served as a prelude to other Warren Court decisions that expanded the scope of constitutional guarantees of equal protection of the laws, First Amendment freedoms of speech and religion, and a variety of rights of criminal suspects.

Warren was a warm, conspicuously decent man, with the easy charm and political nature of a former governor of California. During his tenure, the Court assumed something of his personality. From the bench Warren would sometimes ask counsel who had made technical legal points whether they thought that the results that they urged were fair – not whether they were supportable by legal argument, but whether they were just or decent in a deeper sense. Some thrilled to the approach of the Warren Court. Many law professors were perplexed, often sympathetic to the Court's results but skeptical of the soundness of its constitutional reasoning. And some of course were horrified. By any fair account, the Supreme Court was once again at the center of national political controversy through most of the Warren years.

The 1968 presidential election marked the end of the Warren era. In that year's campaign, the Republican nominee, Richard Nixon, took clear aim at the Warren Court's decisions, especially those that had expanded the rights of criminal suspects. According to critics, the Warren Court's decisions repeatedly loosed dangerous criminals onto the streets on newly minted legal technicalities. If elected, Nixon promised, he would appoint "law and order" Justices with a "strict constructionist" philosophy. Nixon's appeal struck a resonant chord. He won. By 1972 he had appointed four new Justices, and the Warren Court was no more.

In the years since Nixon began the process of transformation, the Supreme Court has grown progressively more conservative. The conservative turn began under the Chief Justice that Nixon appointed, Warren Burger, and it has continued under Burger's successor, William H. Rehnquist. It is not always easy to say exactly what it means for the Court to be "conservative," any more than to say what it means for the Court to be "liberal." But a simple measure commonly used by political scientists will suffice for current purposes: Judicial decisions count as conservative when they reach substantive outcomes that those with conservative political views could be expected to applaud.[28]

One measure of the current Supreme Court's conservatism comes from the way it was put together. As of the writing of this book, seven of the nine Justices have been appointed by Republican Presidents. Chief Justice William H. Rehnquist was first nominated to the Court by Richard Nixon in 1972 and then was elevated to the post of Chief Justice by President Ronald Reagan in 1986. At least during his early years on the bench, Rehnquist – who made his early career in Arizona, where he allied himself with the crusadingly conservative Barry Goldwater – was widely viewed as the most conservative Supreme Court Justice since the 1930s. If Rehnquist has lost the title of "most conservative," it is only because of the subsequent appointments of Antonin Scalia in 1986 and Clarence Thomas in 1991. Both take the position, at least much of the time, that constitutional interpretation should reflect the "original understanding" of those who wrote and ratified particular constitutional provisions. On a broad range of issues, a return to eighteenth- and nineteenth-century understandings would support outcomes favored by political conservatives. The "originalism" of Scalia and Thomas also admits exceptions, however, and many of those exceptions permit Scalia and Thomas to take substantively conservative positions not firmly rooted in the original understanding – for example, in opposition to affirmative action by the federal government (to which the Equal Protection Clause does not apply) and in support of broadly defined "property" rights.

Also numbering among the Court's conservative bloc are two more Justices appointed by Ronald Reagan – Sandra Day O'Connor and Anthony Kennedy. O'Connor, the first female Justice in the nation's history, served for a time as a Republican member of the Arizona legislature, and she has been a leader in the Court's modern efforts to protect states' rights. On other issues, she is sometimes less conservative than Rehnquist, Scalia, and Thomas, but on more issues than not her voting record would tend to please Reagan Republicans. The same could be said of Anthony Kennedy, named to the Court by Reagan in 1987 after Senate Democrats had mustered the votes to reject an even more conservative nominee, Robert Bork.

Although O'Connor and Kennedy count as conservative in the eyes of nearly all liberals, they are also sometimes described as "swing Justices," or the two who are mostly likely to break with the other conservatives to give liberals occasional victories in high-profile cases (involving, for example, affirmative action, gay rights, and abortion). In my view, those victories create a public impression that the Court is more liberal than it actually is; by any fair account, the Court's stands on a few especially visible and divisive issues explain why staunch political conservatives can sometimes be as disappointed in the current Court as liberals often are. The two other current Justices to have been nominated by Republican Presidents – John Paul Stevens, who was named to the Court by Gerald Ford, and David Souter, who was nominated by the first President Bush – are sometimes regarded as having abandoned their conservative principles. To some extent this may be so. To some extent it may be a measure of where the Court's center of gravity lies that Justices thought to be at least moderately conservative at the time of their appointment could now be classified as relative liberals. The Court's other two Justices as I write in 2004 are Ruth Bader Ginsburg and Stephen Breyer, both nominated to the Court by the Democratic President Bill Clinton.

If the modern Supreme Court is substantively conservative, in recent years it has also grown increasingly methodologically self-conscious and attentive to analytical detail. Nonetheless, most observers do not believe that the current Court – despite its occasional reliance on "originalist" analysis – has collectively renounced an approach to adjudication under which the Justices weigh considerations of fairness and practicality in reaching their decisions. *Bush v. Gore* offers a famous example. Subsequent chapters will discuss others.

An Outline of What Is to Come

Constitutional law is a sprawling subject that does not respect neat divisions. In rough terms, however, the Constitution performs two main functions. First, it creates and structures the government of the United States. Second, it guarantees individual rights against the government.

For the most part, the organization of this book reflects this crude distinction, although it deals with the Constitution's two functions, as I just described them, in reverse order. Part I considers constitutional doctrines involving individual rights. Chapters One through Six consider central topics concerning freedom of speech, freedom of religion, economic liberties, rights to fair criminal and civil procedures, the equal protection of the laws, and so-called "fundamental rights" that are not "enumerated" in the Bill of Rights. (It would be impossible to deal with all of the rights created by the Constitution and to keep the book even reasonably short, and I have therefore had to accept some painful omissions of other important topics.)

Part II of the book discusses constitutional doctrines involving the structure of government under the Constitution. Chapters Seven, Eight, and Nine deal, respectively, with the powers of Congress under Article I, of the President under Article II, and of the judiciary under Article III of the Constitution. Besides summarizing relevant constitutional doctrine, the chapter on judicial power contains the book's principal discussion of debates about interpretive methodology and about how the power of judicial review ought to be exercised. I postpone consideration of these important debates until Chapter Nine so that readers will be able to assess the various positions against the background of substantive discussions contained in earlier chapters.

The chapters in Part III address topics in which issues of individual rights are not easily separated from issues of constitutional structure and governmental power. Chapter Ten discusses elections, political democracy, and the Constitution. Chapter Eleven addresses limits on state power resulting from the Constitution's structure and the individual rights to which those limits give rise. Chapter Twelve is about the Constitution in war and emergency. Chapter Thirteen deals with the reach of the Constitution, which generally applies only to the government and not to private conduct, and Congress's power to "enforce" the Constitution by enacting laws designed to protect constitutional rights. Finally, Chapter Fourteen summarizes the themes developed in earlier chapters.

PART ONE

Individual Rights Under the Constitution

ONE

Freedom of Speech

Congress shall make no law . . . abridging the freedom of speech.
– The Free Speech Clause of the First Amendment

The most stringent protection of free speech would not protect a
man in falsely shouting fire in a theatre and causing a panic.
– Justice Oliver Wendell Holmes, Jr.[1]

IN THE WAKE OF THE 9/11 ATTACKS ON THE UNITED STATES,
imagine that an Al Qaeda sympathizer stands before a crowd and
urges *jihad* against the United States. He denounces westerners, zion-
ists, and Americans as devils reviled by God. He calls for suicide
bombings and other terrorist attacks against infidels, throughout the
world but especially in the United States. He urges all lovers of God
to try to devise, and if possible to execute, plans of attack against
nuclear power plants, water supplies, bridges, and synagogues.

If this imagined Al Qaeda sympathizer did his speech-making elsewhere in the world, the United States would likely convey a protest
to the appropriate government and demand that it stop such preaching of hate and violence. Speech, we know, often triggers action. We
would dislike having a foreign government sit by until an attack actually occurred. But if the speaker were an American citizen, living
in the United States, our government would need to adopt a different
posture. The imagined speech would be protected by the First Amendment to the Constitution, as interpreted by the Supreme Court of the
United States – at least unless and until the Court could be persuaded
to change its mind.

The Foundations of Modern Doctrine

Broad protection for freedom of speech has emerged as one of the defining features of American constitutional law. Interestingly, however, modern doctrine does not reflect the original understanding of the First Amendment. Historians have often emphasized the narrowness of the framers' vision. According to most accounts, the one clear purpose of the Free Speech Clause was to prohibit systems of so-called prior restraint, under which authors had to get the approval of administrative censors before they could publish their works.[2] Somewhat curiously from a modern perspective, a constitutional prohibition against prior restraints would not, by itself, immunize speakers or writers from being punished for their speech *after* it was spoken or published. Although such a prohibition bars pre-clearance requirements, it does not stop the government from outlawing speech that is lewd or profane, for example, provided that the punishment does not come until after a speaker has had his or her say.

Beyond systems of prior restraint, some historians believe that the First Amendment was originally understood to forbid after-the-fact punishments for "seditious libel" or criticism of the government.[3] Other historians either take the other side, believing that the founding generation meant to outlaw prior restraints and nothing more, or regard the evidence as doubtful.[4] Almost no one, however, contends that the framers and ratifiers widely understood the Free Speech Clause as doing more than outlawing licensing schemes and, possibly, as protecting critics of the government from punishment for seditious libel. Some among the founding generation may have had broader views, possibly linked to a belief in the existence of "natural rights," but there is little or no evidence of any concrete consensus.[5]

Today, much has changed. As interpreted by the Supreme Court, the First Amendment protects nearly every form of expression from profanity to commercial advertising to flag-burning. What is more, virtually no participant in contemporary constitutional debates seems to object to the departure from the Constitution's originally understood meaning with respect to freedom of speech.

With modern free-speech doctrine lacking firm foundations in the original understanding of the Constitution, it might be thought that the Supreme Court's approach must reflect consensus judgments about the necessary content of a universal human right to free speech. But this suggestion would be mistaken. The United States recognizes speech rights that are substantially broader than those protected by most liberal democracies. To take the most vivid example, most liberal democracies have ratified an international human rights convention that commits signatory nations to banning speech that incites racial hatred.[6] Although the United States participated in the drafting of that convention, this country has never ratified it, largely because of concerns that the convention would violate the First Amendment. Far from suppressing speech that attempts to incite racial hatred, American free-speech doctrine holds racist utterances to enjoy First Amendment protection in most circumstances.

A number of forces have contributed to the development of modern First Amendment law. The Supreme Court has played the principal role in shaping and reshaping a complex body of rules, often in response to the lessons it has gleaned from experiences both happy and unhappy. Cultural forces have also exerted an enormous influence. Supreme Court decisions have proved durable when they resonate with broadly shared values and attitudes, less so when they sound dissonant themes. For the most part the doctrine reflects a robust optimism about "the marketplace of ideas." People get to decide for themselves what to believe and what not to believe. Some ideas can be deeply hurtful – racist utterances being a prime example – but neither the surrounding culture nor the judicial doctrine tends to offer much sympathy: American school children are taught, and many believe, that "sticks and stones can break my bones, but names will never hurt me." Ours is a highly commercialized society, and our First Amendment now protects commercial advertising nearly as fully as it protects political oratory. But this is also a pragmatic nation, skeptical of absolutes, and when the Court believes a particular type of speech to be severely harmful, speech-protective principles will often yield. As Justice Oliver Wendell Holmes wrote in the Supreme Court's first major case interpreting the First Amendment, "The most stringent protection of free speech would not protect a man in falsely shouting fire in a theatre and causing a panic."[7]

Proximate Origins of Modern Doctrine

The origins of modern free-speech doctrine lie in a series of cases decided by the Supreme Court under the 1917 Espionage Act. Before the outbreak of World War I, Congress had enacted little legislation restricting speech, and the Court's discussions of freedom of speech had consisted largely of sweeping, mostly unsympathetic, generalities. Nor had the Supreme Court applied the First Amendment to strike down state laws. (Only during the 1920s did the Court begin to enforce the First Amendment against the states, on the theory that it had been made applicable to them by the Fourteenth Amendment, which was enacted in the aftermath of the Civil War.) In assessing whether the Espionage Act violated the First Amendment, the Court thus found itself relatively free to craft free-speech doctrine as it saw fit.[8]

Enacted during World War I, the Espionage Act made it a crime to cause, attempt to cause, or conspire to cause insubordination in the American armed forces or obstruction of military recruiting. The Supreme Court first encountered the statute in *Schenck v. United States*[9] (1919). Schenck and some companions had distributed leaflets to roughly 15,000 men accepted for military service. On one side the leaflets compared conscription with slavery; on the other they implored recipients to "Assert Your Rights." Justice Holmes, who would later emerge as a crusading champion of speech rights, wrote the unanimous opinion upholding the defendants' conviction for attempting to cause and conspiring to cause interferences with the American war effort. He first established Schenck's intent: "Of course the document would not have been sent unless it had been intended to have some effect, and we do not see what effect it could be expected to have upon persons subject to the draft except to influence them to obstruct the carrying of it out."[10]

Turning then to the First Amendment issue, Holmes brusquely dismissed any suggestion that *all* speech might enjoy constitutional protection, even though the First Amendment says literally that "Congress shall make *no* law ... abridging the freedom of speech." As shown by the imagined case of a false cry of fire in a crowded theater, an absolutist interpretation was simply out of the question. Nor, it might be added, does the Amendment's language necessarily call for such an approach. As John Marshall had pointed out in an out-of-court debate in the 1790s, the First Amendment does not protect all speech, but only "the freedom of speech." The courts must define "the freedom of speech" and thus distinguish speech that is protected from speech that is not.

There are many possible grounds on which the Court might have sought to distinguish protected from unprotected speech. It might, for example, have looked to the original understanding of the First Amendment. But the Court conducted no historical inquiries in *Schenck*. Instead, Justice Holmes – who had been wounded three times in the Civil War and was very much a hard-eyed realist – seized on the criterion of actual or likely harmfulness as the key to identifying speech that lies outside "the freedom of speech" that the First Amendment protects. Speech can be used to deceive, to threaten, and to provoke lawless violence as well as to inform, amuse, and debate. Focusing on speech's capacity to cause harm, Holmes wrote that "[t]he question in every case is whether the words are used in such circumstances and are of such a nature as to create a clear and present danger that they will bring about the substantive evils that Congress has a right to prevent."[11]

With these words, Holmes launched the famous "clear and present danger" test for identifying speech *not* protected by the First Amendment. In applying that test, however, Holmes did not initially demand much evidence of the clarity or even the presence of danger. In *Schenck*, the government had not proved that the leaflets distributed by the defendants had caused insubordination or resistance to the draft or that they were likely to do so. Nonetheless, the Court upheld the convictions. The possibility of serious harm, coupled with intent to produce it, was enough.

Holmes applied the "clear and present danger" test with similar laxity in another case decided in 1919, *Debs v. United States*.[12]

Eugene V. Debs was a leading political figure of his day, a four-time Socialist Party candidate for President who got six percent of the total votes cast in 1912. Despite or possibly because of his stature, Debs was indicted and prosecuted under the Espionage Act based on a speech that he addressed to an Ohio state Socialist Party Convention on a Sunday afternoon. In that speech, he criticized the war, expressed sympathy for those who had opposed and resisted the draft, and said to his audience that "you need to know that you are fit for something better than slavery and cannon fodder."[13] On no more evidence than this, Holmes found the "clear and present danger" test to be satisfied. Debs had used words with a tendency to obstruct war recruiting, even if that result never actually occurred.

Schenck and *Debs* got free-speech doctrine off to a bad start. Holmes was surely right that likely harmfulness is a relevant consideration in defining "the freedom of speech." But there cannot be any very robust free-speech doctrine without some focus on why free speech might deserve constitutional protection (or, if not all speech deserves special protection, why some of it does). In *Schenck* and *Debs*, Holmes ignored the value of speech or, perhaps more precisely, the values in light of which speech might merit protection even when it poses a risk of producing bad consequences.

The facts of *Schenck* and especially *Debs* illustrate one of the reasons why free speech is important: Vivid, passionate, occasionally hyperbolic speech about moral and political matters is vital to public debate in a political democracy. As Holmes himself would write in a later case, it would be intolerable for the government first to declare war and then imprison those who criticize its policies.[14] Democracy requires the freedom to dissent. Admittedly, speech criticizing the government's policies might mislead the voters, dishearten soldiers, or otherwise lead to bad results. But protection of political speech is part and parcel of the Constitution's commitment to democracy. In a democracy, the voters need to be trusted to hear all sides of a debate. In the light of history, the affirmance of Eugene Debs's conviction for making a speech to a political convention was a travesty of the First Amendment.

Within less than a year, Justice Holmes had shifted his perspective and begun to emphasize the values served by freedom of speech. He accepted the mantle of "the great dissenter" beginning in *Abrams v. United States*[15] (1919), involving another prosecution under the Espionage Act, in which he advanced his celebrated "marketplace of ideas" rationale for broad protections of freedom of speech:

> If you have no doubt of your premises or your power and want a certain result with all your heart you naturally express your wishes in law and sweep away all opposition. . . . But when men have realized that time has upset many fighting faiths, they may come to believe even more than they believe the very foundations of their own conduct that the ultimate good desired is better reached by free trade of ideas – that the best test of truth is the power of the thought to get itself accepted in the competition of the market, and that truth is the only ground on which their wishes safely can be carried out.

Holmes's "marketplace of ideas" rationale for broadly protecting free speech stood in some tension with the "clear and present danger" test to which he still said he adhered: If the Constitution aspires to create an open marketplace in ideas, why would it permit speech – including political criticism of the government – to be censored when it began to prove persuasive enough to pose a clear and present danger? Nevertheless, Holmes surely seems right that speech should be deemed *presumptively* valuable and thus protected by the First Amendment, based on the theory that ideas and debate promote the kind of society in which people will be well situated to decide for themselves which ideas deserve acceptance and which do not. He also seems persuasive in his reinterpretation of the "clear and present" danger test to require an evidentiary showing that harm is in fact likely to occur in the relatively immediate future. Those who wish to censor speech about political matters should not be able to rely on speculations about possible consequences in the remote future, but should need to advance evidence of specific, possibly imminent, harms.

A few years later, Justice Louis Brandeis made a further, enduring contribution to the free-speech tradition in an eloquent concurring opinion in *Whitney v. California*[16] (1927). Brandeis argued that "freedom to think as you will and to speak as you think are means indispensable to the discovery and spread of political truth." The First Amendment, he continued, reflected assumptions "that order cannot be secured merely through fear of punishment for its infraction; that it is hazardous to discourage thought, hope and imagination; that fear breeds repression; that repression breeds hate; that hate menaces stable government; that the path of safety lies in the opportunity to discuss freely supposed grievances and proposed remedies; and that the fitting remedy for evil counsels is good ones."[17] Like Holmes, Brandeis accepted the clear and present danger test, but he too proposed to construe it narrowly: "Only an emergency can justify repression"; the "imminent danger" must be clearly apprehended, likely to occur, and "relatively serious."[18]

For more than a decade, Holmes and Brandeis wrote mostly in dissent as majority opinions continued to uphold convictions of those who advocated unlawful action to promote political goals – resistance to the draft, or mass strikes that would cripple wartime production, or the overthrow of industrial capitalism. Nonetheless, the power of their arguments rallied opinion gradually to their side, as they personally became heroes of American constitutional culture. Among the shades of conservative gray that defined most Supreme Court Justices of the era, Holmes stood out as a handsome patrician with a rare gift for judicial eloquence and an infectious desire to meet and know the young as well as the old. Possessing perhaps the sharpest legal mind of any Justice ever to sit on the Court, Holmes drew admiring attention as "the Yankee from Olympus." Brandeis possessed an equal capacity to inspire. The first Jew ever to serve as a Supreme Court Justice, he had championed causes of the poor and disadvantaged before his appointment. He too wrote with unusual flair. By the 1930s and 1940s, the Supreme Court frequently applied the "clear and present danger" test in the searching way that Holmes and Brandeis had said that it should be applied, to protect radical dissenters from mainstream opinion.

A major test for the emerging tradition of speech protectiveness came in *Dennis v. United States*[19] (1951). *Dennis* arose at the height of Cold War anxiety about militant, subversive Communism. It involved prosecutions of leaders of the American Communist Party for advocating the overthrow of the government of the United States by force, not immediately but at some remote future time. A divided Supreme Court upheld the convictions entered by a lower court. Although the evil of a Communist insurrection seemed remote, the Court determined that "imminent" threats were not needed to justify conviction under the "clear and present danger" test. Rather, courts "must ask whether the gravity of the 'evil,' discounted by its improbability, justifies such invasion of free speech as is necessary to avoid the danger."[20]

Like *Schenck* and *Debs*, which were decided in the flush of fear and patriotism accompanying American entry into World War I, *Dennis* was very much the product of its fearful time in the McCarthy era, so-called after the bullying Senator Joseph McCarthy who briefly mesmerized the nation with chilling and often baseless allegations of Communist infiltration into the highest levels of American government. Seen in that context, the Court's decision in *Dennis* was "quite understandable," as John Ely has written, but also very disturbing, because the suppression of speech even loosely about politics "mocks our commitment to an open political process."[21] If any lesson can be drawn, it would seem to be this: First Amendment protections of political speech cannot depend on case-by-case judicial judgments of whether particular utterances by particular speakers pose a clear and present danger. In frightened times, judges are as prone as legislators to overestimate the risk that speech criticizing the government's policies or structure may occasion calamity. Some types of speech deserve more nearly categorical protection.

Before little more than another decade had passed – and after vigorously protected rights of speech and assembly had proved vital to the success of the civil rights movement of the 1950s and 1960s – the Supreme Court had apparently drawn this conclusion. The Court inscribed its lesson into law in *Brandenburg v. Ohio*[22] (1969). Brandenburg, a Ku Klux Klan (KKK) leader, was prosecuted and convicted under a state statute making it a crime to advocate criminal activity as a means of accomplishing political reform. By a unanimous vote, the Court reversed his conviction. The Court's opinion made no reference to the "clear and present danger" test, which it effectively swept away. Instead, the Court purported to extract from prior decisions "the principle" that a state may never punish the mere advancement of ideas, as opposed to express calls for violation of the law, and that it may not "forbid or proscribe advocacy of the use of force or of law violation except where such advocacy is directed to inciting or producing imminent lawless action and is likely to incite or produce such action."[23]

Despite the Court's suggestion to the contrary, a majority of the Justices had never previously endorsed any "principle" affording so much protection to free speech. Although earlier cases had suggested that only advocacy of violence can be punished, and not the advocacy of abstract political ideas, the Court had never before held that even the express advocacy of violence was protected by the First Amendment unless it was likely to produce "imminent lawless action." Had the *Brandenburg* test been applied in previous cases, the speakers in *Schenck, Debs,* and *Dennis* would all have gone free. In *Schenck* and *Debs,* it is at least arguable that the defendants did not expressly advocate violation of the law, and in neither of those cases nor in *Dennis* had the government proved that the speech at issue was likely to incite "imminent," or nearly immediate,[24] violence. Far from merely making explicit a principle already reflected in prior decisions, *Brandenburg* gave broader protection to speech advocating violation of the law than either Holmes or Brandeis had ever defended. To fall outside the protective reach of *Brandenburg,* speech must expressly advocate law violation, not merely create a clear and present danger that such violation may occur, and it must be likely to produce its effects imminently.

Although the *Brandenburg* rule protects more speech than did any previous formulation ever handed down by the Supreme Court, it does not protect all speech aimed at producing less than imminent violence. A court would not construe the First Amendment as protecting a mob boss who directs a "hit" at some relatively distant future time.

Nor would *Brandenburg* necessarily protect terrorist cells or those carrying the instructions to activate terrorist plans. Speech used to form or advance the ends of a "conspiracy" – a private agreement to pursue unlawful ends – is almost certainly not protected by the First Amendment, *Brandenburg* notwithstanding. Moreover, just as the Supreme Court devised the *Brandenburg* rule in 1969, it could reject or modify that rule at any time. For now, however, *Brandenburg* furnishes the First Amendment rule applicable to speech publicly advocating violence or other violation of the law, at least when the end to be promoted is even loosely "political."

It may or may not be ironic that the first beneficiary of the *Brandenburg* rule was a member of the KKK preaching hatred of racial and religious minorities. As noted in the introduction to this chapter, most other liberal democracies have put speech inciting racial and religious hatred into a category of its own and have prohibited it. The Supreme Court might have followed a parallel course, treating racially and religiously bigoted speech as unprotected by the First Amendment because it is incompatible with an underlying constitutional assumption of human equality. *Brandenburg*, however, drew no such lines. Possibly the Court considered Brandenburg's speech to be loosely political and deserving of protection on that ground. Possibly the Justices believed, contrary to fact, that "names can never hurt." Or possibly the Court recalled, although it did not advert to, a thought uttered by Justice Brandeis in *Whitney v. California*: "that fear breeds repression; that repression breeds hate; [and] that hate menaces stable government." Better to let the hate-mongers talk openly, the Court may have thought, than to drive them out of the public square and into unseen caldrons. If so, the Court was making an empirical and predictive judgment, quite possibly correct but also contestable.

Whatever its motivating concerns, *Brandenburg* vividly symbolizes the extent to which the First Amendment currently protects freedom to express what Holmes termed "the thought that we hate."[25] For over thirty years now, it has stuck as the law because it reflects a broadly shared cultural commitment to protect the expression even of the most remotely political ideas, even when doing so entails palpable costs – for example, to the targets of hate speech such as Brandenburg's – and larger risks to the society as a whole.

Expressive Conduct

Although the First Amendment refers to freedom of speech, not conduct, the distinction between speech and conduct often proves elusive. Among other things, some conduct is expressive – the rolling of eyes, the making of gestures, and the burning of flags and draft cards as forms of political protest. It might thus be tempting to say that all expressive conduct enjoys the protection, or at least the presumptive protection, of the First Amendment. But rock throwing, the destruction of property, and even murder and assassination sometimes convey messages too. Plainly, therefore, some way must be found to determine which kinds of expressive conduct deserve First Amendment protection and which do not.

For much of the twentieth century, the Supreme Court struggled to distinguish expressive activities that were principally speechlike from those that principally involved conduct. In *United States v. O'Brien*[26] (1968), a case involving the burning of a draft card as a mode of political protest, the Court embarked on a new course. O'Brien, who had publicly burned his draft card to protest the Vietnam War, was convicted under a federal statute making it a crime to mutilate or destroy a draft certificate. In assessing his First Amendment defense, the Court began by denying "that an apparently limitless variety of conduct can be labeled 'speech' whenever the person engaging in the conduct intends thereby to express an idea."[27] Almost immediately, however, the Court picked up a different theme, by focusing on whether the government's reason for prohibiting the destruction of draft cards was "unrelated to the suppression of free expression."[28] If the statute's only purpose was to stifle critics of the Vietnam War, the Court suggested that it would be invalid. To permit governmental censorship of ideas merely because many people find them offensive or because the government does not trust the public to evaluate them would threaten the central First Amendment principle that people should be able to decide for themselves which ideas to believe (at least in matters of politics and opinion). By contrast, the Court sensibly suggested, if the government were trying to stop harms unrelated to the *messages* being conveyed by political protestors – such as the destruction of items necessary to the efficient operation of the draft – the protective policies of the First Amendment would be less centrally engaged. To put the point only slightly differently, the Court concluded that the First Amendment condemns deliberate governmental censorship of ideas, but does not disable the government from banning conduct, such as the destruction of governmental property, that is harmful for reasons independent of any message that it may express.

The approach adopted in *United States v. O'Brien* continues to govern First Amendment cases involving a mixture of speech and conduct. If the government bars a form of conduct as a means of stifling messages that it finds offensive, the courts will almost invariably find a constitutional violation. To cite one vivid example, the Supreme Court invalidated prohibitions against flag burning in *Texas v. Johnson*[29] (1989) and *United States v. Eichman*[30] (1990). The Justices ruled that the government's interest in prohibiting this conduct related to the message that flag burning conveyed and to the offense that it generated. The Court found no sufficient justification for governmental suppression of an attempt to convey ideas.

By contrast, governmental regulation even of expressive conduct will be upheld, *O'Brien* established, "if it furthers an important or substantial governmental interest ... unrelated to the suppression of free expression; and if the incidental restriction on alleged First Amendment freedoms is no greater than is essential to the furtherance of that interest."[31] Finding the government's purposes to be unrelated to suppression of ideas, the Court has upheld a ban against sleeping on the National Mall in Washington, even as it applied to protestors who wished to dramatize the plight of the homeless.[32] The Court concluded that interests in maintaining the beauty of the Mall justified an across-the-board ban on sleeping and camping there, even when the effect was partly to thwart expressive conduct.

Over time, *O'Brien* has proved to be among the Supreme Court's most influential free-speech decisions of the modern era. Its significance reaches beyond the special problems posed by expressive conduct. As commentators quickly noticed, even when the government regulates "pure" speech, it may sometimes act for reasons unrelated to the suppression of ideas.[33] For example, a rule barring sound trucks in residential neighborhoods after 9 P.M. forbids the dissemination of speech, not expressive conduct, but the purpose is to preserve residential tranquility in the nighttime, not to stifle any particular message. Subsequent cases make clear that rules of this kind – justified by reasons unrelated to the suppression of ideas – will receive deferential treatment from the courts under a test similar to that laid down in *O'Brien*. At the same time, by emphasizing that not all regulations of speech necessarily embody censorial purposes, *O'Brien* helped to crystallize the presumptive offensiveness of those that do. As the Court now routinely recites in a variety of contexts, when the government regulates speech on the basis of its content, a censorial motive most likely explains why some speech is banned but other speech is not, and a strong presumption of constitutional invalidity applies.[34] In nearly all contexts, "content-based" regulations of speech – which try to stop the public from hearing some messages but not others – can be justified only by an exceedingly weighty governmental interest, if at all.

Shocking and Offensive Speech

Another signal step in the development of modern First Amendment law came in *Cohen v. California*[35] (1971). During the era of protests against the Vietnam War, Cohen walked into a courthouse wearing a jacket emblazoned with the legend "Fuck the Draft." The state of California prosecuted and convicted him under a statute that forbade disturbing the peace. The Supreme Court reversed the conviction. In defending Cohen's conviction, the state argued that it had no intent to censor his antiwar message: He was free to express that message however he liked, as long as he did not disturb the peace of his fellow citizens by conveying that message through shocking and offensive words. The Court rejected this argument. It deemed Cohen's message inseparable from the words that he chose to express it. Linguistic expression, the Court wrote, has "emotive" as well as "cognitive force,"[36] and Cohen's chosen words conveyed a depth of emotion that other formulations might not have communicated. "[W]e cannot indulge the facile assumption that one can forbid particular words without also running a substantial risk of suppressing ideas in the process," the Court said.[37]

Cohen's reasoning is compelling, even if its conclusion is jarring: The First Amendment protects a right to shock and offend as inseparable from the right to express opinions. Like the partial protection of racist speech in *Brandenburg*, the doctrine established by *Cohen* is not cost free. Apart from its possible coarsening effect on common sensibilities, shocking speech often confronts unwilling listeners, not just those who thrill to see conventional standards flouted. What is more, the right to shock and offend can be, and sometimes is, exercised maliciously against the most vulnerable groups in American society, including racial minorities. Lines can be drawn in some cases, and prohibitions upheld when language not only shocks but also conveys a physical threat,[38] but the line drawing grows difficult once *Cohen*'s compelling reasoning is accepted: There is often no distinction between a constitutionally protected substantive message and the form, however shocking or hateful, in which the message is expressed.

Remaining Unprotected Categories, Including Obscenity

In *Chaplinsky v. New Hampshire*[39] (1942), the Supreme Court offered the much-quoted observation that "[t]here are certain well-defined and narrowly limited classes of speech, the prevention and punishment of which has never been thought to raise any Constitutional problem." The Court continued: "These include the lewd and obscene, the profane, the libelous, and the insulting or 'fighting' words – those which by their very utterance inflict injury or tend to incite an immediate breach of the peace."[40]

As illustrated by cases such as *Cohen v. California*, which involved profanity, the list of categories of speech that are excluded from First Amendment protection has proved historically variable. ("Libelous" or defamatory speech, another category listed in *Chaplinsky* as outside the protective reach of the First Amendment, has also received an important measure of protection in more recent decisions.) Yet virtually no one has ever suggested that the First Amendment should protect threats, solicitations of bribes, or verbal agreements to fix prices, any more than it protects false cries of fire in a crowded theater. The question is not whether there should be any categories of speech excluded from the First Amendment, but which categories lie beyond the constitutional pale. Among the most interesting disputes has involved "obscenity" – a term that the Court has viewed as somehow linking the sexually explicit with the disgusting, but that has proved astonishingly difficult to define precisely. (Refusing to be stymied by the problem of definition, Justice Potter Stewart once remarked of the hard-core pornography that he thought should be subject to prohibition, "I know it when I see it."[41])

Although obscenity had long been assumed to lie outside the First Amendment, the Supreme Court did not face a case squarely presenting the question until the middle of the twentieth century. In *Roth v. United States*[42] (1957), the Court held obscenity to lack First Amendment protection, partly because of evidence concerning the original understanding, partly because obscenity contributed little or nothing to the search for truth, and partly because it threatened the social interest in order and morality.

But the Court's surprisingly careless opinion did not define "obscenity" with any care. The absence of a clear definition proved troublesome when, as the 1950s spilled into the 1960s, magazines and motion pictures pressed the boundaries of constitutional protection. Two Justices, Hugo Black and William Douglas, who sometimes styled themselves as First Amendment literalists or absolutists, could see no basis for holding sexually explicit speech and pictures to be less protected than other kinds and consistently voted to reverse all obscenity convictions. (Black liked to carry a copy of the Constitution in his pocket, to be available whenever he wanted to make the point with all possible dramatic force that the Constitution says "Congress shall make ... *no law* ... abridging the freedom of speech.") The other Justices continued to wrestle with the definitional issue, with three

Justices ultimately concluding that for material to be obscene and thus subject to legal prohibition, prosecutors must prove it to be "utterly without redeeming social value."[43] Few prosecutions could meet this standard.

In 1973, the more conservative "Burger Court" – which took its name from Warren Burger, who became Chief Justice in 1969, and included three other Justices newly appointed by President Richard Nixon following his "law and order" election campaign – reexamined the issue. In *Miller v. California*,[44] the Court laid down a test for constitutionally unprotected obscenity that has endured through the current day. It defines obscenity as material that (1) "taken as a whole, appeals to the prurient interest," that (2) "depicts or describes, in a patently offensive way, sexual conduct specifically defined by... applicable state law," and that (3) "taken as a whole, lacks serious literary, artistic, political, or scientific value." In defining obscenity that Congress and the states are entitled to regulate (if they choose to do so), the current doctrine makes no exception for sales or displays of obscene materials only to consenting adults. Adult theaters that admit only people over twenty-one years old are vulnerable to prosecution.[45]

The Court's toleration of governmental attempts to stifle sexually explicit messages is exceptional in modern First Amendment doctrine. It probably reflects a continuing prudishness, both among the Justices and among significant segments of the population, about the rawest forms of sexual explicitness. In other contexts, the Court permits the content-based regulation of speech only to prevent palpable and serious harms, such as damage to reputation arising from libelous speech and incitements to imminent lawless violence. In contrast, the Court has demanded no proof that obscenity causes any harm apart from its allegedly debasing effects on the character of those who view it. Social scientists have produced some evidence, which is admittedly disputed, suggesting that materials that are not only sexually explicit, but also violent, may tend to promote increased violence toward women, at least among some populations.[46] Significantly, however, the Supreme Court has not shaped its definition of prohibitable obscenity to materials plausibly likely to promote sexual violence. Not all obscene films and photographs include violence, and many materials that do eroticize violence are not obscene under the Supreme Court's definition, either because they are not predominantly "prurient" in their appeal or because they possess some "serious" value.

The Supreme Court's obscenity doctrine is peculiar in another way as well. Although it permits the prohibition of obscenity, the definition of obscenity is relatively narrow. As a result, *Miller* has done little to stem a mounting flood of sexually explicit materials into American popular culture. The Court's conservative stand against sexually licentious material thus appears to have little practical significance.

The one exception, if that is the proper term, involves child pornography. In *New York v. Ferber*[47] (1982), the Supreme Court upheld a state law prohibiting the production, distribution, and sale of so-called child pornography, defined to include the presentation or depiction of live "sexual conduct" by a child under sixteen years old. A state court had held the statute unconstitutional, because it applied to all materials showing children engaged in sexual conduct, without regard to whether the material satisfied the obscenity test of *Miller v. California*. The Supreme Court disagreed. Emphasizing the severe harm to children forced to engage in live sexual performances, the Court unanimously upheld the challenged statute. The Court obviously views child pornography, as defined, as not only smutty but dangerous to children in the highest degree, and it has invited vigorous enforcement of child pornography laws.[48]

Commercial Speech

Before the 1970s, the Supreme Court accorded no First Amendment protection to commercial advertising.[49] A change of course began in *Virginia State Board of Pharmacy v. Virginia Citizens Consumer Council Inc.*[50] (1976). The Virginia Pharmacy Board forbade pharmacists to advertise the prices that they charged for prescription drugs. The Board had adopted its policy to preserve the competitive position of small drug stores, which often needed to charge higher prices than large chains because their costs were higher. According to the Board, small neighborhood pharmacies were likely to be more knowledgeable about their individual customers, and thus to give better service and advice, than chain stores. In striking down the Virginia regulation, the Supreme Court majority emphasized the interest of consumers in having access to information, so that they could decide for themselves what to buy and where to buy it. The Court declined to articulate a clear test governing when the regulation of advertising might be permissible. It doubted, however, that the government could ever be justified in barring the dissemination of truthful information simply for the purpose of keeping consumers in the dark.

At the time of the *Virginia Pharmacy* case, the Supreme Court's most liberal Justices were those most eager to extend First Amendment protection to commercial advertising, just as they were generally the Justices most protective of First Amendment rights in other contexts. Justice William Rehnquist, then the Court's most conservative member, dissented. As a policy matter, he worried that "[u]nder the Court's opinion the way will be open not only for dissemination of price information but for active promotion of prescription drugs, liquor, cigarettes, and other products the use of which it has previously been thought desirable to discourage."[51] Rehnquist dissented again from the Court's ruling in *Central Hudson Gas & Electric Corp. v. Public Service Commission*[52] (1981), which established a test for the permissibility of restrictions on commercial advertising that the Supreme Court has never abandoned. Under that test, for commercial speech to be entitled to First Amendment protection at all, it "must concern lawful activity and not be misleading." If that threshold is crossed, government may regulate commercial advertising only if the regulation directly promotes a "substantial" governmental interest and "is not more extensive than is necessary to serve that interest."[53]

From a loosely political perspective, the Justices in *Virginia Pharmacy* and *Central Hudson* might easily have seemed misaligned, but in a way not much noticed at the time. In both cases, the challenged restrictions on speech were parts of a broad framework of economic regulation. The state of Virginia licensed pharmacies such as that involved in the *Virginia Pharmacy* case and closely regulated their business practices. Similarly, the party claiming free-speech rights in

Central Hudson was a highly regulated electric power company, indeed a licensed monopolist, challenging a restriction on the promotional aspect of its business. As the Nobel Prize-winning economist Ronald Coase pointed out, in the decades following the New Deal, liberals generally championed broad regulation of economic markets, but maintained that the government had no business regulating speech under the First Amendment.[54] During the same period, conservatives protested governmental intervention in economic markets, but tended to support the regulation of speech in a variety of contexts (including the prohibition of obscenity and the suppression of speech by subversive organizations such as the Communist Party). According to Coase, both positions were inconsistent. On the one hand, if the government was good at regulating economic markets (as liberals thought), it was unlikely to be much less good at regulating speech markets, or at least at regulating the advertising of economic transactions. On the other hand, if government intervention into economic markets tended to bring bad consequences (as conservatives maintained), the government was unlikely to perform better when it regulated speech.

Since Coase offered his comment, the position of judicial liberals has not changed a great deal, but that of judicial conservatives has. In recent years they have emerged as enthusiastic champions of commercial speech rights. Indeed, in *Lorillard Tobacco Co. v. Reilly*[55] (2001), the Court's five most conservative Justices outvoted four typically more liberal dissenters to invalidate a Massachusetts statute barring billboard advertising of tobacco products within 1,000 feet of a school or playground.[56] Without disputing the state's claims that tobacco advertising helps attract children to addictive and deadly products, the Court's majority ruled that the burdens on speech imposed by the state law were too "onerous" to survive constitutional scrutiny.

The decision in *Lorillard Tobacco Co.* demonstrates the tendency of legal doctrine to deal in abstraction. In the eyes of the law, companies engaged in the business of selling cigarettes became "speakers" protected under the First Amendment even though the sole aim of their "speech" – consisting mostly of misleading images of healthy and sexy-looking people on billboards – was to promote the sale of a deadly product. But *Lorillard* also represents a weighing of competing values. No more today than in Holmes's time is all speech absolutely protected under the First Amendment. False cries of fire in crowded theaters of course remain subject to prohibition. And the same Justices who joined the *Lorillard* majority continue to hold that the states can regulate obscenity, simply to preserve state interests in morality. In *Lorillard*, the Justices might have held that the state's interest in protecting its children outweighed the speech interests of tobacco companies eager to market their products. Instead, the majority concluded that the balance of considerations tipped the other way.

The Broadcast Media

Perhaps surprisingly, different First Amendment rules sometimes apply to different media of communication. As long as newspapers and magazines do not print material that is altogether outside the protection of the First Amendment, such as obscenity or false advertising, the First Amendment gives them nearly complete immunity from governmental regulation. By contrast, the broadcast media (radio and television) have historically enjoyed less protection. The original justification for differential treatment of the print and broadcast media lay in public ownership of the airwaves. In order to prevent a chaos of competing voices attempting to broadcast over the same frequencies, the Federal Communications Commission (FCC) licenses use of the broadcast spectrum, and the Supreme Court has held that the FCC may use its licensing power to demand programming in the public interest.[57] For example, the FCC can require that the broadcast media provide news coverage. In *Red Lion Broadcasting Co. v. FCC*[58] (1969), the Court also upheld the constitutionality of the Commission's now-abandoned "fairness doctrine," which required balanced coverage of public issues.

In *FCC v. Pacifica Foundation*[59] (1978), the Supreme Court went further in holding that the FCC may enforce regulations prohibiting broadcast over the public airwaves of speech that the Commission deems "indecent," even if it is not "obscene" under the test of *Miller v. California*, at least during times when children may be listening. The *Pacifica* case arose when a San Francisco radio station played a recorded monologue by the comedian George Carlin titled "Filthy Words," featuring seven words that Carlin himself described as barred from the public airwaves – "the ones that will curve your spine, grow hair on your hands and maybe, even bring . . . peace without honor . . . and a bourbon."[60] The monologue repeatedly used the seven "filthy" words to comic effect, but not to the amusement of the FCC. When the Commission threatened to enforce a regulation barring the broadcast of "indecent" material, Pacifica claimed a violation of its rights under the First Amendment. The Supreme Court disagreed. Although Carlin could not have been punished for delivering his monologue in a theater or a nightclub (because it was not "obscene" under the test of *Miller v. California*), a majority of the Justices concluded that Pacifica could be penalized for broadcasting it over the public airwaves. Relying on different arguments from those they had advanced in *Red Lion*, the Justices emphasized two considerations in holding that the First Amendment gives less protection to the broadcast media than to other kinds of speakers: Radio and television broadcasts come directly into the home, and they are uniquely accessible to children.

Having held that the radio and television stations broadcasting over the public airwaves are subject to different First Amendment rules than the print media, the Supreme Court has recently been pressed to clarify the rules applicable to *cable* television. Like the over-the-airwaves media, cable television comes directly into the home and is widely accessible to children. But, unlike the traditional broadcast media, cable operators deliver their signals through privately owned wires, not publicly owned and licensed airwaves. Most if not all of the current Supreme Court Justices therefore agree that the special First Amendment rules permitting federal regulation of the broadcast media do not apply to regulation of cable companies.[61]

In the long run, as cable television spreads to more and more homes, it seems doubtful that a sharp distinction between the First

Amendment status of broadcast television and cable television will continue to make any practical sense (if it does now). And although predictions are hazardous, in a variety of contexts the Court seems increasingly insistent that all content-based regulations are invalid unless "necessary" to promote "compelling" governmental interests. It may be only a matter of time until the regulation of over-the-air broadcasting must also meet this standard.

This already appears to be the case with regulation of speech on the Internet. In *Reno v. American Civil Liberties Union*[62] (1997), the Court struck down a federal statutory provision barring the sending or display of "patently offensive" (but not necessarily "obscene") material in a manner available to anyone under eighteen years of age. As the Court noted, this prohibition effectively restricted the messages that could be sent to chatrooms or newsgroups, and it would have imposed prohibitively expensive burdens on speakers with websites to verify that all of their users are adults. The Court thus ruled that the prohibition swept too broadly and thereby violated the First Amendment, despite serious concerns about children's access to inappropriate materials.[63]

Freedom to Associate and Not to Associate

The First Amendment contains no explicit reference to freedom to associate for expressive purposes. Nonetheless, the Supreme Court has held that such a right exists, largely because of the role of association in helping to promote speech: People often join groups in order to be able to advocate their causes more effectively. An important case in the development of the doctrine was *NAACP v. Alabama*[64] (1958), in which the state had demanded that the local chapter of the National Association for the Advancement of Colored People (NAACP), a civil rights organization, disclose its membership lists. In Alabama in 1958, public identification of NAACP members would predictably have subjected them to widespread hostility and possibly worse. In addition, the threat of future identification would have discouraged membership in civil rights organizations. Confronted with these facts, the Court held that the Constitution protects a right to associate for expressive purposes. It then ruled that for Alabama to force public disclosure of the NAACP's membership rolls would impose a burden on that right and that the Constitution forbade the imposition of such a burden in the absence of a powerful reason, which the state had not demonstrated.

Once recognized, the right to freedom of association for expressive purposes implies a right *not* to associate. Like-minded people who join expressive groups have at least a presumptive right to exclude people who hold different views. To cite an obvious example, the NAACP should not have to admit white racists (nor should the KKK have to admit blacks). At the same time, the right not to associate should not be defined too broadly. Otherwise it would threaten the government's power to bar discrimination on the basis of race, religion, and gender whenever an affected group or business claims an expressive purpose. A bigoted employer who prefers not to hire blacks or Jews should not be able to claim a constitutional right of freedom of association strong enough to override obligations imposed by the nation's civil rights laws. To date, the precise scope of the constitutional right not to associate remains uncertain.

Roberts v. United States Jaycees[65] (1984) presented a question about the right of expressive organizations to discriminate on the basis of gender. The Jaycees are a nonprofit national corporation, organized to promote educational, charitable, and civic purposes. By rule, the Jaycees restricted regular membership to men between the ages of eighteen and thirty-five. When Minnesota enacted an antidiscrimination statute forbidding the Jaycees to exclude women, the Jaycees claimed a violation of their right to freedom of association. The Supreme Court disagreed. It rested its conclusion on two considerations, without making clear whether either alone would have sufficed. First, the government had a "compelling" interest in preventing discrimination on the basis of gender.[66] Second, the Jaycees had failed to establish that the challenged statute impeded their ability to communicate their "preferred views," because they had presented no evidence that "women might have a different attitude" from men concerning the political, economic, and charitable issues on which the group sometimes spoke.[67]

To be contrasted with *Roberts* is *Boy Scouts of America v. Dale*[68] (2000), in which the Court found that a state antidiscrimination statute did violate the First Amendment by abridging rights to freedom of association. The Scouts removed Dale as an assistant scout master upon learning that he was gay, was the copresident of the Rutgers University Lesbian/Gay Alliance, and had been quoted in the press on the need for gay role models. After a New Jersey court ordered Dale's reinstatement under a state antidiscrimination statute, the Scouts pressed a freedom of association claim in the Supreme Court. By 5–4, the Court upheld the Scouts' claim. The majority opinion found that the Scouts were an expressive organization, seeking to instill moral values. It also accepted the Scouts' claim, vigorously contested by the dissenting opinion, that the Scouts had a long-standing position that homosexual behavior was morally inappropriate. With these findings in place, the Court held in essence that Dale's continued presence in the Scouts would have sent a progay message at odds with the message that the Scouts wished to send. It distinguished *Roberts* on the ground that forcing the Jaycees to admit women did not "materially interfere with the ideas" that the Jaycees wished to express.[69]

Concluding Note

For better or for worse, *Boy Scouts of America v. Dale* illustrates the "firstness" of the First Amendment within contemporary constitutional doctrine. In a collision with core principles of free speech and freedom of association, competing values – including those associated with ideals of human equality – typically give way. But a concluding note of caution is also in order. If my carefully framed conclusion about the firstness of the First Amendment is correct, it is because it captures the First Amendment's frequently absolute pretensions ("Congress shall make *no* law . . . abridging the freedom of speech"), while also acknowledging its capacity for occasional compromise and equivocation through recognition that only "core principles" are unyielding. ("The most stringent protection of free speech would not protect a man falsely shouting fire in a theatre.") In determining the outer boundaries of First Amendment protections, judges and Justices must make difficult, often contestable, judgments.

TWO

Freedom of Religion

Congress shall make no law respecting an establishment of religion, or prohibiting the free exercise thereof....

> – The Religion Clauses of
> the First Amendment to the Constitution

[Freedom of religion] embraces two concepts, – freedom to believe and freedom to act. The first is absolute but, in the nature of things, the second cannot be.

> – *Cantwell v. Connecticut*[1]

IN 1966, THE FORMER HEAVYWEIGHT BOXING CHAMPION of the world, Muhammad Ali, was sentenced to five years in jail for refusing to report for induction into the army. The country was then at war in Vietnam. The nation had a draft. But when called, Ali refused to take what the Supreme Court described as "the traditional step forward,"[2] and he was prosecuted as a result. His defense was straightforward: The draft law then in force provided exemptions for those who, because of sincere religious belief, were conscientiously opposed to war in any form. As a newly converted member to the Nation of Islam faith, Ali claimed entitlement to "conscientious objector" status.

Although the appeals process took five years, in *Clay, aka* [also known as] *Ali v. United States*[3] (1971), the Supreme Court overturned Ali's conviction. The Court based its decision entirely on the draft laws then in effect. It held that the draft authorities had erred in their consideration of whether Ali was entitled to a draft exemption as a religiously motivated conscientious objector. Nevertheless, constitutional issues were not far in the background. What is more, those background constitutional issues were difficult, controversial, and tangled. To see why is to understand perhaps the central issue in constitutional doctrines involving freedom of religion.

The First Amendment includes two clauses dealing with religion. The first, the Establishment Clause, provides that "Congress shall make no law respecting an establishment of religion." The second, the Free Exercise Clause, immediately adds that neither may Congress "prohibit[] the free exercise thereof." Taken together, the two Religion Clauses reflect a commitment to religious voluntarism or freedom of religious conscience. The Establishment Clause forbids governmental efforts to impose religious beliefs or practices. The Free Exercise Clause stops the government from barring or discouraging religious observance.

The difficulty is that general propositions do not resolve hard cases, as the statute at the center of *Clay v. United States* nicely illustrates. From one side, a serious argument could be mounted that Ali had a constitutional right to be excused from the draft, enforceable even if Congress had not provided an exemption. If the government had required him to fight in violation of his religious beliefs, or sent him to jail for refusing to do so, it would arguably have violated his right to the free exercise of his religion. According to some, the Free Exercise Clause establishes that people cannot be punished for doing what their religion dictates that they must do, at least in the absence of a compelling governmental interest supporting the imposition of punishment.

From another side, however, others protest that for the government to provide a draft exemption *only* for religiously motivated objectors (and not, for example, for those opposed to war on philosophical but not religious grounds) creates a preference for religious believers over nonbelievers in violation of the Establishment Clause. According to this view, a law that takes note of religious belief for purposes of affording favored treatment (as in the form of draft exemptions) "respect[s] an establishment of religion" in contravention of the Constitution.[4]

When the debate is framed in these terms, there is something to be said for both of these nearly polar arguments – and perhaps, thus, a natural disposition for the Supreme Court to adopt a mediating position. But a mediating position clearly could not satisfy everyone, and any particular mediating position risks pleasing no one. Perhaps as a result, there is nearly pervasive disagreement about how the Religion Clauses ought to be interpreted, even though some points of doctrine are reasonably clear.

Although issues under the Religion Clauses are often interconnected, the Supreme Court typically resolves Establishment Clause issues within one doctrinal framework, Free Exercise Clause issues within another. In tracing the outlines of contemporary doctrine, I begin by following the same approach, treating first the Establishment Clause and then the Free Exercise Clause, before reconnecting the discussions at the end.

Introduction to the Establishment Clause

Disputes about the Establishment Clause, like disputes about the meaning of most constitutional provisions, begin (although they do not necessarily end) with efforts to identify the Clause's originally understood meaning. It is easy to discover statements by members of the founding generation demanding rigid separation of church and state. Yet the federal government had scarcely begun operation before both Houses of Congress hired chaplains, to be paid from public funds, and before President George Washington proclaimed a national day of prayer and thanksgiving.[5] In modern disputes, those who favor strict separation of church and state, and who believe that the government should not become entangled with religious institutions or accord preference to those with religious motivations, point to expressions of separationist ideals as the best evidence of the original understanding. On the other side, those who believe that religion ought to play a greater role in American public life, and who think that the government should be able to make laws that accommodate religious beliefs (by furnishing draft exemptions, for example), cite historical practice as evidence that the Establishment Clause must originally have been understood relatively narrowly – perhaps barring only the official designation of a single state church, explicit coercion of religious practice, and taxes specifically to fund a single established religion.[6]

There are no early Supreme Court decisions interpreting the Religion Clauses. Indeed, only two Establishment Clause cases received any significant consideration by the Supreme Court before 1947,[7] which commentators typically treat as the beginning of the "modern" era.[8] Challenges to federal action under the Religion Clauses were rare if not nonexistent during the early years, and those clauses – like other provisions of the Bill of Rights – were originally understood not to apply to the states.[9]

Two slightly overdrawn positions will help to illuminate current controversies about the Establishment Clause. "Strict separationists" believe that the government has no business supporting religious beliefs or institutions in any way – for example, by providing tax breaks to churches, assisting parochial schools, including prayers or benedictions in public ceremonies, or inscribing "In God We Trust" on the currency. But strict separationists struggle with the significance of long-standing practice. If the first Congress hired and paid chaplains and if "In God We Trust" has been on the currency from the beginning of the Republic without either the founding generation or most of their successors seeing a problem, then how can these and similar practices be deemed unconstitutional today?

Opposed to the strict separationists are a loose coalition of what might be called "religious accommodationists."[10] Emphasizing historical practice, they maintain that the Establishment Clause forbids governmental efforts to coerce the citizenry to practice or support any single religion, but deny that it mandates hostility or even indifference to religion in general. As long as the government does not favor one sect above others, but shows equal respect for a plurality of faiths, religious accommodationists believe that the Constitution tolerates noncoercive acknowledgments and accommodations of religious beliefs. Religious accommodationists can well explain why certain entrenched social practices (such as the inscription of "In God We Trust" on the currency) were not historically perceived as presenting constitutional difficulties: The relevant practices are not coercive and do not prefer one narrow sect over another. But accommodationists

60

have a harder time explaining, and indeed may have to reject, Supreme Court rulings that now seem well accepted, including the decision that prayer in the public schools violates the Establishment Clause.[11]

To date, neither the strict separationists nor the religious accommodationists have achieved their fullest aspirations. Supreme Court doctrine reflects a contested mix of competing views. In recent years, however, the Court has tilted increasingly away from strict separationism and toward a religious accommodationist approach.

Religion in the Public Schools

In path-breaking decisions in the 1960s, the Supreme Court held that officially organized prayer and Bible readings in the public schools violate the Establishment Clause.[12] The decisions sparked immediate controversy. Their historical foundations were doubtful. Nevertheless, the decisions manifested a compelling ideal of religious voluntarism that can reasonably be ascribed to the Religion Clauses: Just as the government should not directly coerce its citizens into practicing a religion that they do not believe, neither should it intentionally subject them to social pressures to adapt their beliefs to a prescribed norm. Children in the public schools are peculiarly impressionable. School-sponsored prayer sends a signal to children that prayer is not only normal, but also viewed as normatively desirable within our society.

From the 1960s through the mid-1980s, the Supreme Court exhibited considerable sensitivity to the social effects of governmental policies in promoting religion, especially in the public schools, and found Establishment Clause violations rather readily. During this period the Court developed a stringent test for Establishment Clause violations – often referred to as "the *Lemon* test" – under which a statute would be deemed invalid if either its "purpose" or its "principal or primary effect" was to promote religion, or if it promoted excessive "entanglement" between church and state.[13] In *Epperson v. Arkansas*[14] (1968), the Court struck down a statute forbidding public schoolteachers to teach the theory of evolution. A majority found it "clear that fundamentalist sectarian conviction was and is the law's reason for existence."[15] In *Stone v. Graham*[16] (1980), the Court similarly invalidated a Kentucky statute mandating the posting of the Ten Commandments on the wall of public school classrooms. Once again the Court determined that the statute's likely purpose and effect were to advance religion.

Near the high tide of strict separationism, in 1985 the Court held unconstitutional a state law authorizing a moment of silence in the public schools "for meditation or voluntary prayer." The opinion in *Wallace v. Jaffree*[17] (1985) emphasized that a previously enacted statute called for the school day to begin with a one-minute period of silence "for meditation." By taking the further step of authorizing "voluntary prayer," the legislature manifested a "purpose" of promoting religion. The Court suggested, but did not expressly hold, that a statute simply prescribing a moment of silence, without reference to prayer, would pass constitutional muster.

The Court's opinion in *Wallace v. Jaffree* provoked strong dissenting opinions arguing that the Court should drastically revise its interpretation of the Establishment Clause.[18] These opinions protested, accurately, that if the Court were serious about invalidating every statute with either the purpose or the primary effect of promoting religion, as it purported to do under the *Lemon* test, a variety of historically entrenched practices would need to fall. There could be no more national days of prayer, "In God We Trust" would need to be banished from the currency, and so forth.

In the years since *Wallace v. Jaffree*, the Supreme Court has grown less quick to find Establishment Clause violations, even in the context of public education, where school children remain notoriously impressionable. For example, the Court has held that when public schools open their classrooms and gymnasiums to use by nonreligious groups (such as chess and drama clubs) they not only may, but must, permit religious organizations to use the same facilities on a nondiscriminatory basis, notwithstanding any possible effects in promoting religion.[19]

More generally, a majority of the Justices have apparently adopted the view, first urged by the moderate conservative Justice Sandra Day

O'Connor, that governmental policies that aid religion should not be condemned under the Establishment Clause unless a "reasonable observer"[20] would view them as "endorsing" religious beliefs or practices. The "endorsement test" is a vague one. As the Court's efforts to apply it have made clear, some of the Justices virtually never find endorsement, whereas others are readier to do so. Justice O'Connor, who pioneered the test, has tried to draw very fine lines. In one important case, she held that an objective observer would not view an outdoor Christmas display that included a creche as constituting an endorsement of religion,[21] though she reached a different conclusion about another creche, which stood by itself at the top of a courthouse staircase, in a different case.[22]

Although the Court has generally been reluctant to find forbidden endorsement in most contexts, a majority of the Justices have continued to treat public schools and impressionable schoolchildren as triggering elevated concerns under the Establishment Clause. In *Lee v. Weisman*[23] (1992), for example, the Court held that it was constitutionally impermissible for a public school graduation ceremony to include a religious invocation or benediction. Because the graduation ceremony was a public event, including adults as well as children, the cases that had forbidden school prayer on ordinary schooldays did not obviously dictate the outcome. As lawyers say, they were "distinguishable." Nevertheless, a narrow majority of the Justices concluded that the context placed impermissible "public pressure, as well as peer pressure, on attending students" to participate in the school-sponsored prayer[24] – even though an earlier decision had found that a state legislature did not violate the Establishment Clause by hiring a chaplain to lead prayers at the beginning of legislative sessions attended predominantly, if not exclusively, by adults.[25]

Governmental Aid to Religious Institutions

Throughout American history, religious institutions have received governmental benefits. Some of these benefits, such as police and fire protection, have flowed to churches on the same basis as to other groups and individuals. But other traditional benefits have gone to churches on more selective terms. For example, from the beginning of constitutional history, churches have been widely exempted from state and local property taxes. Charitable institutions other than churches may also qualify for tax relief, but in comparison with noncharitable organizations, churches stand on a preferred footing. Noting the traditional status of tax benefits for churches, the Court found in *Walz v. Tax Commission*[26] (1970) that a state law exempting churches from property taxes (along with other educational and charitable institutions) did not violate the Establishment Clause. The *Walz* decision is notable in part because it comes from the same era in which the Court formulated the so-called *Lemon* test and in which it manifested sturdily separationist views in other settings. Even for Justices otherwise committed to strict separation, the combination of history and entrenched expectations gave pause. But the Court's opinion in *Walz* was narrow. It suggested that although the government could permissibly exempt churches from taxes, it would be problematic under the Establishment Clause for the government to give money directly to a religious institution. Even though the cash value of a tax exemption and a government check might be precisely the same, the Court thought that there was a symbolic difference between them: For the government to transfer money directly to a religious institution somehow looked like a stronger form of endorsement than did excusing churches from tax obligations imposed on most but not all others.

Through most of constitutional history, it was uncommon for the government to give money or other items of value (other than broadly shared public services and tax breaks) directly to religious institutions. But the permissibility of direct governmental aid emerged as an important political issue beginning in the 1960s. Parochial schools, nearly all operated by the Roman Catholic Church, initially lay at the center of the controversy.[27] Citing a desire to promote the public interest in effective education, local and national governments began to furnish aid to parochial schools or to parents who wished to send their children to parochial schools. But public support for parochial schooling also attracted strong opposition. Some regarded the public initiatives as special-interest legislation, enacted for the benefit of

Catholics. Others feared that bidding by churches for public support would provoke an entanglement of state and churches that was likely to prove unhealthy for both.

The Supreme Court initially reacted with a mix of skepticism and confusion. During its relatively strict separationist period from the 1960s through the mid-1980s, the Justices invalidated numerous governmental programs aiding parochial schools. But the Court did not strike down every aid program that came before it. Even constitutional specialists had a hard time making sense of the pattern of decisions.

Then, in the 1980s and 1990s, the social and political climate changed.[28] First, American national politics veered to the right, with religious conservatives playing a prominent role in the emerging governing coalition. Second, conservative Protestant denominations began to operate parochial schools in larger numbers. As they did so, the issue of aid to parochial schools increasingly affected Protestants as well as Catholics. Third, central elements of the conservative coalition that formed during the 1980s and 1990s believed that private institutions, including churches, could provide a variety of services more effectively than could a bureaucratic public sector, which seemed to some to have done a peculiarly poor job with public education, especially in urban school districts. From this perspective, it made good sense for the government to subsidize private service organizations, including churches, as an alternative to direct public provision of education and other traditional public services (such as treatment for drug and alcohol abuse).

Against the background of these trends, an increasingly conservative Supreme Court has gradually relaxed the Establishment Clause restrictions on governmental aid to parochial schools and other religious organizations. The emerging doctrine is difficult to describe with both brevity and precision, because of divisions within the conservative majority. But a central theme involves "neutrality": When the government offers benefits to secular schools or drug-abuse programs, it ought not be required to discriminate against religious ones, but may extend benefits on a neutral basis to secular and religious institutions alike. Within the evaluative framework favored by Justices at the center of a divided Court, an objective observer would not typically view programs that provide benefits on a "neutral" basis as constituting a forbidden "endorsement" of religious beliefs. The relevant cases divide into two general categories.

One involves the direct provision of governmental aid to religious schools and other organizations. Overturning several decisions from earlier decades, that Supreme Court held in *Mitchell v. Helms*[29] (2000) that it was constitutionally permissible for the government to provide educational materials directly to parochial schools on the same basis that it provided those materials to other private schools. No opinion garnered five votes. The plurality opinion joined by the Court's four most conservative Justices found no Establishment Clause violation where two conditions were met: The materials distributed by the government were "secular," not inherently religious, and they went to parochial and nonparochial schools on a "neutral" basis.[30] Justice O'Connor's concurring opinion, which was necessary to make the majority, added the further requirement that the secular materials provided by the government must not be "diverted" for use in specifically religious indoctrination.[31] (For example, an overhead projector could be used in math or history classes, but not in a class on religious dogma – even though there would be no way to stop a religious school from using the money saved by the government's donation of an overhead projector to buy specifically religious instructional materials out of its own, rather than the government's, budget.) A dissenting opinion protested that the Court set a dangerous precedent by allowing the government to provide direct aid to religious institutions, supported by the taxes of those who objected to such aid.

A second category of cases involves the government's provision of financial aid to *parents* who prefer to send their children to religious rather than to public schools. The most important case is *Zelman v. Simmons-Harris*[32] (2002), which upheld the constitutionality of a school voucher program. Under the program, parents of school-age children receive governmental vouchers, worth a certain number of dollars toward school tuition, which they can use at either a parochial school or at a secular private school (if they choose not simply to send their children to public school). Challengers argued that the scheme involved in *Zelman* would promote religion by encouraging increased attendance at parochial schools and, what is more, that it would effectively coerce taxpayers to pay for explicitly religious instruction. By 5–4, the Supreme Court disagreed. According to Chief Justice William Rehnquist's majority opinion, the crucial point involved the "neutrality" of the voucher program: Parents could qualify for vouchers regardless of their religious beliefs, and the vouchers could be cashed at secular as well as at religious schools. The voucher program thus did not promote religion or coerce the payment of tax dollars for the purpose of promoting religion, but merely facilitated "the genuine and independent choices of private individuals,"[33] regardless of whether those choices were religious or nonreligious. A dissenting opinion joined by four Justices argued, to no avail, that the majority's talk of neutrality blinked the reality that most vouchers were cashed at religious schools and that vouchers would therefore tend to promote religious belief.[34]

The "neutrality" rationale of *Mitchell v. Helms* and *Zelman v. Simmons-Harris* does not lack appeal, at least on the surface. If the government provides aid to private secular schools (as well as operating secular public schools), a mandatory exclusion of religious schools smacks of discrimination. It would be a mistake, however, to believe that an ideal of neutrality has emerged as the centerpiece of the current Court's overall approach to Establishment Clause issues. As long as legislatures can employ chaplains, the currency is inscribed with "In God We Trust," and Presidents can proclaim national days of prayer, the overall body of law reflects religious accommodationism at least as much as it does strict neutrality between religion and nonreligion.

The Free Exercise Clause

The Supreme Court's first major decision interpreting the Free Exercise Clause came in *Reynolds v. United States*[35] (1878). At issue was whether the Free Exercise Clause precluded the enforcement of a federal antipolygamy statute against a religious Mormon at a time when the Mormon Church considered polygamy a religious duty. The Court rejected Reynolds's claim of right under the Free Exercise Clause and upheld the prosecution.

Reynolds exemplifies the central issue in interpreting and applying the Free Exercise Clause: When, if ever, must the government make exceptions to generally applicable laws (such as a law against polygamy) for people who have religiously motivated reasons to engage in conduct that those laws make illegal or otherwise burden? To answer that question, the *Reynolds* Court invoked a distinction between religious belief, which was immune from regulation, and religiously motivated conduct, which was not: "Congress was deprived of all legislative power over mere opinion, but was left free to reach actions which were in violation of social duties or subversive of good order."[36] This is a plausible position, but also a harsh one. The government confronts its citizens with what the late Justice Potter Stewart – one of the Court's most lucid writers and clever phrase-makers – once termed "a cruel choice" when it demands that they either breach their religious duties (for Mormons, at the time of *Reynolds*, thought it the religious duty of men to have multiple wives) or violate the secular law.[37] It is not implausible to read the Free Exercise Clause as requiring the government to make reasonable accommodations to spare its citizens choices of this kind.

During the 1930s and 1940s, the Supreme Court gradually softened the harsh stance it had adopted in *Reynolds* and began to hold that the Free Exercise Clause sometimes protects conduct, at least when religiously motivated conduct is coupled with speech. The Court required an especially striking exemption for religiously motivated conduct in *Wisconsin v. Yoder*[38] (1972), which held that a state must exempt the Old Order Amish from a requirement that parents send their children to school through the age of sixteen. An Amish parent, whose fifteen-year-old daughter had already completed the eighth grade, argued that for him to subject her to further public schooling would violate his religious obligation to maintain his family apart from the world and worldly influences. Although acknowledging the importance of education, the Court concluded that the state's interest in compelling an additional year or two of high school attendance was insufficient to outweigh the interests of the Amish community under the Free Exercise Clause.

The decision in *Yoder* followed a similar ruling in *Sherbert v. Verner*[39] (1963). *Sherbert* involved a claim to unemployment benefits by a Sabbatarian who had lost her job because she refused to work on Saturday. (When she was hired, the work week was five days, but her employer subsequently added mandatory Saturday shifts.) The government denied benefits on the ground that Sherbert was voluntarily, rather than involuntarily, unemployed. But the Supreme Court held, in essence, that Mrs. Sherbert was entitled to an exemption from the otherwise applicable rule barring unemployment benefits to those who had left their jobs voluntarily unless the government could demonstrate that enforcement of the rule against her (and others who acted on the basis of perceived religious duties) was necessary to promote a "compelling state interest."[40]

If *Reynolds* had adopted a narrow interpretation of the Free Exercise Clause, *Yoder* and *Sherbert* articulated a far-reaching one. Under the "strict scrutiny" test laid out in *Sherbert*, people claiming to act on the basis of religious duties were entitled to exemptions from otherwise applicable laws unless the government could demonstrate a "compelling interest" that necessitated denying such exemptions. Although this test is easy enough to state, its application gave rise to impressive difficulties. As a succession of cases demonstrated, conflicts between legal duties and religious duties abound in our religiously diverse nation. In some contexts, *Sherbert*'s compelling state interest test seemed to the Supreme Court to ask the government to bend too much. In one case, for example, the Old Order Amish asserted a religious objection to paying Social Security taxes.[41] To have to allow religious exemptions from ordinary tax obligations would be an administrative nightmare for the government. The Court therefore rejected the claim. But if the result was sensible, the reasoning was more troublesome. If "administrative convenience" counts as a compelling governmental interest, then that strict-looking standard has been diluted quite considerably.

What is more, an interpretation of the Free Exercise Clause that *mandates* preferential treatment for those claiming religious motivations may lead to tension with other constitutional values, notably including those embodied in the Establishment Clause.[42] If the government grants exemptions to otherwise applicable legal duties for religious believers but not for nonbelievers, it arguably promotes religion.

In light of concerns such as these, the Supreme Court reversed course once again and held that the Free Exercise Clause generally does *not* mandate exemptions for religiously motivated conduct, in *Employment Division v. Smith*[43] (1990). At issue was whether a state that criminalized possession of the mildly hallucinogenic drug peyote must make an exception for those who wished to use the drug as part of Native American religious rituals. In holding that no exemption was required, the Court refused to apply *Sherbert's* compelling interest test. According to Justice Antonin Scalia's majority opinion, the Free Exercise Clause does not create a right to exemptions from "neutral, generally applicable laws," such as a bar against peyote use.[44] Instead, much more narrowly, the Free Exercise Clause *only* forbids the government to single out religiously motivated practices and to prohibit them simply because "they are engaged in for religious reasons, or only because of the religious belief that they display."[45] Within this framework, neutral and generally applicable laws, such as laws prohibiting peyote use by everyone, simply raise no issue under the Establishment Clause; their enforcement against religiously motivated conduct does not trigger a compelling state interest test or otherwise require special justification.

Having laid down this general rule, Justice Scalia's majority opinion in *Employment Division v. Smith* recognized a small set of exceptions. These exceptions were crafted mostly to permit the Court to reconcile its newly prescribed approach with the outcomes reached in, though not with the reasoning of, prior cases. (Under doctrines requiring courts to respect "precedent," the Supreme Court is generally believed to have a greater obligation to accept that prior cases reached the correct outcome than to accept that prior cases reasoned soundly in arriving at that outcome.) Apart from defined exceptions, the *Smith* rule holds, and the Free Exercise Clause does not mandate exemptions to otherwise applicable laws for religious believers.

Employment Division v. Smith has drawn angry objections from constitutional scholars,[46] among others. (Among the others were large majorities in both Houses of Congress, who enacted a statute called the Religious Freedom Restoration Act that directed the courts to assess claims to religious exemptions from general statutes under a compelling interest test. As discussed in Chapter Thirteen, however, the Supreme Court held that statute to be unconstitutional.) One criticism holds that *Smith* misunderstands the original understanding of the Free Exercise Clause – a claim disputed by both the Supreme Court majority and by other scholars. Another protests that the Court's approach treads callously on religious minorities, whose interests are less likely to be accommodated by legislatures than are those of mainstream religions. For example, during the Prohibition era, when the possession of alcohol was otherwise illegal, the government made an exception for Communion wine. By contrast, the Oregon statute barring peyote use that was involved in *Employment Division v. Smith* provided no comparable accommodation for the religious rites of the Native American Church. (Interestingly, in the *aftermath* of the *Smith* decision, the Oregon legislature amended the state's drug laws to permit possession and use of peyote for religious purposes only.) Emphasizing concerns such as these, several members of the Supreme Court have refused to accept *Smith*'s rule of decision and have argued that the Court should reconsider and overrule it.[47] For now, however, *Smith* states the law: Although the Free Exercise Clause bars the government from prohibiting religious conduct "only because of the religious belief" that prompts it, the Clause does nothing to ameliorate the "cruel choice" that arises when a neutral, generally applicable statute forbids conduct (such as the sacramental use of peyote) that some citizens think it their religious duty to perform.

Voluntary Governmental Accommodations of Religion

A final set of difficult issues arises under the Religion Clauses when the government *voluntarily* exempts persons engaged in religiously motivated conduct from otherwise applicable duties. As I noted in the introduction to this chapter, an issue of this kind lay in the background in *Clay v. United States*. A comparable issue would be raised by Oregon's amended drug laws, which still include a general prohibition against peyote use, but now make an exception for persons using peyote for religiously motivated purposes. Do exemptions specifically and solely applicable to religiously motivated conduct violate the Establishment Clause?

Only a few Supreme Court cases directly address issues of this kind. Although some are difficult to reconcile with others,[48] their general tenor suggests that when the government imposes a burden – for example, by forbidding conduct – it may selectively lift that burden to accommodate religious beliefs, at least as long as its doing so does not impose substantial burdens on others and could not reasonably be understood as endorsing the underlying beliefs.[49] It perhaps bears emphasis, however, that the cases are few and their teachings less than wholly clear. In cases decided during the era of the Vietnam War, the Court construed the statute granting draft exemptions to those who opposed war on religious grounds to make the same exemptions available to people who were not religious in the traditional sense, but who nevertheless opposed all wars for reasons of conscience.[50] The Court may have believed that granting an exemption only to believers in a traditional God would have created difficulties under the Establishment Clause.

Tensions Between the Free Exercise and Establishment Clauses

For anyone who believes both (1) that the Establishment Clause forbids the government to prefer or promote religion and (2) that the Free Exercise Clause requires the government to spare its citizens the "cruel choice" between obeying the law and obeying their religion whenever it can reasonably do so, the two Clauses will often be in conflict. The Free Exercise Clause will require exemptions from otherwise applicable legal duties that the Establishment Clause will forbid (because exemptions for the religiously observant may tend to promote religion). To put the same point another way, it is impossible to maintain what might be regarded as "strong" interpretations of both

Clauses – a strict separationist view of the Establishment Clause and a demand that the government accommodate religious beliefs under the Free Exercise Clause.

Although there are various ways in which a conflict between the two Clauses might be avoided, the current Supreme Court has dealt with the situation by adopting relatively "weak" interpretations of both. *Employment Division v. Smith* gives a weak reading of the Free Exercise Clause, under which the government virtually never needs to accommodate religious believers by exempting religiously motivated conduct from generally applicable laws. The Court's interpretation of the Establishment Clause, which allows the government to inscribe "In God We Trust" on the currency and to supply valuable goods and services to religious institutions as long as it does so on a "neutral" basis, is similarly weak. Indeed, the Court's interpretation of the Establishment Clause appears to allow the government voluntarily to lift the burden that governmental regulations impose on religiously motivated conduct on a *nonneutral* basis, without providing comparable exceptions for others, at least some of the time.

The conjunction of weak Free Exercise Clause doctrine with weak Establishment Clause doctrine gives elected governmental officials a great deal of discretion in dealing with matters involving religion: The government is seldom required to accommodate religious beliefs, but it has relatively broad freedom to do so if it chooses.

This doctrinal structure well serves the interests of those with mainstream religious beliefs. The political process will seldom impose significant burdens on mainstream views, and mainstream believers are unlikely to be affronted by such practices as putting "In God We Trust" on the currency and making Christmas Day a national holiday. If the doctrinal structure should be faulted, it is for failing to provide adequate protection of religious minorities.

It should be remembered, however, that the category of "religious minorities" includes two subgroups. One consists of the religiously devout who would wish greater governmental accommodation of their beliefs – more exemptions from generally applicable laws, expanded voucher or other programs to facilitate the religious education of their children, and so forth. The other subgroup comprises religious or irreligious outsiders who feel demeaned and marginalized by governmental programs supporting and accommodating religious beliefs that they do not share. Religion Clause doctrine could give fuller protection to the interests of either of these minority subgroups, but it could not give fuller protection to both.

THREE

Protection of Economic Liberties

The Constitution was essentially an economic document based upon the concept that the fundamental private rights of property are anterior to government and morally beyond the reach of popular majorities.

– Charles A. Beard[1]

[A] constitution is not intended to embody a particular economic theory.... It is made for people of fundamentally differing views....

– Justice Oliver Wendell Holmes, Jr.[2]

WHEN THE HISTORIAN CHARLES BEARD WROTE IN 1913 that "[t]he Constitution was essentially an economic document," he claimed too much. The founders intended the Constitution to protect many values, not just property rights. Nevertheless, property and contract rights ranked high among the rights that the Constitution was initially designed to safeguard. Prominent framers and ratifiers worried particularly about legislation excusing debtors from obligations to their creditors.[3] They viewed such legislation as immoral because it violated the sanctity of promises and as imprudent because it discouraged commercial lending. (If the legislature could excuse promises to repay money, banks would be less willing to loan money in the first place.) Article I, Section 10 thus provides that "[n]o State shall ... pass any ... Law impairing the Obligation of Contracts." The Fifth Amendment forbids the taking of "private property ... for public use, without just compensation."

Curiously, however, the Supreme Court's most important and sustained effort to protect economic liberties occurred under a provision of the Constitution that was not clearly designed to restrict *substantive* legislation at all – the Due Process Clause of the Fourteenth Amendment, which says that "no state shall deprive any person of life, liberty, or property, without due process of law." During the late nineteenth and early twentieth centuries, the Court's protection of economic rights under the Due Process Clause (during the so-called *Lochner* era, which took its name from the case of *Lochner v. New York*[4]) occasioned enormous controversy and ultimately helped bring the Court, if not the country, to the edge of disaster in the 1930s. The tale of the Court's retreat from that disaster was briefly told in the Introduction. In the aftermath, judicial efforts to protect economic liberties have subsisted under a cloud. To understand that cloud, and how it developed, is crucial to understanding current doctrine. This chapter, therefore, takes a relatively historical approach. Significantly, however, the Supreme Court has never renounced the protection of economic rights. In recent years, its more conservative Justices have shown renewed interest in restraining governmental interference with property rights, but not so far in protecting other asserted economic liberties.

Early History

Before the Civil War, the Takings Clause of the Fifth Amendment – which prohibits the taking of private property for public use without just compensation – did not apply to the states. Nor did the federal government engage in many uncompensated expropriations. As a result, few early cases arose under the Takings Clause.

By contrast, decisions under the Contract Clause loomed relatively large in the early history of the Supreme Court. *Sturges v. Crowinshield*[5] (1819) invalidated a state bankruptcy law that excused debtors from contractual obligations created before the law's adoption. Under the statute, debtors who declared bankruptcy and surrendered all of their property for division among their creditors could be discharged from further obligation to pay their old debts. The Court ruled that the law impaired the obligation of contracts.

In another famous case, *Fletcher v. Peck*[6] (1810), Chief Justice Marshall rejected a state's effort to withdraw property rights that it had previously granted in exchange for the payment of money. He found the state's nullifying effort to be condemned by the Contract Clause and by "general principles which are common to our free institutions."[7] The latter phrase is telling. Many of the Justices of the early Supreme Court viewed the Constitution as embodying "natural rights," including rights to property and economic liberty, that they regarded as given by God or nature or as otherwise morally self-evident.[8] These Justices naturally read provisions such as the Contract Clause in light of their moral and constitutional theories. For them, the more difficult question was whether the Court should invalidate legislation that violated moral rights even if it did not transgress specific constitutional limitations (such as the Contract Clause). Justice Samuel Chase offered a celebrated statement that the courts should decline to enforce morally wrongful legislation in *Calder v. Bull*[9] (1798), in which he cited as an example "a law that takes property from A and gives it to B: It is against all reason and justice, for a people to entrust a Legislature with SUCH powers; and, therefore, it cannot be presumed that they have done it."

A rare Contract Clause case to divide the Marshall Court – and also to reveal a potential gap in the natural rights philosophy – was *Ogden v. Saunders*[10] (1827). Like *Sturges v. Crowinshield, Ogden* involved a bankruptcy law providing for the discharge of debts. The contracts at issue in *Ogden*, however, had all come into existence *after* the enactment of the state statute providing for cancellation of debts in cases of bankruptcy. Over the sharp dissent of Chief Justice Marshall, the Court reasoned that state laws existing at the time of a contract's formation in effect became part of the contract. Under this reasoning, the debtor in *Ogden* had not promised categorically to pay the money that he owed, but only to pay unless he became insolvent and was discharged in a bankruptcy proceeding as contemplated by the state's bankruptcy law. The state bankruptcy law thus did not impair the obligations created by preexisting contracts; instead, it conditioned or regulated the obligations that subsequent contracts could create.

It is easy to understand the allure of *Ogden's* reasoning. Surely private parties should not be able to escape the reach of state regulatory legislation simply by making a contract. Suppose, for example, that state law prohibits the use of a pesticide that is damaging to the environment. Suppose, further, that I enter a contract to pay Jones $500 to treat my lawn with that forbidden chemical. Under these circumstances, surely neither Jones nor I should be able to claim successfully that the state's regulatory legislation "impairs" the obligation created by our contract and thereby violates the Constitution. Rather, the state law must be allowed either to operate as a condition of the contract, forcing the substitution of some other pesticide, or to bar the contract from ever taking effect.

It is equally plain, however, that the reasoning of *Ogden v. Saunders* threatens to drain nearly all substance from the Contract Clause. If state regulatory legislation always forms a part of all subsequently enacted contracts, and if there are no constitutional limits on the legislation that states may enact, then the states can effectively limit contract rights in any way that they choose – as long as they do so prospectively, before a contract has been formed. Chief Justice Marshall dissented for this reason.

Viewed together, the majority and dissenting opinions in *Ogden v. Saunders* frame a central issue in defining constitutionally protected economic liberties: How can the courts distinguish permissible governmental *regulation* of the terms on which parties may contract from constitutionally forbidden *impairments* of the right to make contracts and have them enforced? As *Ogden* demonstrates, that issue arises under the Contract Clause. But it can also be framed as arising under other provisions of the Constitution, as subsequent constitutional developments have demonstrated.

The Fourteenth Amendment

In the aftermath of the Civil War, Congress proposed and the states ratified the Fourteenth Amendment to the Constitution. Although principally intended to guarantee the civil rights of former slaves and their descendants, the Fourteenth Amendment deliberately speaks in more general terms: "[i] No State shall make or enforce any law which shall abridge the privileges or immunities of citizens of the United States; [ii] nor shall any State deprive any person of life, liberty, or property, without due process of law; [iii] nor deny to any person within its jurisdiction the equal protection of the laws."

At the very least, there is a serious historical argument that the Fourteenth Amendment's framers and ratifiers intended the first quoted clause, prohibiting state abridgement of the "privileges or immunities" of citizenship, to protect certain basic economic liberties. The language of the Privileges *or* Immunities Clause of the Fourteenth Amendment closely parallels the Privileges *and* Immunities Clause of Article IV. As will be discussed in Chapter Twelve, the Privileges *and* Immunities Clause is essentially an antidiscrimination provision: It contemplates the existence of a set of privileges and immunities of state citizenship, leaves it to the states to define their content, and says that a state may not withhold those privileges and immunities, however it chooses to define them, from citizens of other states who happen to be within its borders. During congressional debates leading to adoption of the Fourteenth Amendment, prominent members of Congress cited a judicial decision listing the privileges and immunities of *state* citizenship under Article IV as identifying the privileges or immunities that would henceforth be recognized as rights of *national* citizenship, and thus defined by the Supreme Court of the United States, under the proposed new Privileges or Immunities Clause.[11] In that decision in *Corfield v. Coryell*[12] (1823), Justice Bushrod Washington – the nephew of George Washington – said that Article IV protected all privileges "which are, in their nature, fundamental; which belong, of right, to the citizens of all free governments."[13]

The crucial judicial test of the meaning of the Fourteenth Amendment's Privileges or Immunities Clause came in *The Slaughter-House Cases*[14] (1872). The state of Louisiana licensed a slaughterhouse monopoly for the city of New Orleans and barred all others from the profession. In the Supreme Court, challengers maintained that the right of butchers "to exercise their trade" was protected against unreasonable state regulation by the newly ratified Privileges or Immunities Clause of the Fourteenth Amendment and that the Court must therefore judge the reasonableness of the state legislation creating a slaughtering monopoly. By 5–4, the Court disagreed. In a tortured opinion, the Court simply refused to believe that the Fourteenth Amendment had elevated the traditional privileges or immunities of state citizenship under Article IV, such as the right to pursue a lawful trade, to the status of privileges or immunities of national citizenship, which would need to be defined and enforced by the federal courts. Instead, it held, the Privileges or Immunities Clause of the Fourteenth Amendment had merely ratified the existence of a few rights of national citizenship already implicit in the original Constitution, such as the right to travel from one state to another.

The Court's reluctance to recognize a set of newly conferred privileges or immunities of national citizenship is easy to understand in its historical context. In the aftermath of the disastrous *Dred Scott* decision and the following Civil War – both briefly discussed in the Introduction – the Court understandably felt vulnerable and uncertain. It was reluctant to claim large new responsibilities likely to enmesh it in further controversy, such as those that the Privileges or Immunities Clause appeared to thrust upon it. If the Fourteenth Amendment created judicially enforceable privileges or immunities of national citizenship, it would have fallen to the Court to define those privileges or immunities and to give them substantive content. Historical understandings might have provided some guidance. Nonetheless, the Court's new responsibilities would have been large, the implications for the states – which would have been subjected to a potentially sweeping array of constitutional limitations for the first time – nearly revolutionary. As the majority put it, "such a construction . . . would constitute this court a perpetual censor upon all legislation of the States."[15] Again, it bears emphasis that before the Civil War the Constitution created very few judicially enforceable rights against the states.

Even so, the Court's reasoning in *The Slaughter-House Cases* is difficult to defend. As the Court had to acknowledge, the Privileges or Immunities Clause plainly says that no state may abridge the privileges or immunities of citizenship; and when it says so, it unmistakably refers to privileges or immunities of *national* citizenship. By holding that the Privileges or Immunities Clause only ratified the existence of privileges or immunities of national citizenship that were already implicit in the Constitution (such as the right to travel from state to state), the *Slaughter-House* majority ruled that a principal provision of the Fourteenth Amendment, adopted specifically to alter the relationship between state and national governments in the wake of a bloody Civil War, essentially changed *nothing*. It was, as a dissenting opinion protested, "a vain and idle enactment."[16] This position was and remains intellectually untenable. It also remains unaltered. Since *The Slaughter-House Cases*, the Court has treated the Privileges or Immunities Clause of the Fourteenth Amendment as a virtual constitutional nullity.[17]

Ironically, however, within a few years of *The Slaughter-House Cases*, the Court began to do under the Due Process Clause what it had refused to do under the Privileges of Immunities Clause: The Court began to scrutinize state legislation to determine whether it unreasonably interfered with liberty or deprived people of property without due process of law (rather than depriving citizens of "the privileges or immunities" of national citizenship).

Substantive Due Process

The era of "substantive due process" review of economic legislation under the Due Process Clause began around 1890. The assumptions that underlay the Court's decision-making are hard to recapture. The Court took for granted that the states are entitled to enact regulatory legislation to promote the public health, safety, and morals. But the Court also assumed that regulation lacking in fundamental fairness should be deemed to deprive their targets of liberty or property "without due process of law." Critics have challenged the very idea of "substantive due process" as a contradiction in terms – "sort of like 'green pastel redness,'" as John Ely once put it.[18] According to those who take this line, the Due Process Clause is obviously a guarantee of fair procedures, and it was a flat-out mistake to use this clause to invalidate legislation on grounds of substantive, rather than procedural, unfairness. Perhaps so, perhaps not – there may be some outcomes that are so substantively unfair that no process that produced them could count as "due." In any event, in hundreds of substantive due process cases from the late nineteenth century through the 1930s the Court asked either or both of two questions. First, does state regulatory legislation have a valid or legitimate public purpose? Second, if so, does the challenged regulation represent a fair and sensible means of pursuing that purpose?

If the notion of substantive due process makes sense at all, the Court's approach sounds reasonable. Certainly it would have sounded reasonable if the Court had conducted precisely the same inquiries to determine whether legislation violated the Privileges or Immunities Clause – as, but for *The Slaughter-House Cases*, it might well have done. In practice, however, acute difficulties arose because the Court's administration of substantive due process review reflected narrow, grudging views of what counted as valid public purposes and as reasonable means of promoting them.

The Court began implementing substantive due process review near the dawn of the so-called Progressive Era. During that period, legislatures recurrently enacted regulatory legislation aimed particularly to protect miners and factory workers, including children, from brutally long hours, low wages, and oppressive conditions of employment. With considerable frequency, the Court found the legislative efforts invalid.

Lochner v. New York[19] (1905), the decision from which this era of judicial history takes its name, exemplifies the Court's approach. *Lochner* struck down a New York statute imposing a sixty-hour limit on bakery employees' work weeks. In finding the statute invalid, the Court first imagined that it might have been passed for the special benefit of bakery workers, to give them an advantage in bargaining with bakery owners. But for the state simply to try to benefit one class of citizens (bakery workers) at the expense of another (their employers) was not, in the Court's view, a valid public purpose. To the Court, legislation designed to benefit only one otherwise competent group of citizens, especially by improving their situation relative to others, aimed to promote class interests, not the general public interest. It was the equivalent of a statute taking from A and giving to B simply because the state preferred B to A.[20]

Alternatively, the *Lochner* Court imagined that the statute limiting bakery workers to sixty-hour weeks might have been enacted for the purpose of protecting bakers' health (rather than their more general well-being). For the state to promote the health of its citizens was a permissible public purpose, the Court acknowledged, but it then scrutinized the state's chosen means and found them wanting. There was insufficient evidence, the Court ruled, that working more than sixty-hours a week as a baker posed a significant threat to health. Absent such evidence, the state's regulation was unreasonable and potentially tyrannical. Under the state's theory, the Court wrote, "[n]ot only the hours of employees, but the hours of employers, could be regulated, and doctors, lawyers, scientists, all professional men, as well as athletes and artisans, could be forbidden to fatigue their brains and bodies by prolonged hours of exercise."[21] Three Justices dissented on this point. They believed the evidence sufficient to uphold the statute as a health measure.

Justice Oliver Wendell Holmes, later to emerge as a champion of free-speech rights, dissented on more fundamental grounds. The Court, he objected, was reading the Constitution through the lens of a particular, controversial economic philosophy that looked skeptically on all governmental regulation of economic markets. As did others who shared that philosophy, the majority Justices assumed that everyone – from the poorest child seeking factory work to the wealthiest employer paying subsistence wages – operated in a condition of natural liberty: If factory owner and factory laborer wished to contract for seventy-hour work weeks at pennies an hour, they had a right to do so. The difficulty, Holmes wrote, was that this was "an economic theory which a large part of the country does not entertain."[22] Where the Court saw voluntary transactions among willing contractors, others saw self-sustaining social structures conspiring to keep the poor poor and the rich rich. Where the Court saw natural liberty, others saw socially constructed inequality in which some had too much bargaining power and others had too little. Given the division of views, Holmes thought that elected officials and ultimately the voters, not the Justices of the Supreme Court, should chart the nation's economic and regulatory policy.

From the 1905 decision in *Lochner* through 1937, the Supreme Court applied substantive due process review to roughly 400 economic regulatory statutes. The Justices invalidated about half. The decisions do not form a pattern of perfect consistency. The Court had difficulty distinguishing legislation promoting genuine "public" interests in protecting those not competent to protect themselves (such as children and sometimes, in the Court's view, women) from legislation that impermissibly attempted to promote some citizens' interests at the expense of others'. The Court also varied in its willingness to credit evidence showing that legislation reasonably promoted worker health and safety. But the Court maintained its basic framework with remarkable consistency in the face of unrelenting public and legislative resistance.

That resistance grew angrier as time passed. *Lochner* was a due process case, invalidating economic regulatory legislation enacted by a state. But the *Lochner* era featured Supreme Court invalidations of regulatory legislation under other provisions of the Constitution as well. Most notably, the Court frequently struck down federal legislation regulating economic activity as lying beyond Congress's power to enact under Article I (the provision from which Congress derives most of its powers). When anger and frustration with the Court reached an apex in the mid-1930s, and with the fate of the New Deal apparently hanging in the balance and President Roosevelt proposing to "pack" the Supreme Court (as discussed in the Introduction), the Court sharply altered its course.

With respect to substantive due process, the signal decision came in *West Coast Hotel Co. v. Parrish*[23] (1937), which upheld a state law mandating a minimum wage for women. Reflecting its dramatic rejection of the *Lochner*-era assumption that an unregulated market economy provided fair opportunities for the exercise of natural liberty, the Court wrote, "The exploitation of a class of workers who are in an unequal position with respect to bargaining power and are thus relatively defenseless against the denial of a living wage is not only detrimental to their health and well-being, but casts a direct burden for their support upon the community."[24] In this formulation, an unregulated "free market" is neither sacrosanct nor even presumptively just. The government violates no protected liberty when it identifies economic "exploitation" and enacts regulatory legislation to correct it.

In the wake of *West Coast Hotel* and parallel decisions sustaining Congress's regulatory power under the Commerce Clause, the principal monuments of the *Lochner* era all tumbled within a few short years. The Court's conservative stalwarts departed the bench. Leading decisions proclaimed that all economic regulatory legislation would enjoy a presumption of constitutionality and would be upheld as long as it was supported by any conceivable rational basis. What is more, the Court shortly announced the verdict that *Lochner*'s underlying theory was not only erroneous, but disgracefully so. Summarizing the lessons that the Court had drawn from the *Lochner* experience, Justice Hugo Black – the first man named to the Supreme Court by Franklin Roosevelt and a constitutional literalist who believed that the Due Process Clause conferred no *substantive* guarantees of property rights – wrote in 1963 that "[u]nder the system of government created by our Constitution, it is up to legislatures, not courts, to decide on the wisdom and utility of [economic regulatory] legislation."[25] He continued: "There was a time when the Due Process Clause was used by this Court to strike down laws which were thought unreasonable, that is, unwise or incompatible with some particular economic or social philosophy.... [That approach] has long since been discarded.... It is now settled that States have power to legislate against what are found to be injurious practices..., so long as their laws do not run afoul of some specific federal constitutional prohibition, or of some valid federal law."[26]

Perhaps significantly, the Supreme Court has never wholly renounced the scrutiny of economic legislation under the Due Process Clause. It continues to ask whether such legislation is rationally related to a legitimate public purpose. Yet, not since 1937 has the Court invalidated economic regulatory legislation on "substantive due process" grounds.[27] More than sixty years later, the taint of the *Lochner* era remains strong.

Modern Contracts Clause Doctrine

Since the demise of *Lochner*, the Supreme Court has not shown much more enthusiasm for invalidating economic regulatory legislation under the Contract Clause than under the Due Process Clause. Indeed, the Court's retreat from strong enforcement of the Contract Clause actually began before the end of the *Lochner* era, in *Home Building Loan Association v. Blaisdell*[28] (1934). At the height of the Great Depression, the state of Minnesota enacted a statute barring mortgage foreclosures for a two-year period. On the surface, this might have appeared to be precisely the kind of debtor relief legislation that the Contracts Clause was meant to forbid: It effectively stopped banks and other creditors from enforcing their contractual rights to foreclose on the property of nonpaying debtors. Nonetheless, the Court upheld the statute.

The Court's *Blaisdell* opinion emphasized two themes. The first involved the statute's emergency nature. The Court quoted Chief Justice John Marshall's opinion in *McCulloch v. Maryland*[29] (1819) for the proposition that the Constitution was "intended to endure for ages to come, and consequently, to be adapted to the various crises of human affairs."[30] The second crucial strand in the Court's reasoning expanded the doctrine, traceable to *Ogden v. Saunders*, that private contracts must be read to incorporate preexisting legal rules and regulations. According to *Blaisdell*, "the reservation of essential attributes of sovereign power" – that is, the right of the state to enact *subsequent* legislation adjusting contract rights – "is also read into contracts as a postulate of the legal order."[31]

This formulation bears close attention. Under it, the Contracts Clause no longer establishes an absolute barrier to state laws that retroactively impair the obligation of contracts; even after contracts have been formed, the state may exercise its "sovereign power" to enact regulatory legislation with the effect of nullifying or adjusting contract rights, as long as that legislation is itself reasonable. The duty to distinguish reasonable from unreasonable adjustments of contract rights falls of course to the Supreme Court, which has tended to judge reasonableness with a tolerant disposition. In only one subsequent case have the Justices invalidated state legislation adjusting rights under contracts solely involving private parties.[32]

The Takings Clause

The so-called Takings Clause of the Fifth Amendment says that "private property [shall not] be taken for public use, without just compensation." As the language makes plain, the Takings Clause does not absolutely bar the taking of private property for public use; on the contrary, it presupposes that governments must possess the power to take what they need. The Takings Clause only requires that *if* the government takes private property for public use, it must pay just compensation.

Although many questions arise under the Takings Clause, the most recurring and difficult involve whether a "taking" has occurred at all. The easiest cases involve governmental occupation and use of private property. If the government takes control of private property to build a fort or a road, and then occupies the fort or maintains a road, a "taking" has unquestionably occurred. More difficult questions are presented when the government engages in activities that interfere with the enjoyment of private property, but does not physically occupy it. In *United States v. Causby*[33] (1946), the government's recurrent use of airspace for military flights made it impossible for Causby to continue to use his land as a chicken farm. The Supreme Court found a taking. According to the Court, the taking was "as complete as if the United States had entered upon the surface of the land and taken exclusive possession of it."[34]

To be distinguished from cases involving the government's occupation and use of property are cases involving the *regulation* of property uses. The leading case is *Pennsylvania Coal Co. v. Mahon*[35] (1922). In Pennsylvania coal country, coal companies commonly purchased or retained underground mining rights, separate from the ownership rights in surface property held by others. Against this background, the Pennsylvania Legislature enacted a statute prohibiting the mining of coal in any manner that would cause the "subsidence" of surface property. The statute effectively barred coal companies from exercising some of their mining rights, even though they technically retained ownership of all the subsurface coal that they had previously purchased.

In legal doctrinal terms, the question posed by cases such as *Mahon* is this: When, if ever, should governmental regulatory legislation that diminishes the value of property rights (in this case by forbidding any use of those rights that would cause "subsidence") be deemed to constitute a "regulatory taking" that requires just compensation? The question arises in innumerable contexts. For example, it comes up whenever the government enacts land-use or zoning regulations. Has a taking occurred whenever a zoning ordinance prohibits the operation of gasoline stations in residential neighborhoods and a property owner who would like to open a gasoline station is forbidden to do so? Whenever environmental protection statutes prohibit the filling of wetlands to make them suitable for housing lots? According to legal historians, the Takings Clause was not originally understood to create a barrier to, or to require the payment of just compensation for, regulatory legislation affecting land use (and thereby diminishing the value of particular properties).[36] But members of the founding generation almost surely did not anticipate either the scope of modern land-use regulation or the problems that have spurred its enactment.

Confronting the issue in *Mahon*, the Supreme Court found that the Pennsylvania antisubsidence legislation constituted a taking. In an opinion by Justice Holmes, the Court did not question that the government enjoyed broad regulatory powers. (Holmes had dissented in *Lochner*.) Nor did Holmes suggest that landowners were entitled to just compensation whenever governmental regulation of permissible property uses diminished the value of their property. But there must be a limit, he wrote. If governmental regulation goes "too far," it becomes effectively indistinguishable from appropriation or destruction of property, and just compensation must be paid.[37]

Since *Mahon*, the Supreme Court has developed a complex body of doctrine guiding the judicial inquiry into when governmental regulation of property uses goes "too far" and thus triggers a just compensation requirement under the Takings Clause. The Court's inquiries are largely "ad hoc," it has said, but in recent years it has noted that "three factors... have 'particular significance': (1) the economic impact of the regulation on the claimant; (2) the extent to which the regulation has interfered with distinct investment-backed expectations; and (3) the character of the governmental action."[38] For the most part, the Court has applied this test in a deferential manner and has allowed the enforcement of land-use regulations even when they dramatically reduce the economic value of land. In doing so, it has followed an approach that closely parallels its post-*Lochner* jurisprudence under the Due Process and Contracts Clauses: Just as the Court does not absolutely prohibit regulatory legislation adjusting contractual and property rights, neither will it make regulation economically infeasible by too readily requiring payments of "just compensation" to regulated parties.

It should probably be no surprise, however, that in recent years an increasingly conservative Supreme Court has shown a renewed interest in the Takings Clause.[39] (In ordinary political parlance, those who generally disfavor economic regulatory legislation, including environmental legislation, are almost invariably described as "conservative.") The Court has agreed to hear a number of Takings Clause cases, and it has upheld the challengers' claims in a fair proportion of them,[40] but mostly on narrow grounds. So far, it has not altered the main elements of a doctrinal framework that gives the government broad regulatory flexibility before it can be said to have gone "too far."

Concluding Thoughts

The central difficulty confronting the Supreme Court under the Takings Clause is in many ways the same as the central difficulty confronting it under the Due Process and Contracts Clauses. From the perspective of fairness, it might appear disturbing when a landowner loses millions of dollars as a result of being denied the "right" to build on wetlands, for example. But a logically prior question is whether the landowner should be seen as having that claimed "right" in the first place. If it is assumed that there is a natural or constitutional "right" to be absolutely free from governmental regulation, then land-use regulation of course violates that right and constitutes a "taking" of property – just as other economic regulatory legislation interferes with the "right" to do whatever one wants or to enter whatever contracts on whatever terms one chooses. As the Supreme Court recognized in renouncing *Lochner*, however, to *assume* that the economy should operate on laissez-faire principles or that there is a general right to freedom from regulation is to assume a controversial economic philosophy that many people do not share and that the Constitution does not necessarily impose.

In the context of the Takings Clause, the philosophy that views all regulation as a deprivation of natural or constitutional rights is particularly untenable. A wetlands owner undoubtedly possesses a property right, but the answer to whether that right includes a privilege to haul in landfill and disrupt drainage and environmental ecosystems cannot be extracted from the necessary meaning of the concept of "property." Property and contract rights need to be defined before they can be protected. It is possible to own a parcel of land without, for example, having the right either to store hazardous wastes there or to fill up its watery areas with soil. With property rights needing to be defined, Congress, the state legislatures, and city councils all have a role in defining them.

Under the Constitution, the Courts must oversee the political process, to ensure that legislative judgments are reasonable and do not intrude on prerogatives that constitutional guarantees minimally and necessarily entail. But the enduring lesson of the *Lochner* debacle is that economic rights invite specification and adjustment by the political branches of government, exercising their regulatory powers, and not merely interpretation by the courts. As Holmes wrote in his famous *Lochner* dissent, the Court should hesitate to read into the Constitution a single, restrictive economic philosophy that reasonable political majorities need not share.

Rights to Fair Procedures

No person shall be ... deprived of life, liberty, or property, without due process of law.
           – The Due Process Clause of the Fifth Amendment

No State shall ... deprive any person of life, liberty, or property, without due process of law.
           – The Due Process Clause of the Fourteenth Amendment

THE CONSTITUTION GUARANTEES VARIOUS RIGHTS to fair procedures for those who are accused of crimes, involved in lawsuits, or subject to other threats of adverse governmental action – for example, being fired from certain government jobs or suspended from public schools. Perhaps the most important and basic procedural rights come from the Due Process Clauses of the Fifth and Fourteenth Amendments, which forbid governmental actions that deprive any person "of life, liberty, or property, without due process of law."

Constitutional guarantees of fair procedures serve at least two functions. One is to promote accurate decision-making. The police may believe that they know who committed a crime and that a trial would be a waste of time and money, but the police may be wrong. The Constitution therefore guarantees the defendant a trial, with the right to hear and confront adverse witnesses. Similarly, a school principal may think, based on a teacher's report, that a child deserves to be suspended. Again, however, the story may have another side. The Due Process Clause guarantees the child at least an informal hearing, to make sure that the decision-maker has all relevant facts.[1]

A second value served by procedural guarantees involves the dignity of those subject to adverse governmental action. Consider, for example, the Fifth Amendment's guarantee that "[n]o person . . . shall be compelled in any criminal case to be a witness against himself." One reason to forbid coerced confessions is that they are likely to be unreliable; people subject to torture may say almost anything. Another reason, however, is that the very process of coercion violates human dignity. Dignitary interests also furnish grounds (in addition to those involving accuracy in fact-finding) supporting rights to hearings under the Due Process Clause. People threatened with adverse governmental decisions deserve to be treated with respect. In many settings, respect means giving people an opportunity to be heard.

Like many ideals, the ideal of perfect procedural justice can never be completely attained. No scheme could guarantee total accuracy of fact-finding. In addition, the costs of various procedural safeguards need to be taken into account. Almost no one thinks that a public school should need to conduct a trial, with lawyers and opportunities for appeal, before giving detention to a student for a minor disciplinary infraction (even though detention probably constitutes a deprivation of "liberty" and even though the school's decision might rest on a factual mistake). Rather, the basic premise of the Constitution's procedural provisions is that the more serious the consequences for an affected person, the more guarantees of procedural fairness that person should have before being deprived of liberty or property. Procedural guarantees therefore reach their maximum in criminal cases.

Procedural Rights in Criminal Cases

As originally written and amended by the Bill of Rights, the Constitution conferred a number of procedural guarantees on defendants in *federal* criminal prosecutions. These included a right to trial by jury in criminal cases involving crimes punishable by imprisonment; a right to confront opposing witnesses; a right to compel the attendance and testimony of favorable witnesses; a right not to be compelled to testify against oneself; and a right to a speedy and public trial.[2] In addition, the Due Process Clause guaranteed other core elements of procedural fairness, including an unbiased judge and jury and fair opportunities to introduce and challenge evidence. But the federal government defines and punishes relatively few crimes (for reasons to be discussed in Chapter Seven). As long as the Bill of Rights applied only to the federal government, and not to the states, the Court's decisions interpreting the procedural guarantees of the Bill of Rights (other than the general guarantee of due process of law) did not have a broad impact.

The modern era for constitutional doctrines involving rights to fair criminal procedures began during the 1960s, under the liberal and controversial Warren Court, in a series of decisions holding that the Fourteenth Amendment "incorporates" or makes applicable against the states all of the "fundamental" guarantees of the Bill of Rights.[3] Starting in the 1930s, the Court had held that the Due Process Clause of the Fourteenth Amendment "encompass[ed] many of the same basic principles as the Bill of Rights guarantees"[4] that were specifically applicable to trials in federal court. During this era, however, the court "generally assumed that due process limits on state action derived from those principles were narrower than the limits imposed on the federal government."[5] In other words, the same right – for example, the right to the assistance of counsel – meant less in state court than in federal court. By contrast, the Court's "incorporation" decisions of the 1960s not only held that the "fundamental" provisions of the Bill of Rights created exactly the same rights against the states that they created against the federal government, but also tended to give broad interpretations of the underlying guarantees. Those decisions, which helped both to define the legacy of the Warren Court and to make it so controversial, imposed widespread changes on the practices of police, prosecutors, and judges.

The story of the Warren Court is a fascinating one, not easily captured in a book such as this one, that is more concerned with constitutional doctrine than with constitutional history. Following the fiasco of the *Lochner* era, the Supreme Court's reigning philosophy for a generation was substantially one of deference to Congress and state legislatures. In appointing the Justices who buried *Lochner*, President Franklin Roosevelt had wanted a court that would stand out of the way of progressive social legislation, not embark on crusades of its own. The Warren Court, which began to take shape after the appointment of Earl Warren as Chief Justice in 1953, broke with the pattern that the Roosevelt-appointed Justices had established, though not so dramatically as is sometimes imagined.

Even in its period of deepest retreat, the Supreme Court had not committed itself to judicial "passivism" in all contexts. An especially influential discussion of when the Court should defer and when it should assert itself came in *United States v. Carolene Products Co.*[6] (1938). On its facts, the *Carolene Products* case involved the constitutionality of a federal statute barring interstate shipment of a milk substitute called "filled milk." The core of the Court's reasoning in upholding the statute has long since faded into obscurity. What etched itself more lastingly into the memory of lawyers and judges was a remarkable footnote in which Justice Harlan Fiske Stone, in the midst of applying a highly deferential standard of judicial review, paused to reflect on the circumstances under which a more assertive judicial role might be appropriate. In that footnote, Stone suggested that the Court should be more aggressive when assessing legislation "which appears on its face to be within a specific prohibition of the Constitution, such as those of the [Bill of Rights], which are deemed equally specific when held to be embraced within the Fourteenth [Amendment]."[7] He also noted that the Court might have a special role in scrutinizing "statutes directed at particular religious or national or racial minorities."[8]

Whether consciously or unconsciously, the Warren Court – which stood at a widening historical remove from the demands for an end to *Lochner*-style judicial activism – substantially adopted the philosophy of the *Carolene Products* footnote.[9] Under the Court's "incorporation" rulings, its criminal procedure decisions enforced the "specific" prohibitions of the Bill of Rights governing such matters as freedom from "unreasonable searches and seizures" and the right of criminal defendants to the "Assistance of Counsel." In addition, the principal beneficiaries of its decisions were the largely disadvantaged classes, disproportionately including "racial minorities" in some regions of the country, who found themselves in the maw of the criminal justice system.

It is impossible to give a full account of contemporary doctrine defining constitutional rights to fair criminal procedures. But a brief survey of three lines of cases may give a flavor of broader developments, beginning with the Warren Court and continuing into the present day. The unfolding story includes a number of important lessons involving the possibility of doctrinal innovation by the Supreme Court, the importance of public and political responses to the Court's decisions, and the apparently limited capacity of decisions involving criminal *procedure* to produce fundamental changes in out-of-court behavior.

One important line of cases involving constitutionally required procedures in criminal cases holds that the Sixth Amendment right to be represented by counsel not only applies to criminal prosecutions in state courts, but also entitles people who cannot afford a lawyer to have one appointed on their behalf. Like the other lines that I shall trace, this one begins with a decision of the Warren Court, *Gideon v. Wainwright*[10] (1963). *Gideon*'s transparently driving concern was equal justice for the poor.[11]

Another line of cases enforces the right against compelled self-incrimination by requiring that police provide specific warnings before engaging in custodial questioning of criminal suspects. The crucial decision came in *Miranda v. Arizona*[12] (1966), which prescribes that for a confession to be admissible into evidence, a suspect must be advised "that he has the right to remain silent, that anything he says can be used against him in a court of law, that he has the right to the presence of an attorney, and that if he cannot afford an attorney one will be appointed for him prior to any questioning if he so desires."

Miranda reflected the Warren Court's characteristic approach in at least two ways. First, the Court undoubtedly saw *Miranda*, like *Gideon* before it, as ensuring that those who were too poor or unsophisticated to ask for lawyers would benefit from constitutional guarantees on a more nearly equal basis with those who were better off. Second, without worrying too much about the niceties of constitutional "interpretation," the Court set out to devise a rule that would work effectively in practice to vindicate underlying constitutional values. Not every confession obtained in the absence of a *Miranda* warning would constitute compelled self-incrimination in the literal sense. As the Court saw it, however, modern techniques of "custodial police interrogation"[13] brought risks of both psychological and physical coercion that it could not detect effectively on a case-by-case basis. To forestall the risk, the Court laid down the rule, which has as little foundation in the constitutional text as it does in constitutional history, that suspects must receive *Miranda* warnings or their equivalents.

A third line of decisions, beginning with the Warren Court's ruling in *Mapp v. Ohio*[14] (1961), applies the so-called exclusionary rule to state criminal prosecutions. The exclusionary rule is a judge-made rule holding that if the police obtain evidence by violating a person's constitutional rights, the illegally acquired evidence cannot be used against that person in a criminal case. In cases governed by the exclusionary rule, a constitutional violation has already occurred – commonly a police search for evidence in violation of the Fourth Amendment right to be free from "unreasonable searches and seizures." Significantly, the Fourth Amendment does not say that evidence obtained through unreasonable searches or seizures cannot be admitted in court. Other remedies might exist. For example, the police officer who conducted the unreasonable search might be subjected to discipline or sued for damages. Nevertheless, the Supreme Court has introduced the exclusionary rule as a rule of criminal procedure, barring the use of illegally obtained evidence to prove the commission of a crime. In making the exclusionary rule applicable to prosecutions in state court, the Warren Court again adopted an approach designed to work effectively in practice to protect underlying constitutional values – in this case, by deterring police from violating constitutional rights in the first place. (Police are less likely to engage in "unreasonable" searches if they know that the fruits of such searches cannot be used to convict a criminal defendant.) Again, the Court's decision came at an obvious cost to other values. When a court applies the exclusionary rule, a person whose guilt could have been established by the excluded evidence often goes free.

Time, Elections, and Change

Although some observers applauded the Warren Court's commitment to equal justice, and indeed were inspired by it, others were disturbed by the Court's willingness to be path-breaking. Indeed, in the turbulent 1960s, when traditional values and institutions seemed to many to be under siege, the Warren Court actually frightened some Americans, who perceived its decisions as undermining law enforcement and releasing known criminals on legal "technicalities" (involving, for example, police failures to give *Miranda* warnings or to observe Fourth Amendment prohibitions against "unreasonable" searches and seizures).[15] As I noted in the Introduction, Richard Nixon made an issue of the Warren Court in the 1968 presidential election campaign, in which he pledged to appoint "strict constructionist" Justices to the Supreme Court. Within a year of his inauguration as President, Nixon had nominated the conservative Warren Burger to replace Earl Warren, who retired, as Chief Justice. In less than four years, three more Nixon appointments had substantially reshaped the Court.

In the era of the Burger Court (1969–86) and the Rehnquist Court that has succeeded it (upon Burger's retirement and replacement as Chief Justice by William Rehnquist), the Warren Court's pattern of expanding the procedural rights of criminal defendants has come to a halt. Indeed, notable cutbacks have occurred in many areas.[16] For example, the Court has created a variety of exceptions to the *Miranda* rule, and it has pared Fourth Amendment doctrines defining unreasonable and thus constitutionally impermissible searches and seizures. In addition, both the Court and Congress have reduced opportunities for people convicted of crimes in state court to obtain review of their convictions for constitutional error in so-called habeas corpus proceedings in lower federal courts.[17]

Nevertheless, there has been no full counterrevolution broadly reversing the decisions of the Warren Court.[18] In particular, the extension of Bill of Rights guarantees to defendants in state criminal prosecutions now seems secure and irreversible, for reasons involving a mix of law, sociology, and psychology. As the legal system adjusts to changes, procedural requirements that once seemed shocking can

97

begin to seem obvious necessities of basic fairness. The right to counsel in state criminal prosecutions may offer a case in point.

Miranda, too, is now securely entrenched. For some time, conservatives held up *Miranda* as a textbook example of judicial "activism," threatening to public safety, and called for the Supreme Court to overrule it. But when the Court finally did expressly reconsider *Miranda* in *Dickerson v. United States*[19] (2000), some of the most conservative Justices joined a 7–2 majority sustaining *Miranda*'s authority. Over time, *Miranda* has woven itself into the fabric of constitutional law. What is more, police practice has adjusted to it, and it has emerged as among the best known symbols of American constitutional law in films and on television. For a Court that relies on the doctrine of precedent, or respect for prior rulings, to sustain its own decisions in the future, the costs of overruling *Miranda* plainly looked larger than the benefits. The Court has also continued to apply the exclusionary rule in both federal and state criminal prosecutions.

The Law on the Books versus the Law in Practice

Although the Burger and Rehnquist Courts have left standing the principal landmark decisions of the Warren Court involving constitutional criminal procedure, it would be a mistake to assume that those decisions have effectively achieved all of their aims. While *Gideon v. Wainwright* continues to guarantee the appointment of lawyers for impoverished defendants, appointed lawyers are typically underpaid and overworked. They have more clients than they can handle. And they respond, in a huge proportion of cases, by steering their clients into a "plea bargain," under which the defendant pleads guilty to a crime but receives some consideration from the prosecutor in return. The prosecutor may charge a less serious offense than he or she might otherwise have done or may recommend a lower sentence. According to recent figures, ninety-two percent of convictions for felonies, or serious crimes, come from guilty pleas. In the absence of a more serious commitment by state governments to fund criminal defenses, poor defendants may thus get little more than an agent to help with plea negotiations, not a committed defender. As is illustrated by highly publicized trials of celebrities such as O. J. Simpson, the gap between criminal justice for the poor and criminal justice for the rich remains huge.

The subsequent histories of *Miranda* and the "exclusionary rule" are harder to chart, in part because the Supreme Court has introduced a number of complex, important exceptions, the details of which are too complex for consideration here. An equally important element of the story is easier to identify in broad terms, though harder to document with full precision. In both *Miranda* and in its exclusionary rule cases, the Warren Court attempted to use constitutional rules involving the evidence that can be introduced *in court* (confessions and the fruits of illegal searches) to alter what it believed to be wrongful and abusive police practices *out of court* (coercive interrogation techniques and unreasonable searches and seizures).[20] There is abundant reason to question how far the Court's rules have achieved their intended out-of-court results. Of perhaps most critical importance, criminal suspects are free to waive their *Miranda* rights and to confess to a crime without speaking to a lawyer or to consent to searches that would otherwise be unreasonable (and thereby take them out of the constitutionally forbidden "unreasonable" category). Americans, it turns out, waive their *Miranda* rights and consent to police searches with remarkable frequency.

Although most Americans have probably heard the *Miranda* warning often enough on television to be able to recite it verbatim, a recent study found out that nearly eighty percent of suspects waived their right to an attorney and agreed to answer police questions immediately.[21] Nor was it only the innocent who talked: Nearly two-thirds of the suspects who waived their *Miranda* rights gave incriminating statements, partial admissions of guilt, or full confessions to their interrogators.[22]

Waiver is an even larger problem, if that be the word, with respect to Fourth Amendment rights. If a police officer approaches a random person on the street and asks to search her purse or backpack, for example, the officer has no obligation to advise her that in the absence of her consent the search would be unreasonable and that any fruits of an unreasonable search could not be admitted in court to prove her guilty of a crime. Nor need the officer ask nicely or explain to the target of his requests (or demands) that she has a right to say no. Under these circumstances, many people in many circumstances may well think that they have no choice but to "consent" to searches and seizures. A recent study of warrantless highway stops in Maryland found that ninety-six percent of drivers consented to have their cars searched, including many who were transporting large quantities of illegal drugs.[23] In these and other contexts, "consent" comes even to the kind of unreasonable and invasive searches that the Fourth Amendment was designed to prevent, and it comes especially often from the poor and the legally uninformed. In the rare cases in which consent is not forthcoming, some observers claim that the police frequently lie and say that it was.[24]

In the eyes of some, experience with *Miranda* and the exclusionary rule illustrates the difficulty, if not the impossibility, of using in-court rules of procedure (involving the admissibility of evidence) to reform the out-of-court practices of institutions such as the police. The same experience highlights a point too often overlooked in legal scholarship: There can be, and frequently is, a large gap between constitutional law as it appears on the books and constitutional law as it operates in practice.

Procedural Rights in Civil Cases

Although some constitutional rights to fair procedures apply only to criminal cases, the central guarantee of procedural fairness – that no one may be deprived of life, liberty, or property without due process of law – retains its force in civil disputes. The Due Process Clause applies most obviously to civil trials, including suits by one private person against another, in both state and federal courts. Both parties have a right to an impartial judge, to fair notice of scheduled proceedings and judicial rulings, and to opportunities to present and challenge evidence. To a small but significant extent, the requirements of due process in civil trials vary with the importance of affected interests. For example, in almost all civil cases, the plaintiff will win and the defendant lose if the plaintiff can prove pertinent facts "by a preponderance of the evidence" – that is, as being more likely than not. But the Supreme Court has recognized an exception for a few cases in which the stakes for the defendant are very high, including those in which the government seeks to remove children from their parents' custody based on alleged abuse or incompetence.[25] Emphasizing the "fundamental interest" of parents in custody and control of their children, the Court has held that due process requires the state to prove the need to terminate parental rights by "clear and convincing evidence."[26] The Court has similarly ruled that a state may not commit a person to an institution on grounds of mental illness without proving by "clear and convincing evidence" that the person is dangerous to himself or herself or to others.[27]

Due Process in Administrative Proceedings

In a variety of contexts, the government sometimes takes adverse action against people, and deprives them of liberty or property, without going to court. For example, customs collectors seize suspected contraband at the border. Health inspectors may impound food that they believe to be contaminated. Or, to cite some different kinds of examples, welfare officials may cut off benefits to those who previously received them, or a public school may fire a teacher or suspend a student for alleged misconduct. In all of these cases, the adverse action depends on informal fact-finding. In each case, the victim could probably go to court and challenge the decision. But filing a lawsuit is costly and difficult. The question thus arises whether the Due Process Clause requires the governmental officials who are directly involved to hold a fact-finding hearing, either before or swiftly after they deprive someone of what the Supreme Court now calls a liberty or property "interest."

The Court's traditional approach, which prevailed well into the twentieth century, included a number of complexities. At its center, however, lay a distinction between "rights" on the one hand and "privileges" or "gratuities" on the other. Within the terms of this distinction, the Due Process Clause conferred procedural guarantees only in cases involving rights to liberty or property – and, crucially, there was no "right" to benefits that the government voluntarily bestowed but could, if it so chose, eliminate altogether. Welfare fell within the latter category (because the government could abolish welfare programs if it wished to do so), as did public employment and opportunities to attend public schools.[28]

Then, especially in the 1970s, the framework changed dramatically. The pivotal decision came in *Goldberg v. Kelly*[29] (1970). Upon concluding that a welfare recipient no longer qualified for benefits, welfare officials frequently struck recipients from the rolls with little advance notice and with no opportunity for an oral hearing on the underlying facts. Kelly protested that this policy was not only unfair, but deprived her of "property" without the constitutionally guaranteed "due process of law." The Supreme Court agreed. Rejecting the old distinction between rights and privileges, the Court held that before officials could withdraw welfare benefits on grounds of ineligibility they needed to offer hearings at which affected people could present their version of the facts.

The Court's decision in *Goldberg v. Kelly* had two key elements. First, the Court assumed that welfare benefits were a form of "property" within the meaning of the Due Process Clause. In this part of its opinion, the Court quoted academic writing emphasizing that statutory "entitlements" to income and other benefits – including not only welfare but Social Security, military pensions, and expected income from government employment – play the same functional role in modern society that more traditional property played in past times.[30] Given the importance of statutory entitlements as many citizens' principal source of wealth, the Court recognized that "interests" in such entitlements could count as property protected by the Due Process Clause's procedural guarantees. Second, the Court stressed that due process is a flexible concept, the requirements of which vary with context. After noting the "brutal need" of many welfare recipients,[31] the Court examined a variety of considerations before ruling that welfare officials must provide hearings *before* they can terminate welfare benefits on the ground that a claimant is not eligible for them. (So-called "postdeprivation" hearings will not suffice.)

In general terms, *Goldberg* sketched the framework that the Court has continued to apply in cases involving claims to administrative due process, or due process rights to hearings before government officials other than judges. One line of cases has struggled with the question of when people have liberty or property "interests" that trigger a right to due process. The cases in this line reflect vexation and frequently confusion and are not easily summarized. In loose terms, people have "property interests" in jobs and benefits when, but only when, state or federal law gives them a right to continuation of those jobs or benefits subject to certain conditions being met.[32] For example, if a statute specifies that certain government employees can be fired only for "good cause," those employees have a property interest in continued employment. Should one of them be fired, the firing would constitute a deprivation of the property interest and trigger rights to procedural due process to determine whether "good cause" really existed. By contrast, probationary employees who have no legal assurance of continued employment, no matter how well they perform, do not have property interests in their jobs.[33]

In defining "liberty" interests, the Supreme Court sometimes looks to rights expressly conferred by state or federal law, just as it does in defining property rights. But the Court has also found some liberty interests to arise directly under the Constitution. It has held, for example, that students in the public schools have a constitutionally protected liberty interest in not being subjected to corporal punishment, even if state or local law should provide otherwise.[34] The existence of this liberty interest does not mean that a student has an absolute right never to be spanked or otherwise physically punished by a school official. It does mean, however, that students cannot be deprived of that liberty interest without being afforded due process of law in the form of an informal hearing before school officials (rather than a judge).

The other crucial question within the *Goldberg* framework arises after a protected liberty or property interest has been found to exist: Exactly what procedural safeguards are "due"? For example, must the hearing precede a deprivation, or will a postdeprivation hearing (which could lead to the correction of an erroneous initial decision) suffice? Can the official who makes an initial decision also conduct the hearing, or must a more disinterested person preside? Must there be a right to present and cross-examine witnesses? Are lawyers allowed to participate?

Once again, the Supreme Court's efforts to answer these questions in specific cases are not always easy to reconcile with one another. In *Goldberg*, the Justices required a hearing *before* the government could cut off welfare payments. In other cases, the Court has found it adequate for the government to provide a hearing after terminating Social Security benefits.[35] Similarly, the Court has sometimes applied more demanding standards and sometimes less demanding standards in determining who will count as an impartial decision-maker once a hearing occurs.

If the Court occasionally reaches surprising conclusions, however, it consistently employs the same analytical approach. The Court's formula, first articulated in *Mathews v. Eldridge*[36] (1976), calls for the "balancing" or weighing of three factors:

> First, the [importance of the] private interest that will be affected by the official action; second, the risk of an erroneous deprivation of such interest through the procedures used, and the probable value, if any, of additional or substitute procedural safeguards; and finally, the Government's interest, including...the fiscal and administrative burdens that the additional or substitute procedural requirement would entail.

The *Mathews* formula highlights a painful but inescapable fact about rights to fair procedures, as already noted at the beginning of this chapter: No process is ever perfect, and in determining how many procedural guarantees to require, the Supreme Court needs to weigh interests in fairness to individuals against the government's interest in being able to make decisions swiftly, without excessive costs of time or money. Nor is weighing the government's interest merely hard-hearted. If the budget for a welfare agency is fixed, then money spent on lawyers and hearings, and in retaining undeserving recipients on the rolls pending the completion of hearings, may actually result in a reduction in substantive payments to the needy.[37] In weighing the competing interests, the Court seeks guidance from history, from prior judicial decisions, and from widely shared public values. At the end, however, the Court must make difficult and often controversial judgments with profound moral and economic implications.

Goldberg v. Kelly, decided in the afterglow of the Warren Court, cited the "brutal need" often faced by welfare recipients as a reason to require predeprivation hearings with relatively broad procedural rights. *Mathews*, decided six years later by a more conservative Court, adopted a more expressly cost-conscious tone. It permitted cutoffs of Social Security benefits without a prior hearing, and it required fewer procedural safeguards when a postdeprivation hearing finally occurs. Since *Mathews*, the Court has grown even more conservative, as the country has too. Subsequent development of the doctrine has reflected those trends, though without dramatic changes. The basic framework remains unaltered, as does the difficulty of determining how much procedural fairness the Constitution can sensibly require.

FIVE

Equal Protection of the Laws

No State shall...deny to any person within its jurisdiction the
equal protection of the laws.
 – The Equal Protection Clause of the Fourteenth Amendment

IN 1994, JENNIFER GRATZ APPLIED FOR ADMISSION to the University of Michigan. Gratz was a good student. Her adjusted high
school grade-point average was 3.8 on a 4-point scale, and she had
achieved a solid but not top-notch score on a standardized college
admissions test. At many colleges this record would have ensured
admission. At the University of Michigan, it did not. After applying
in the fall of 1994, Gratz received a letter in January 1995 notifying
her that she would need to wait until April for a final decision: Although she was "well qualified," she was "less competitive than the
students who have been admitted on first review." In April a second
letter arrived, this one with the news that Gratz had been rejected.

Unwilling to accept this result, Gratz filed suit in federal court,
alleging that the University of Michigan had deprived her of "the
equal protection of the laws" guaranteed by the Equal Protection
Clause of the United States Constitution. In particular, Gratz, who is
white, argued that Michigan unconstitutionally discriminated against
her by granting race-based admissions preferences to members of
historically underrepresented minority groups.

The facts of *Gratz v. Bollinger*[1] (2003) were complicated, in
part because the University of Michigan's undergraduate admissions
policy – like those at many elite colleges – took a number of factors
into account. Under the system that Gratz challenged in the Supreme
Court, applicants were ranked on a scale that included 150 possible

points. Of these, 110 were based on high school grades, standardized test scores, and the rigor of an applicant's high school program. Beyond that, it was possible to earn points for leadership, the quality of an application essay, or residence within the state of Michigan. Applicants whose parents had attended the University of Michigan received 4 points. One category grouped together, and provided 20 points for, being a member of an underrepresented racial minority group, coming from a socioeconomically challenged background, being a recruited athlete, or being designated by the provost for special treatment.

Under this system, Gratz would have been admitted if she had come from a socioeconomically challenged background, was a recruited athlete, or was assigned a preference by the provost (perhaps because of family ties or family wealth, some of which might have been dangled as available for donation to the University). She would also have earned admission if she had recorded sufficiently better grades or test scores and possibly if she had demonstrated more leadership or had a parent who was a Michigan graduate. But Gratz did not complain about being "discriminated against" on any of these bases. She argued solely that the University of Michigan denied her the equal protection of the laws by giving a 20-point preference to members of racial minority groups.

The Supreme Court agreed and held Michigan's undergraduate admissions scheme to be unconstitutional – although, as I subsequently explain, in a separate case decided on the same day the Justices upheld the different affirmative action program used by the University of Michigan Law School, in which race was taken into account but made a smaller and less rigid difference. Many complications thus lie ahead. Even without those complications, however, *Gratz v. Bollinger* illustrates the central features of modern equal protection doctrine and raises many of the questions that surround it. A few bear noting at the outset.

The Equal Protection Clause does not prohibit all forms of governmental discrimination, nor do all bases for governmental discrimination trigger searching judicial scrutiny. The University of Michigan gives preferences to applicants with high grades over applicants with low grades and to Michigan residents over residents of other states. It prefers athletes to nonathletes and the children of alumni to applicants who are not the children of alumni. Had Gratz argued that the University of Michigan cannot discriminate on any these grounds, her argument under the Equal Protection Clause almost surely would have failed. (This, presumably, is why Gratz raised no such challenges.) But why does the Equal Protection Clause permit so much governmental discrimination? Why would the Court have upheld governmental policies that discriminate against applicants who have relatively weak grades or test scores, come from states other than Michigan, or are not the children of alumni?

In contrast with nearly all other bases for governmental decision making, race-based classifications draw heightened judicial scrutiny. When Gratz claimed that she was discriminated against on the basis of race, she had a winning argument. The Court treats race-based classifications as "suspect," unlike classifications based on test scores or, in some contexts, family background (as in the case of alumni children). But what is so different and special about race? Or if it is obvious what is "special" about race, what other grounds for governmental classification, if any, should be viewed as similarly "suspect" and thus as presumptively unconstitutional? Should classifications based on gender be treated as suspect? Classifications based on homosexuality?

In treating some bases for discrimination as "suspect" and others as not, modern equal protection doctrine does not reflect the original understanding of the Equal Protection Clause. There is little or no evidence that the Equal Protection Clause was originally understood to bar race-based *preferences* for racial minorities – the kind of "race discrimination" challenged by Jennifer Gratz. Indeed, although many Americans might be surprised to learn it, the evidence suggests that the framers and ratifiers of the Equal Protection Clause did not even view it as banning all laws discriminating *against* racial minorities. This is one reason, though by no means the only one, that it took until 1954 – nearly 100 years after the ratification of the Equal Protection Clause – for the Supreme Court to invalidate legally segregated education in *Brown v. Board of Education*.[2] How, then, did the

Court arrive at its celebrated decision in *Brown*? Do the arguments supporting the result in *Brown* point clearly to the conclusion that the affirmative action program at issue in *Gratz* violated the Equal Protection Clause?

Whether the Supreme Court admits it or not, it inevitably makes lots of moral judgments in applying the Equal Protection Clause. But are those pure judgments of personal morality, or do other considerations come into play? If the latter, what considerations tend to influence the Court's decisions?

In the course of surveying modern equal protection doctrine, this Chapter will elaborate the points that I have highlighted and attempt to answer the questions that I have just raised.

Equal Protection and the Constitution

Although the Declaration of Independence proclaimed that "all men are created equal," the original Constitution included no general guarantee of equal protection of the laws. Indeed, as noted in the Introduction, the original Constitution contemplated the continued existence of slavery. Following the Civil War, however, Reconstruction Congresses proposed and the states ratified the Thirteenth Amendment, which abolished slavery, and then the Fourteenth Amendment, which provides that "[n]o State shall...deny to any person within its jurisdiction the equal protection of the laws." Today, the equal protection guarantee ranks among the centerpieces of the Constitution. No provision more profoundly reflects national ideals. As with some other constitutional guarantees, however, current doctrine under the Equal Protection Clause owes far more to historically unfolding cultural forces than to original understandings.

As perhaps the most obvious measure of cultural influence, the Supreme Court today applies the equal protection guarantee to *federal* as well as to state legislation, even though the Equal Protection Clause refers only to what "no *State*" may deny. This practice traces to a 1954 decision in which the Court pronounced it simply "unthinkable" that the Constitution could tolerate race-based discrimination by the federal government while condemning identical discrimination by the states.[3] To justify its conclusion, the Court held that the Due Process Clause of the Fifth Amendment includes a guarantee of basic governmental fairness that condemns race discrimination. This ruling drew no support from original history, and the Court did not pretend otherwise. The Fifth Amendment was adopted at a time when the Constitution provided for slavery; then, no one thought it barred race discrimination.

Cultural forces have played nearly as large a role in shaping judicial doctrine under the Equal Protection Clause itself. By all accounts, the principal purpose of the Fourteenth Amendment (in which the Equal Protection Clause appears) was to protect the former slaves and their descendants against the most invidious forms of state discrimination. But the framers and ratifiers of the Fourteenth Amendment inhabited a pervasively racist world, much of which they apparently did not intend to challenge, at least immediately. As one example, Congress maintained segregated galleries throughout its debates about the Fourteenth Amendment. In addition, almost no one appears to have thought that the Fourteenth Amendment barred state and local governments from operating racially segregated public schools.[4] Among the states then operating segregated schools, none changed its practices upon the Amendment's ratification.

In attempting to explain the original meaning of the Fourteenth Amendment, historians have emphasized that the principal drafters intended the centrally operative provision to be the Privilege or Immunities Clause: "No State shall make or enforce any law which shall abridge the privileges or immunities of citizens of the United States." According to the most widely accepted account, the framers recognized at least two categories of "rights" – fundamental rights on the one hand, and lesser rights, including "social" rights, on the other.[5] They apparently expected the Privileges or Immunities Clause to guarantee fundamental rights to everyone, including African Americans, but not necessarily to mandate equality in all spheres of governmental conduct. According to this same account, the framers regarded the Equal Protection Clause as reinforcing the demand for equality with respect to fundamental rights, but not necessarily as guaranteeing that all rights, including rights to sit in public galleries or to attend public schools, must be distributed equally.

Although this is the most commonly accepted view, it should probably not be pressed too dogmatically. No more with the Fourteenth Amendment than with other constitutional provisions did the framers and ratifiers reach consensus on their expectations and write those expectations into law. On many points, they undoubtedly disagreed among themselves. They also worked against the background of a moral tradition opposing slavery and celebrating the ideal of natural rights, shared by all human beings. Some historians and constitutional theorists thus maintain that the Equal Protection Clause constitutionalizes a moral ideal and that it is the moral ideal of equality, not the framers' specific expectations, that ultimately ought to matter in constitutional adjudication.[6] Again, however, virtually no one contends that a majority of the framers and ratifiers specifically expected or intended the Fourteenth Amendment to outlaw all forms of race-based discrimination.

As discussed in Chapter Three, the Supreme Court dashed the framers' expectations for the Privileges or Immunities Clause in *The Slaughter-House Cases*[7] (1872): *The Slaughter-House Cases* construed the Privileges or Immunities Clause so narrowly as to be almost meaningless. Within a few years, however, the Equal Protection Clause took on a life of its own and has achieved a significance apparently never contemplated by the framing generation. Under current doctrine, most governmental classifications are subject to judicial scrutiny under a "rational basis" test similar to that applied to economic regulatory legislation under the Due Process Clause in the post-*Lochner* era. But the Court deems a few bases for classification, such as race, to be constitutionally "suspect." Suspect classifications attract "strict" judicial scrutiny and will be upheld only if "necessary to promote a compelling governmental interest."

Rational Basis Review

Most if not all laws create classifications and provide different treatment for people in different categories. Tax laws sometimes require those who earn larger incomes to pay higher rates than those who earn smaller incomes. The blind cannot get driver's licenses. Even criminal laws have a classificatory effect. A law against theft sorts people into two categories, thieves and nonthieves. The government punishes the lawbreakers, but not the law-abiding. Examples such as these demonstrate that the Equal Protection Clause cannot sensibly command that the government treat everyone "the same." The rich can be treated differently from the poor for purposes of taxation, the blind differently from the sighted in the distribution of driver's licenses. Instead of insisting that everyone be treated "the same," the Equal Protection Clause mandates only that "like cases," or those who are the same in relevant ways, should be treated alike. In other words, its guiding principle condemns discriminations only among those who are relevantly similar. Thus comes the central question for equal protection analysis: When are cases "alike," or when are people sufficiently similar in relevant respects, so that they must be treated the same?

In its central range of operation, equal protection doctrine answers this question by applying a test of means–ends rationality to governmental *classifications*. The government can award drivers' licenses to those with good vision, while withholding licenses from the blind, because this classificatory scheme rationally advances a legitimate governmental interest in highway safety. Viewed in light of that interest, the blind and the sighted are not similarly situated: The blind are less likely to be safe drivers. By the same token, the government can classify thieves differently from nonthieves, and impose restraints on the former but not on the latter, because this difference in treatment promotes an interest in deterring theft.

As already noted, the rational basis test used to test ordinary or nonsuspect classifications under the Equal Protection Clause closely parallels the rational basis test used in the post-*Lochner* era to assess economic regulatory legislation under the Due Process Clause. Perhaps for that reason, the equal protection test is similarly deferential in most applications.[8] The Supreme Court hesitates to say either that the government's ends or purposes are not legitimate or that there is no rational connection between ends and means. In a post-*Lochner* world, if the government chooses to tax the rich at a higher rate than the poor, or to assist dairy farmers but not cranberry growers, the Court will not second-guess its judgments.

This is why, as I have suggested, the Court would almost certainly have upheld most if not all of the criteria used by the University of Michigan in its undergraduate admissions process. The University wants to admit good students, who will make the best use of a college education – a legitimate purpose, to which selection based on high school grades and test scores is rationally related. It is legitimate for the University to want competitive athletic teams. Preferences for recruited athletes promote this goal. Preferences for alumni children may pose slightly greater difficulties, but they too are probably acceptable. Within a highly deferential framework for evaluation, alumni preferences might be thought to advance legitimate interests in maintaining good relations with past graduates (who may be good candidates to make financial contributions to the school). Such preferences might also be defended by reference to an interest in admitting those students who are likely to have the longest-standing desires to attend the University of Michigan. Nor is it a problem that the University's policies promote a variety of purposes, not just one. A single law or policy may aim to advance multiple goals, and a classification will be upheld if it is rationally related to any.

Although the Supreme Court almost always accords great deference to legislative judgments in applying rational basis review, there are occasional exceptions. According to a recent study, the Court applied the rational basis test in 110 cases during the twenty-five-year period from 1971 to 1996.[9] In 100 of those cases, the Court upheld the challenged statute or regulation, but in 10 cases, or about 9 percent of the total, the Court found a constitutional violation. What is more, the Court appeared to apply what the study's author termed "heightened rationality" review in all of the cases in which it found an equal protection violation.[10]

United States Department of Agriculture v. Moreno[11] (1973) illustrates the pattern. *Moreno* held that a federal statute offended equal protection principles by denying food stamps to "any household containing an individual who is unrelated to any other member of the household."[12] The Court might easily have upheld the statute by ruling that Congress could permissibly choose to subsidize only households that resemble traditional families. In determining eligibility for spending programs, Congress generally enjoys great flexibility to protect the public treasury by drawing lines, and lines that give preferences to families and family members are permissible in many contexts. Instead, despite its frequent assertions that legislation will be upheld if there is any *imaginable* basis on which it might be supported, the Court focused on what it said was the statute's real purpose – to exclude "hippy" communes from achieving eligibility. Pronouncing that "a bare congressional desire to harm a politically unpopular group cannot constitute a *legitimate* governmental interest,"[13] the Court invalidated the challenged statutory exclusion.

In contrast with the Court's dominant line of highly deferential decisions, *Moreno* exhibits what might be termed an occasional or recessive willingness to engage in serious review of the substantive fairness of legislative classifications, even in "rational basis" cases. Plainly implicit in this approach is an assumption that fairness is at least not wholly in the eye of the beholder. Although most legislative judgments may fall within a permissible range, some do not. It bears emphasis that the morally judgmental disposition reflected in *Moreno* is recessive only, at least in rational basis cases. The Court's dominant tendency is to perform review so deferential as to amount to a rubber stamp. But the recessive disposition to assess the substantive fairness of legislative classifications refuses to disappear entirely. It crops up from time to time, sometimes in unexpected cases.

Race and the Constitution: Invidious Discrimination

In contrast with the rational basis review that the Supreme Court applies in most cases, the modern Court treats all race-based classifications as "suspect" or presumptively unconstitutional. As discussed above, this approach appears not to reflect the original understanding of the Equal Protection Clause. Nor did the Supreme Court always take the modern view.

In the notorious case of *Plessy v. Ferguson*[14] (1896), the Court upheld a Louisiana law requiring that passenger railroads provide "equal but separate accommodations for the white, and colored races." After being excluded from the "white" car, Homer Plessy argued first that he carried only a small proportion of black blood and thus was white, not black, within the meaning of the law. That claim failing, he argued next that the race-based classification violated the Equal Protection Clause. The Supreme Court disagreed. Asserting that the Fourteenth Amendment was not "intended to abolish [all] distinctions based upon color, or to enforce social, as distinguished from political, equality,"[15] the Court held that the legislature had the power to enact race-based classifications – at least within the domain of "social" rights – as long as those classifications were "reasonable."

In this aspect of its ruling, *Plessy* appears to have tracked what many believe to be the historically understood meaning of the Equal Protection Clause: It barred governmentally mandated race-based discrimination with respect to a limited class of fundamental rights, but not with respect to social rights. Almost immediately, however, the Court encountered a complication. It assumed that all governmentally mandated discriminations – those based on race, just like those between the educated and the uneducated, the old and the young, or the rich and the poor – must at least be "reasonable" to be legally permissible. Applying this requirement, the Court readily accepted that it was reasonable for Louisiana to accommodate prevailing social attitudes by mandating "separate but equal" railroad cars for whites and blacks. The difficulty involved whether the separate accommodations could really be adjudged equal. As a matter of fact, the white cars were often more comfortable than the black cars. Increasing the awkwardness was that whites were in fact permitted to sit in the black cars, which often doubled as smoking cars, if they so chose, whereas blacks were wholly excluded from the white cars. The Court dealt curtly with objections such as these: "We consider the underlying fallacy of the plaintiff's argument to consist in the assumption that the enforced separation of the two races stamps the colored race with a badge of inferiority. If this be so, it is not by reason of anything found in the act, but solely because the colored race chooses to put that construction upon it."[16]

From a modern perspective, this assertion is hard to take seriously. Among all of the opinions of the Supreme Court, this may be the point, as Charles Black once wrote, at which "[t]he curves of callousness and stupidity intersect at their respective maxima."[17] At the time of its decision, however, *Plessy v. Ferguson* attracted no stir. During the last two decades of the nineteenth century, race relations in the United States sank toward a historic low, especially in the South. For most of the country, as for most of the Justices, it may have been almost unimaginable that the Constitution could mandate what the Court described as the enforced "commingling" of the races. Justices of the Supreme Court tend to embody the characteristic outlooks of their time and to see constitutional issues in light of them. For people who perceived racial discrimination as natural, not invidious, it may even have been possible to believe that the accommodation of white preferences for separation carried no necessary message of black inferiority.

But it was plainly also possible to perceive the reality of the situation. "The thin disguise of 'equal' accommodations for passengers in railroad coaches will not mislead any one," Justice John Marshall Harlan wrote in a solitary dissenting opinion.[18] Very much a man of his time, Harlan spoke unapologetically of the special virtues and accomplishments of "[t]he white race."[19] "But in view of the constitution," he wrote in the same paragraph, "there is in this country no superior, dominant, ruling class of citizens. . . . Our constitution is color-blind."[20]

Despite Harlan's protest, *Plessy*'s regime of "separate but equal" endured for more than fifty years. Over time, its morally shameful character – a matter by no means wholly dependent on the original understanding of any constitutional provision – grew ever more apparent to increasing numbers of Americans. Not surprisingly, the Supreme Court manifested acute discomfort with race-based discriminations in its next major consideration of their constitutionality.

Nevertheless, the Court expressly upheld a race-based military order excluding all persons of Japanese ancestry from designated areas of the West Coast in *Korematsu v. United States*[21] (1944).

The exclusion order followed the Japanese attack on Pearl Harbor of December 1941. Fearing that people of Japanese descent posed a sabotage risk, military officials ordered all persons of Japanese ancestry to leave the West Coast and to submit to detention in "relocation centers." The military orders applied to roughly 112,000 people, of whom more than 65,000 were American citizens. Confronted with a challenge to the exclusion order, the Court began its *Korematsu* opinion by announcing that "all legal restrictions which curtail the civil rights of a single racial group are immediately suspect" and subject to "the most rigid scrutiny."[22] This assertion was in one way remarkable. Even though the Equal Protection Clause does not apply to the federal government, the Court effectively held the federal government to equal protection norms: With no bow in the direction of the original understanding, it assumed that race-based classifications are so presumptively offensive to basic principles of fairness that they trigger "the most rigid scrutiny."

In *Korematsu*, however, the reality of the Court's analysis did not match its language. The majority upheld the race-based exclusions based on scanty evidence contained in what a dissenting Justice termed an "unsworn, self-serving statement, untested by any cross-examination," offered by the general who had ordered the exclusion.[23] Writing for the Court, Justice Hugo Black insisted that "[t]o cast this case into outlines of racial prejudice . . . merely confuses the issue."[24] Critics have charged otherwise.

In the aftermath of *Korematsu*, social attitudes concerning race and race discrimination did not stand still. Following World War II, President Harry Truman ordered the desegregation of the American armed forces, which had remained segregated throughout the war. Increasing numbers of blacks assumed positions of prominence. The 1948 platform of the Democratic Party included a strong civil rights plank for the first time. Meanwhile, lawyers for the NAACP had begun a brilliant legal campaign attacking segregation in public education.[25] At the beginning, NAACP lawyers accepted the "separate but equal" framework traceable to *Plessy v. Ferguson*. In one setting after another, they demonstrated that the separate educational facilities maintained for racial minorities were not at all equal to those enjoyed by whites. Having won a number of victories with this strategy, they prepared to argue that racially discriminatory education was inherently unequal and thus unconstitutional.

The NAACP pressed this argument before the Supreme Court in *Brown v. Board of Education*[26] (1954). In their initial deliberations, the Justices found themselves troubled and divided. However wrong segregation might be, some worried that they lacked an adequate legal basis to upset the rule that had prevailed for more than fifty years under *Plessy v. Ferguson*. They also worried that it might lie beyond the proper reach of judicial power to decree a revolutionary change in racial relations in a significant portion of the United States. (The disgrace of the *Lochner* era and the threat of Court packing lay less than twenty years in the past.) With early discussions "indicat[ing] a vote somewhere between five to four for sustaining school segregation and six to three for striking it down,"[27] the Justices decided to take the unusual step of asking for a second round of arguments in the case. Before the second argument occurred, Chief Justice Fred M. Vinson – who was generally unsympathetic to the challengers' case – died, to be replaced by Earl Warren. With the *Brown* case in mind, Justice Felix Frankfurter is said to have remarked, "[T]his is the first solid piece of evidence I've ever had that there really is a God."[28]

Under Warren's leadership, the Court ruled by a stunning vote of 9–0 that legally mandated segregation in public education violated the Equal Protection Clause. Historical inquiries, conducted by the parties at the Court's request, gave the Justices little help in reaching that conclusion: At best, the history revealed no clear intent to abolish discrimination in public education. At worst, it showed an understanding of education as a less than fundamental right with respect to which race-based separations were permitted. But the Court refused to be deterred. "In approaching this problem, we cannot turn the clock back to 1868 when the [Fourteenth] Amendment was adopted, or even to 1896 when *Plessy v. Ferguson* was written," Warren wrote.[29] Focusing on the present day, he emphasized that education had become "perhaps the most important function of state and local governments"[30] and that segregation, as a matter of social and psychological fact, communicated a message of race-based inferiority.[31] In an opinion lacking further rhetorical flourishes, the Court held that "in the field of public education the doctrine of 'separate but equal' has no place."[32]

Brown numbers among the most important and socially revolutionary decisions in Supreme Court history. But the Court did not insist that the revolution begin immediately. Instead of ordering immediate school desegregation, the Court called for yet a third argument in the case. Nearly a year later, the Justices issued a second decision, devoted solely to the issue of remedies for school segregation.[33] In that decision the Court pronounced that responsibility for school desegregation rested in the first instance with state and local officials, not the federal courts, and said that such officials must proceed, not necessarily immediately, but with "all deliberate speed."[34] A long period of foot-dragging ensued. Not for a decade or more did the Supreme Court begin to insist firmly on immediate, effective desegregation of the public schools. (A few courageous judges on the lower federal courts took firmer stands, sometimes at considerable personal risk to themselves and their families.)

To some extent, the Supreme Court appears to have been waiting, attempting to create as few waves as possible, hoping for public opinion to rally to its side. In a number of decisions throughout the 1950s, the Justices quietly applied the rule of *Brown v. Board of Education* to end publicly mandated segregation in facilities such as parks, golf courses, and playgrounds. In doing so, they subtly expanded *Brown*'s rationale. As originally written, the Court's decision had emphasized the special character of education and had expressly banished "separate but equal" only from the realm of public schooling. But even while broadening its antidiscrimination mandate, the Court went out of its way – some would say shamefully so – to avoid a collision over the issue of interracial marriage. In *Naim v. Naim*[35] (1955), the Court essentially refused to rule on an appeal challenging a Virginia statute that forbade interracial marriage. Justice Frankfurter apparently persuaded his fellow Justices that interracial marriage aroused such "deep" and hostile feeling that a Court pronouncement would undermine support for *Brown* and school desegregation.[36] On a pretext, the Court dismissed the appeal and permitted the statute to be enforced.

Over time, support for *Brown* increased, as did support for a broader constitutional principle of racial equality. In roughly the decade following *Brown*, the civil rights movement, led by Dr. Martin Luther King and others, helped to inspire broad-based national sentiment, if not a consensus, that race-based discrimination was a serious moral wrong. Congress enacted a civil rights bill in 1957 and followed by adopting the 1964 Civil Rights Act, the most sweeping and important guarantee of equal rights since Reconstruction. Emboldened by the rising tide of public opinion, the Supreme Court stiffened its commitment to protecting racial minorities in the 1960s and early 1970s. In a series of cases, the Court began to demand immediate steps to abolish school segregation. Indeed, the Justices altered their view about what previously segregated school systems had to do to satisfy the Constitution. In *Brown*, the Court had apparently contemplated that it would suffice merely to end expressly race-based assignments of whites to all-white schools and of blacks to all-black schools. By the late 1960s and early 1970s, the Court insisted on more: Previously segregated school districts needed to achieve meaningful integration, with substantial numbers of white and black students actually attending the same schools.[37] Where necessary to achieve this effect, the Court – in a highly controversial development – began to uphold lower court orders requiring the busing of some students away from the closest schools to schools in other neighborhoods.[38]

By 1967, the Court was finally prepared to deal with the constitutionality of state statutes prohibiting interracial marriage. In *Loving v. Virginia*,[39] the Justices ruled unanimously that such statutes violated the Equal Protection Clause. Within a few more years, the Court had formulated the still-applicable test under which it will invalidate all statutes that discriminate on the basis of race unless they are "necessary to promote a compelling government interest."

The Court's modern stance is also reflected in *Palmore v. Sidoti*[40] (1984). *Palmore* arose from the efforts of a divorced white father to have his daughter removed from the custody of his ex-wife after she married a black man. A state court ruled in favor of the father on the ground that the transfer of custody would promote the best interests of the child – the usual legal standard in child custody matters – because if the daughter remained in a biracial household, "social stigmatization...is sure to come." The Supreme Court rejected this reasoning. By a unanimous vote, the Court ruled that even if private prejudices might lead to "social stigmatization," they could not be permitted to influence a child custody decision: "The Constitution cannot control such prejudices but neither can it tolerate them. Private biases may be outside the reach of the law, but the law cannot, directly or indirectly, give them effect."[41]

Although the Court did not use the language of "strict scrutiny" in *Palmore*, its approach also helps to illustrate what strict scrutiny means. In some minimal way, it might have been "rational" for a court to consider whether a child is likely to suffer social stigmatization from living in a biracial household as one factor among many relevant to determining the child's best interests. Under strict scrutiny, however, the mere fact that it would be "rational" (in some minimal sense) to take race into account will not suffice. Race-based decision making is strongly disfavored and will be permitted only where "necessary" to promote a compelling interest.

When the social and doctrinal developments are viewed in hindsight, it is remarkable how fast a firm national consensus emerged that publicly enforced race discrimination, which had been a familiar feature of American life from the very beginning, was morally and constitutionally intolerable. In the 1950s, the correctness of *Brown v. Board of Education* was a much-debated issue. Southern politicians protested that the Supreme Court misunderstood local customs and sensibilities; prominent professors maintained that the Court had not adequately justified its decision to overrule *Plessy v. Ferguson* as a matter of law. Within little more than a generation, *Brown* was embraced from all sides as a symbol of the Supreme Court at its best. Especially if that judgment is accepted, it bears noting that *Brown* came only in 1954, nearly 100 years after the ratification of the Fourteenth Amendment, and that the Court did not enforce *Brown* aggressively for another decade, when Congress's enactment of the 1964 Civil Rights Act signaled a political as well as judicial commitment to the protection of minority rights.

Professor Alexander Bickel surely had *Brown* in mind when he offered a much quoted, but also much debated, commentary on the role of the Supreme Court in American government: The Court's job is to lead public opinion, but it must genuinely lead, not pretend to be able to command. The Court, he wrote, "should declare as law only such principles as" it can reasonably expect "will – in time, but in a rather immediate foreseeable future – gain general assent."[42] The Court's ruling in *Brown v. Board of Education* appears to have achieved that much. In the overall pattern of its decisions involving race-based discrimination, the Court attempted no more.

Race and the Constitution: Disparate Impact

Governmental statutes and policies can disadvantage racial minorities in at least two ways. As in *Plessy v. Ferguson* and *Korematsu v. United States*, they can withhold benefits or impose burdens on an expressly racial basis. Or, even if they do not formally mention race at all, they may have a greater adverse impact on one racial group than another.

Washington v. Davis[43] (1976) exemplifies the phenomenon of racially "disparate impact." Under a rule adopted by the District of Columbia, candidates to become police officers had to record a specified score on a test designed to measure verbal ability and reading comprehension. Black candidates failed the test at four times the rate of whites. Citing the test's racially skewed impact, challengers argued that it was racially discriminatory in effect, even if not in form, and that it should receive heightened judicial scrutiny under equal protection principles (rather than being subject merely to rational basis review). The Supreme Court disagreed.

According to the Court, racially disparate impact does not by itself constitute forbidden race discrimination. Nor are statutes with a racially disparate impact constitutionally "suspect" and therefore invalid unless necessary to promote a compelling governmental interest.

Such statutes do not even trigger a heightened burden of governmental justification. Instead, rational basis review applies *unless* a challenger can prove that a statute or policy with a racially discriminatory impact was enacted for the discriminatory *purpose* of harming a racial minority group.

Washington v. Davis was an extremely important case. Racial minorities may suffer two kinds of disadvantage. One arises from hostility. The other is a relative dearth of sympathy, empathy, or concern. If a test systematically disadvantaged whites, rather than blacks, then public officials might well reconsider whether the test was a good one or otherwise readjust governmental policy. Under *Washington v. Davis*, the Equal Protection Clause bars legislation that reflects race-based hostility, but it leaves the problem of racially selective sympathy and indifference wholly unaddressed.

The Court's reasoning in *Washington v. Davis* was relatively explicit. In American society, there are likely to be many rules and policies under which blacks on average fare less well than whites. If all were invalid absent a compelling justification, courts could expect challenges to "a whole range of tax, welfare, public service, regulatory, and licensing statutes that may be more burdensome to the poor and [thus] to the average black [who is more likely to be poor] than to the more affluent white."[44] What is more, governmental bodies (for better or for worse) would feel a subtle pressure to pay attention to race in order to avoid racially disparate impacts that could cause them to be sued. In light of its assessment of the costs and benefits, the Supreme Court refused to license serious constitutional challenges to every statute or policy with a racially skewed effect. It defined the race discrimination forbidden by the Constitution as purposeful race discrimination (only) and read the Equal Protection Clause as requiring no special judicial scrutiny of statutes with racially disparate effects.

Affirmative Action

When the Supreme Court began to treat race-based classifications as constitutionally "suspect," it did so in cases involving discriminations directed against racial minorities. Within less than twenty years of the decision in *Brown v. Board of Education*, however, the courts began to confront race discrimination cases of a different kind – suits brought by whites challenging "affirmative action" programs. Under such programs, members of minority groups receive a preference in the award of jobs, admissions to selective colleges and universities, or government contracts.

Defenders advance a broad range of arguments in favor of affirmative action. Some see a need to remedy historical injustices that have led to a current situation in which whites, on average, are substantially better educated and earn significantly higher incomes than blacks, on average. Others cite continuing discrimination in contemporary society. Others contend that a racially diverse society requires racially diverse leadership to function effectively: Opening doors to traditionally disadvantaged minorities manifests the society's openness to diverse excellences, inspires hope and confidence among minority populations, and ensures representation of diverse viewpoints. Without affirmative action, many maintain that representation of blacks in elite educational institutions – traditional training grounds for leadership positions in business, the professions, and politics – would plummet. According to one recent study, "[u]nder race-blind policies, Blacks would make up only 1.6 to 3.4 percent" of the students in accredited law schools, and "[e]liminating affirmative action from medical education would reduce Black enrollment by 90 percent."[45]

Virtually no one claims that the Constitution requires affirmative action. In constitutional law, questions about affirmative action therefore arise only after a governmental body has voluntarily adopted an affirmative action program. Coming before courts in this posture, affirmative action cases present distinctive questions of constitutional principle and judicial role. In explaining why strict scrutiny was appropriate in cases involving discriminations against minorities, commentators often cited the theory of the *Carolene Products* case (which I briefly discussed in Chapter Four): Heightened judicial scrutiny is needed to protect "discrete and insular" minority groups from the effects of "prejudice" in the political process.[46] Under this process-based view, which identifies the purpose of strict scrutiny under the Equal Protection Clause as protecting minority groups against prejudice, affirmative action programs should not occasion judicial concern. Such programs benefit members of minority groups, rather than harm them, and they are not likely to be motivated by "prejudice" against the white majority.

It is also possible, however, to take a more substantive view of the Equal Protection Clause as prohibiting (or at least making "suspect") all discriminations that are particularly unfair or socially dangerous or divisive. Under this approach, the crucial question about affirmative action programs is whether race-based preferences for racial minorities are morally objectionable or at least sufficiently suspect to trigger strict judicial scrutiny. Some believe that all race-based classifications are unfair. Others think that race-based classifications are objectionable only when used to demean, suppress, or stigmatize. According to those who take this "antisubordinationist" view, the Equal Protection Clause affirms that racial minorities should not be held down on account of their race, but it does not signal that race should never be taken into account (any more than it requires that other traits, including such "immutable" characteristics as blindness, gender, age, and possibly IQ should never be taken into account).

There is no indication that the framers and ratifiers of the Equal Protection Clause regarded race-based preferences for racial minorities as unfair or constitutionally impermissible. In the years immediately surrounding enactment of the Fourteenth Amendment, Congress repeatedly enacted statutes providing benefits for "colored" soldiers and sailors, women and children. A judicial decision to subject affirmative action programs to strict judicial scrutiny therefore cannot rest on the original understanding, any more than it can reflect a process-based commitment to protecting discrete and insular minorities. Such a decision can only reflect a judicial judgment about fundamental fairness.

In a lengthening string of cases, the Supreme Court has held – often by narrow majorities – that affirmative action programs are as constitutionally suspect as any other form of race-based discrimination and thus trigger strict judicial scrutiny. For many years now, the leading case has been *Regents of the University of California v. Bakke*[47] (1978), involving an affirmative action program by the Medical School of the University of California at Davis. Each year the Medical School enrolled 100 students. Some years there were no minority students; without affirmative action, the school never admitted more than a handful. In response to this situation, the Medical School decided to set aside sixteen places solely for minorities. Alan Bakke, a white who applied and got rejected, brought a challenge under the Equal Protection Clause.

Four Justices would have rejected the equal protection challenge and upheld the Medical School's admissions policy as an acceptable remedy for historic and continuing societal discrimination. Four other Justices would have held any use of race in the admissions process to be forbidden by a federal statute.

Justice Lewis Powell, who cast the decisive vote, tried to carve a middle way between blanket acceptance and blanket condemnation of affirmative action programs. In his opinion, much of which was joined by no other Justice, but which nonetheless stated the controlling position (because the other Justices were split 4–4), Powell held that race-based affirmative action triggered strict judicial scrutiny: It was permissible under the Equal Protection Clause only if necessary to promote a compelling governmental interest. But Powell, unlike complete opponents of affirmative action, recognized at least two circumstances under which race-based preferences might pass that test. First, he believed that affirmative action could be permissible as a remedy for specifically identified past discrimination by particular institutions, but not, he emphasized, as a remedy for general, possibly pervasive societal discrimination. Second, he found that educational institutions had a compelling interest in achieving a diverse student body–one that would produce rich classroom discussions and help to educate students for success in a racially diverse world. Powell thus authorized affirmative action, but only on a narrow basis. He insisted that the Equal Protection Clause requires that any affirmative action program be no more sweeping than necessary to achieve its purpose. He specifically pronounced rigid racial "quotas" constitutionally impermissible (and thus invalidated the minority set-aside employed by the University of California at Davis Medical School).

He said that educational institutions seeking diversity could take race into account as one relevant factor among many, but that they must give individualized consideration to every applicant.

Subsequent decisions have generally followed the path laid out in *Bakke*. In *Richmond v. J. A. Croson Co.*[48] (1989), involving affirmative action preferences in the award of government contracts, a clear Court majority affirmed that affirmative action programs would trigger strict scrutiny. *Croson* also enforced Justice Powell's conclusion in the *Bakke* case that a governmental body such as the City of Richmond has no "compelling" interest in remedying past race discrimination by the society at large. For affirmative action programs to be justified as a remedy, a governmental body must identify specific patterns or incidents of past discrimination in which it was somehow implicated, either through its own wrongful actions or through a failure to take preventive measures that it could and should have taken.

For a time, the Supreme Court took the position that affirmative action programs implemented by the *federal* government should not draw the same "strict" scrutiny as affirmative action by state and local governments.[49] As a historical and textual matter, the Equal Protection Clause evinces a distrust of states but not of Congress, and it might be thought that Congress should have greater flexibility than the states to provide race-based remedies for past race-based wrongs. In 1995, however, the Court overruled itself on this question and held that federal as well as state affirmative action programs should be strictly scrutinized.[50]

The Court's most recent word on affirmative action came in 2003 in two separate cases that involved undergraduate and law school admissions at the University of Michigan. The undergraduate admissions case was *Gratz v. Bollinger*,[51] the facts of which were presented at the beginning of this chapter. In *Gratz*, a 6–3 majority struck down a rigid program under which applicants from underrepresented minorities received a large (and fixed) total of 20 points out of a possible 150 on the school's admissions index. Although the Court assumed that the University had a "compelling" interest in achieving a diverse student body, it ruled that the uniform 20-point bonus was too large and mechanical to be narrowly tailored to a legitimate interest in the kind of diversity that the University could legitimately claim to value under Justice Powell's *Bakke* opinion.

The law school admissions case, *Grutter v. Bollinger*,[52] was probably even more important than *Gratz*. In *Grutter*, at least six Justices expressly followed Justice Powell's approach in *Bakke* and held that educational institutions have a "compelling interest" in achieving a diverse student body.[53] The same six Justices agreed that educational institutions may permissibly take race into account as one factor contributing to diversity, as long as they do so on an individualized basis and without racial quotas. In an opinion by Justice Sandra Day O'Connor, a moderate conservative who has often tried to follow in the footsteps of Justice Powell, a narrower majority of 5–4 also held that in seeking diversity a school may strive self-consciously to enroll a "critical mass" of traditionally underrepresented minorities. Justice O'Connor insisted, however, that assessment of candidates must be individualized and that quotas are impermissible. She affirmed that expressly race-based decisions would not be "necessary" (and thus would be unconstitutional) if practicable race-neutral alternatives would allow an institution to achieve the "diversity" that it sought. She also added a requirement that affirmative action programs "must be limited in time" and said, provocatively if not with legally binding effect, that "[w]e expect that 25 years from now, the use of racial preferences will no longer be necessary to further the interest [in diversity] approved today."[54]

In sometimes caustic dissenting opinions, the four Justices in the minority argued that in its search for a critical mass the University of Michigan Law School – whose affirmative action program the majority upheld – made race count for too much. In their view, the numbers proved that the school in practice sought to achieve rough racial proportionality, rather than merely making race a modest "plus" in achieving the kind of diversity that enhances educational quality.

Although *Grutter* was a decision of enormous importance, it leaves many questions to be resolved in future cases. Much of the opinion emphasized the special interest of educational institutions in achieving the kind of diverse student body that improves the quality of education. It would therefore be possible to read *Grutter* as limiting the "diversity" interest that can justify affirmative action to the context of university admissions. Other parts of the opinion, however, can be read as containing hints that the compelling governmental interest in diversity might sweep more broadly. For example, Justice O'Connor quoted approvingly from a brief by a group of retired generals and admirals, who asserted that "a 'highly qualified, racially diverse officer corps...is essential to the military's ability to fulfill its princip[al] mission to provide national security.'"[55] If the military has a compelling interest in a racially diverse officer corps, perhaps other governmental institutions have comparably compelling interests in achieving and maintaining diverse work forces. Further litigation clearly awaits.

Gender and the Constitution

Through most of constitutional history, discrimination against women was accepted as a matter of course. The Supreme Court reviewed gender-based classifications under the rational basis test but invariably approved them. In an 1873 case upholding a statute that denied women the right to practice law, the Court observed that "[t]he natural and proper timidity and delicacy which belongs to the female sex evidently unfits it for many of the occupations of civil life."[56] The Court's tone had not changed notably by 1948, when it upheld a law barring most women from obtaining bartender's licenses: "The fact that women may now have achieved the virtues that men long claimed as their prerogatives and now indulge in vices that men have long practiced, does not preclude the State from drawing a sharp line between the sexes."[57]

The first decision invalidating a statute that discriminated on the basis of sex came in 1971.[58] The timing reveals much. By 1971 cultural attitudes about women's roles were changing dramatically. Shortly afterwards, in a case challenging the military's policy of automatically providing "dependency" or spousal support allowances to married male but not to married female members of the armed forces, Ruth Bader Ginsburg – later to be named a Supreme Court Justice herself – forcefully argued that sex-based classifications should be deemed constitutionally suspect, just like those based on race. Ginsburg maintained that sex, like race, was an immutable trait, crucial to self-identity, "which the dominant culture views as a badge of inferiority justifying disadvantaged treatment." Ginsburg won the case, *Frontiero v. Richardson*[59] (1973), with eight of the nine Justices agreeing that women were disadvantaged unfairly. But she could persuade only four Justices, one short of a majority, that statutes that discriminate on the basis of sex should be analyzed in the same way as statutes that discriminate based on race.

The Court's hesitation was understandable. Ginsburg was right that sex, like race, is a highly salient characteristic: People always notice the gender of others. She was also right that women have historically been disadvantaged on the basis of sex and that the disadvantages remained palpable in 1973: Women on average earned lower incomes than men, remained subject to various forms of formal and informal employment discrimination, and had achieved few prominent positions of political leadership. But if the struggle for gender equality has obvious parallels to the struggle for racial equality, there are important differences as well. For one thing, the physiological differences between men and women are more than skin deep: Only women can get pregnant, men on average are stronger and heavier than women, and so forth. For another, whereas race would likely be irrelevant in an ideal world, gender would not. Sexual attraction would remain, as might sex-linked desires for privacy (for example, in separate restrooms, showers, and so forth), and there would continue to be correlations between sex and average height, strength, and weight. A third complicating factor is that women are a (small) majority of the American population, not a "discrete and insular minority." None of these considerations remotely suggests that sex discrimination is not a problem of constitutional dimension – only that issues of sex-based discrimination present distinctive complexities.

With respect to the "standard" for judicial review, the Supreme Court ultimately decided to split the difference between the strict scrutiny applied to race-based classifications and the rational basis review used in most other cases. In *Craig v. Boren*[60] (1976), the Court held that gender-based discriminations should be deemed invalid unless they "serve important governmental objectives" and are "substantially related to achievement of those objectives." To this formula it later added the gloss that gender-based discriminations are impermissible unless supported by "an exceedingly persuasive justification."[61]

At issue in *Craig* was an Oklahoma statute that forbade men between the ages of eighteen and twenty-one, but not women of the same age, to buy low-alcohol beer. The state defended the statute as a means of stopping drunk driving, to which it said that young men were more prone than young women. The Court, however, found the supporting evidence insufficient to justify the differential treatment. Its decision reveals a good deal about both the "intermediate" scrutiny to which gender-based discriminations are subject and the Court's underlying concerns.

Although many of the arguments for treating gender-based classifications as suspect involve historic discrimination against women, in *Craig* the Court applied elevated scrutiny to invalidate a statute that discriminated against young *men*. Nor was *Craig* unusual in this respect: The Justices regularly scrutinize statutes that disadvantage men under precisely the same test applicable to statutes that disadvantage women. In insisting on parallel treatment, the Court may believe statutes that discriminate against men to be as presumptively unfair as those that discriminate against women. It may also believe that gender stereotypes are the mirror images of one another. If so, a statute based on a stereotype of males as prone to engage in risky behavior such as drinking and driving may tend to reinforce a parallel stereotype of women as cautious and risk averse. In the long run, gender-based stereotypes probably tend to limit the opportunities open to men and women alike.

It also bears notice that although the statute involved in *Craig* failed "intermediate" scrutiny, it would almost certainly have passed the rational basis test. The state had a legitimate interest in reducing drunk driving. It was not irrational to try to reduce drunk driving by prohibiting alcohol sales to a group who might reasonably be thought prone to drink and then to drive. Indeed, the state actually had some evidence suggesting that although men between the ages of eighteen and twenty-one displayed at least a modest tendency to drive while drunk, women of the same age almost never did. In short, it was probably "rational," in a narrowly instrumental sense, for the state to forbid the purchase of low-alcohol beer to eighteen- to twenty-one-year-old men, and equally "rational" to exclude women from the prohibition. Nevertheless, the Court refused to permit the discrimination between men and women. Even when gender-based discrimination is otherwise rational, the Court apparently concluded, it can have a moral and perhaps a social cost – possibly, once again, by reinforcing cultural stereotypes. To put the point somewhat more bluntly, *Craig v. Boren* appears to construe the Equal Protection Clause as committed to fighting gender-based stereotypes by forbidding gender-based discriminations, even when they are otherwise rational, unless they are "substantially related" to an "important" governmental objective.

Although *Craig* both established a test for the constitutionality of statutes that discriminate on the basis of gender and highlighted the Court's concern with gender-based stereotypes, subsequent decisions do not form a simple pattern. The Court has invalidated formulas that designate men for higher pay. Nearly all statutes that expressly exclude women from jobs and opportunities are also invalid, but there are exceptions. The Court has upheld a statute effectively excluding women from employment as prison guards in "contact" positions in facilities with all male prisoners.[62] It also upheld a statute providing that men, but not women, must register for the draft.[63] In both cases a majority of the Justices thought that physiological differences between men and women (rather than unconsidered stereotypes) justified differential treatment.

In *United States v. Virginia*[64] (1996), the Court – in an opinion authored by Justice Ruth Bader Ginsburg, who became the second woman ever to serve on the Supreme Court when she was nominated by President Bill Clinton in 1993 – held that a state violated the Equal Protection Clause by excluding women from a prestigious state college offering a distinctive educational program, at least without offering a comparably excellent program exclusively for women. In a footnote, the Court said that it did not mean to rule on the question whether separate classes for men and women would be permissible as long as equally good opportunities existed for both.[65] But it emphasized that states may not discriminate between men and women on the basis of stereotypes or overbroad generalizations.

The difficulty, of course, is that stereotypes and overbroad generalizations can be difficult to distinguish from the reasoned awareness of "real differences" that can sometimes justify gender-based classifications. On the one hand, real physiological differences between men and women probably justify single-sex athletic teams (although the Court has not had occasion to say so expressly). On the other, the Court held in *United States v. Virginia* that the state relied on an impermissible stereotype in concluding that women could not profit from the physically and psychologically arduous educational method employed at Virginia Military Institute.

Against this backdrop, *United States v. Virginia* – decided by a Supreme Court that included two female Justices – may be especially important for its emphatic location of the burden of justification in cases of gender-based discrimination: "Parties who seek to defend gender-based government action must demonstrate an 'exceedingly persuasive justification' for that action. . . . The burden of justification is demanding and it rests entirely on the State."[66]

Discrimination Against Homosexuals

The past twenty years have witnessed widespread, often heated debates about the constitutionality of statutes that discriminate against homosexuals. At one level, these debates have involved a relatively straightforward clash of moral and social outlooks. From the perspective of gay rights advocates, homosexuals are a classic discrete and insular minority that is the victim of prejudice: Traditional taboos against homosexuality lack reasoned justifications. Gays should be as free to find gratification and fulfillment through openly gay relationships as heterosexuals through heterosexual relationships. Nor, once having done so, should they be discriminated against. By contrast, cultural conservatives believe that open gay sexuality threatens traditional moral values built around monogamous marriage (between a man and a woman) and the two-parent family. In their view, gay sex reflects a perversion of the order of nature (and in the eyes of many, the order ordained by God). For those who take this view, discrimination against homosexuals seems natural and appropriate, whether to show moral disapproval or to protect society from the spread of corruption.

As is the case with the equal protection doctrine involving discriminations based on race and sex, the Supreme Court's approach to discriminations against homosexuals has shifted over time, at least partly in response to changing social attitudes. But the doctrine is difficult to sort out, because the loose category of "gay rights litigation" has involved challenges to at least three different kinds of statutes: (1) those involving explicit discriminations against homosexuals – for example, barring homosexuals from certain jobs or opportunities (such as service in the United States military); (2) laws that apply only to same-sex behavior (such as prohibitions against same-sex sodomy and gay marriage); and (3) statutes with a discriminatory effect on gays, such as statutes that prohibit all sodomy (heterosexual as well as homosexual). The Supreme Court has dealt with cases in the third category under the Due Process Clause, rather than the Equal Protection Clause, and the hardest cases in the second category are ones in which the discrimination involves what the Court has termed "fundamental rights." Although this division is not wholly satisfactory, I therefore postpone consideration of due process and fundamental rights issues until Chapter Six and deal here only with governmental classifications that expressly discriminate against homosexuals.

The Supreme Court's single major pronouncement on discriminations of this kind came in *Romer v. Evans*[67] (1996). A bit of background is necessary. Lower courts traditionally held that governmental discriminations against homosexuals triggered only rational basis review and in the vast majority of cases sustained them against constitutional attack. What is more, a 1986 decision by the Supreme Court, *Bowers v. Hardwick*,[68] had upheld a prohibition against homosexual sodomy. Although the Court divided 5–4 in *Bowers*, the majority opinion was unusually caustic and dismissive. Many champions of gay rights were therefore fearful, believing the time not to be ripe, when the Supreme Court agreed to hear *Romer v. Evans*.

Romer arose when Colorado voters approved a ballot question amending the state's constitution to bar the enforcement of either state or local legislation affording homosexuals "any minority status, quota preferences, protected status or claim of discrimination." That Colorado voters would have been asked to approve such an amendment showed that cultural attitudes were shifting: The proposed amendment reflected a reaction by cultural conservatives against an emerging tendency by state and local governments not only to repeal antisodomy statutes, but also to pass legislation barring discrimination against homosexuals. By any standard, however, the Colorado amendment was poorly written and unclear. At a minimum, it prohibited the enactment within Colorado of legislation specifically protecting homosexuals against public or private discrimination (in the way that civil rights legislation frequently bars discriminations on the basis or race or gender, for example). It arguably, but only arguably, took the further step of leaving homosexuals without legal redress under Colorado law if they were discriminatorily denied rights otherwise conferred on *all* Colorado citizens, such as the right to ride a bus (after paying the fare) or to receive protection from the police and fire departments.

In a decision that surprised many observers, the Supreme Court held by 6–3 that the Colorado amendment violated the Equal Protection Clause. In so ruling, the Court pointedly assumed that discriminations against homosexuals are subject only to rational basis review, not strict judicial scrutiny. But Justice Anthony Kennedy's opinion found that the Colorado amendment failed rational basis review because it was "at once too narrow and too broad": "It identifies persons by a single trait and then denies them protection across the board. . . . A law declaring that in general it shall be more difficult for one group of citizens than for all others to seek aid from the government is itself a denial of equal protection of the laws in the most literal sense."[69] The only explanation for such a law, Justice Kennedy wrote, was that it "was born of animosity toward the class of persons affected"[70] and thus lacked the *legitimate* purpose required by rational basis review.

The narrowness of *Romer*'s holding left many questions, some now resolved and others not. By applying only rational basis review and by finding that the particular form of discrimination involved in *Romer v. Evans* was irrational and thus forbidden, the Court appeared to acknowledge the possibility that certain other discriminations against homosexuals may be rational and thus constitutionally acceptable. And if one had to speculate, the best guess would be that the discrimination the Court would most hesitate to invalidate would be the discrimination reflected in the United States military's "don't ask, don't tell" policy, under which those who identify themselves as homosexuals are barred from military service. Justifiably, the Court dislikes meddling in military affairs. What is more, the Justices almost surely recall the furious opposition that President Bill Clinton encountered, from Congress and much of the public as well as from the uniformed services, when he briefly suspended the military's traditional antigay stance.

In the sweep of history, it is possible, probably likely, that *Romer v. Evans* will be viewed as a way station on the road to a ruling that all discriminations against homosexuals are suspect or semisuspect. A subsequent decision in *Lawrence v. Texas*[71] (2003), which I discuss in Chapter Six, would tend to support this prediction: *Lawrence* flatly overruled *Bowers v. Hardwick* and held that states have no legitimate interest in prohibiting homosexual sodomy. But predictions are risky (especially, Yogi Berra has said, when they are about the future). For now, the doctrine requires distinctions between irrational discriminations against homosexuals and rational ones, and the Court has given no clear signal that it views the latter category as necessarily an empty one.

Conclusion

It is often suggested that modern equal protection doctrine reflects a theory, traceable to *United States v. Carolene Products Co.*[72] (1938), under which the courts defer to legislative judgments except when classificatory schemes reflect prejudice against discrete and insular minorities. The *Carolene Products* theory explains the correctness of the Court's approach in *Brown v. Board of Education*: African Americans are the paradigmatic "discrete and insular minority," long victimized by prejudice. The *Carolene Products* rationale also helps to justify most applications of rational basis review: In cases *not* involving discrete and insular minorities, the political process can usually be relied on to do at least rough justice, and searching judicial review would risk repeating the mistakes of the *Lochner* era by intruding unnecessarily on legislative prerogatives.

Increasingly, however, the Supreme Court has adopted positions that are incompatible with the *Carolene Products* theory. On one hand, the Court treats certain classificatory schemes as suspect or semisuspect even when they disadvantage majority rather than minority groups. For example, it strictly scrutinizes race-based affirmative action schemes that disadvantage whites, not blacks. Similarly, it treats all gender-based classifications as semisuspect, even though women are a statistical majority (not a minority) of the population and even though it would be bizarre to think that men, as a class, are the victims of widespread prejudice. On the other hand, the Court refuses to confer suspect status on a number of classifications involving genuine minority groups against whom prejudice seems very real – persons with mental retardation, for example[73] – when it believes that classificatory legislation is likely to be both practically sensible and morally acceptable.

For better or worse, the Supreme Court has treated equal protection as a moral ideal to which the courts must give content, partly in light of their personal judgments and partly in light of the evolving understandings of the American people. Seldom if ever does the Court describe its function in these daunting terms. But that, in essence, is what the Court does.

SIX

Fundamental Rights

"[L]iberty" is not a series of isolated points pricked out in terms of...freedom of speech, press, and religion...and so on. It is a rational continuum which, broadly speaking, includes a freedom from all substantial arbitrary impositions and purposeless restraints.

       – Justice John Marshall Harlan[1]

The Court is most vulnerable and comes nearest to illegitimacy when it deals with judge-made constitutional law having little or no cognizable roots in the language or design of the Constitution.

       – Justice Byron White[2]

AS THE SUPREME COURT NOTED IN THE FIRST SENTENCE of its opinion, *Skinner v. Oklahoma*[3] (1942) "touche[d] a sensitive and important area of human rights." The state of Oklahoma was about to sterilize Jack T. Skinner against his will. In the view of Oklahoma, Skinner was a "habitual criminal," convicted three times of crimes involving "moral turpitude" – twice for "robbery," once for stealing chickens. The state's "Habitual Criminal Sterilization Act" called for repeat offenders to be sterilized in order to stop people with manifest criminal tendencies from passing those tendencies to future generations.

In doctrinal terms, Skinner was not an easy case. Or, perhaps to state the same thing differently, from one perspective it seemed too easy. To Skinner and indeed to the Justices of the Supreme Court, Oklahoma's Habitual Criminal Sterilization Act may have looked cruel and offensive, jarringly similar in some respects (though not, of course, in all) to the "eugenics" then being practiced in Nazi

Germany. But what provision of the Constitution, if any, did the Oklahoma law violate? So close to the ignominious *Lochner* era, the Supreme Court would not have been willing to find a violation of substantive due process. And although the Eighth Amendment forbids "cruel and unusual punishments" for crimes, in 1942 the Court had not yet held that the Eighth Amendment imposes limits on the states, as well as on the federal government. So Skinner's lawyer emphasized the Equal Protection Clause: The statute's defect, Skinner said, was that it singled out some three-time convicts, but not others, for sterilization. More particularly, it rather systematically excluded white-collar criminals, for example, such as those who "embezzle" money that has been entrusted to them, from the sterilization imposed on three-time chicken thieves.

To a person not versed in constitutional law, this might seem a sound basis for objection. The problem, for the Supreme Court, lay in the rational basis test normally applied under the Equal Protection Clause. To prevent the inheritance of criminal tendencies was a "legitimate" governmental purpose. And for the state to single out some criminals as more likely than others to pass on dangerous criminal tendencies was probably not wholly irrational either. (Surely neither chicken thieves nor any other subcategory of criminals, defined by their offenses, constitutes a suspect class, discrimination against which would trigger strict judicial scrutiny.) As Chief Justice Harlan Fiske Stone wrote in a concurring opinion, "[I]f we must presume that the legislature knows... that the criminal tendencies of any class of habitual offenders are transmissible..., I should suppose that we must likewise presume that the legislature, in its wisdom, knows that the criminal tendencies of some classes of offenders are more likely to be transmitted than those of others."[4]

To raise this argument, however, is to presuppose that the rational basis test applies. *Skinner v. Oklahoma* held that it did not. In an opinion by Justice William O. Douglas, the Court began and ended by emphasizing the obvious fact that the challenged legislation intruded on a "basic civil right[]," involving "[m]arriage and procreation," that was "fundamental to the very existence and survival of the race."[5] When legislation draws lines that affect so fundamental a right, the Court ruled, "strict scrutiny" rather than "rational basis" review applies – even in cases such as *Skinner* that involve no "suspect classification." Applying strict scrutiny, the Court invalidated the Oklahoma Habitual Criminal Sterilization Act, substantially on the ground that it was unfair to sterilize Skinner while exempting white-collar criminals. Again, however, the decision to apply strict scrutiny was itself a crucial, doctrinally innovative step in the Court's analysis. It was only because the Supreme Court classified the right to procreate as what the Justices would now call a "fundamental right" that strict scrutiny applied and Skinner won his case.

The Idea of Fundamental Rights

When *Skinner* was decided, the notion of "fundamental" rights was a doctrinal novelty on which the Court did little to expand in the years immediately following. Although the authors of the Fourteenth Amendment contemplated the existence of fundamental rights constituting the privileges or immunities of national citizenship, the Supreme Court effectively buried the Privileges or Immunities Clause in *The Slaughter-House Cases*[6] (1872), as discussed in Chapter Three. Nor did the idea of fundamental rights play any role during the era symbolized by *Lochner v. New York*[7] (1905), when the Court purported to inquire equally into the reasonableness of all restrictions on all liberties, nor in the immediate aftermath of the *Lochner* era. Beginning in the late 1950s, however, and especially during the 1960s and 1970s, the Court began to designate some rights protected by the Due Process and Equal Protection Clauses as more "fundamental" than others. Among the rights assigned to this category were the rights to vote, to marry, to raise one's children, and to have an abortion. Under modern doctrine, statutes that infringe judicially identified fundamental rights trigger "strict" judicial scrutiny and are invalid unless "necessary to promote a compelling governmental interest." (Statutes thus attract the same "strict" scrutiny if they *either* discriminate on "suspect" bases, as discussed in Chapter Six, *or* burden fundamental rights.)

The Supreme Court's fundamental rights jurisprudence is deeply controversial, with some maintaining that the Court has no business identifying and giving robust protection to "unenumerated" rights – so called because they are not specifically listed in the Constitution – such as the rights to vote, to marry, and to have an abortion. From the critics' perspective, the Court properly protects "enumerated" rights such as freedom of speech, but "unenumerated" fundamental rights are illicit judicial creations. Although not uncommon, the distinction between "enumerated" and "unenumerated" rights is more misleading than informative.[8] The Constitution refers specifically to "the freedom of speech" but not to the freedom of association. Should recognized rights to freedom of association be deemed unenumerated and therefore suspect or even illegitimate? Virtually no one seems to think so. Are recognized rights to engage in expressive conduct, such as picketing and displaying signs, unenumerated because the First Amendment mentions only "speech"? Again, virtually no one seems to think so. It might be suggested that certain rights are properly recognized as implicit in the First Amendment and thus should count as enumerated even if not identified specifically, but that other provisions of the Constitution cannot similarly generate implicit rights. But this position is arbitrary and untenable. The right to travel from state to state, which is discussed at greater length in Chapter Eleven, furnishes a historically recognized example of a right implicit in the structure of the Constitution as a whole. Although the right to travel is not listed anywhere in the Constitution, it is presupposed by the Constitution's structure, which creates a unified nation. In this as in other cases, a categorical distinction between enumerated and unenumerated rights is more likely to confuse than enlighten. What matters is whether a right is implicit in the Constitution in some meaningful sense or is presupposed by it. If so, a second question arises, involving how weighty or important that right is.

In the current day, judicial conservatives often insist that tradition provides the exclusive touchstone for the identification of fundamental rights. Liberals are more open to the possibility that historical understandings, although relevant, are not necessarily controlling.

Sexual Privacy or Autonomy

The Supreme Court's most enduringly controversial fundamental rights cases have involved sexual privacy or autonomy. *Skinner v. Oklahoma*, which was decided in 1942, laid the foundation for these cases, but no further building occurred for more than two decades. Doctrinal development, and the controversies surrounding it, began in earnest in *Griswold v. Connecticut*[9] (1965). *Griswold* presented a challenge to a state statute that barred the distribution or use of "any drug...or instrument for the purpose of [contraception]." As interpreted, the statute allowed doctors to prescribe contraceptives to protect physical and psychological health – a loophole widely exploited by physicians serving middle- and upper-class patients. But the law posed a threat to clinics expressly offering family planning assistance to a predominantly lower-class clientele. In *Griswold*, two doctors challenged their convictions for prescribing contraceptives for use by married couples for no purpose other than contraception. By a vote of 7–2, the Court invalidated the statute, despite obvious anguish about the rationale for the result. (In contrast with *Skinner*, in *Griswold* the Court could not rest the decision on the Equal Protection Clause, because the challenged statute prohibited everyone, not merely one particular class, from using birth control devices solely for purposes of contraception.)

Writing for the Court, Justice Douglas – the author of *Skinner* and a Justice who had been named to the Court in the near aftermath of the discredited *Lochner* era and was pledged not to repeat its mistakes – flatly denied that the decision involved the identification of a fundamental right protected by the Due Process Clause: "Overtones of some arguments suggest that *Lochner*...should be our guide...[b]ut we decline that invitation,"[10] he wrote. In a brisk but confusing opinion that skirted gibberish at crucial points, Douglas instead reasoned that several provisions of the Bill of Rights give rise to "peripheral" or "penumbral" rights that "create zones of privacy."[11] As an example, he cited the recognized the First Amendment right to freedom of association, which is not expressly mentioned in the Constitution, as constituting a "penumbra where privacy is protected from governmental intrusion."[12] Similar "penumbras" of privacy surround other constitutional guarantees, Douglas continued, and the relation of marital intimacy – which Connecticut sought to regulate by denying contraceptives to married couples – fell "within the zone of privacy created by" one or more of those guarantees or penumbras,[13] though Douglas did not say which. Concurring opinions in the case thought it less necessary to establish that the Connecticut statute violated "some right assured by the letter or penumbra of the Bill of Rights."[14] In the view of one of the concurrences, "the concept of liberty" protected by the Due Process Clause "protects those personal rights that are fundamental, and is not confined to the specific terms of the Bill of Rights."[15]

Although confusing in other respects, *Griswold* clearly suggested that the most disturbing feature of the Connecticut statute was its intrusion into intimate aspects of the marital relationship, some protection for which the Constitution could fairly be said to presuppose: Surely those who wrote and ratified the Constitution took it for granted that people would be able to marry and to enjoy sexual intimacy within marriage. Without explanation, the Court simply abandoned that limitation on *Griswold*'s rationale in *Eisenstadt v. Baird*[16] (1972), in which it invalidated a Massachusetts law that forbade the distribution of contraceptives to *single* people. "If the right of privacy means anything," the Court wrote, "it is the right of the individual, married or single, to be free from unwanted governmental intrusion into matters so fundamentally affecting a person as the decision whether to bear or beget a child."

The decision in *Eisenstadt* came near the height of what has been described as a sexual revolution. It expressed the prevailing spirit of the age. It also reflected a jurisprudential assumption, which is more nearly timeless, that the Constitution presupposes, and thus authorizes the Supreme Court to identify and protect certain fundamental liberties that it does not expressly mention. It perhaps deserves repeated emphasis that this jurisprudential assumption is very broadly shared, at least when it is not made explicit. To recur to an example discussed already, the First Amendment refers only to freedom of speech, but it is fairly read to presuppose a right to freedom of expressive association. Most commentators also believe that *Griswold v. Connecticut* reached the right result. A Constitution that protects speech and religion and that creates a right to be free from unreasonable searches and seizures (among other firmly recognized rights) should be read as presupposing a right to marry and to enjoy marital intimacy. The difficult questions all involve application: Which rights should the Supreme Court identify as fundamental, and to which criteria should it look in reaching its judgments?

Roe v. Wade and Abortion Rights

If ever concealed, the difficulty of those questions burst into prominence in *Roe v. Wade*[17] (1973). As is well known, *Roe* held that the Due Process Clause protects a fundamental right to abortion. The Court's analysis unfolded in two crucial steps. First, the Court found that "the right...to be free from unwanted governmental intrusion into matters so fundamentally affecting a person as the decision whether to bear or beget a child" – which was prefigured in *Skinner v. Oklahoma* and expressly recognized in *Eisenstadt v. Baird* – encompasses a fundamental right to abortion. Second, the Court then asked whether restriction of that right could be justified under the strict scrutiny test as necessary to promote a compelling governmental interest. Only when a fetus reached the stage of viability, the Court ruled, does the state's interest in fetal life become "compelling." Before that, a woman has a protected constitutional right to terminate an unwanted pregnancy.

Roe's reasoning is controversial at both steps. At the first, critics maintain that the Court's definition of the right to decide whether "to bear or beget a child" omits the most morally important point: Abortion inherently involves the destruction of a human fetus. Abortion opponents claim that there can be no right, fundamental or otherwise, to cause the loss of an innocent life. At the second step, critics assert that the state's interest in preserving fetal life is morally compelling from the moment of conception.

As an enormous literature has abundantly demonstrated, there are many things that can be said in *Roe*'s defense, just as there are many things that can be said in opposition. Amid the continuing debate, it remains remarkable that seven Justices of the generally conservative Burger Court could have joined the *Roe* opinion. The Court's majority obviously failed to anticipate how endlessly divisive the abortion issue would prove to be. In contrast with some of their successors, even the most conservative Justices on the Burger Court were predominantly secular in orientation. From their perspective, *Roe* must have seemed a judicious compromise: It protected a woman's right to control the use of her body before the point of fetal viability, while permitting the state to protect unborn life thereafter.

It may also bear emphasis that *Roe*, like *Skinner* and *Griswold* before it, had an "equal rights" as well as a "fundamental rights" dimension. For one thing, only women can become pregnant, and virtually never does the law require anyone other than a pregnant woman to risk his or her life, or make bodily sacrifices comparable with those exacted by pregnancy, to protect or preserve the life of another. (The closest analogy may involve compelled military service in wartime – a burden that was imposed on men but not on women in the past.) In addition, because many states did not prohibit abortion, a woman with sufficient funds and sophistication could always procure a lawful abortion by traveling to a state where abortion was legal. By contrast, women who were poor and unsophisticated often lacked access to legal abortion. Thousands sought illegal abortions instead. According to some estimates, the mortality rate for illegal, unlicensed abortions was more than ten times higher than the mortality rate for legal abortions.[18]

Whatever the Justices may have thought, *Roe v. Wade* sparked a furor that has still not subsided more than thirty years later. Abortion opponents have never accepted *Roe*'s legitimacy. Conservative presidential candidates shortly thereafter began to promise to appoint prolife Justices to the Supreme Court. The Republican Party platform called for *Roe* to be reversed. By 1992, after Republican Presidents Ronald Reagan and George Bush had appointed five new Justices to the Supreme Court (and Democrats none), *Roe* appeared ripe for overruling.

The Court thus surprised most observers when it affirmed "*Roe's* essential holding" in a bitter 5–4 decision in *Planned Parenthood of Southeastern Pennsylvania v. Casey*[19] (1992). Three themes dominated the plurality opinion in *Casey* that was jointly authored by Justices Sandra Day O'Connor, Anthony Kennedy, and David Souter, all of whom were nominated to the Court by Presidents pledged to seek prolife Justices. First, if *Roe* was a mistake at the time of its decision, it was at least not an obvious one. An unwanted pregnancy subjects women to enormous burdens. Decisions such as *Skinner*, *Griswold*, and *Eisenstadt* made it plausible to hold as a matter of law that women had a fundamental right to decide whether to bear a child.[20] Second, a generation of women had shaped their lives in partial reliance on *Roe*. They had entered relationships and built careers in the expectation that unplanned pregnancies would not force them into unwanted childbearing. Third, the plurality worried openly that the Court's "legitimacy" would be compromised if it were to overrule *Roe* "under fire" and thus foster an impression that political pressure could trigger a change in constitutional law.[21] Precisely because the authors of the *Casey* plurality opinion had been appointed to overrule *Roe*, they felt, when the occasion actually arose, that they ought not do so. *Casey* marked the first time that the Supreme Court ever openly expressed such a thought.

Although preserving *Roe's* "central holding," *Casey* grants the states more flexibility than before to regulate and discourage abortion. Under *Roe*, nearly all impediments to abortion attracted strict judicial scrutiny. Under *Casey*, the states can impose waiting periods and require the provision of information on alternatives to abortion as long as their efforts do not amount to what the Court judges an "undue burden" on the ultimate abortion right.

No more than *Roe*, however, could *Casey* authoritatively proclaim that its word about abortion rights would be the last. Abortion cases continue to come to the Court, as state legislatures and Congress enact statutes that test the meaning of the undue burden standard and even invite the Court to reconsider *Roe* and *Casey*. Nor should it be thought categorically inappropriate for legislatures to press the Court to reverse itself. Legislatures did so throughout the

Lochner era. In yet an earlier period, Abraham Lincoln argued eloquently that Congress should continue its efforts to ban the spread of slavery in territories not yet admitted into the Union as states, notwithstanding the Supreme Court's ruling in *Dred Scott v. Sandford*[22] (1856) that Congress lacked authority to do so.[23] In the final analysis, the justifiability of legislative refusals to accept that the Supreme Court has settled a matter definitively depends at least in part on the moral and constitutional merits of the underlying position. The moral and constitutional merits of *Roe v. Wade* remain subject to dispute.

Gay Rights

In 1986, while conservative opposition to *Roe v. Wade* mounted, the Supreme Court confronted a challenge to a Georgia statute forbidding sodomy. As written, the statute drew no distinction between homosexual and heterosexual sodomy. In practice, however, prosecutions for consensual heterosexual sodomy never occurred. Criminal prosecutions for homosexual sodomy were also rare, but unusual circumstances resulted in the filing of charges against Michael Hardwick: When police arrived at his home to question him about another matter, a roommate led them directly to Hardwick's bedroom, where they observed him engaged in homosexual sodomy. Although the state ultimately dropped the prosecution, Hardwick decided to press the issue. He sought a judicial ruling that the antisodomy statute deprived him of a constitutionally protected fundamental right to sexual autonomy in the privacy of his bedroom.

In *Bowers v. Hardwick*[24] (1986), the Supreme Court rejected that claim. Several threads ran through the Court's opinion and the concurring opinions of the Justices in the 5–4 majority. The first involved anxiety about the judicial role in recognizing fundamental rights amid the fallout from *Roe v. Wade*. Writing for the Court, Justice Byron White, one of the two original dissenters in *Roe*, observed that "[t]he Court is most vulnerable and comes nearest to illegitimacy when it deals with judge-made constitutional law having little or no cognizable roots in the language or design of the Constitution."[25] He further maintained that the Court could properly treat as "fundamental" only those rights that were either "implicit in the concept of ordered liberty" or "deeply rooted in this Nation's history and tradition."[26] This formulation would have justified the ruling in *Griswold v. Connecticut*, but seemed intentionally ambiguous about *Roe v. Wade*.

The second, sometimes latent, theme in the Court's opinion reflected contempt for homosexual conduct. The Court refused to consider whether the Constitution would permit application of the Georgia statute to heterosexual sodomy.[27] In a concurring opinion, Chief Justice Warren Burger quoted an earlier legal writer who had termed sodomy a crime worse than rape.[28] Citing historical prohibitions against sodomy, the majority opinion caustically concluded that "to claim that a right to engage in [homosexual sodomy] is 'deeply rooted in this Nation's history and tradition' or 'implicit in the concept of ordered liberty' is, at best, facetious."[29]

A third strand in the Court's opinion involved an unwillingness to recognize a fundamental privacy or autonomy right embracing all forms of private, voluntary sexual conduct. The Court said that "it would be difficult, except by fiat, to limit the claimed right to homosexual conduct while leaving exposed to prosecution adultery, incest, and other sexual crimes even though they are committed in the home."[30]

Justice Harry Blackmun wrote a powerful dissenting opinion in *Bowers*. He derided the majority's preoccupation with the anatomical details of private, consensual acts of sexual intimacy. At stake, he wrote, was not an isolated right to engage in homosexual sodomy, but "the fundamental interest all individuals have in controlling the nature of their intimate associations with others."[31] In his view, the Constitution presupposed a right of all persons to control "the most intimate aspects of their lives,"[32] at least through voluntary conduct in the privacy of their homes that posed no palpable threats to themselves or others. He thought it cruel and bigoted to deny to homosexuals the lawful opportunity for sexual intimacy that others take for granted.

Seventeen years later, the Court largely adopted Blackmun's position when it squarely overruled *Bowers v. Hardwick* in *Lawrence v. Texas*[33] (2003). The Court's decision in *Lawrence* was bold. The Justices could have ruled in favor of the challengers on narrow equal protection grounds. The Texas statute involved in the case prohibited homosexual, but not heterosexual, sodomy. The Court thus might have held that even if all sodomy could be prohibited, the distinction between homosexual and heterosexual sodomy was simply irrational and thus unconstitutional. (Justice Sandra Day O'Connor took this position in a concurring opinion.) But Justice Anthony Kennedy, who wrote the majority opinion joined by four other Justices, insisted on going further, to make clear that a state could not prohibit homosexual sodomy even if it also barred heterosexual sodomy. He also made clear the Court's central concern with the dignity of homosexuals: "When homosexual conduct is made criminal by the law of the State, that declaration in and of itself is an invitation to subject homosexual persons to discrimination both in the public and in the private spheres. The central holding of *Bowers* has been brought in question by this case, and . . . [i]ts continuance as precedent demeans the lives of homosexual persons."[34] The three Justices generally viewed as the Court's most conservative – Chief Justice William Rehnquist and Associate Justices Antonin Scalia and Clarence Thomas – filed a strident dissent.

The readiest explanation for the Court's movement from *Bowers* to *Lawrence* involves a shift in personnel. The precedents on which the *Lawrence* majority principally relied all dated to before *Bowers*. Justice Kennedy thus said pointedly that "*Bowers* was not correct when it was decided, and it is not correct today. . . . *Bowers v. Hardwick* should be and now is overruled." But Justice Kennedy also noted that whereas in 1961 all states outlawed sodomy and twenty-four continued to do so in 1986 (when *Bowers* was decided), by 2003 the number was down to thirteen, of which four barred only homosexual sodomy. The social trend may have fortified the majority's confidence that it reflected an emerging moral consensus of the American people when it concluded that the "liberty" protected by the Due Process Clause should embrace broad rights of sexual autonomy.

In describing the constitutionally protected "liberty" that *Lawrence* upheld, Justice Kennedy departed from precedent in a small but potentially significant way: He did not use the terminology of fundamental rights or strict judicial scrutiny. This was surely a deliberate choice. In making it, he may have meant to undermine the sharp distinction between strict scrutiny and rational basis review and to claim a judicial authority to make more nuanced judgments. Justice Kennedy also took pains to describe the protected liberty as one involving the conduct of "*private* lives in matters pertaining to *sex*." This formulation appeared designed to distinguish the right upheld in *Lawrence* from the right that is sure to be claimed in subsequent cases – a right to homosexual marriage. The Court has previously described marriage as a "fundamental right," denials of which would trigger strict judicial scrutiny, but it remains uncertain how the protected right to "marriage" will be defined. It might be defined by reference to tradition as referring exclusively to a relationship between a man and a woman, or it might be viewed as a status of legal union from which homosexual couples cannot be excluded. For the Court to adopt the latter view would put it in a vanguard position. (The Massachusetts Supreme court has recognized a right to same-sex marriage under the Massachusetts *state* constitution, but it stands alone in this controversial stance as of the writing of this book.) With thirty-seven states already having granted the right of sexual liberty that the Court protected in *Lawrence*, *Lawrence* imposed no comparable demand.

Dissenting in *Lawrence*, Justice Antonin Scalia protested that the Court had abused its authority by taking a partisan position in a "culture war" between liberals and social and religious conservatives and "largely sign[ing] on to the so-called homosexual agenda ... [of] eliminating the moral opprobrium that has traditionally attached to homosexual conduct."[35] Scalia may have intended this comment as hyperbole, though possibly he did not. There seems little doubt, and the Court did not deny, that it had made a judgment of fairness: It was wrong to deny to those wishing to engage in homosexual conduct the same opportunities for lawful sexual intimacy that the Court's precedents had previously ensured to heterosexuals. If this issue is the subject of a culture war, neutrality may not be an option.

Rights Involving Death and Dying

In 1997 the Supreme Court decided two important cases rejecting claims of what the press recurrently termed a constitutional "right to die." This was a misnomer. Die we all shall, with or without a right to do so. To speak technically and precisely, the issues before the Court involved the constitutionality of state laws forbidding people to receive the assistance of a willing physician in committing suicide. In *Washington v. Glucksberg*[36] (1997) and *Vacco v. Quill*[37] (1997), the Court ruled that the Constitution creates no general right to physician-assisted suicide.

Chief Justice William Rehnquist wrote the majority opinions in both cases. In considering whether patients who were already terminally ill had a fundamental right to assisted suicide, Rehnquist employed substantially the same narrow test that the Court had used in *Bowers v. Hardwick*. Under it, he found no fundamental right to assisted suicide because no such right was "deeply rooted in this Nation's history and tradition."[38] On the contrary, all states had once prohibited assisted suicide, and all but one continued to do so.

In denying any right to assisted suicide, however, Rehnquist drew an important distinction. Most states traditionally have acknowledged the right of competent persons to refuse unwanted medical treatment – even when the refusal of treatment, including life support or dialysis or chemotherapy, would predictably lead to death. Because that more limited right to refuse treatment had the support of "tradition[]," Rehnquist and the rest of the Court assumed (although they had no need to hold expressly) that it occupied the status of a fundamental right guaranteed under the Due Process Clause.[39]

Five Justices of the Court, in concurring opinions not joined by the Chief Justice, also appeared to believe that terminal patients have a constitutional right to the assistance of a willing physician in obtaining medication adequate to control their pain.[40] For some patients whose suffering is especially acute, it may be predictable that a dosage sufficient to bring pain relief will also cause death. Doctors and theologians have developed the so-called doctrine of double effect to deal with this situation. Under it, doctors may permissibly administer medication necessary to alleviate pain, even if a secondary and unintended effect is to occasion death.

With the Court having recognized a fundamental right of competent persons to refuse unwanted medical treatment, and with at least five Justices apparently believing that there is a fundamental right not to be deprived of medication necessary to alleviate terminal suffering, the doctrinal picture emerging from *Washington v. Glucksberg* is somewhat complex. Within it, seeming anomalies may exist. A terminal patient may direct a doctor to turn off a respirator; that step would count as the exercise of a fundamental right to refuse treatment, even if death will result immediately. But a terminal patient not on a respirator has no right to the assistance of a physician in obtaining drugs for suicide.

If disparities such as this seem troubling, at least two considerations support the Court's piecemeal approach. First, the likely effects of authorizing physician-assisted suicide are much debated. Some believe that legalized physician-assisted suicide would corrupt the doctor–patient relationship. It might also give rise to cruel pressures on the elderly to choose suicide as an alternative to expending all their assets or consuming scarce medical resources. Under the circumstances, it may be prudent to wait to see what happens in states or countries that may voluntarily choose to authorize physician-assisted suicide, as Oregon and The Netherlands have currently done. Second, as Justice O'Connor wrote in her concurring opinion in *Washington v. Glucksberg*, "[e]very one of us at some point may be affected by our own or a family member's terminal illness."[41] Issues involving assisted suicide have recently drawn public attention. The Court can expect to profit from deliberation in the political arena. The words that the Court has spoken so far will not necessarily be its last.

Fundamental Rights Involving the Family

Fundamental rights involving the family are among the most firmly rooted in tradition and thus among those most uncontroversially protected by the Due Process and Equal Protection Clauses. In several cases the Court has characterized the right to marry as "fundamental."[42] The Court has also held that parents have constitutionally protected fundamental interests in the care, custody, and control of their children. The precise scope of protected parental rights requires careful definition. The state can forbid parents to treat their children abusively. The state can also enforce compulsory education laws and require that all children be vaccinated,[43] parental wishes to the contrary notwithstanding.

The recent case of *Troxel v. Granville*[44] (2000) presented a novel question involving parents' rights to control who could visit with their children. A Washington statute permitted "any person" to petition a court for visitation rights and authorized the court to grant such rights whenever "visitation may serve the best interest of the child." In a case involving no determination of parental unfitness, the Supreme Court held that the statute gave too much discretionary power to judges and retained too little for parents. Interestingly, however, the Court could not agree on a majority opinion specifying when, if ever, a state might permissibly grant visitation rights to nonparents, including grandparents, despite a parent's objection. Nor did the plurality opinion in the case, joined by four Justices, invoke the strict scrutiny formula often applied in other fundamental rights cases. Instead, the plurality inquired more loosely into the reasonableness of this particular infringement on parents' traditional rights.

This approach made practical sense under the circumstances. Like the rights to property that were discussed in Chapter Four, fundamental liberty rights need to be defined before they can be enforced. Again as with property rights, state law has at least some role to play in the process of definition. If a state requires that schoolchildren observe a dress code, and if parents object that the code interferes with their fundamental right of control over their children, the issue should not be whether the infringement on parental rights is "necessary to promote a compelling governmental interest." The logically prior question is whether this modest limitation on parental powers actually intrudes on a parent's fundamental right – as that right has historically been understood or would sensibly be defined – at all. A similar analysis helps to explain many familiar and familiarly accepted restrictions on the right to marry. As Justice Potter Stewart once wrote, "[s]urely ... a State may legitimately say that no one can marry his or her sibling, that no one can marry who is not at least 14 years old, that no one can marry without first passing an examination for venereal disease, or that no one can marry who has a living husband or wife."[45] Rules such as these do not infringe the right to marry so much as define it – even though, as Justice Stewart continued, surely "there is a limit beyond which a State may not constitutionally go"[46] in confining the definition of fundamental rights.

Conclusion

As illustrated by cases involving the misnamed "right to die" and parents' rights to control their children's upbringing, a strong majority of the Supreme Court accepts that the Constitution in general and the Due Process Clause in particular protect certain basic human liberties to which the Constitution does not refer by name. Especially since *Roe v. Wade*, controversy abounds about which rights should be regarded as implicit in the Constitution or as presupposed by it. There are similar debates, equally heated, about whether "fundamental rights" must be grounded in history or can be identified by direct appeal to moral fairness or changing social norms. On the most basic point, however, more agreement exists than is often acknowledged, even if that agreement is sometimes obscured in debates about whether particular rights ought to be recognized: In creating individual rights against the government, the Constitution implies or presupposes more than it says expressly.

PART TWO

The Constitutional Separation of Powers

SEVEN

The Powers of Congress

The powers delegated by the proposed Constitution to the federal
government are few and defined.

                                        – The Federalist No. 45

IN 1994, IN SEPTEMBER OF HER FRESHMAN YEAR at Virginia Poly-
technic Institute, Christy Brzonkala reported that she had been raped
by two members of the school's varsity football team, one of whom
allegedly told her, "You'd better not have any diseases." When Brzonkala pressed a complaint against the two men in the college's disciplinary system, the charges against one were dismissed. The other
student was found guilty and initially suspended for two semesters,
but the school's provost overturned that punishment as "excessive"
in light of the penalties in similar cases.

Rape is of course a crime under the laws of Virginia, and Brzonkala
might have sought action by the state's criminal justice system. Generally, however, private citizens cannot force prosecutors to bring
criminal charges. For a variety of reasons, prosecutors sometimes
hesitate to press rape charges, perhaps especially against college athletes. So Brzonkala filed a *civil* (rather than criminal) lawsuit of her
own in which she sought not to have her alleged assailants sent to
jail, but to have them required to pay money damages directly to her.
She did so under the Violence Against Women Act, a federal statute
enacted by Congress in 1994.

In *United States v. Morrison*[1] (2000), the Supreme Court of the
United States ordered the dismissal of Brzonkala's lawsuit. The Court
made no finding that Brzonkala had not been raped, nor that the
defendants were not her rapists. By 5–4, the Court ruled instead that

the federal statute that authorized her to sue was unconstitutional – not because the defendants would have had a right to rape Brzonkala (they would not), but because Congress had no power under the Constitution to enact a statute generally forbidding or penalizing violence against women.

From several perspectives, *United States v. Morrison* reveals a good deal about congressional power under the Constitution of the United States. The government of the United States continues to be what the Supreme Court, echoing the Constitution's framers, calls one of "limited powers." Unlike state governments, which can generally pass any law that they wish unless the Constitution forbids them to do so, for Congress to be able to enact legislation it must point to some specific provision of the Constitution that authorizes it to do so. Article I lists Congress's powers in a long string of clauses. (A few other grants of congressional authority are scattered in other parts of the Constitution, including the Thirteenth, Fourteenth, and Fifteenth Amendments.) The length and specificity of Article I's list support the inference that other powers are withheld. The Tenth Amendment makes that conclusion unmistakable. It provides that "[t]he powers not delegated to the United States by the Constitution, nor prohibited by it to the States, are reserved to the States respectively, or to the people."

In *United States v. Morrison*, it was conceded that no clause in the Constitution said expressly that Congress could prohibit or punish violence against women. In their eighteenth-century world, the framers and ratifiers of the Constitution apparently assumed that the states, rather than the federal government, would have responsibility for punishing most acts of violence. Defenders of the Violence Against Women Act therefore had to stretch a bit in arguing that the statute was constitutionally valid. They claimed that Congress had authority to enact the Violence Against Women Act under the Commerce Clause, which says that "[t]he Congress shall have Power . . . to regulate Commerce . . . among the several States."[2]

Although it might initially seem far-fetched to argue that the Commerce Clause empowers Congress to prohibit violence against women, that argument was at least plausible under previous cases decided by the Supreme Court. (Indeed, four Justices of the Supreme Court accepted it in *Morrison*.) When no other provision of the Constitution clearly empowers congressional action, yet Congress believes regulatory legislation to be desirable or even urgently necessary, both Congress and the courts have recurrently looked for some connection, however tenuous, between a regulated activity and interstate commerce. It is under the Commerce Clause that Congress, for example, has enacted minimum wage legislation, environmental protection statutes, and civil rights laws prohibiting discrimination by private employers (which, unlike the government, are not directly covered by the Equal Protection Clause).

Like the Justices of the Supreme Court, constitutional law "experts" disagree about whether *United States v. Morrison* is consistent with the Court's prior cases. Either way, the case frames questions of great constitutional importance. How did we get to the current situation, in which many of the most important statutes enacted by Congress need to be justified by reference to the Commerce Clause, even when they do not straightforwardly regulate the movement of goods in commerce from one state to another? Does a great deal of modern law rest on an outright evasion of the Constitution's language and intent? Does the Court's recent invalidation of the Violence Against Women Act mean that a lot of other federal legislation, including prohibitions against race discrimination by restaurants and private businesses, is now at risk of being struck down as well?

These questions arising under the Commerce Clause have parallels in some other constitutional provisions conferring powers on Congress. In this chapter, however, I focus almost entirely on the commerce power, both because it is centrally important and because debates about congressional authority under other provisions have often tracked Commerce Clause debates. At the very end of the chapter I say a few words about Congress's power to lay taxes and spend money to "provide for the...general Welfare of the United States."[3]

Elements of "The Original Understanding"

In thinking about the reach of congressional power, as about most constitutional questions, the starting point lies in the constitutional text and its historical purposes. But the historical purposes of the Commerce Clause are hard to reconstruct in a neutral way, because the framers and ratifiers inhabited a political, economic, and intellectual world so different from ours. On the one hand, the framers clearly anticipated that the states, not Congress, would be the principal lawmakers. They also appeared to contemplate that the states would retain what they called the "police power" – probably to the exclusion of Congress – to enact legislation to protect the public health, safety, and morals. On the other hand, the framers viewed the Constitution as empowering Congress to deal with all matters of genuinely national dimension.[4]

Formidable intellectual puzzles arise in the effort to integrate the various elements of the framers' views and to discern their relevance to modern problems. To be slightly more concrete, today there are many problems that appear genuinely national in scope that the framers could never have anticipated. Some, such as interstate trafficking in child pornography, may involve threats to the public safety and morals that, as thus categorized, the framers might have thought the exclusive concern of the states. But suppose that Congress attempts to address the problem, which centrally involves the abuse of children, by forbidding the shipment of child pornography across state lines. Legislation of this form arguably regulates "commerce" (or trade "among the several States") in the most literal sense, even if its purpose involves considerations of safety and morality that the framers might have expected to be the province of state rather than federal regulation.

An additional element of the framers' worldview further complicates the picture insofar as their expectations occupy center stage. The founding generation regarded each of the states as a "sovereign," which had retained its sovereignty even after the ratification of the Constitution. To the eighteenth-century mind, "sovereignty" implied supremacy. Reconciliation of state sovereignty with national sovereignty thus would appear to have required that there be no overlap of state and national powers: If the federal government could regulate the same conduct as a state, and thereby displace state legislation, this would have implied that the state was not really sovereign or supreme. Operating with this categorical scheme, at least many members of the founding generation appear to have assumed that there was a distinction between the manufacture of products, which was subject only to state and not to congressional regulation, and the shipment and sale of goods in interstate commerce, which came within Congress's commerce power. But suppose that a manufacturing plant spews pollution into the atmosphere, that the pollution flows across state lines, and that it damages agriculture, health, and thus economic productivity in other states. Should Congress be deemed powerless to enact regulatory legislation because of an anachronistic eighteenth-century understanding that the regulation of manufacturing is a power reserved to the states? Isn't pollution a genuinely national problem today, even if it was not in 1787? And didn't the framers and ratifiers intend to empower Congress to deal with all genuinely national problems?

As modern lawyers and judges struggle with questions such as these, more is at stake than abstract issues of fidelity to the Constitution's "original understanding."[5] On the whole, political liberals tend to favor a broad interpretation of Congress's commerce power. Liberals generally support environmental, economic, and workplace safety regulation. Liberals also emphasize that for regulation of this kind to be effective, and sometimes even possible, it must occur at the national level. For example, it may be impossible for any one state to protect its environment effectively if air pollution from other states sweeps across its borders. It may be almost equally impossible for one state to require employers to provide pensions or medical benefits to their employees if surrounding states do not do likewise. If a single state were to impose such obligations, many businesses might flee to other states, where their costs would be lower. This being so, no state might dare be the first to mandate that employers provide health insurance to their full-time workers, even if a majority of the voters in all or nearly all states would wish to see such a mandate enacted *if* it would not drive businesses out of state. In a case such as this, national legislation may be the only kind that is practically and politically feasible.

Whereas liberals tend to favor broad congressional power, conservatives characteristically regard it with more skepticism, and not just because they have different views about the nature or significance of the Constitution's original understanding. Part of their opposition reflects resistance to one-size-fits-all national regulation. In at least some cases, state and local governments may enjoy distinctive advantages in tailoring legislation to local problems and values. Conservatives also tend to believe that "that government is best which governs least," at least in the area of business regulation. Recognition of sweeping federal regulatory power increases the likelihood that regulation will be enacted at some level of government. According to conservatives, regulation not only diminishes liberty, but also threatens to create costly economic inefficiency.[6]

As in other areas of constitutional law, it could be argued, of course, that these liberal and conservative views should be irrelevant to matters of interpretation. But for judges and Justices needing to decide which strand of the "original understanding" to emphasize and how to construe relatively vague constitutional language in light of history and precedent, considerations of which interpretation would be "best" probably exert a pervasive influence.

Doctrinal and Conceptual History

Supreme Court decisions interpreting the Commerce Clause have followed a long and twisting path. Roughly speaking, the Supreme Court of John Marshall's era took an expansive view. In the early years, however, Congress did not enact much national regulatory legislation. The Court thus had no occasion to measure the precise scope of congressional authority.

When testing cases began to arise in the late nineteenth and early twentieth centuries, at least two evaluative frameworks suggested themselves. One was "formalist," or concerned with the form of federal regulation. It focused on whether Congress had directly and

specifically regulated the movement of goods in commercial enterprise across state lines. By the narrowest of margins, the Court followed a formalist approach in *Champion v. Ames*[7] (1903), which
upheld Congress's power to forbid the interstate transportation of
lottery tickets. According to the Court, the statute was valid because
it regulated commerce, the shipment of an item of sale from one
state to another, in the literal or formal sense. A dissenting opinion protested that the purpose of the statute was to protect the
public morals from the evil of gambling and that the regulation
of morality was a state function, not delegated to Congress by the
Commerce Clause.[8] The *Champion* majority brushed this objection
aside.

An alternative approach to analyzing congressional power under
the Commerce Clause could be described as "realist," focused not
on the form of legislation but on its real consequences or purposes.
The Court employed a realist framework in *The Shreveport Case*[9]
(1914). At issue was whether Congress could authorize the Interstate
Commerce Commission (ICC) to set rates for the intrastate shipment
of rail freight between two cities in Texas. It was undisputed that the
ICC could regulate rates charged by a railroad for shipments from
Texas to Louisiana. But when the railroad began to charge lower
rates for shipments along longer routes within the state of Texas,
those lower rates had a skewing effect on interstate trade: Because it
was cheaper to ship and sell goods in Texas than to transport them
out of state, interstate commerce diminished. In light of this real
effect on what was ultimately shipped in interstate commerce, the
Court upheld the ICC's regulation of rates on what were formally
intrastate rail routes.

Taken by themselves, both the formalist and the realist approaches
appeared to make sense. For the Supreme Court and ultimately for
the country, the problem involved fitting both into a coherent overall
framework. Just as either a formalist or a realist test could be used
to uphold congressional power, as in *Champion v. Ames* and *The
Shreveport Case*, either could also be used to restrict congressional
power. By the early twentieth century, there were Supreme Court decisions citing realist grounds for invalidating legislation that would

have passed a formalist test. For example, in *Hammer v. Dagenhart*[10] (1918) the Court struck down a federal statute forbidding the shipment in interstate commerce of items that had been produced by child labor. Although the statute dealt formally with shipment in interstate commerce, and thus would have passed a formalist test, it was invalid, the Court said, because Congress's real purpose and intended effect involved the regulation of manufacturing activities occurring wholly within individual states. Other decisions found that legislation regulating activities with real effects on interstate commerce could not be justified because it formally involved the regulation of manufacturing. To explain when regulation could be justified under a realist theory, the Court distinguished between activities with "direct effects" on interstate commerce, which Congress could regulate, and activities with only "indirect" effects, which it could not. But the line between direct and indirect effects proved elusive, the Court's judgments difficult to predict. The doctrine subsisted for decades in this confused state.[11]

Crisis and Revision

The confusion came to a crisis during the Great Depression of the 1930s. As businesses failed and unemployment mounted, an increasingly desperate public looked to the national government for solutions. In the eyes of large political majorities, the experimental policies of the New Deal offered the nation's best hope. The New Deal's programs were eclectic, but many rested on the idea that the way to renewed prosperity lay in national economic regulatory legislation, adopted under the Commerce Clause and justified on the "realist" theory that otherwise intrastate activities pervasively influence and ultimately determine what is bought and sold in interstate commerce.

Despite the emergency, despite the availability of plausible doctrinal arguments for upholding the main elements of the New Deal, a determinedly conservative Supreme Court initially struck down one piece of New Deal legislation after another. Having won an overwhelming reelection mandate, Roosevelt, in near desperation, proposed his notorious Court-packing plan in 1937. And the Court, for whatever reason, almost immediately climbed down and began to uphold the same type of legislation that it had previously been invalidating. The Court's changed approach to the Commerce Clause was especially dramatic. Within a few years it had reshaped Commerce Clause doctrine so that it would now hold federal legislation to be permissible whenever it satisfied *either* a formalist or a realist test. Under what has been termed "the New Deal settlement,"[12] legislation passed constitutional muster if it regulated or forbade shipments in interstate commerce, even if the plain purpose was to regulate manufacturing (for example, by forbidding the shipment in interstate commerce of any goods produced by firms that failed to pay their employees a minimum wage).[13] But regulatory legislation could equally be defended on the ground that the activity being regulated had substantial effects on interstate commerce[14] – a test that the Court interpreted very loosely. In one celebrated case, the Court unanimously upheld a prohibition against a farmer's exceeding a federal quota for the production of wheat by growing an extra 239 bushels for home consumption.[15] If every farmer did the same, the Court reasoned, the *cumulative* effect on the purchase and sale of wheat in interstate commerce would be substantial. Congress therefore enjoyed regulatory authority under the Commerce Clause.

Further testimony to the breadth of Congress's commerce power came in the 1960s, when the Supreme Court upheld central provisions of the 1964 Civil Rights Act – which prohibits race discrimination by restaurants and places of public accommodation, as well as by public and private employers – under the Commerce Clause. In *Katzenbach v. McClung*[16] (1964), the Court applied the statute against a restaurant whose customers admittedly included few or no travelers in interstate commerce. The Court reasoned that much of the food bought and served by the restaurant traveled across state lines and that restaurant patronage by excluded minorities would increase, and that purchases connected to interstate commerce would therefore increase as well, if discrimination by all restaurants were forbidden. These linkages sufficed to justify regulation under the Commerce Clause.

The Rehnquist Court: A Shift of Direction?

Under precedents such as these, which began with the Supreme Court's "switch in time" in 1937 and continued for more than a half-century, Congress's regulatory power under the Commerce Clause came very close to being unbounded – despite the original understanding and the Constitution's plain structural aim to endow Congress with limited powers only. Had the Court simply abdicated its responsibilities in the face of political pressures? At least three powerful arguments supported the Court's approach. First, if the Commerce Clause was originally understood to empower Congress to deal with all genuinely national problems, prevailing understandings of what constituted genuinely national problems had changed between 1787 and 1937. By 1937, the national economy was pervasively interconnected. Nearly all economic matters affected commerce among the states, at least indirectly. Second, in its pre-1937 efforts to draw lines restricting Congress's power, the Court had failed dismally. It had not developed a doctrinal framework capable of yielding sensible and predictable results. Surely the Constitution does not require a jurisprudence of confusion.

Third, and perhaps most important, before its 1937 turnaround the Court had sounded constitutional alarms and signaled its belief to both Congress and the public that Congress was overreaching its constitutional powers. Viewing the situation as it did, the Court was right to raise its objection and to enforce constitutional limits as it understood them. But whether the Court was right on the merits was at least debatable, and on debatable points not involving individual rights many believe that the Justices sitting at any one time not only cannot, but should not, prevail in a sustained collision with aroused public opinion. By 1937, the Justices had stood up for too long and created too much confusion and frustration by doing so. It was past time for the Justices to adjust their interpretation of the Commerce Clause.[17] The so-called New Deal settlement – permitting Congress broad if not unbounded authority to enact regulatory legislation under either formalist or realist tests – reflected a reasonable adjustment under the circumstances. Its reasonableness helps to explain how it could endure for so long.

To cite the reasonableness of the New Deal settlement is not, however, to deny the availability of reasonable grounds for objection to the resolution of a disputable constitutional issue on such distinctly "liberal" terms. Conservative critics could cite the Constitution's plain policy of limiting congressional power in a meaningful way, the diminished role for the states that substantially unbounded congressional power implies, and the general adage that all governmental power poses a threat to individual liberty.

Perhaps it is therefore not surprising that in 1995 a Supreme Court that had grown increasingly more conservative since the late 1960s moved to unsettle "the New Deal settlement," at least to some extent. In *United States v. Lopez*[18] (1995), the Court held by 5–4 that Congress lacked power under the Commerce Clause to enact a statute that criminalized the possession of a gun within a school zone. The government argued that guns near schools diminished school attendance and disrupted education, with adverse long-term effects on economic productivity and thus on the interstate movement of goods. But the Court's conservative majority said that the chain of reasoning needed to link school violence to commerce was too attenuated and that the likely effects on commerce were not sufficiently "substantial." A few years later came *United States v. Morrison*[19] (2000), finding that Congress lacked the power to enact the Violence Against Women Act. The majority opinion in *Morrison* emphasized that Congress had not regulated a principally "economic activity." It suggested that Congress could regulate intrastate economic activities (such as manufacture and sales of goods), but not noneconomic intrastate activities (such as acts of domestic violence against women), based on their substantial cumulative effects on the flow of goods in interstate commerce.

Although the Supreme Court has clearly undertaken a doctrinal reassessment, the line that it has apparently drawn between economic and noneconomic activities has not so far threatened the heart of the governmental regulatory power that emerged during the New Deal era – the power to regulate economic enterprises based on an assumption that the national economy is pervasively interdependent. In concurring opinions in *Lopez* and *Morrison*, one of the Justices, Clarence Thomas, said that the Court should consider more sweeping revisions, aimed at bringing current doctrine more nearly in line with the original understanding of congressional power.[20] But no other Justice has publicly joined this call. Judicial precedent constitutes one obstacle to the course urged by Justice Thomas. The Court's disastrous experience in resisting the New Deal also raises a caution flag. In addition, any very stringent limitation on congressional power would threaten the constitutionality of the 1964 Civil Rights Act, banning race-based discrimination throughout the national economy, which the Supreme Court has specifically upheld as a valid exercise of the commerce power. Today, the 1964 Civil Rights Act stands as an entrenched and cherished symbol of the nation's commitment to racial equality. No national politician could attack the 1964 Civil Rights Act without triggering widespread ridicule and contempt. A Supreme Court inhabiting the prevailing political, moral, and intellectual culture seems unlikely to mount such an attack either.

Perhaps, then, the doctrine has reached a temporary equilibrium, under which Congress enjoys very broad but not wholly unbounded power under the Commerce Clause. Clearly, however, caution is in order. The current Court would plainly like to do more to revitalize constitutional federalism, if only it could find legally, economically, and politically acceptable ways of doing so.

Congressional Regulation of State and Local Governments

Among the reasons for the Constitution to limit congressional power (besides protecting individual liberty) is to preserve a central role for state and local governments. Congress can threaten the importance of state and local governments in two distinct ways. First, as already discussed, it can assume regulatory powers in traditional domains of state and local responsibility. Second, Congress can directly regulate state and local governments' activities.

The unfolding history of the Fair Labor Standards Act (FLSA) – a statute mandating that employers pay minimum wages – illustrates the distinction between these two types of congressional action. As originally enacted by Congress in 1938 and upheld by the Supreme Court in 1941, the FLSA regulated private employers engaged in manufacturing, which was once viewed as an exclusively state responsibility, but it did not directly regulate the states themselves. In 1966, Congress amended the law to take the further step of regulating the wages and hours of state and local governmental employees. By doing so, it raised the question whether the Commerce Clause or principles of constitutional federalism limit Congress's power to regulate the activities of state and local governments, even when the comparable activities of private employers would be subject to regulation.

The Supreme Court's answers to this question have veered back and forth. In 1968, the Court gave a negative answer: Legislation that would otherwise be valid under the Commerce Clause does not become invalid insofar as it imposes obligations on state and local governments.[21] A scant eight years later the Court reversed itself by the narrow vote of 5–4. In *National League of Cities v. Usery*[22] (1976), it ruled that general principles of constitutional federalism, as reflected in the Tenth Amendment, forbade Congress "to directly displace the States' freedom to structure integral operations" – for example, by determining the wages and hours of state employees – "in areas of traditional governmental functions." But the regime of *National League of Cities* lasted less than a decade. The decision to overrule it, again by 5–4, came in *Garcia v. San Antonio Metropolitan Transit Authority*[23] (1985). According to *Garcia*, if Congress enacts general legislation that permissibly regulates an activity, the Constitution does not mandate exemptions for state and local governments.

When the Court decided *Garcia* in 1985, Justice William Rehnquist (who would be elevated to the position of Chief Justice a year later) wrote a four-sentence dissenting opinion, distinctly haughty and vaguely taunting in tone. Although Rehnquist did not say so expressly, the trend in national politics appeared to favor conservatives, so that the appointment of more conservative Justices could be expected over time. In his opinion, Rehnquist confidently predicted that the day would come when the "principle" of the *National League of Cities* case would "again command the support of a majority of this Court"[24] and when, presumably, *Garcia* would be overruled.

In several ways, the developing picture when the Court decided *Garcia* was not a happy one. Part of the Court's responsibility is to develop a coherent, reasonably stable body of constitutional law. The Justices must of course consider how the Constitution would ideally be interpreted and implemented, a matter about which they might understandably differ by shifting divisions of 5–4, but they also need to weigh competing interests in order and predictability. In this case, Justices on both sides of the issue plainly believed that those on the other side had engaged in misguided, if not irresponsible, overreaching in overruling recent decisions by only the narrowest of margins. Nevertheless, judicial tit-for-tat in overruling recent precedents by 5–4 majorities sows confusion, imposes costs on those who must adjust to the successive rulings, and breeds disrespect for the Supreme Court and the authority of its decisions.

Since the decision of *Garcia* in 1985, changes in the Court's composition have made it more conservative, and more interested in protecting federalism, than it has been since before the New Deal – as witnessed, for example, by its decisions in *United States v. Lopez* and *United States v. Morrison*. Significantly, however, the conservative majority has made no move formally to overrule *Garcia*. On the contrary, the Court has continued to uphold federal statutes that impose identical obligations on private companies and governmental bodies.[25]

Although avoiding a frontal attack on congressional power to impose regulations on state and local governments, the Court has pursued a strategy of barring a particular subcategory of federal regulations: It has held that implicit constitutional principles command respect for state and local governments and bar Congress from enacting legislation that singles out state and local governments and requires them to perform functions – such as enacting legislation[26] or enforcing the law – that *only* the government and its agents can perform. A leading case articulating this principle, *Printz v. United States*[27] (1997), thus ruled that Congress could not compel local sheriffs to enforce a federal statute restricting the sale of guns.

It remains to be seen whether the Court will go further in protecting state and local governments against direct federal regulation under the Commerce Clause. When the Court previously tried to do so, the standard laid down in the *National League of Cities* case – forbidding Congress "to directly displace the States' freedom to structure integral operations in areas of traditional governmental functions" – proved frustratingly vague and unpredictable in application. By contrast, the narrower limit on congressional power adopted in more recent cases (forbidding Congress to single out state and local governments and require them to perform uniquely governmental functions) is relatively clear. Clarity and predictability are important legal virtues, to which some of the Justices who are most profederalism in principle are also strongly committed.[28]

The Spending Power

As important in some ways as the commerce power is Congress's power to tax and spend under Article I, Section 8. As with the Commerce Clause, the original understanding of this provision is uncertain. James Madison, who played a peculiarly influential role in drafting the Constitution, maintained that Congress was empowered to tax and spend only in order to fund the exercise of other powers specifically conferred by the Constitution (such as raising armies and maintaining post offices).[29] By contrast, Alexander Hamilton, another prominent participant in the Constitutional Convention who like Madison was a coauthor of *The Federalist Papers*, contended that the taxing and spending power was an independent one, permitting Congress to expend funds in any way that it thought appropriate to promote the general welfare.[30] Since the New Deal era, the Court has adhered to the latter, broader view, which was crucial to its rulings upholding the Social Security system,[31] a massive social welfare bureaucracy that the founding generation could not have imagined. In upholding the old-age pension program, Justice Benjamin Cardozo wrote that Congress has broad discretion to identify what the general welfare requires. He added: "Nor is the concept of the general welfare static. Needs that were narrow or parochial a century ago may be interwoven in our day with the well-being of the nation."[32] Today Social Security and other federal spending programs funded out of tax revenues seem too deeply rooted to be vulnerable to constitutional attack even if, for example, historians were to demonstrate that Madison's view, not Hamilton's, reflected the predominant understanding of the Constitution's framers and ratifiers.

Concluding Thoughts

The government of the United States remains a government of limited powers. But the limits to which Congress is subject have evolved greatly over the course of American history. As the Supreme Court struggles to accommodate competing considerations of constitutional relevance, including varied strands within the "original understanding" of Congress's powers, its role has often been, and indeed continues to be, controversial. The controversy hit its zenith during the New Deal, after which the Court, in retreat, effectively treated Congress's powers as boundless for more than a half-century. Today, a more conservative Court that cares more about federalism has imposed renewed restraints, and it has attracted criticism for doing so from, for example, supporters of the Violence Against Women Act. So far, however, the current Court has not threatened Congress's central modern powers to regulate private economic enterprise. The Court's future course of action is difficult to predict. All that seems certain is this: The process of evolution that produced the body of existing doctrine has surely not come to an end.

EIGHT

Executive Power

Energy in the Executive is a leading character in the definition of good government. It is essential to the protection of the community against foreign attacks; it is not less essential to the steady administration of the laws.

– The Federalist No. 70

OVER THE SWEEP OF AMERICAN HISTORY, power has almost steadily flowed to the President.[1] Congress is a large, often divided, institution. All members must seek election by themselves. All have constituencies to which and for which they attempt to speak. By contrast, the Executive Branch is headed by a single President of the United States, who is much more capable of decisive and accountable leadership. As such leadership has seemed increasingly important, the President has accumulated responsibility to provide it, typically with the acquiescence of Congress and the courts.

These developments have not occurred in defiance of the Constitution, at least when the Constitution is understood in the way that John Marshall, author of *Marbury v. Madison* (1803), once commended – as "intended to endure for ages to come, and consequently, to be adapted to the various *crises* of human affairs."[2] But when adaptation is the order of the day, no firm guides exist as to which elements of the constitutional text should be read strictly and which loosely. When Congress and the President have concurred that the President needs to exercise a power, the courts have most often deferred to that judgment. Indeed, as is emphasized in Chapter Thirteen, dealing with the Constitution in war and emergency, many of the most important issues involving the constitutional separation of powers have been resolved through informal give and take between Congress and the President, with the courts not being involved at all. Some issues have come to court, however, and the judiciary has struggled to develop and enforce limiting principles fit for a world that the Constitution's framers and ratifiers could not have foreseen.

The Youngstown Case

Constitutional lawyers typically regard the Steel Seizure Case, *Youngstown Sheet & Tube Co. v. Sawyer*[3] (1952), as the leading Supreme Court decision involving presidential power. Curiously, however, they treat the concurring opinion of Justice Robert Jackson as more authoritative than the majority opinion. More generally, they explain the result in terms that disavow nearly everything that the majority opinion says.

Youngstown arose when, with the nation at war in Korea, President Harry Truman ordered federal officials to seize and operate the nation's steel mills to avert a planned strike. Truman maintained that an interruption in steel production would threaten the war effort and the safety of troops in the field. Had he wished to do so, Truman could have invoked a federal statute, the Taft–Hartley Act, and obtained a judicial order forbidding a strike for 80 days, during which time he could have sought emergency legislation from Congress. But Truman was a Democratic President with an important union constituency. The Taft–Hartley Act, which the unions despised, had been passed over his veto. Spurning the course available under the Taft–Hartley Act, Truman claimed power directly under the Constitution to seize the steel mills and to run them, presumably on terms acceptable to the Steelworkers Union, until the dispute was settled. As authority for his action, Truman cited his constitutional power as Commander-in-Chief[4] and provisions of Article II empowering the President to "take Care that the Laws be faithfully executed"[5] and vesting him with "[t]he executive Power."[6]

By a vote of 6–3, the Supreme Court held that none of these provisions either individually or collectively empowered the President to take over the steel mills. Justice Hugo Black – who always claimed to take the Constitution at its literal word – wrote the majority opin-ion. According to Black, the steel mills were too remote from any battlefield for the President's Commander-in-Chief power to be rel-evant. Black further maintained that the "take care" power and the grant of executive power both limited the President to executing laws that Congress had enacted. According to Justice Black, the Constitu-tion carefully and specifically assigns lawmaking power to Congress and restricts the President to executing congressionally enacted laws. For the President to order seizure of the steel mills in the absence of authorizing legislation was too much like lawmaking.

Justice Black's stated approach reflects what scholars have termed a "formalist" approach to separation-of-powers issues.[7] He assumed that a bright, categorical divide exists between the lawmaking powers given to Congress and the law-executing powers given to the exec-utive, with the content of both categories fixed by historical under-standings. In this way of thinking about separation-of-powers issues, crisis and felt needs play no central role. If this approach were pressed to its logical extreme, it would probably yield the conclusion (as pointed out by the dissenting opinion) that Abraham Lincoln acted unconstitutionally when he issued the Emancipation Proclamation freeing southern slaves in the midst of the Civil War. In the exercise of his Commander-in-Chief power, Lincoln claimed the right to alter the legal relationship between slaves and their masters, not merely to carry out statutes passed by Congress.

Sharply contrasting with Justice Black's opinion was that of Justice Robert Jackson, a former Attorney General under Franklin Roosevelt and a special prosecutor at the Nuremberg trials of Nazi war crimi-nals. More pragmatic than doctrinaire, Jackson was also perhaps the best writer ever to serve on the Supreme Court, the author of many much-quoted epigrams, including an observation that the Constitu-tion should not be converted into "a suicide pact." Although Jack-son agreed with Black about how the *Youngstown* case should come out, his opinion argued that the President's powers are not rigidly fixed under the Constitution, as Justice Black maintained, but at least partly adjustable.[8] Within Jackson's framework, one crucial variable involves the stance taken by Congress. When Congress authorizes the President to act, the politically accountable branches of the national government accord in their judgment about the practical necessity or desirability of executive authority, and courts should give strong deference to their determination. In polar contrast with cases in which Congress has authorized presidential action, Jackson identified a category of cases in which Congress has acted to curb presidential authority. In such cases Jackson thought that presidential power sank to its lowest ebb. Between the poles of congressionally authorized and congressionally forbidden assertions of executive authority, Jackson identified a third category that he dubbed a "zone of twilight."⁹ Within it, he suggested, presidential power might depend on practical considerations, including the gravity of the problem that the President confronted.

Commentators have often pointed to Justice Jackson's opinion as epitomizing a "functionalist" approach to separation-of-powers issues (in contrast with Black's "formalism"). As the term is usually used, "functionalism" recognizes that the lines separating executive from legislative from judicial power are often blurry and variable; that ebbs and flows of power are permissible as long as each branch retains its truly core functions and a capacity to check and balance power grabs by other branches; and that practical considerations matter in determining what the Constitution requires and permits, at least in otherwise doubtful cases.

Under Justice Jackson's framework, a presidential seizure of the steel mills might well have appeared defensible in a true national emergency, if no practical alternative existed. In *Youngstown*, however, the President had another, statutorily authorized means to protect the national interest: He could have got an injunction barring a strike for eighty days under the Taft–Hartley Act and, if the union still threatened to walk out at the end of that period, could have sought congressional authorization for a seizure. What is more, by enacting the Taft–Hartley Act, Congress had at least implicitly signaled its intent to deny the President the broader, more drastic power simply to order federal takeovers of important industries.

As is suggested by the fact that Justice Black's formalism and Justice Jackson's functionalism both pointed to the same result, the

Youngstown Court almost surely reached the right decision. But which of these two formidable Justices had the better of the argument? This is a debatable question, on which reasonable minds can differ. As will be seen, however, there can be no question that Justice Jackson's framework better explains the overall pattern of the Supreme Court's decisions, both before and after *Youngstown*.

Foreign Affairs

The "functionalist" tradition of flexibility in construing presidential power, especially in light of practical needs and congressional acquiescence, manifests itself perhaps most dramatically in the domains of war, which is discussed in Chapter Twelve, and foreign affairs. The President has repeatedly claimed authority to act unilaterally in matters of foreign affairs, largely on the theory that the United States must be able to speak with a single decisive voice on the world stage. For the most part, both courts and Congress have acceded to this claim.[10] The Constitution provides that the President can negotiate treaties "by and with the Advice and Consent of the Senate... provided two thirds of the Senators present concur."[11] This prescribed process makes secret negotiations difficult; it also permits as little as one-third of the Senate to block a treaty. At the end of World War I, for example, a relatively small band of senators succeeded in blocking ratification of the Treaty of Versailles and in keeping the United States out of the League of Nations. As an alternative to the treaty process, Presidents have subsequently claimed an authority to enter into "executive agreements," with the same force of law as treaties, without seeking Senate approval. In important cases decided during the 1930s and 1940s, the Supreme Court held that an executive agreement between the Roosevelt administration and the Soviet Union was legally valid and that it both created judicially enforceable federal rights and overrode competing claims based on state law.[12] By permitting an executive agreement to nullify otherwise applicable state law, the Court upheld a power of unilateral presidential lawmaking, the scope of which remains uncertain.

During the 1980s, the Supreme Court again held that the President could eliminate rights to sue a foreign government in American courts, this time under an executive agreement concluding a crisis that had involved the seizure of American hostages by the government of Iran. The Court's opinion in *Dames & Moore v. Regan*[13] (1981) sounded the pragmatic themes of Justice Jackson's concurring opinion in the *Youngstown* case. The Court emphasized the need for executive flexibility in matters involving foreign relations. It was vital to get back the American hostages, desirable to get the deal done swiftly on terms acceptable to the Iranians. The Court also found implicit congressional authorization for the President to act unilaterally, but acknowledged that no statute conferred the power directly.

Today, it is no longer clear when the President must seek Senate ratification of a treaty in order to conclude a legally binding agreement with a foreign government altering the rights of American citizens.

Delegated Power in Domestic Affairs

In domestic affairs, perhaps the central historical development involving the separation of powers has concerned the growth of the executive branch and the flow to it of delegated lawmaking power. The Constitution's framers and ratifiers could not have anticipated federal benefit-dispensing agencies on the scale of the Social Security Administration, nor regulatory agencies administering complex workplace safety or environmental protection legislation. In the twentieth century, however, both federal benefit programs and regulatory regimes seemed increasingly imperative. What is more, as the number and scope of federal programs grew, Congress proved unable, and sometimes unwilling, to write statutes at the necessary level of detail to guide their implementation. In the environmental area, for example, Congress can decide that factories may not emit dangerous amounts of toxic waste into the air or water, but it may lack the resources to determine exactly which wastes should be deemed toxic at exactly which concentrations. To bridge the gap between general policies and the details of their application, Congress began to vest executive agencies with rule-making power – the authority to write rules or regulations, with the force of law, specifying how vague statutory directives should be applied.

The leading case upholding the delegation of rule-making authority to executive agencies, *Yakus v. United States*[14] (1944), came out of World War II. To combat wartime inflation, Congress established a federal agency charged with limiting wage and price increases to those that would be "fair and equitable." The statute, the Emergency Price Control Act, obviously left enormous discretionary authority in the implementing agency, which needed to develop detailed codes specifying permissible and impermissible price increases for various jobs and commodities throughout the country. In practical effect, the Act provided for lawmaking to occur within the executive branch. Nonetheless, the Supreme Court upheld the delegation. Its reasoning had two parts. First, the Court suggested that Congress had already done all the required lawmaking in the constitutional sense, because it had established a legislative policy – that only fair and equitable price increases should be permitted – and left the agency with the job of implementing the law, not making it. The Court thus purported to honor the so-called nondelegation doctrine, which holds that Congress may not delegate its core legislative powers. In fact, however, the scope of delegated power was enormous, as the second strand of the Court's reasoning acknowledged. That second strand was avowedly pragmatic: "The Constitution as a continuously operative charter of government does not demand the impossible or the impracticable."[15] Congress and the President had reasonably concluded that the stresses of wartime required the development of anti-inflation rules. To develop those rules in their necessary details – determining, for example, how much could be charged for a used car or a loaf of fresh (or day-old) bread – lay beyond Congress's practical competence. The Court thus approved a significant delegation of rule-making power to the executive branch.

Yakus set a precedent much exploited by subsequent Congresses and extending well beyond wartime demands. Today a host of agencies possess the power to issue legally binding regulations involving such matters as entitlement to federal benefits, workplace safety, environmental quality, and forbidden employment practices.

In delegating lawmaking authority to the executive branch, Congress sometimes acts for sound reasons, involving its own lack of technical expertise. But sometimes, too, Congress may find it politically more expedient to legislate in general terms and to transfer the responsibility for making some of the hardest, most contentious decisions to the executive branch. In either case, the executive branch grows more powerful, and the stakes of presidential elections increase. When the White House changes hands, executive agencies can revise the rules issued by predecessor administrations to give concrete meaning to vague statutory directives. To cite just one particularly notable example, Republican administrations tend to construe environmental protection laws more loosely than do Democratic administrations.

Legislative Vetoes and Line-Item Vetoes

As Congress delegated increasing rule-making power to the executive branch, especially in the period from the 1930s through the 1970s, it predictably looked for new ways to oversee and influence the exercise of executive power. In particular, it began to rely increasingly on statutory provisions authorizing so-called legislative vetoes. In a typical statutory design, Congress would authorize executive rule-making, but provide that the rules drafted by an executive agency – such as environmental regulations – could not take effect if either the House or Senate enacted a "veto resolution" expressing its disapproval.

The Supreme Court addressed the constitutionality of legislative vetoes in *Immigration and Naturalization Service v. Chadha*[16] (1983). By 8–1, the Court held the arrangement unconstitutional. In an opinion by Warren Burger – who served as Chief Justice from 1969 through 1986 – the Court reasoned that legislative vetoes violated the plain language and structural design of the Constitution. Congress is the legislative branch, charged with lawmaking. When Congress enacts a veto resolution, it must be presumed to act legislatively, Chief Justice Burger wrote; it could not, for example, exercise executive power. But for Congress to legislate, Article I of the Constitution requires that both Houses of Congress must approve the same bill or resolution, which must then be presented to the President for his possible veto. Legislative vetoes were unconstitutional, the Chief Justice reasoned, because they departed from this precise, constitutionally mandated scheme. There might be good policy reasons supporting legislative vetoes, the Court said, but it had no business weighing policy arguments. The Court pronounced itself bound by "[t]he choices...made in the Constitutional Convention."[17]

Chadha exhibits the enormous challenges facing the Supreme Court in applying the Constitution to the circumstances of the modern world and to governmental structures that have evolved, often with the Court's approval, to address modern problems. Defenders advanced forceful functionalist arguments that the legislative veto actually helped to realize the basic premise underlying Article I: The valid enactment of federal law requires the joint concurrence of both Houses of Congress. When Congress delegates rule-making authority to the executive branch, the risk arises that the executive will promulgate rules that Congress does not in fact approve. Legislative vetoes, the argument continues, defuse this risk and restore the original constitutional balance by ensuring that Congress actually concurs in, or at least does not reject, agency rules possessing the force of federal law. Against arguments such as these, wooden invocation of "choices...made in the Constitutional Convention" rings slightly hollow. The modern governmental framework departs from original constitutional understandings in many ways. As demonstrated by the *Yakus* case, which upheld rule-making by the executive branch, the Court is perfectly capable of viewing constitutional norms as adaptable to modern practical imperatives when it wishes to do so.

When all of the complexities of modern government are taken into account and are judged against the Constitution's most fundamental presuppositions, the decision in *Chadha* was very likely the correct one. The ready availability of legislative vetoes created a subtle incentive for Congress to shirk its constitutional responsibility for making hard policy choices. Members were encouraged to enact broad language and pass the buck to administrative agencies. The choice to do so was essentially cost-free, as long as each House of Congress retained the chance to veto rules that it especially disliked. Without the legislative veto, the delegation of essentially open-ended rule-making authority looks less attractive. Following the Court's decision in *Chadha*, Congress has a greater incentive to do its job responsibly at the legislative stage.

If this or similar analysis is correct, however, it calls for subtle thinking about how constitutional doctrine is best shaped by courts to protect underlying values, not mechanical recitations about the Constitution's plain text and original understanding. It is possible, of course, that the Court thought about whether to invalidate legislative vetoes in far more sophisticated ways than its *Chadha* opinion revealed. But the formalist methodology of *Chadha*, which is reminiscent of Justice Black's approach in *Youngstown*, is difficult if not impossible to reconcile with the flexible approach taken in *Yakus*.

One attempt at reconciliation would proceed as follows: *Chadha* rightly assumes that the Court should prefer narrow, literalist interpretations of the constitutional text and adhere closely to original understandings unless there is some very good reason, arising from changed contexts or practical exigencies, for it not to do so. A good reason arguably existed in *Yakus*, but not in *Chadha*. Strikingly, however, the Court did not explain its invalidation of legislative vetoes in these terms.

Clinton v. City of New York[18] (1998), another recent separation-of-powers case, stands out as one of the few post-New Deal cases to invalidate a congressional effort to delegate power to the executive branch. Nearly everyone agrees that Congress regularly includes wasteful spending items in the federal budget. Powerful members demand projects for their states or districts, or favors for preferred constituencies, and spending bills get loaded with excess. To deal with the problem, a bipartisan congressional majority enacted the Line Item Veto Act, which authorized the President – after first signing a bill into law – subsequently to determine particular authorized expenditures to be wasteful and thus to decline to make them. The Act labeled the President's notifications to Congress of planned non-expenditures as line-item vetoes.

The Supreme Court struck down the Line Item Veto Act in *Clinton v. City of New York*. In reasoning similar to that of *Chadha*, the Court pointed out that the Constitution provides very specifically for the process by which bills become law and by which presidential vetoes may occur – before a bill becomes law, not after. If the vetoes exercised by the President under the Line Item Veto Act were "vetoes" in the constitutional sense, this reasoning would deserve to carry the day. As two dissenting opinions emphasized, however, the title of the Line Item Veto Act was misleading. In determining to withhold spending on wasteful or exorbitant projects, the President did not need to be seen as "vetoing" legislation; he could be viewed, instead, as simply exercising a statutorily conferred authority to withhold unnecessary spending. If, for example, a bill authorized the President to spend up to $100 billion to meet the nation's defense needs, and if he spent only $90 billion, no one would say that he had "vetoed" $10 billion worth of spending. The Line Item Veto Act could easily have been viewed in the same way – as creating a discretion to withhold spending of otherwise authorized funds, not as licensing a "veto" of line items in the federal budget.

Perhaps, as Justice Antonin Scalia wrote in dissent, the title of the Line Item Veto Act "fak[ed] out" the Supreme Court.[19] Because the Act purported to confer a veto power, the Court assumed that a veto power must be at stake, even though another description of its effect would have been more apt. Perhaps the title troubled the Court for other, partly symbolic reasons. The title may have sent a disturbing signal that Congress meant to evade or even flout the Constitution. Or perhaps the Court thought that the Line Item Veto Act threatened to distort the constitutional scheme of checks and balances by giving the President too much discretionary power. However public spirited the Act's goals, it would have greatly enhanced the President's capacity to reward friends (by permitting spending on their preferred projects, however profligate) and punish enemies (by withholding spending on projects of great importance to them, wasteful or not). Only this much seems clear: The Line Item Veto Act presented complex questions of constitutional judgment, not a simple issue about whether Congress can give the President a "veto" power withheld by the Constitution.

Appointments and Removals

Although Article II begins by saying that "the executive Power shall be vested in a President of the United States," the President cannot execute that power all alone. He (or she) needs subordinates, whose offices must be established by law. Responsibility to establish agencies and departments lies in Congress. And Congress, in establishing agencies and departments, has sometimes attempted to limit the President's power to appoint and remove those who run them. Intricate constitutional questions have thus arisen about whether, when, and to what extent Congress can limit presidential power to appoint and remove high executive officials.

One prominent view is notable for its elegant simplicity. The so-called unitary executive theory holds that the Constitution establishes one President, vested with the whole "executive power," and that he must therefore be able to supervise and control all who work for him.[20] According to the unitary executive theory, presidential control requires that the President should possess exclusive power to appoint high federal officials and that the President should also have unrestricted authority to dismiss officials whose performances displease him. This theory promises to deliver coherent, accountable presidential administration.

On the whole, the Supreme Court has agreed with unitary executive theorists that the President must have the power to appoint all high federal officials charged with executing the law.[21] In doing so, the Court has relied on the plain language of Article II, Section 2, Clause 2, which directs that the President "shall nominate, and by and with the Advice and Consent of the Senate, shall appoint" certain named officials and "all other Officers of the United States, whose Appointments are not herein otherwise provided for."

Even under the "unitary executive" thesis, the President's appointment power is not, of course, unbounded: The Constitution specifically provides that presidential appointees can take office only upon confirmation by the Senate. In deciding whether to "consent" to the appointment of *executive* officials, however, the Senate has historically given the President considerable latitude. (The implied contrast is with appointments to the *judicial* branch, a subject briefly discussed in Chapters Nine and Fourteen.) Members of the executive branch work for the President. The President is accountable for their performance in office. Nevertheless, over the course of history the Senate has refused to confirm at least nine nominees for Cabinet positions.[22] Some rejections have rested on concerns about the nominees' ethical conduct. Others have reflected the Senate's simple judgment that a particular nominee was temperamentally or otherwise unfit to hold high federal office.

The scope of the President's inherent constitutional authority to fire high executive officials is the subject of recurring constitutional debate. Following the Civil War, in the midst of a struggle between Congress and President Andrew Johnson over Reconstruction policy, the House of Representatives voted to impeach Johnson for unilaterally dismissing a Cabinet officer in defiance of the short-lived Tenure of Office Act, which purported to limit the President's ability to fire members of his own Cabinet without Senate approval. But the Senate refused by a narrow margin to find Johnson guilty of an impeachable offense, apparently because some Senators agreed with him that the Tenure of Office Act was unconstitutional, because it crippled the President's capacity to administer the executive branch.

Since the failed Johnson impeachment, disputes about the President's constitutional authority to remove federal officials have moved from impeachment debates into the courts. Two classic cases exhibit the complexity of the resulting judge-made doctrine. *Myers v. United States*[23] (1926) grew from the President's insistence on removing a postmaster, despite a federal statute protecting postmasters from dismissal except for good cause. In an opinion by Chief Justice William Howard Taft, himself a former President, the Court invalidated the statutory limitation on the President's removal power. The President was responsible for the administration of the entire executive branch, Taft reasoned, and he must therefore be able to dismiss any subordinate who did not enjoy his full confidence.

A few years later the Court confronted *Humphrey's Executor v. United States*[24] (1935), involving a statute that limited the President's power to remove commissioners of the Federal Trade Commission.

Taking a distinctly flexible or "functionalist" approach, the Court distinguished *Myers* based on the duties performed by Federal Trade Commissioners. Whereas Myers performed traditional executive functions, the Court emphasized that Congress had empowered the Federal Trade Commission to issue rules and regulations defining unfair trade practices and, in some cases, to adjudicate in the first instance – subject to review in a regular federal court created under Article III of the Constitution – whether violations of federal law had occurred. According to the Court, when Congress creates "quasi legislative or quasi judicial agencies,"[25] it can limit the President's removal powers in order to protect the independence of those performing legislative and especially judicial functions. Such agencies, the Court said, are "wholly disconnected from the executive department."[26]

Read literally, *Humphrey's Executor* would be an example of constitutional adaptation run riot. It is one thing to say that Congress can confer rule-making and adjudicative powers on administrative agencies; it is another to suggest that Congress can create agencies wholly outside the executive branch and presumably outside the legislative and judicial branches as well. The Constitution provides for just three branches. Three are enough. Although it has now become common to refer to agencies such as the Federal Trade Commission as "independent agencies," it is better to think of them as "relatively independent" agencies within the executive branch.

The crucial point, however, involves substance, not terminology. In the wake of *Humphrey's Executor*, the Supreme Court must decide which federal officials perform predominantly executive functions, and thus come under the rule of *Myers* that the President must have unrestricted power to fire high officials performing purely "executive" functions, and which have duties that are sufficiently judicial or legislative to warrant restraints on the President's removal authority. These questions lack sharp answers. If Congress chooses to do so, it can assign rule-making and quasi-adjudicative functions to Cabinet Departments such as the Department of State (which has principal responsibility for foreign affairs); the Constitution does not mandate the use of quasi-independent officials. Yet it seems unimaginable that

Congress could limit the President's power to dismiss a Secretary of State in whom he had lost confidence. If this conclusion is correct, then the labels quasi-judicial and quasi-legislative may guide judicial thinking in some cases, but they are not the only relevant factors. The Court must assess when the benefits of presidential control of official decision-making, and the political accountability that it brings, are outweighed by competing values. An unrestricted removal power ensures clear presidential accountability for the performance of government – a strong presumptive good. But there may be special reasons to think that a few governmental functions are best insulated, at least in part, from the sphere of presidential politics and political calculation.

As *Humphrey's Executor* suggests, certain quasi-adjudicative functions may occupy the category in which insulation from presidential politics makes both practical and constitutional sense. When the Federal Trade Commission determines whether the specific trade practices of specific companies violate the law – subject to further review in a court – its thinking should not be influenced by political pressure to reward the President's allies or to punish his opponents. The quasi-independent Federal Reserve Board may furnish another example of a federal agency whose functions should be insulated as far as possible from political pressures, including those that a President would predictably bring to bear if he could fire members at will. Through its control over the money supply and interest rates, the Federal Reserve Board has a considerable power to stimulate a lagging economy or, conversely, to dampen inflationary tendencies in an economy that is overheated. In the latter case, its job is to administer painful medicine; in the former, the optimal dosage may be one that brings a gradual improvement, not an immediate recovery. Congress made a deliberate, considered decision to give the powers of the Federal Reserve to a quasi-independent agency, rather than to the President or to officials immediately subject to the President's direction. An incumbent President will always have a strong political incentive to try to cause the economy to boom in election years. If the consequence of presidential control would predictably be a costly cycle of boom followed by bust, then removing certain decisions from direct political control again makes practical sense. Congress made this calculation when it first established the Federal Reserve Board early in the twentieth century. By nearly everyone's calculation, that judgment has served the nation well.

Admittedly, however, "functional" assessments of this kind require calculations of costs and benefits that are inherently contestable. By upholding congressional power to impose limits on the President's power to remove some officials but not others, the Supreme Court has assumed a responsibility for making judgments in an area where the line between law and policy blurs and sometimes vanishes.[27]

NINE

Judicial Power

[T]he judiciary, from the nature of its functions, will always be the least dangerous [branch of government]. . . . It may truly be said to have neither FORCE nor WILL, but merely judgment.
        – The Federalist No. 78

The Imperial Judiciary lives.
   – Justice Antonin Scalia, protesting a Supreme Court decision
                     upholding abortion rights[1]

IN 1973, DURING A CONGRESSIONAL INVESTIGATION into abuses of power by the presidential administration of Richard Nixon and illegal activities by the Nixon reelection campaign, it came to light that Nixon had secretly recorded a large number of conversations in the Oval Office. The special prosecutor charged with investigating wrongdoing by administration and campaign officials demanded access to the tapes. When Nixon refused, the special prosecutor sought a court order directing Nixon to hand them over.

Whatever his personal motivations, Nixon had a serious constitutional argument that the tapes were protected by "executive privilege" – a prerogative of the President, as head of the executive branch, to protect papers, tapes, and other evidence of what his advisors had said to him and he to them in the course of making presidential decisions. According to Nixon, it would harm the presidency, and thus the country, if Presidents could not receive truly confidential advice and probe policy options on an absolutely confidential basis. Nixon, of course, acknowledged that Presidents could disclose any information that they saw fit. But he maintained, in essence, that the management of presidential deliberations was the exclusive business of the

President, not the courts. What is more, White House officials hinted that if the Supreme Court ordered Nixon to surrender the tapes, he might simply refuse as a matter of constitutional principle.

On July 24, 1974, the Supreme Court issued its ruling in *United States v. Nixon* (more commonly known as *The Nixon Tapes Case*),[2] commanding the President to give the tapes to a federal judge, for the judge, rather than the President, to determine which conversations should and which should not be made available to the special prosecutor. Despite his prior bluster, and despite the plausibility of his arguments, Nixon meekly complied. He really had no choice. If Nixon had refused to surrender the tapes in response to a Supreme Court order, the public would have been outraged. Congress would almost certainly have treated the defiance as a ground for his impeachment and removal from office.

The Nixon Tapes Case made a rather stunning contrast with the earlier case of *Marbury v. Madison*[3] (1803), discussed in the Introduction. In *Marbury*, if the Supreme Court had issued an order directing Secretary of State James Madison to take an action that President Thomas Jefferson had ordered him not to take, Jefferson and Madison let it be known that they would defy the Court's command. What is more (and makes the greater contrast with *The Nixon Tapes Case*) it was widely believed in 1803 that if the Supreme Court ruled against Madison and the Jefferson administration, thereby provoking defiance, then Congress – which supported the President – would actually have impeached Chief Justice John Marshall and removed *him* from office. In *Marbury*, it was the Chief Justice who needed to make a tactical retreat; in *The Nixon Tapes Case* it was the President.

Differences in the facts of the cases undoubtedly matter, as do differences in the legal arguments. It also probably matters that Jefferson was a very popular President in 1803, whereas by 1974 Nixon was a very unpopular one. But the stature of the Supreme Court had also changed immeasurably. In 1803, the Court was a weak and vulnerable institution, with the reach of its authority in doubt. By 1974, the Court had achieved a remarkable potency, which it retains today.

This chapter, involving judicial power under the Constitution, unfolds in three main parts. The first deals with the character of the judicial role within American constitutional practice. The second explores the debates and anxieties that surround the exercise of judicial power: How can so much judicial power be justified under a Constitution committed to democratic self-government, not government by judiciary? The third part of the chapter discusses limits on judicial power, some self-imposed by the courts and others stemming from surrounding cultural and political forces.

The Character of Judicial Power

Writing in 1936 in an important case invalidating the centerpiece of the New Deal's farm program, Justice Owen Roberts tried to blunt criticism by saying that the Supreme Court's job was not to exercise any independent judgment about the wisdom or even the possibly urgent necessity of challenged legislation, but simply "to lay the article of the Constitution which is invoked beside the statute which is challenged and to decide whether the latter squares with the former."[4] The Constitution's meaning, he implied, was almost invariably plain. In cases of doubt, others have suggested, research into the "original understanding" will ordinarily resolve any uncertainty.

As previous chapters of this book have probably suggested, Roberts' portrait of the judicial role was more fanciful than realistic. (One wonders whether Roberts himself would not have acknowledged as much in less defensive moments – if not in 1936, then surely a year later, when his so-called "switch in time that saved nine" ended the constitutional crisis that had provoked Franklin Roosevelt's Court-packing plan.) Often the Constitution's plain text will give no simple answer to modern constitutional questions: Which utterances lie within and without "the freedom of speech"? When is a search or seizure "unreasonable" and thus forbidden (rather then reasonable and thus permissible)? Which governmental classifications are consistent and inconsistent with "the equal protection of the laws"?

When the text gives no obvious answer, few would deny that the original understanding of constitutional language is relevant, but it is often hard to apply eighteenth- and nineteenth-century understandings to modern problems. I emphasized this point in Chapter Seven, involving the Supreme Court's historic struggles to interpret and apply the Commerce Clause, but other examples could also be cited.

What is more, many strands of judicial precedent seem inconsistent with the original understandings of constitutional language, and once precedents have been established, nearly everyone acknowledges that they, too, need to be reckoned with in constitutional adjudication. A particularly clear example involves the constitutionality of paper currency. The issuance of paper money very arguably exceeds the original understanding of Congress's power, conferred by Article I, Section 8, Clause 5 of the Constitution, to "coin Money."[5] Had the framers wished to empower Congress to issue "greenbacks," they could easily have said so; the authorization to "coin Money" seems to speak more narrowly. But the Supreme Court held otherwise in 1871,[6] and a reversal on this issue would provoke economic chaos.

Another example involves race-based discrimination by the federal government. Although it seems clear that no provision of the Constitution, even as amended, was originally understood to bar discrimination by Congress (as the Equal Protection Clause, enacted in the aftermath of the civil war, only limits action by the *states*), the Supreme Court has treated race-based discriminations by the federal government as "suspect" for more than sixty years now and has subjected such discriminations to "strict" or "searching" judicial scrutiny.[7] Regardless of whether the earliest cases were rightly reasoned, the matter is now considered by nearly everyone to be settled by precedent and evolving moral understandings. Indeed, even Supreme Court Justices who maintain in other contexts that constitutional adjudication should reflect "the original understanding" of constitutional language have accepted judicial precedents applying equal protection norms to the federal government (and, more controversially, have cited those precedents as authority for condemning federal affirmative action programs).[8]

It is true, of course, that the Supreme Court is not absolutely bound by precedent. Sometimes it chooses to "overrule" itself. But the largely discretionary judgment of when to follow precedent and when to overrule it only adds a further judgmental element to constitutional adjudication in the Supreme Court.

When the various relevant considerations are all put into play, I have suggested repeatedly now – largely following Professor Ronald Dworkin on this point[9] – that Supreme Court Justices typically decide how the Constitution is *best* interpreted in light of history, precedent, and considerations of moral desirability and practical workability. All of these factors are relevant. No clear rule specifies which will be controlling in a particular case. In this context, political scientists repeatedly emphasize that the voting patterns of Supreme Court Justices tend to be relatively (though not perfectly) predictable on the basis of their political ideology.[10] In view of the judgmental character of constitutional adjudication, it would be astonishing if the results were otherwise.

To say this is not to imply that the decisions of Supreme Court Justices are crudely political. The Justices function in what I described in the first chapter of this book as a constitutional "practice," which subjects them to a number of role-based constraints. They must reason like lawyers and take account of text and history as well as precedent. They work in the medium of constitutional law, not partisan politics, and the medium of law – with its characteristic techniques of reasoning – limits, shapes, and channels the Justices' search for the best interpretation of the Constitution.[11] Nevertheless, the nature of constitutional interpretation leaves abundant room for the exercise of legal and sometimes moral imagination.

Nor, in assessing the scope of judicial power, is it always helpful or even strictly accurate to think of the Supreme Court as engaged solely in constitutional "interpretation." Among the Court's characteristic modern functions is to formulate rules and tests for application by lower courts in future cases. This process of course begins with an interpretive search for "the meaning of the Constitution." Before research's conclusion, however, the Court frequently needs to make a lot of practical judgments, informed by its sense of likely consequences. In my view many of the Court's rules are better viewed as devices to "implement" constitutional values than as "interpretations" of constitutional language.[12] Among the clearest examples of constitutional "implementation" as a function distinct from pure "interpretation" comes from *Miranda v. Arizona*[13] (1966), which introduced the requirement that the police give so-called *Miranda* warnings. Although admittedly an extreme case, the *Miranda* decision exemplifies a broader phenomenon. Many of the doctrinal tests canvassed in earlier chapters lack clear roots in either the Constitution's language or its history. The Supreme Court has devised them in order to implement constitutional values, but they do not emerge from the Constitution through a process that would naturally be described as one of interpretation.

One final detail about the role of the Supreme Court deserves mention in a discussion of judicial power. Under the current statutory scheme, the Supreme Court enjoys almost complete discretion about which cases to hear and not to hear. Courts in the United States decide tens of thousands of cases every year. The Supreme Court could not possibly review every decision involving a federal constitutional question. After experimenting with various other schemes, Congress, by statute, has provided that the Supreme Court simply gets to choose which cases decided by lower courts it would like to review. In a typical year, the Court is asked to review more than 7,000 cases, out of which it has recently selected fewer than 100. For the most part, the Court agrees to decide those cases that the Justices think most important. The Supreme Court's power to choose its own cases is an important one, which permits the Court to establish and pursue any agenda that it may wish to adopt – for example, by expanding constitutional rights or powers in some areas or pruning them in others.

Anxieties About Judicial Power

The breadth of the power exercised by courts, and especially by the Supreme Court, naturally gives rise to recurrent debates and anxiety. As lawyers and judges worry about whether and when it is legitimate for courts to invalidate legislation based on their interpretation (which others may not share) of a very old constitution, they have at least two concerns in mind. One involves public acceptance of judicial review: Under what circumstances, if any, might the American people simply refuse to put up with having courts invalidate legislation that popular majorities support? What would happen if a popular President defied a very unpopular judicial ruling? Might the people line up behind the President, rather than behind the Court? A second question involves the moral and political justifiability of judicial review, especially in light of the relatively free-wheeling way in which it is sometimes practiced: How, if at all, should courts go about deciding constitutional issues such that the American people *ought* to put up with their doing so?

These are perennial questions in American constitutional law and American politics. But they have arisen with special sharpness at some times in constitutional history – for example, during the *Lochner* era and then when Richard Nixon promised to appoint "strict constructionist" Justices who would halt the excesses (as he saw them) of the Warren Court. In recent years conservative critics of the Supreme Court have found a focal point for criticism in the Court's 1973 decision in *Roe v. Wade*,[14] which held that absolute prohibitions against abortion violate the Constitution during the period before a fetus becomes viable or capable of surviving outside the womb. Although restrictions on abortion undoubtedly curtail "liberty," no one believes that the Due Process Clause – the provision on which the Court based its decision – was originally understood or intended to protect abortion rights. The Court based its ruling partly on precedent, partly on a contestable judgment that it is unreasonable to make women bear an unwanted fetus.

In objecting to decisions such as *Roe*, critics often maintain not just that the Court reached the wrong decision, but that it is not fair or "legitimate" for the unelected Justices of the Supreme Court to exercise a power to thwart the judgments of political majorities – at least when legislation is not in flat contravention of the Constitution's originally understood meaning. This challenge, to which Alexander Bickel gave the label of "the counter-majoritarian difficulty,"[15] deserves to be taken seriously. But it bears emphasis that charges of "countermajoritarianism" can be leveled at conservative as well as liberal judicial decisions. As discussed in Chapter Seven, in recent years, the five Justices of the Supreme Court who are generally labeled most "conservative" have invalidated numerous pieces of federal regulatory legislation, including the so-called Violence Against Women Act,[16] on the ground that Congress lacks authority to enact it. Conservative Justices have also voted to subject federal affirmative action programs to strict judicial scrutiny, even though no provision of the Constitution was originally understood to bar affirmative action (or other forms of race-based discrimination) by the federal government. Conservative Justices have also voted to strike down popularly enacted restrictions on commercial advertising, even though it seems highly doubtful, at best, that the First Amendment was originally understood to protect commercial advertising.

Against the background of the countermajoritarian difficulty and related anxieties, judges and Justices openly debate questions of judicial role and interpretive methodology, often in the course of opinions deciding actual cases. Nor are debates about constitutional methodology confined to the courts. When Presidential candidates talk about the kind of judges and Justices that they would like to appoint, issues of proper interpretive methodology enter a broader public arena. Similar debates occur when the Senate considers whether to approve the nominations of candidates put forward by the President to become federal judges.

In recent years, at least two (highly conservative) Justices of the Supreme Court, Antonin Scalia and Clarence Thomas, have occasionally maintained that judges and Justices should renounce interpretive methodologies that require them to decide how the Constitution would "best" or most fairly be applied to modern conditions and should decide cases based solely on the original understanding of constitutional language – what it was understood to mean by those who ratified it.[17] Because virtually no one denies that the original understanding is *relevant* to constitutional adjudication, it is often hard to gauge the precise scope of the difference between so-called originalists and their opponents. But originalists often claim that their methodology is sharply distinctive.

Insofar as originalism is sharply distinctive, however, critics urge two forceful objections. First, the "original understanding" of some constitutional provisions may be far out of touch with current realities.[18] For example, as discussed in Chapter Seven, the principal basis for claims of federal authority to regulate the economy is a constitutional provision empowering Congress to regulate "Commerce . . . among the several States." It is highly questionable whether Congress's regulatory authority in this vital area should depend entirely on the understanding that prevailed in what President Franklin Roosevelt, in championing the need for federal power to defeat the Great Depression, referred to as "horse and buggy" days.[19]

A second problem, to which I have called attention already, is that a great deal of modern constitutional doctrine that is now too entrenched to be given up seems impossible to justify by reference to the original understanding. Originalists do not maintain otherwise. They generally concede that their theory must make an *exception* for issues settled by past, entrenched judicial decisions[20] – or at least some of them. It is issues of consistency that give originalists trouble, for they do not contend that all erroneous precedents should be immune from correction. To take perhaps the best known example, prominent originalists insist tirelessly that *Roe v. Wade*'s recognition of constitutional abortion rights ought to be overruled. But what distinguishes *Roe* from the precedents that originalists would leave unaltered? In essence, originalists reserve the right to pick which precedents to reject and which to accept, largely on the basis of their own judgments concerning which are important, desirable, and undesirable. Once it is recognized that Justices must make judgments of this kind, originalism fails in its own aspiration to exclude the Justices' moral and political views from constitutional adjudication. It is a philosophy available to be trotted out in some cases and ignored in others.

Confronted with objections such as these, originalists commonly insist that it takes a theory to beat a theory. Many originalists believe the best defense of their method is that it is the least bad of an imperfect lot. Others believe that alternative approaches to constitutional adjudication are better.

Another prominent theory of constitutional adjudication rests on the premise that the Constitution embodies "moral" rights.[21] According to this view, the Constitution's framers and ratifiers did not invent such rights as those to freedom of speech and religion and to the equal protection of the laws. Rather, they recognized that such rights already existed as moral rights, and they incorporated those moral rights into the Constitution. Those holding this view would say, for example, that the Equal Protection Clause extends as far as the moral right to treatment as an equal and thus justifies the result in *Brown v. Board of Education*, even if the framers and ratifiers of the Fourteenth Amendment would have thought otherwise. At its foundation, a "moral rights" approach to constitutional adjudication must posit that the courts are better at identifying moral truths than are members of Congress and the state legislatures, perhaps because the latter are subject to political pressures to which the former – who have more opportunity to be long-sighted and deliberative – are not. Critics of course maintain that this approach invites judges simply to impose their personal moral views. Judges, they insist, have no monopoly on, and indeed no special insight into, moral truth.

In view of the objections to both originalism and a "moral rights" approach, some observers call for greater "judicial restraint" in invalidating legislation. When members of Congress and state legislators enact statutes, they have presumably considered whether the legislation violates the Constitution and determined that it does not. In light of this presumption, advocates of judicial restraint have long contended – since the *Lochner* era and even before – that the Supreme Court should accord "deference" to the constitutional judgments of other branches of government. According to one famous formulation of this position, the Court should invalidate statutes only when Congress or a state legislature has made a "clear mistake" about what the Constitution permits.[22] This is by no means a wholly implausible position, but it would call for a dramatically reduced judicial role. It would also cast retrospective doubt on many of the Supreme Court's most celebrated decisions, including some that have protected the rights of racial minorities, safeguarded political speech, and enforced voting rights.[23]

Believing that the Court should retain a robustly protective role in these areas, the late constitutional scholar John Hart Ely argued for deference to majorities *except* in cases involving claims of minority rights or rights to participate in the political process.[24] He justified this approach by arguing that the Constitution's predominant commitment is to political democracy, and that courts should therefore intervene to make sure that the processes of political democracy function fairly. Among its implications, Ely's theory would stop courts from invalidating affirmative action programs (which disadvantage the white majority, not a racial minority) and recently enacted statutes that discriminate against women (who are a numerical majority, not a minority, of the population). Ely did not claim that the Supreme Court actually follows his theory, only that it should.

Other participants in constitutional practice defend a more flexible approach to constitutional adjudication, such as they believe the Court has characteristically practiced, partly based on an analogy to the way that judges decided cases under the so-called common law.[25] Well into the nineteenth century, Congress and the state legislatures still had enacted comparatively few statutes, and the most basic law – called the common law – was developed by judges on the basis of custom and reason. In deciding cases at common law, judges begin with the rules as formulated in prior judicial decisions, but they also enjoy some flexibility to adapt those rules as circumstances change or as custom and reason require. Under the approach advocated by common-law constitutionalists, Supreme Court Justices should employ a comparably flexible approach in deciding constitutional issues. They should always begin with the text of the written Constitution, with which any interpretation must at least be reconciled. And they should treat the original understanding as always relevant and often decisive. But, it is argued, judges and especially Justices should also give weight to previous judicial decisions, including those that depart from original constitutional understandings, and they should take express account of what is fair, reasonable, workable, and desirable under modern circumstances, because we will get better constitutional law if they do so than if they do not. Critics, notably including originalists, argue that the common-law approach gives too large a role to judges, who are invited to thwart the wishes of democratic majorities based on their personal notions of justice and workability.

As the seemingly endless debate perhaps suggests, it may well be that questions of appropriate interpretive methodology admit no *general* answer – and that there can be no categorically persuasive rejoinder to the countermajoritarian difficulty either. The justification of the Supreme Court's role and interpretive methodology, if any, may well depend on the substantive fairness and popular acceptability of the particular decisions that it makes across the sweep of time.[26] For now, at least, the people of the United States appear to have accepted a judicial role in adapting the Constitution to changing perceptions of need and fairness. But their acceptance of a flexible judicial role should surely be regarded as contingent, based on an assumption – grounded in our traditions – that judicial review as historically practiced has tended to produce good results overall: It is a useful device for promoting substantive justice and for reaching results that are broadly acceptable to the American public in ways that are at least tolerably consistent with the constitutional ideal of "a government of laws, and not of men."[27]

Alexander Bickel may have had a thought such as this in mind when he wrote, somewhat enigmatically, that the Court "labors under the obligation to succeed."[28] If the Court must somehow succeed in order to justify the role that it plays, and if success depends on reconciling the contestable demands of substantive justice with sometimes competing imperatives of adhering to settled rules of law and of rendering decisions that the public deems acceptable, it is easy to understand why the practice of judicial review should provoke ongoing anxieties and debate.

Limits on Judicial Power

Partly because of its potency, the judicial power needs to be reined in, at least to some extent. It is. Some of the restraints on judicial power come from legal doctrines. Others arise from interaction between the judiciary and other, more overtly political, forces and institutions.

To begin with, Article III of the Constitution says clearly that the "judicial power" extends only to "Cases" or "Controversies," or to what the delegates to the Constitutional Convention described as "cases of a Judiciary nature."[29] Although the Supreme Court has developed numerous doctrines defining the necessary elements of a constitutional "case" or "controversy," perhaps the most important involves the requirement of "standing": To have standing to press a constitutional claim, the challenger must demonstrate that he or she has suffered a concrete "injury" as a result of an allegedly unconstitutional act.[30] Mostly, standing doctrine requires that a lawsuit be brought by a proper party. Imagine that I, a male citizen of Massachusetts and not a doctor, read in the newspaper that Alabama has imposed a restriction on abortions that I believe to be unconstitutional. I would lack standing to challenge the Alabama law, because I have not suffered concrete injury as that term is used in the legal sense. The proper parties to challenge the imagined statute would be women in Alabama who want or are likely to want abortions and doctors who are threatened with penalties if they perform abortions.

In another application of the case or controversy requirement, the Supreme Court has held that a few disputes about constitutional issues present "political questions" to be decided by either Congress or the President, not the courts. One thread of this doctrine maintains that some constitutional provisions specifically confer interpretive responsibility on a branch of government other than the judiciary. For example, Article I, Section 3, Clause 6 provides that "[t]he Senate shall have the sole Power to try all Impeachments" – actions to remove certain high federal officials from office on the ground that they have committed "Treason, Bribery, or other high Crimes and Misdemeanors."[31] In *Nixon v. United States*[32] (1993), the Court held that this language barred judicial review of whether the Senate had properly discharged its constitutional responsibilities in removing a federal judge named Walter Nixon. The Constitution authorized the Senate, not the courts, to determine the requisites of a fair impeachment trial.

Another thread of the political question doctrine emphasizes that some legal questions are not well suited for judicial resolution, either because of the absence of "judicially manageable standards" or because a judicial answer might create confusion or national embarrassment, especially in foreign affairs.[33] Invoking this rationale, a number of lower courts refused to rule on challenges to the constitutionality of the Vietnam War. (Opponents argued that the war was unconstitutional because Congress had never formally declared war, as they said it was required to do under Article I, Section 8, Clause 11 of the Constitution.) For obvious reasons, a judicial order to withdraw troops from battle would not only embarrass the government, but also sow confusion and put lives at risk.

Apart from the case or controversy requirement, which governs whether a constitutional claim can be adjudicated at all, the Supreme Court has crafted a number of doctrines that call for judicial "deference" to the judgments of other officials in determining what the Constitution requires.[34] For example, the Court has said repeatedly that courts should nearly always accept the judgments of military authorities in assessing constitutional challenges to military regulations and discipline.[35] As was discussed in Chapter Three, the Court has also said that it will almost always defer to the judgments of Congress and the state legislature in determining whether economic regulatory legislation survives challenge under the Equal Protection and Due Process Clauses. Doctrines of judicial deference obviously reduce the tensions that can result from collisions between the courts and other branches of government.

Beyond doctrines that call generally for deference to other branches of government, it appears that the Supreme Court may occasionally respond in a self-conscious way to public opinion or to the anticipated reactions of elected political officials. In *Marbury v. Madison*, for example, the Court may well have determined that William Marbury had to lose, lest an explosion of outrage by Thomas Jefferson and the Congress produce a devastating backlash against the Court. Scholars have also identified at least a few other instances in which the Court may deliberately have steered away from rendering decisions that it thought likely to be defied.[36]

For the most part, however, Supreme Court Justices probably do not need to think self-consciously about public opinion or risks of defiance in order to reach conclusions that the public, or most of it, is likely to find at least minimally acceptable. The Justices are creatures of the time in which they live (as are the rest of us). Their views are not likely to stray too far from the political mainstream. If the Court stakes out positions that the public finds objectionable, either generally or with respect to a particular, politically charged issue, the President, in nominating new Justices, is likely to look for candidates who will pull the Court back into line.

The extent to which the Supreme Court tends to march in step with popular attitudes should not be overstated. Many of the issues decided by the Court draw little or no political interest. With respect to these, the Court can chart its own course without attracting much notice. In addition, individual Justices not only are expected to vote their consciences, but are also personally insulated from political retaliation. (Apart from the remote risk of impeachment, the Constitution mandates that all federal judges "shall hold their Offices during good Behaviour," which in essence means that they enjoy life tenure, and their salaries cannot be reduced during their time in office.[37]) As a result, it is by no means impossible for the Court temporarily to find itself misaligned with the views of political majorities pending the "lag" before appointments and confirmations restore the balance. What is more, Presidents making nominations to the Supreme Court may actually try to push it in either a politically liberal or a politically conservative direction, depending on their own outlook, rather than seeking nominees who are squarely in the political center. When the Senate is controlled by the President's own party, Presidents usually tend to get their way. When the opposing party has a majority in the Senate, which must confirm nominees before they can take office, resistance is more likely. Beginning in 1795, with a senatorial rejection of George Washington's nomination of John Rutledge, the Senate has refused to consent to twenty-six Supreme Court nominations, or about one in every six, made by Presidents.[38] Overall, perhaps the most that can be said is that the views of the Supreme Court with respect to constitutional issues of substantial political significance are unlikely to diverge *very far* from those of aroused political majorities for more than a relatively brief period.[39]

It is unclear how this state of affairs should be judged. On the one hand, the dependence of the judiciary on presidential nominations and Senate confirmation diminishes the risk of a runaway judiciary. It also reduces the practical significance of the so-called countermajoritarian difficulty, which I introduced earlier. On the other hand, a judiciary that tends to share prevailing cultural norms, and thus to decide cases in light of them, is not likely to be a very robust guarantor of minority rights – at least until a particular minority's claim of rights is one that the mass public is generally prepared to accept.[40] It is surely no accident that the Supreme Court generally accepted race-based segregation as constitutionally permissible throughout the Jim Crow era of the late nineteenth and early twentieth centuries. Nor is it coincidental that the Court's path-breaking decisions forbidding gender-based discrimination did not come until the 1970s, when the movement for women's rights had already begun to transform traditional attitudes.

To maintain that the Court seldom diverges far from the mainstream is not to claim that the Court's rulings make no difference. Sometimes they make a great deal of difference. The point here is simply that the difference made by the Supreme Court, both for better and for worse, almost invariably occurs within a politically and culturally bounded range.

PART THREE

Further Issues of Constitutional Structure and Individual Rights

Elections, Political Democracy, and the Constitution

[S]tatutes distributing the franchise [or right to vote] constitute the foundation of our representative society. Any unjustified discrimination in determining who may participate in political affairs or in the selection of public officials undermines the legitimacy of representative government.

– Chief Justice Earl Warren[1]

IN 1980, WHEN *City of Mobile v. Bolden*[2] came before the Supreme Court, the city of Mobile, Alabama, had been governed since 1911 by a City Commission consisting of three members, all elected by the voters at large. Slightly more than one-third of those voters were African American. Yet in the sixty-nine years between 1911 and 1980, not a single African American had ever won election to the City Commission. Two factors handicapped African American candidates. First, white voters tended to vote for whites and against blacks. Indeed, the pattern appears to have been one of "racially polarized voting" in which white voters tended to vote against African Americans' candidates of choice even when most African Americans supported a white candidate. Second, the city's at-large voting structure permitted white votes to dominate black votes for every seat on the Commission. If the city had been divided into three separate voting districts, each electing its own city commissioner, it would have been easy to create a predominantly African American district. The city's African American minority then would have had a chance at electoral representation. In their suit in the Supreme Court, a group of African Americans argued that the Equal Protection Clause required the city to revise its electoral system in just this way.

The Supreme Court might have looked at *Mobile v. Bolden* through either or both of two lenses. Seen through one, *Mobile v. Bolden* was a straightforward case involving alleged race discrimination, to be resolved under the equal protection principles discussed in Chapter Five. Within the equal protection framework most often applied in race discrimination cases, the crucial question was whether Mobile's electoral scheme, which did not openly classify on the basis of race, was nevertheless established or maintained for a racially discriminatory purpose. Under *Washington v. Davis*[3] (1976), a statute is generally not invalid, and does not even trigger heightened judicial scrutiny, merely because it has a racially discriminatory impact (such as, in *Mobile v. Bolden*, making it more difficult for blacks than for whites to elect a candidate of choice). For a constitutional challenge to succeed, a racially discriminatory purpose must be proved. It was not obvious, however, that the equal protection framework of *Washington v. Davis* should have applied.

Seen through another lens, *Mobile v. Bolden* raised more general issues, not limited to race, involving the appropriate design of democratic institutions. Voting rights were at stake, and the Supreme Court has repeatedly characterized voting rights as "fundamental" under the Equal Protection Clause. In *Mobile v. Bolden*, the city had adopted an electoral structure in which a minority always lost. Within the context of democratic theory, it might be observed that electoral minorities are *supposed* to lose; "majority rule" implies that minorities must accept defeat. In *Mobile v. Bolden*, however, the issue was not whether a minority ought ultimately to lose, but whether it ought to be *represented*, or at least have a fair chance to win representation. When the question is framed this way, there is clearly something to be said for the idea that the city should have had to give African Americans a better chance of electing at least one representative to the City Commission. But there is also reason to be concerned about whether the deepest issues involving the design of political democracy are well handled by courts under judge-made constitutional rules. Would the same arguments for a structure that permits minority representation apply if the disadvantaged minority consisted not of African Americans, but of Republicans or Democrats, the wealthy, or those who stood on one side of a contested local issue (such as where a garbage dump ought to be located)? And how big would a minority have to be before it could claim a constitutional right to a voting system that permits it to elect a representative? What if African Americans had constituted only one-fifth or one-ninth of the population of Mobile, rather than one-third?

Shrinking from questions such as these, the Supreme Court opted to look at *Mobile v. Bolden* solely through the first lens, as a race discrimination case. So viewing the case, a majority of the Justices applied the familiar equal protection rule under which statutes that do not employ explicitly race-based classifications but nonetheless have a racially disparate impact are unconstitutional only if they are adopted or retained for a racially discriminatory *purpose*. On the facts, the controlling opinion in *Mobile v. Bolden* found no discriminatory intent, though it left the door open to findings of discriminatory intent in other cases. The city of Mobile was thus allowed to maintain a governmental structure under which a substantial African American minority was never able to elect a representative to the City Commission.

To a considerable extent, the Court's approach in *Mobile v. Bolden*, as in other cases presenting voting-rights claims, reflects the limitations of the Constitution itself. Although the Constitution requires elections, and indeed makes them events of fundamental importance, it does not go into much detail about how elections should be conducted. As a result, most of the work of designing electoral schemes occurs through statutes, some enacted by Congress and most by the states, that create offices and voting districts, determine how candidates qualify for appearance on the ballot, and regulate a few electoral practices such as the giving of money to candidates. Like other statutes, those that establish electoral structures and otherwise regulate elections and campaigns must be tested for constitutionality. The Supreme Court doctrines developed to assess such statutes form the subject of this chapter – one that many commentators now put under the heading of "election law."

I have begun this chapter on election law with *Mobile v. Bolden* because the Supreme Court's approach in that case typifies its approach in many other cases. If the Court thought that the Constitution embodied a general theory of democracy, it could resolve election law cases under that theory. But the Justices have been unable to discern or develop such a theory. Without one, they typically conduct more narrowly framed investigations to identify violations of specific provisions not centrally concerned with elections or the structure of political democracy. The Court thus folded *Mobile v. Bolden* into the familiar framework of rights to freedom from race discrimination under the Equal Protection Clause. Cases involving restrictions on the financing of political campaigns, which I discuss at the end of this chapter, get treated similarly, as calling for the application of established First Amendment rights to freedom of speech and political association.

Many commentators believe that the Court misses a vital dimension of the problems in election law cases when it talks exclusively in the vocabulary of individual rights and fails to focus directly on issues of how best to structure political democracy under the Constitution. Perhaps for this reason, the Court's analysis in election law cases often seems shallow and unsatisfying, even when the rules that it lays down are serviceably clear.

Voting Rights: The "One-Person, One-Vote" Cases

The Supreme Court's most celebrated cases involving voting rights are the so-called one-person, one-vote cases, symbolized by *Reynolds v. Sims*.[4] Like *Mobile v. Bolden*, *Reynolds* arose from the state of Alabama. When the Court considered the case in 1964, the Alabama legislature had not once "reapportioned" itself since 1901. Over the intervening sixty-three years, shifting population patterns had made it possible for voters in districts that included only about twenty-five percent of the state's population to elect a majority of the members in both the state senate and state house of representatives. Cities, which had grown larger, were underrepresented. Rural areas had disproportionate influence. Nor was the Alabama legislature likely to fix the problem. Fair reapportionment would have required many legislators to vote themselves out of jobs. Similar situations existed in other states.

In *Reynolds,* Alabama voters in underrepresented areas claimed that the state's electoral scheme violated the Equal Protection Clause. At the time the case was argued, *Reynolds* appeared to raise extraordinary difficulties. On the one hand, voting arrangements that let minorities dominate state politics seemed inherently unfair. On the other hand, it was far from clear that any provision of the Constitution, as historically understood, authorized the Supreme Court to remedy the unfairness. Neither was it obvious that the right to an "equally weighted" vote should be regarded as implicit in the Constitution's overall theory or structure. With each state entitled to two Senators in the United States Senate, voters in small states have relatively more voting power in senatorial elections than do voters in large states.

Finally, many observers shared a concern to which Justice Felix Frankfurter gave passionate voice: that judicial oversight of legislative districting would plunge the Court into a dangerous "political thicket." In Alabama or any other state, there are many ways that lines might be drawn to create voting districts of roughly equal population. That being so, any selection was likely to advantage either Democrats or Republicans. If the courts got involved at all, Frankfurter feared that they would quickly become embroiled in partisan controversies. Beyond a few plain constitutional limits, such as those forbidding discrimination on the basis of race or gender in the distribution of voting rights, he also doubted the availability of judicially manageable standards to make decisions about how political power ought to be allocated. For Frankfurter, electoral districting questions were political to the core. He thought that courts should treat them as coming within the "political question" doctrine, discussed in Chapter Nine, and thus as committed entirely to the "political branches" of government.

In *Reynolds v. Sims* and a series of other one-person, one-vote cases during the 1960s, the Supreme Court dismissed these concerns. Basing its rulings on the Equal Protection Clause, it held that "seats in both houses of a bicameral state legislature must be apportioned on a population basis,"[5] following each decennial census, with each citizen's vote having equal weight. The Court's analysis rested on the notion that voting rights are "fundamental" rights under the Equal

Protection Clause. Its methodology was loosely consistent with that in other fundamental rights cases, as discussed in Chapter Six: Read as a whole, the Constitution presupposes that people will have the right to vote. Given the fundamental importance of voting rights, the Court held that when voting rights are distributed, they must be distributed so that each person's vote counts roughly equally.

Although the one-person, one-vote cases provoked fierce controversy at the time of their decision, within as little as a decade they had won nearly universal acceptance. A rule demanding equal populations in electoral districts turned out to pose few problems in implementation: Legislatures know the standard that they must meet to achieve judicial acceptance of their plans. When tempers had cooled, the idea that everyone's vote should have equal weight also accorded with almost everybody's notion of basic fairness.[6]

Beyond "One-Person, One-Vote"

The one-person, one-vote cases resolved one problem, but as it turned out only the simplest one, in ensuring that voting power is fairly distributed. A further question involves the proper role of the courts, if any, in ensuring that equally sized legislative districts (which thus satisfy the one-person, one-vote requirement) permit fair representation of all relevant groups. *Mobile v. Bolden*, the case that introduced this chapter, reflects the Court's approach to claims that voting schemes unfairly disadvantage racial minorities. Although African Americans were consistently unable to elect a representative to the Mobile City Commission, the Court held that the city had no obligation to adopt a districting scheme that would have permitted African Americans to elect a representative of choice. Under the framework that a majority of the Justices adopted, racial minorities may establish constitutionally forbidden "vote dilution" only by proving that a voting scheme was adopted or maintained for racially discriminatory purposes.

The Supreme Court has also had to consider claims that the design of electoral districts unfairly disadvantages, or dilutes the voting strength of, one or another political party. *Davis v. Bandemer*[7] (1986) exemplifies the problem. In the aftermath of the 1980 census, when legislatures throughout the nation needed to be reapportioned to comply with the one-person, one-vote requirement, the Republican Party controlled the Indiana legislature. In a time-honored process known as "gerrymandering," Indiana Republicans set out to do what Democrats tried to do in states in which they had legislative majorities – create voting districts that would help their candidates and disadvantage the other party. Employing well-known techniques, the Indiana Republicans "packed" as many likely Democratic voters as possible into some legislative districts. These districts became "safe" seats for Democrats, but their design also ensured that the Democrats, in winning them by huge margins, would "waste" many votes that might have helped elect Democrats in other districts. Having arranged for lots of Democratic votes to be "wasted," the Indiana Republicans then drew a series of district lines that "split" other geographic concentrations of Democrats by assigning some to one district and some to another, each with a Republican majority. The design worked. In the 1982 elections, Republican candidates captured fifty-seven seats in the Indiana State House of Representatives to the Democrats' forty-three, even though Democratic candidates won fifty-two percent of the total votes cast statewide.

When Indiana Democrats challenged the constitutionality of the Republicans' gerrymander, the Supreme Court could not agree on a majority opinion. In *Davis v. Bandemer*, three Justices would have held that challenges to partisan gerrymandering present "political questions" not fit for judicial decision at all; this would have meant that party-based gerrymanders violate no judicially enforceable constitutional rights.[8] Nearer to the opposite extreme, two Justices believed that gerrymanders are inherently unfair and that courts should hold them unconstitutional whenever they are effective.[9] In the middle, a plurality of four ruled that partisan gerrymanders violate the Constitution only when they "consistently degrade a voter's or a group of voters' influence on the political process as a whole."[10]

In essence, *Davis v. Bandemer* recognized a fundamental constitutional right to be free from partisan gerrymanders, but defined that right very narrowly and made violations almost impossible to prove: Proof of "consistent degrad[ation]" could apparently emerge only from a series of elections in which one party was grossly underrepresented in the legislature (relative to the total number of votes won by its candidates). That the Indiana gerrymander had worked for one election in 1982 did not suffice. Writing for the plurality, Justice Byron White adopted that position quite self-consciously. On one hand, he believed that electoral districting was an inherently political exercise and that state legislatures, in performing it, were incorrigibly partisan. He thus thought it would be naive and unworkable to hold that partisan scheming in the design of legislative districts always violated the Equal Protection Clause. On the other hand, he thought that the Court must define some limit, marked by the consistent degradation of the votes of one or the other party. *Davis v. Bandemer* thus reflected an uneasy compromise. Although forbidding the grossest partisan excesses, it did not develop a more affirmative theory concerning the fair distribution of voting power beyond the one-person, one-vote requirement.

Perhaps troubled by this state of affairs, which includes the absence of a majority opinion on a matter of great importance, the Supreme Court agreed to revisit the issues presented by party-based gerrymanders in *Vieth v. Jubilerer* (2004). Once again, however, the Justices proved unable to agree on a majority opinion, and the votes of a divided court left real doubt that a constitutional violation could ever successfully be proved.

Majority–Minority Districting

The Supreme Court has taken a more aggressive stance against deliberate state efforts to create "majority–minority" districts in which statewide racial minorities (such as African Americans) enjoy majority status. States might attempt to create majority–minority districts for a number of reasons, but perhaps the most common involves pressures to comply with a federal statute, the Voting Rights Act (VRA). The VRA was originally enacted to stop states, especially in the South, from deliberately drawing district lines that disadvantaged racial minorities. Congress amended and toughened the VRA when it thought that the Supreme Court, in cases such as *Mobile v. Bolden* (which was discussed in the introduction to this chapter), had done too little to ensure that minorities were treated fairly. As interpreted by the Supreme Court, the amended VRA requires states to create majority–minority districts when (1) a minority community is large and compact enough to constitute the majority in a properly drawn district, (2) the minority community is politically cohesive, and (3) the majority has itself engaged in racially polarized voting.[11]

In a series of cases, the Supreme Court has ruled that although the VRA requires the states to keep race in mind in order to create majority–minority districts when they can readily do so, the Constitution forbids them to make race the "predominant factor" in districting decisions. The predominant factor test emerged gradually from cases involving oddly shaped districts, the strange contours of which defy explanation on grounds other than race. Such districts, the Court wrote in *Shaw v. Reno*[12] (1993), "reinforce[] the perception that members of the same racial group – regardless of their age, education, economic status, or the community in which they live – think alike, share the same political interests, and will prefer the same candidates at the polls."

Dissenting Justices have emphasized that legislatures can and sometimes do create oddly shaped districts to benefit groups other than racial minorities. In *Shaw v. Reno*, Justice John Paul Stevens wrote: "If it is permissible to draw boundaries to provide adequate representation for rural voters, for union members, for Hasidic Jews, for Polish Americans, or for Republicans [as it generally is, as long as the districts observe one-person, one-vote principles,] it necessarily follows that it is permissible to do the same thing for members of the very minority group whose history in the United States gave birth to the Equal Protection Clause. A contrary conclusion could only be described as perverse."[13]

The more conservative Justices reject that reasoning. In their eyes, race is different, because it is peculiarly divisive and unfair as a basis for governmental decision-making, especially when it is plainly the predominant factor in producing decisions. (Recall the Court's ruling, discussed in Chapter Five, that public universities may make racial minority status a "plus" in their admissions processes, but cannot allow race to count for too much or employ racial quotas.) However one judges the majority's position, which is invariably classed as "conservative," it is a principled one that illustrates an important distinction between judicial politics and electoral politics. In recent years, Republican congressional majorities have made no move to repeal provisions of the VRA that pressure states to create majority–minority districts. The reason lies at least partly in partisan concerns. Almost without exception, majority–minority districts are packed with an overwhelming proportion of Democrats and thus "waste" Democratic votes that might help elect more Democratic candidates if some could be distributed elsewhere. In imposing constitutional obstacles to majority–minority districts, conservative Supreme Court Justices read the Constitution in light of views that are "political" in one sense, involving judgments of fairness, but they are not "partisan" in the sense of seeking to promote the fortunes of any political party. By the same token, the Court's more liberal Justices have consistently voted to sustain the constitutionality of majority–minority districts, presumably without regard to the electoral interests of the Democratic Party.

Equality in the Counting of Votes

If the Supreme Court's divisions are reassuringly nonpartisan in cases involving majority–minority districts, *Bush v. Gore*[14] (2000) raised doubts in the minds of some. As discussed in the Prologue, the Supreme Court did not hesitate to plunge into the political thicket when legal controversies enveloped the crucial Florida vote count in the 2000 presidential election. The precise question before the Court involved the rights of voters and candidates with respect to the counting of votes. The case arose when the Florida Supreme Court ordered a controversial recount of ballots for which voting machines had registered no presidential choice, but gave almost no guidance to vote counters. All the court said was that counters should attempt to discern "the intent of the voter." According to the Supreme Court of the United States, a recount conducted with no further direction would have violated the "fundamental" right of Florida voters to have their votes valued equally: "[T]he standards for accepting or rejecting contested ballots might vary not only from county to county but indeed within a single county from one recount team to another."[15]

In issuing its ruling in *Bush v. Gore*, the Supreme Court majority paid no heed to historic practices involving the counting and recounting of ballots. Before the advent of voting machines, all ballots had been counted by hand, often with no more direction than the Florida Supreme Court had given. Nor did the Supreme Court's ruling in *Bush v. Gore* specifically indicate that a state would deny equal protection if, for example, it used more and less accurate voting machines in different parts of the state. Instead the Court said this: "Our consideration is limited to the present" facts involving "the special instance of a statewide recount under the authority of a single state judicial officer" who had the authority to prescribe uniform vote-counting standards but had failed to do so.[16]

The Supreme Court's *per curiam* opinion in *Bush v. Gore* had no identified author. As noted in the Prologue, however, the four Justices generally counted the most liberal all dissented from the outcome in whole or in part. Justices Stevens, Ginsburg, and Breyer wrote or joined opinions flatly denying that an equal protection violation had occurred.[17] Justice David Souter agreed with them in protesting that even if a constitutional problem existed, the Florida Supreme Court should be given a chance to fix it, by issuing clearer vote-counting instructions, rather than having the recount simply halted in its tracks. The five most conservative Justices made up the majority. In other cases under the Equal Protection Clause, the conservatives are those who are usually least likely to find rights violations (except in cases challenging affirmative action). Several members of the conservative majority frequently insist that the Court has no authority to condemn practices that were historically accepted as constitutional – a principle that they ignored in *Bush v. Gore*.

For now, the implications of *Bush v. Gore* remain unclear. Perhaps the decision will usher in a new era of searching equal protection review of electoral practices. If so, it might force states to provide equally good and accurate voting machines in all precincts, so that all voters have an equal chance of having their votes registered correctly.

In many states, there now tends to be better technology in wealthier than in poorer communities, and thus a greater likelihood that the rich will get their votes counted accurately than will the poor.

Alternatively, *Bush v. Gore* may prove comparable to "a restricted railroad ticket, good for this day and train only."[18] The majority Justices may have felt that extraordinary features of the situation justified extraordinary action, unlikely to be called for again. They may have believed that a partisan Florida Supreme Court dominated by Democrats was trying to steal an election that Bush had fairly won, or that a recount under the glare of partisan pressures and a national media spotlight would surely prove unfair, or that continued uncertainty about the election's outcome risked a national crisis that the Court needed to resolve decisively.[19] If so, the rule of *Bush v. Gore* may reach no further than the case's facts.

If the implications of *Bush v. Gore* remain unclear, the wisdom of the Court's decision is just as debatable. Some believe that the Justices in the majority not only supplied cool and disinterested judgment, but also saved the nation from dangerous confusion that could have resulted from continued uncertainty about the election's outcome. Others maintain that the Justices either descended into rank partisanship or at least lost their bearings in resolving what Justice Oliver Wendell Holmes would have called a "great case." "For great cases are called great," Holmes wrote, "not by reason of their real importance in shaping the law of the future, but because of some accident of immediate overwhelming interest which appeals to the feelings and distorts the judgment."[20] We may still stand too close to *Bush v. Gore* for anyone to judge disinterestedly.

Ballot Access

Closely bound up with voting rights in the structuring of political democracy under the Constitution are questions involving the rights of candidates and parties to get onto the ballot. Many of these questions arise from the party system, which grew up despite the hopes of the founding generation. The states rely heavily on political parties to decide which candidates can appear on the ballot, typically by holding so-called primary elections. Republican and Democratic candidates invariably qualify, but what if states impose deliberate obstacles for other parties or independent candidates? What rights do they have to be listed on election ballots?

The Supreme Court's cases yield no sharp answer to these questions. Recently the Court appears to have used a "balancing" test. State interests in restricting ballot access include avoiding voter confusion, ensuring the election of a candidate with majority support, and preserving the stability of the political system. Weighing on the other side are the equal protection and due process interests of disadvantaged parties and candidates, as well as the interest of voters in being able to vote for whomever they wish and First Amendment freedoms of voters and candidates to "associate" with each other on the terms that they choose. Within this framework, states may insist that parties and candidates seeking access to the ballot demonstrate a "significant, measurable quantum of community support," but they cannot impose unreasonable requirements on small or freshly emerging parties. *Munro v. Socialist Workers Party*[21] (1986) upheld a state law allowing minor party candidates onto the general election ballot only if they got at least one percent of the total votes cast in the primary elections for the offices that they sought. By contrast, *Williams v. Rhodes*[22] (1968) struck down a statute that kept minor party candidates off the ballot unless they filed petitions signed by a number of qualified voters equaling fifteen percent of the votes in the previous gubernatorial election.

Other questions arise when the states try to regulate participation in party primaries. For the most part, the Supreme Court has held that the parties have a right to decide for themselves who can vote in their primaries, with the signal exception being that they may not discriminate on the basis of race.[23] Perhaps the most important of the recent decisions, *California Democratic Party v. Jones*[24] (2000), invalidated a state law attempting to create a "blanket primary" in which citizens would have been able to vote for any candidate for any office, regardless of party affiliation. The California Democratic Party objected to the law, which would have let Republicans help to choose Democratic candidates, and the Supreme Court sustained the challenge. Writing for the Court, Justice Antonin Scalia held the blanket primary law to be an impermissible interference with the parties' First Amendment rights to expressive association and nonassociation. He found it unacceptable that one party might have its nominee "determined by adherents of an opposing party" who chose to "cross over" just for the primary.

Campaign Speech and Finance Regulation

Both before and after candidates get on the ballot, they campaign for office. In the modern world, money is the mother's milk of campaign politics. Running an effective campaign requires organization, mailing and phone lists, telephone banks, and paid advertising, often in expensive media. But if money is the mother's milk of election campaigns, it can also distort and corrupt the broader political process of which elections form only a part. In the crudest example of corruption, moneyed interests can trade cash with dishonest politicians for specific, expressly requested political favors. Even in the absence of formal bargains, big donors buy access to politicians, and access often translates into influence. Even when money and access do not buy influence, they may appear to do so and thereby sap faith in the American political system.

Against the background of concerns such as these, congressional efforts to regulate money in politics have unfolded in three principal stages. The first came in 1907. Enacted against the background of crude and notorious attempts by big-moneyed interests to bribe politicians, the Federal Corrupt Practices Act, which still remains in force, makes it a crime for corporations to give money directly to political candidates.

The second regulatory stage began in the 1970s. In the wake of scandals surrounding shakedown fundraising by Richard Nixon's 1972 presidential reelection campaign, Congress enacted the Federal Election Campaign Act (FECA) Amendments. As amended, the FECA imposed two main types of restrictions on the financing of political campaigns. First, it limited the amounts of money that groups and individuals could *contribute* to candidates and their campaign committees. In other words, it restricted outright gifts of money. Second, the legislation regulated the amount of money that candidates, groups, and other individuals could directly *expend* to influence the outcome of political campaigns. In other words, it limited the freedom that groups and individuals, including candidates for office, would otherwise have had to spend their money directly on such things as political advertisements.

Opponents of the amended FECA argued strenuously that both its contribution limits and its expenditure limits violated the First Amendment. Even opponents readily acknowledged that Congress could prohibit outright bribes and explicit trades of money for political favors. They maintained, however, that the FECA Amendments went much further by attempting to limit the influence that wealthy groups and individuals could achieve by using their money to persuade voters – through advertisements, for example – to adopt their preferred points of view. According to the FECA's critics, the First Amendment forbids governmental efforts to limit speech about politics, including political advertising, based on a fear that listeners may be persuaded by it. On the other side, FECA's defenders argued that the legislation restricted the use of money, not speech itself, and that it was unfair for those with great wealth to be able to use their money to purchase political influence, even in the absence of express trades of money for votes or other favors.

In the face of these competing arguments, the Supreme Court essentially split the difference in its 1976 decision in *Buckley v. Valeo*,[25] a case that established the basic framework for the regulation of campaign finance that persisted for the next quarter-century. *Buckley* attached enormous constitutional significance to the distinction between *contributions*, or gifts of money to candidates and their campaign committees, and *expenditures*, or the direct use of money to influence the outcome of political campaigns through, for example, the purchase of political advertising. *Buckley* upheld the FECA's principal *contribution* limits. According to *Buckley*, contributions of money to candidates and campaign committees are not themselves speech, even if their purpose is to permit the generation of speech. In addition, the Court thought that limits on direct gifts of money to candidates and campaign committees were closely tailored to prevent corruption and the appearance of corruption. By contrast, the Court invalidated limits on *expenditures* of money on campaigns and campaign advertising. If a group or individual engages in direct spending to advocate the election of a candidate – for example, by placing an advertisement in a newspaper, rather than by giving money to the candidate so that the candidate can buy advertising – the expenditures constitute protected speech, the Court held. Having equated expenditures with speech, the Court rejected the notion that some speakers could be silenced lest they achieve too much influence: Under the First Amendment, the voters should decide for themselves whom and what to believe.

Whatever might be said for *Buckley*'s difference-splitting approach as a matter of constitutional principle, its effects in practice pleased no one. In the years following the Court's decision, the political system continued to be awash in money, with more being given and spent in each election cycle than in the one that preceded it. With seemingly boundless imagination, candidates and political parties exploited loopholes that permitted money to be poured into political campaigns without triggering the FECA's contribution limits – perhaps most notably by funneling contributions through political parties, many contributions to which the FECA had not attempted to regulate. In addition, groups and individuals who were blocked from "contributing" large sums to political campaigns began to use their money instead to make constitutionally protected "expenditures," often by running supposedly independent "attack" ads targeting candidates whom they wished to defeat. With large sums flowing into politics anyway, some continued to believe that all or nearly all restrictions on campaign contributions should be invalidated as an attempt to interfere with the generation of political speech. Others, who thought that moneyed interests exerted far too much influence over American politics, demanded that Congress try again to impose more effective restrictions on campaign financing.

In the political arena, those who sought to reduce the influence of money on elections gradually gained the upper hand. Spurred by the crusading efforts of Senators John McCain and Russell

Feingold, Congress ushered in the third major stage in federal efforts to regulate campaign finance by passing the Bipartisan Campaign Reform Act (BCRA) in 2002. The BCRA includes two elements of particular importance, both designed to plug perceived loopholes in the prior scheme of regulations. First, it stops the flow of so-called soft or unregulated money to political parties by providing that no one may give a party more than $25,000 per year. In the 2000 election cycle, the staggering sum of $1.2 billion had flowed to the Republican and Democratic parties, much of it in the form of then unregulated gifts from exceptionally wealthy donors, more than 800 of whom gave more than $120,000 apiece. Second, the BCRA attempts to limit corporate and union influence on elections by forbidding corporations and labor unions to run ads that refer by name to a candidate for federal office within sixty days of a primary or general election.

Nearly as soon as it was enacted, the BCRA was challenged in court, but it survived nearly unscathed in *McConnell v. Federal Election Commission*[26] (2003). As is often the case, Justice Sandra Day O'Connor – the only sitting Justice ever to have held elective office (as a member of the Arizona legislature) – cast the decisive vote. With the Court's four most conservative Justices voting to strike down the BCRA's central provisions and with the four more liberal Justices solidly supporting the law, Justice O'Connor coauthored (along with Justice John Stevens) the Court opinion ruling that large donations to political parties present risks of corruption or the appearance of corruption and are therefore subject to regulation without offense to the First Amendment. "[T]he manner in which parties have sold access to federal candidates and officeholders...has given rise to the appearance of undue influence," the Court said,[27] and Congress was entitled to regulate to protect the integrity of American democracy. The five majority Justices reached a similar conclusion about corporate and union *expenditures* on political advertising within sixty days of an election. It was permissible, the Court said, for Congress to enact "legislation aimed at 'the corrosive and distorting effects of immense aggregations of wealth that are accumulated with the help of the corporate form and that have little or no correlation to the public's support for the corporation's political ideas.'"[28] To no avail, the dissenting Justices protested that the majority stretched the notion of "corruption" beyond recognition by holding that corporations and unions somehow "corrupt" the political process when they do no more than purchase advertisements trying to persuade voters to adopt their points of view.

Although *McConnell v. Federal Election Commission* represented a great *legal* victory for the champions of campaign finance reform, the *practical* effects of the BCRA remain to be seen. As the Supreme Court frankly acknowledged in the last paragraph of its opinion, money in the contested field of American politics may be like water in the ground that "will always find an outlet."[29] "What problems will arise, and how Congress will respond, are problems for another day," the Court wrote.[30] For now, however, the limitations established by the BCRA are the law of the land, and if big money finds other avenues to influence the outcome of election campaigns, five Justices have signaled that they will look sympathetically at future regulatory efforts by Congress.

Conclusion

At the end of the day, constitutional doctrines dealing with elections are a bit of a hodgepodge. The Constitution mandates that elections occur, but it provides little in the way of regulatory framework, and it manifests no clear, overarching theory in light of which to judge the constitutionality of regulatory legislation enacted by Congress and the state legislatures. In the absence of a guiding theory, the Supreme Court has established a number of relatively ad hoc rules governing voting arrangements, ballot access, and restrictions on campaign finance. In the main, however, it has given Congress and the state legislatures a relatively free hand to design voting districts, to establish rules governing parties' and candidates' rights to appear on the ballot, and even to regulate the financing of campaigns. Whether its course be wise or otherwise, the Court seems far less committed to pursuing a vision of what democracy ought to be than to stemming a few discrete practices by Congress and the state legislatures that it believes no sound theory of political democracy could sensibly tolerate.

ELEVEN

Structural Limits on State Power and Resulting Individual Rights

[The] principle that our economic unit is the Nation, which alone has the gamut of powers necessary to control of the economy . . . , has as its corollary that the states are not separable economic units. . . . [A] state may not use its admitted powers to protect the health and safety of its people as a basis for suppressing competition.

– Justice Robert H. Jackson[1]

TO RAISE REVENUE AND PERHAPS ALSO to discourage people from leaving its borders, Nevada, back in the 1860s, imposed a tax of one dollar on stagecoach and railway tickets for out-of-state destinations. In *Crandall v. Nevada*[2] (1867), the Supreme Court held that the tax was unconstitutional. In ruling as it did, the Court did not point to the language of any particular constitutional provision. None refers expressly to a right to travel from one state to another, much less to a right to travel without being taxed. Instead, the Court found the right to travel among the states, and a prohibition against state legislation penalizing the exercise of that right, to be implicit in the general structure of the Constitution and in the concepts of nationhood and national citizenship.

From a modern perspective, *Crandall v. Nevada* illustrates two important features of American constitutional law. First, just as existence of the states imposes implied limits on Congress's regulatory powers – a matter discussed in Chapter Seven – so the existence of the federal government and the idea of unitary nationhood impliedly restrict the power of the states. Second, the resulting limits, which might be described as arising from the Constitution's structure, in effect give rise to individual rights against the states (such as the right recognized in *Crandall* not to be taxed or otherwise penalized by the government for traveling from one state to another).

How Federal Power and Federal Law Can Restrict State Power

Limits on the powers of the states flow from a number of constitutional sources besides the expressly rights-conferring provisions discussed in Chapters One through Six. In assigning power to the federal government, the Constitution sometimes explicitly forbids the states to exercise parallel authority. For example, after authorizing Congress to "coin Money" in Article I, Section 8, the Constitution provides separately in Article I, Section 10 that no state shall coin money. After empowering Congress to declare war,[3] Article I again includes a separate provision that "[n]o State shall, without the Consent of Congress,...engage in War, unless actually invaded, or in such imminent Danger as will not admit of delay."[4] When the Constitution empowers the federal government but does not expressly disempower the states, harder interpretive questions arise. As a matter of common sense, the congressional power to levy taxes does not impliedly stop the states from collecting taxes also. Without tax revenues, states could not function. By contrast, the Supreme Court has held that Congress's power to regulate foreign commerce implicitly imposes significant restraints on state regulatory authority.[5] It would be unacceptable for state law to interfere with federal management of the foreign relations of the United States.

Federal statutes, as well as federal constitutional provisions, can override, nullify, or, as lawyers say, "preempt" state law. This effect occurs through the Supremacy Clause of Article VI, which provides that "this Constitution and the Laws of the United States which shall be made in Pursuance thereof...shall be the supreme Law of the Land..., any Thing in the Constitution or Laws of any State to the Contrary notwithstanding." There are two kinds of statutory preemption. *Express preemption* occurs when a federal statute says in so many words that federal regulation is intended to be exclusive. *Implied preemption* happens when, even though a federal statute says nothing about preemption, enforcement of a state law would conflict with a federal law.

An example may illustrate how preemption works in practice. In 1965, Congress enacted a law requiring cigarette manufacturers to put specific warning labels on their packages as well as in their advertisements. The federal law did not, however, say anything about when, if ever, smokers might be able to sue tobacco companies for harms caused by their products. Some years later, a former smoker who was a lung cancer victim sued a cigarette manufacturer in a New Jersey court, claiming an entitlement to damages under New Jersey law. The victim argued in part that New Jersey law required cigarette manufacturers to give fuller disclosures about the dangers of smoking than the federally prescribed warnings provided. When the case came to the Supreme Court, the question was whether Congress, in enacting the federal statute, had meant only to establish a minimum warning that must be given to smokers, or whether it also intended the federally mandated warning to be the maximum that cigarette manufacturers could be required to provide and thus to "preempt" laws, such as New Jersey's, that required fuller warnings. As a matter of constitutional law, no one doubted Congress's power to preempt state law if it wished to do so; the question was solely one of congressional intent, involving whether Congress meant to displace state law or whether state law was incompatible with the aims of the federal statute. On the facts of the case, *Cippolone v. Liggett Group, Inc.*[6] (1992), a divided Court held that the federal statute preempted state law that would have allowed suit and recovery based on a failure to provide further warnings about the dangers of smoking, but not state law permitting suit for affirmative misrepresentations by cigarette manufacturers about the safety of their product.

The Privileges and Immunities Clause

In the early 1970s, Alaska suffered an unemployment problem. Although the state's oil industry was thriving, many of the best jobs went to workers newly arrived from out of state, some of whom had no interest in making Alaska their permanent home. In an effort to improve the lot of Alaskans, the state legislature enacted a statute, dubbed "Alaska Hire," requiring that Alaska residents be given a hiring preference over visiting out-of-staters for all jobs "resulting from" oil and gas leases or pipeline projects to which the state was a party. The Supreme Court invalidated Alaska Hire by a unanimous vote.

The Court's ruling in *Hicklin v. Orbeck*[7] (1978) rested on Article IV's Privileges and Immunities Clause, which provides that "[t]he Citizens of each State shall be entitled to all Privileges and Immunities of Citizens in the several States." Although its language is slightly archaic, the Privileges and Immunities Clause establishes an antidiscrimination rule: Whatever privileges and immunities a state chooses to grant to its own citizens, it must at least presumptively grant to out-of-staters visiting the state. As an express constitutional provision, the Privileges and Immunities Clause has distinctive language and a distinctive history, both of which have informed its application. But the Privileges and Immunities Clause also reflects values or suppositions that are implicit in the Constitution's structure and that extend both further and deeper than its specific language. In *Hicklin v. Orbeck*, the Court held in substance that the state's interest in being able to mandate preferences for its own citizens must yield to the national interest in maintaining equal employment opportunities in an open national economy. Under a national Constitution, state interests had to take second place to national interests.

Obviously, however, there is another side of the coin, as was acutely visible to the Alaska legislature. Although the United States exists as a single nation, states also have a separate existence, and it is part of their function distinctively to help their own citizens. Surely Alaska can enact welfare programs under which it makes payments to Alaska citizens and only to Alaska citizens. Surely the state can give Alaska residents preferences in admissions to the state university, and it can charge lower tuition to in-staters than to out-of-staters. Surely, in other words, there must be some balance of state interests and national interests. The Constitution must forbid some kinds of state actions and discriminations against out-of-staters, because they would be incompatible with nationhood and national citizenship, but it must permit others, because without them statehood and state citizenship would be meaningless. *Hicklin v. Orbeck* put Alaska Hire on the wrong side of a constitutional line. But where exactly is that line? Although the Supreme Court has not responded as clearly as one might wish to that fundamental constitutional question, at least the outlines of an answer emerge from the Court's decisions.

In applying Article IV's Privileges and Immunities Clause in cases such as *Hicklin v. Orbeck*, the Supreme Court has prescribed two sorts of inquiries. The first aims to distinguish the "privileges and immunities of citizens" from other opportunities or benefits. To make this distinction, the Court has adopted a largely historical test, equating "the privileges and immunities of citizens" with those rights that were historically deemed "fundamental" or understood to "belong...to the citizens of all free governments."[8] This historically based test for fundamental rights under the Privileges and Immunities Clause can easily create confusion, because it is *different* from the not always historical tests used to identify "fundamental rights" under the Due Process and Equal Protection Clauses (as discussed in Chapter Six). As a result, a right may be deemed fundamental for purposes of the Privileges and Immunities Clause, but not for the Due Process or Equal Protection Clause, or vice versa. But under the *historical* test used to identify fundamental and nonfundamental rights under the Privileges and Immunities Clause, states can prefer their own citizens when distributing nonfundamental rights. In the leading case of *Baldwin v. Fish and Game Commission*,[9] the Court thus held that a state could charge out-of-staters more than in-staters for elk-hunting licenses because the opportunity to hunt elk was not a historically fundamental right.

The "right" to hunt elk may seem trivial. Other members of the nonfundamental category are more important. Under a historical test, it appears that rights to welfare and education – which I previously suggested that states must be able to provide to their own citizens on a preferential basis – would fall into the nonfundamental category. However important they might be today, they would apparently not have been regarded as fundamental in the eighteenth and early nineteenth centuries.

The second judicial inquiry under the Privileges and Immunities Clause occurs when states attempt to prefer their own citizens in matters involving the recognized "privileges and immunities of citizenship," prominent among which, for historical reasons, is the right (involved in *Hicklin v. Orbeck*) to pursue a lawful trade. Significantly, the Supreme Court has not held that the Privileges and Immunities Clause forbids all discriminations between citizens and noncitizens even when they involve historically fundamental rights. It has said only that such discriminations are presumptively unconstitutional and can be upheld only if the state demonstrates a valid, legitimate, or substantial justification for treating out-of-staters less favorably than in-staters.

In applying this aspect of its test, the Supreme Court has consistently invalidated state laws that flatly forbid out-of-staters from working or seeking jobs in the private sector or that subject them to discriminatory taxes or regulations, as in *Hicklin v. Orbeck*. The Court has distinguished, however, between state laws that impose discriminatory taxes and prohibitions, which it virtually never permits, and those that authorize the distribution of jobs *either as government employees or on projects paid for by the government out of tax revenues*. With respect to the latter, the Court has suggested that a city or state might have "substantial," and thus constitutionally adequate, reasons to prefer its own citizens to out-of-staters.[10]

The justification for this distinction presumably lies in the need to create sensible incentives for state and local governments that, after all, are political communities with a special responsibility to their own citizens. By permitting states to grant hiring preferences to their own citizens when they are spending public funds, the Supreme Court provides an incentive for states to make expenditures that they might not make otherwise. If such preferences were not permitted, then states would be much less likely to fund a variety of beneficial programs – a sad if not disastrous consequence from the perspective of both public policy and constitutional law.

Within the Supreme Court's framework for analyzing claims under the Privileges and Immunities Clause, the hiring preferences mandated by Alaska Hire went too far. The state could have preferred

Alaskans in hiring workers for jobs with the state itself, but it could not force private employers to prefer Alaskans for all jobs "resulting from" leases and projects to which the state was a party.

The "Dormant" Commerce Clause

Apart from the Privileges and Immunities Clause, which guarantees rights of citizenship, it has long been assumed that the Constitution's Commerce Clause – although framed as a grant of power to Congress to regulate interstate commerce – implicitly restricts the states' ability to impose commercial regulations that interfere with interstate commerce. This is an important assumption. It is often tempting for states to try to promote the welfare of their own citizens by discriminating against out-of-state businesses (corporations cannot claim the protection of the Privileges and Immunities Clause) or against goods produced out-of-state. A historically familiar example involves the dairy industry. For decades, the number of dairy farms has been shrinking, especially in the northeastern states, as large milk producers, many from the midwest, have been able to undersell their competition. Rather than watch the collapse of their domestic dairy industries, a number of states have enacted "protectionist" measures aimed at shielding in-state farmers from competition with out-of-staters. Sometimes the protective efforts have taken the form of discriminatory taxes on milk imported from out of state. In other instances, states have imposed minimum price requirements on the sale of milk by farmers to wholesale distributors – forbidding the sale of milk at cheap prices, regardless of where it is produced – to protect in-state farmers by making it impossible for their out-of-state competitors to undersell them. (Even if out-of-state farmers can produce milk more cheaply than in-state farmers, minimum price laws stop them from selling it at cheaper prices, and their competitive advantage is thereby destroyed.)

If Congress wished to do so, its Article I commerce power would permit it to displace or preempt state legislation that makes it harder for out-of-staters to sell their goods. But it would be difficult to craft such legislation in general terms. For example, Congress could not sensibly bar all state legislation that tends to diminish the flow of goods in interstate commerce. State laws as sensible as those forbidding the sale and use of dangerous products – firecrackers, for example – diminish interstate commerce in the regulated products. In theory, Congress could also monitor the enactment of state legislation affecting commerce and displace only those specific laws of which it disapproved. As a practical matter, however, the sheer volume of state lawmaking would make it difficult, if not impossible, for Congress to do so effectively.

Believing that Congress could not realistically oversee all state regulations of commerce and displace those that it found objectionable, the Supreme Court has stepped into the perceived breach by holding that the Commerce Clause impliedly creates presumptive, judicially enforceable limits on state legislation. The resulting body of doctrine is often called "dormant Commerce Clause doctrine," to signify that Congress's regulatory power is dormant, or unexercised. Under this doctrine, the courts determine which state enactments should be deemed invalid because of their effects on interstate commerce. If, however, Congress disagrees with a judicial judgment, it retains its authority to regulate commerce by specifically authorizing a state regulation that the courts have found objectionable.[11]

Under dormant Commerce Clause doctrine, state tax and regulatory statutes that expressly discriminate against goods from other states – for example, by subjecting them to taxes or other regulations to which goods produced in-state are not subjected – are nearly always invalid. The Supreme Court pronounces repeatedly that the Commerce Clause forbids "economic protectionism – that is, regulatory measures designed to benefit in-state economic interests by burdening out-of-state competitors."[12] As the Court said in *Baldwin v. G.A.F. Seelig, Inc.*[13] (1935), a case involving efforts by the state of New York to prop up its dairy industry, if one state, "in order to promote the economic welfare of her farmers, may guard them against competition with the cheaper prices of [farmers in other states], the door has been opened to rivalries and reprisals that were meant to be averted by subjecting commerce between the states to the power of the nation." For a tax or regulatory statute that discriminates against interstate commerce to be upheld, a state must demonstrate that the discrimination is made necessary by a valid and compelling consideration unrelated to economic "protectionism" – for example, by showing that goods shipped in interstate commerce risk spreading a contagion that cannot be effectively contained except by exclusion.[14] A state engages in forbidden "protectionism," as the Supreme Court uses that term, when it tries to protect its citizens or industries from fair economic competition, but not when it tries to protect against hazards such as disease that are unrelated to fair competition.

When a state law does not expressly discriminate against goods or firms from other states, but has an "incidental" effect on the flow of interstate commerce – for example, by forbidding the sale of firecrackers that can be lawfully manufactured and sold in other states – the Supreme Court regularly says that it will determine on a case-by-case basis whether the local benefits are great enough to justify the negative impact on interstate commerce.[15] Virtually never, however, does the Court invalidate a state regulatory statute under the Commerce Clause unless that statute has the *effect* of advantaging in-state economic interests over their out-of-state competitors. Thus, if a state were to ban the sale of all firecrackers, the statute would almost surely be upheld against a challenge under the Commerce Clause, even though fewer firecrackers would be sold in interstate commerce as a result. By contrast, if a state were to ban the sale of some firecrackers but not others, and if it happened that the permitted firecrackers were predominantly manufactured in the state and that the prohibited firecrackers were predominantly manufactured out-of-state, judicial review would be much more searching, aimed at "smoking out" a hidden attempt to advantage the in-state manufacturer in economic competition with out-of-state competitors.

Surveying the obvious pattern of the Supreme Court's cases, which tend to invalidate statutes under the dormant Commerce Clause only when they help in-state economic interests in competition with out-of-staters, Professor Donald Regan has surmised that "protectionism" is all that the Court really cares about.[16] To explain the pretense that the Court "balances" in-state benefits against harms to the flow of interstate commerce, Regan speculates that the Court hesitates to accuse state legislatures of constitutionally forbidden discrimination against out-of-staters; it therefore pretends to balance competing state and national interests, but in fact invalidates state legislation only when it strongly suspects that a state is really trying to protect its own citizens from fair economic competition. The Court may also prefer to preserve its options lest a case come along in which a state law, though not intentionally protectionist, has hugely adverse effects on interstate commerce and achieves virtually no local benefit. In any event, if a state regulatory statute does not advantage state residents at the expense of out-of-state competitors, it is almost certain to survive judicial challenge under the dormant commerce clause.

The States as "Market Participants"

Like the Privileges and Immunities Clause, dormant Commerce Clause doctrine that forbids states to prefer or protect their own citizens raises a fundamental question about the states' role under the Constitution and about the meaning of state citizenship: Once again, aren't states *supposed* to try to advance the interests of their citizens, sometimes in preference to those of outsiders? In response to that question, the doctrinal structure under the dormant Commerce Clause, like that under the Privileges and Immunities Clause, generally prohibits the states from trying to aid their citizens by subjecting out-of-staters to discriminatory regulations and taxes, but permits the states to favor their own citizens when buying or selling goods or services. Under the so-called "market participant exception" to dormant Commerce Clause doctrine, a state that engages in economic activity can hire its citizens on a preferential basis, and it can similarly grant preferences to its own citizens as purchasers of goods sold by the state.

In *Reeves, Inc. v. Stake*[17] (1980), involving a challenge to the practice of a state-owned cement plant in selling cement to in-state customers on a preferential basis, the Court attempted to rationalize the "market participant" exception to dormant Commerce Clause doctrine. *Reeves* intimated that when a state enters the market, it does not act in a sovereign or governmental capacity, and that norms applicable to the state-as-sovereign therefore do not apply. This suggestion will not withstand analysis. A state remains a state, and thus subject to constitutional limits, as much in the market as in any other context. No one contends that a state should be able to discriminate on the basis of race or religion when buying or selling goods. On the contrary, it is *because* the state remains a state that it should be able to prefer its citizens when buying goods and services and when selling or dispensing other goods. As noted earlier, it is the function of states, as political communities, to attempt to benefit their citizens, sometimes in preference to noncitizens. For a variety of sound reasons involving national union and national citizenship, states cannot attempt to protect their citizens by imposing discriminatory taxes that would be likely to cause resentment and trigger retaliation by other states. But states can and should be encouraged to create goods – such as educational opportunities, public housing, and welfare benefits – that would not otherwise exist. In order for states to have an incentive to do so, they are reasonably permitted to prefer their own citizens when they buy, sell, or distribute such goods and opportunities.

Traditionally, states have also been permitted to provide economic subsidies to domestic industries.[18] The line between a discriminatory tax against out-of-staters and a subsidy for domestic industries can often be a fine one – a point that has recently troubled the Court and might possibly trigger a doctrinal rethinking.[19] By tradition, however, a state that has permissibly accumulated revenues through taxes on its own citizens is permitted to prefer its own citizens when making voluntary expenditures.

Conclusion

As I noted at the outset of this chapter, if the concept of unitary nationhood makes it impermissible for the states to favor their own citizens by enacting laws that discriminate against out-of-staters, it effectively creates rights in out-of-staters to be free from discrimination. But not all state discriminations against out-of-staters are forbidden. If they were, the states could not fulfill some of their most basic functions. The doctrine distinguishing permissible from impermissible discriminations is sometimes murky, but its basic aim is crystal clear. Constitutional law must permit an accommodation between the ideal of unitary nationhood and national citizenship on the one hand and the concept of meaningful statehood and state citizenship on the other.

TWELVE

The Constitution in War and Emergency

[While] the Constitution protects against invasions of individual rights, it is not a suicide pact.

          – *Kennedy v. Mendoza-Martinez* (1963)[1]

War is hell.

          – General William Tecumseh Sherman

ON APRIL 12, 1861, CONFEDERATE MILITARY FORCES FIRED on Fort Sumter and within a few days forced the surrender of Union soldiers stationed there. Confronted with the gravest crisis in American history, President Abraham Lincoln knew that he must convene the Congress of the United States. But Congress was large, even then, and opinionated and divided. Lincoln therefore thought that he could manage the crisis better alone. So he called Congress into session but postponed the meeting date until July 4.[2]

In the period between April 12 and July 4, Lincoln ordered a blockade of southern ports – a step almost universally regarded as an act of war. Article I of the Constitution assigns the power "[t]o declare War" to Congress, which had not yet convened.[3] Also before July 4, Lincoln called for volunteers for the army and ordered fifteen ships added to the navy, even though the Constitution specifically gives Congress, not the President, the powers to "raise and support Armies" and to "provide and maintain a Navy."[4] Doubting the loyalty of officials in the Treasury and War Departments, Lincoln directed the Secretary of the Treasury to transfer $2 million in federal funds to three private citizens charged by him to make requisitions "for the defence and support of the government"[5] – notwithstanding the constitutional provision that "[n]o Money shall be drawn from the Treasury, but in Consequence of Appropriations made by Law."[6]

In a further response to secessionist activity, Lincoln, in the language of the Constitution, either suspended or authorized suspension of "the Privilege of the Writ of Habeas Corpus" in selected regions of the country. Technically, this step barred courts from examining the legality of arrests of civilians by military officials. As a practical matter, it permitted military leaders to lay down rules binding on civilians as well as on military personnel and to imprison those believed to be engaged in disloyal activities. Although the Constitution specifically provides for suspension of the writ of habeas corpus "when in Cases of Rebellion or Invasion the public Safety may require it," it does so in Article I, which lists the powers of Congress, not in Article II, which deals with the powers of the President.[7]

Did Lincoln violate the Constitution? Should we care?[8] Did his ends – preservation of the Union and ultimately the extinction of slavery – justify his chosen means? Does the Constitution confer unlimited powers on the government and its officials in times of war and possibly other emergency?

These are timeless questions that historians, lawyers, and concerned citizens continue to debate.[9] For his own part, Lincoln, who was a lawyer, took pains to offer constitutional defenses for nearly every step that he took. In addition, when Congress finally convened, it voted legislation declaring Lincoln's actions "respecting the army and navy of the United States" to be "hereby approved and in all respects legalized and made valid."[10] A few years later, the Supreme Court held that Lincoln also had constitutional authority to order a blockade of southern ports.[11] For all practical purposes, the Court said, the nation was at war, even if no war had formally been declared, and in wartime the decision to order a blockade comes within the President's power as Commander-in-Chief.

Only with respect to the suspension of habeas corpus and resulting assaults on individual liberties did either Congress or the judiciary show much resistance. After Lincoln had suspended the writ of habeas corpus, Union military officials arrested a suspected Confederate sympathizer named John Merryman. Merryman's lawyer went to the Chief Justice of the United States, Roger Taney, and sought "the Writ of Habeas Corpus" to which the Constitution refers – an order directing Merryman's jailer to come to court, bringing Merryman with him, and either justify the imprisonment as a matter of law or release the prisoner. Taney issued the writ. In an opinion explaining his decision, he acknowledged that the President had tried to suspend "the privilege of the writ of habeas corpus" and thereby stop the courts from protecting civil liberties. But Taney ruled that the President had no power to do so: The Constitution gives the power to suspend the writ of habeas corpus to Congress, not to the President.[12]

Lincoln refused to yield. He ordered his military officers to ignore Taney's ruling, and the officers obeyed the President, not the Chief Justice. Merryman thus remained under military arrest. Meanwhile, Lincoln prepared and published a constitutional defense of his actions: The Constitution did not say in so many words that only Congress, not the President, could suspend the writ of habeas corpus. In wartime, with Congress not in session, Lincoln argued that the President could lawfully exercise the power in his capacity as Commander-in-Chief.[13]

Lincoln's argument provides an important perspective on the complex interconnection between constitutional argument and more broadly political argument. Sometimes "political" concerns and values influence the courts. In Lincoln's case, the political tenability of his position depended at least in part on his ability to make a constitutional argument. The American people care about the Constitution. It would not have gone down well, even in wartime, for Lincoln to claim an entitlement to flout the Constitution. Having lost in court, Lincoln made his constitutional case to Congress and the American people. When the President and the courts differ in their interpretations of the Constitution, the American people ordinarily think the President should accept the courts' judgment. In wartime, the situation may sometimes be different. Lincoln's political stature did not suffer much from his defiance of a judicial order in *Ex parte Merryman*, nor has his historical reputation. (Along with George Washington, he is nearly always rated one of the two greatest Presidents.)

Although distinctive in some ways, in others Lincoln's argument that the Constitution is a flexible instrument sounded very much in the tradition of John Marshall, the great Chief Justice, who had emphasized that the Constitution was designed to be adaptable to "crises of human affairs" and should be construed accordingly.[14] This has been the dominant tradition of American constitutional interpretation. I have emphasized that tradition and lauded it throughout this book. Flexibility, I have suggested, is a great virtue, and our Constitution has served so well precisely because it is, and has been interpreted to be, so flexible.

But if flexibility is a virtue, it is sometimes a risky one, because a constitution that is completely flexible is also a constitution that imposes no hard, intractable restraints on governmental power and no hard, unyielding guarantees of individual rights. Especially in time of war and emergency, the Constitution frequently does more to provide a framework for arguments than it does to resolve them. Nor, again, are wartime arguments about constitutional law always addressed exclusively, or even principally, to the courts.

In the remainder of this chapter, I briefly summarize constitutional doctrines and history involving the scope of presidential and congressional power in war and related emergencies. I then consider individual rights in war and emergency before discussing, without pretending to resolve, a few issues arising from the current so-called war on terrorism.

The Power to Initiate War

Throughout American history, Presidents have claimed authority to send troops into battle or otherwise engage in warlike acts without awaiting a congressional declaration of war. Thomas Jefferson sent ships into the Mediterranean to battle the Barbary Pirates. Lincoln took it upon himself to blockade southern ports and otherwise begin fighting the Civil War. By one count, "[f]rom 1798 to 2000, there were over 200 cases where the President transferred arms or other war material abroad or actually sent troops [into hostile environments], all without Congressional involvement."[15]

Some of the arguments supporting unilateral presidential power to enter military hostilities are pragmatic: American lives and interests would be compromised if the President could not take swift, unhesitating action to protect the national interest against foreign threats. Other arguments now appeal to historical practice. Still others claim that those who wrote and ratified the Constitution intended to permit the President to initiate war-making. Although scholars are divided, some maintain that Congress's power to declare war is a narrow one, which merely triggers the international laws of war,[16] and need not be exercised in order to authorize military action by the United States. On this view, the President can launch military operations unilaterally, subject only to constraints arising from Congress's power to deny funding.

Although the Supreme Court has never specified the scope of unilateral presidential authority to commit troops to battle, Congress reviewed the pattern of executive war-making during the early 1970s, when a Democratic Congress sought to impose modest strictures on the President, then a Republican. Enacted in 1973, the War Powers Resolution[17] provides that whenever the President initiates military action he should notify House and Senate leaders within twenty-four hours and that presidentially directed military actions should cease after not more than sixty days unless authorized by Congress. It is noteworthy that although the Resolution aims to limit presidential power, it expressly contemplates presidential authority to engage in hostile military operations for up to sixty days without congressional approval. It is also noteworthy that the War Powers Resolution passed over the veto of President Richard Nixon, and every subsequent President has echoed Nixon in maintaining that limiting unilateral military initiatives by the President to sixty days violates the Constitution. Apart from pressuring the President to consult with congressional leaders, the Resolution has had little practical effect: Congress has typically acceded, however grudgingly, to presidential leadership in matters of war and peace.

Events surrounding the 1991 Persian Gulf War and the 2003 war in Iraq illustrate how the division of war-making powers between Congress and the President has tended to work. In both cases the

President's representatives initially maintained that he could conduct large-scale military operations without needing congressional approval. Had the President insisted on this position, it is at least highly doubtful that a court would have tried to stop him. The "political question" doctrine (discussed in Chapter Nine) arguably applies;[18] troops in the field should not have to await judicial pronouncement on the lawfulness of military orders.

It bears repeated emphasis, however, that the Constitution is not just a document for the courts, especially in matters of war and peace. Even when the judicial branch sits on the sidelines, the Constitution matters to Congress and the President, not least because it matters to the American people. In the case of both the Gulf War and the war in Iraq, the President ultimately found it politically indefensible to begin a war without first obtaining congressional authorization. When the President sought such authorization, Congress followed determined presidential leadership and went along.

The congressional resolutions authorizing these recent conflicts were not labeled as "declarations of war," but the terminology should not matter. The crucial practical point, as resolved in the court of public opinion, was that the country should not launch a major, long-term military action unless the President and both Houses of Congress were solemnly and publicly committed to it.

Federal Powers During Wartime

Once war or its practical equivalent is underway, the courts have usually responded sympathetically to claims that the government possesses all reasonably necessary powers to make the venture succeed. Because the federal government is one of limited powers, courts must ask first whether some provision of the Constitution authorizes Congress or the President to act at all. Only if that question yields an affirmative answer do claims of constitutional rights come into play. As I discuss shortly, questions of governmental powers and individual rights are not always as sharply separate as this sequential consideration might imply. For now, however, it suffices to recall Justice

Robert Jackson's famous observation in the *Youngstown* case,[19] discussed in Chapter Eight, that when Congress and the President concur that governmental action is necessary, the powers of the national government are at their zenith. Never is this more true than in war and emergency. Indeed, I am not aware of any wartime emergency measure, voted by Congress and signed by the President, that the Supreme Court has ever found to lie beyond national regulatory power. For example, it was during World War II that the Court first upheld congressional power to impose nationwide wage and price controls.[20]

When the President asserts a wartime power to take steps not approved by Congress, matters are potentially more difficult, especially if the presidential action occurs at home, rather than abroad. But when wartime Presidents have claimed power, Congress has usually acquiesced – as, for example, when Congress retroactively approved Lincoln's actions regarding the army and navy during the Civil War. To be sure, there are exceptions to this pattern. In the *Youngstown* case, the Court found that the President lacked the power to take over the nation's steel mills. Overall, the President's authority had probably not diminished from Lincoln's time, but the Court in *Youngstown* concluded that Congress had meant to deny the President the power that he claimed. It did not say so, but it probably also believed (as discussed in Chapter Eight) that the emergency was not great enough to justify an otherwise impermissible presidential action.

War and Individual Rights

As governmental powers expand in wartime, individual rights notoriously suffer. The explanation partly reflects doctrinal or conceptual considerations, which sometimes require courts to take conditions of war and emergency into account. Such conditions matter in different ways for different rights.

First, a few rights may wholly disappear when the nation is at war. The Third Amendment provides that "[n]o Soldier shall, in time of peace be quartered in any house, without the consent of the

Owner," but it makes an exception for wartime. To take another plain example, the right to "the Privilege of the Writ of Habeas Corpus" to test the legality of arrests and detentions can be suspended "when in Cases of Rebellion or Invasion the public Safety may require it."[21] Second, some rights are expressly defined by reference to what is reasonable. For example, the Fourth Amendment does not ban all searches and seizures, but only "unreasonable" ones. Some searches and seizures that would be unreasonable in peace may be reasonable in war and emergency.

Third, in probably the most typical case, even rights ordinarily regarded as "fundamental" may yield when "necessary to promote a compelling governmental interest." This is a telling formulation. It suggests that courts must do something like "balancing" the interests of those claiming constitutional rights against the government's interests or those of the public as a whole.[22] In war and emergency, risks to the public interest may be greater than in other times, and they may appear even greater than they are.

Among America's wars, the Civil War was probably the worst for individual rights.[23] First without and later with congressional authorization, Lincoln oversaw the suspension of habeas corpus throughout much of the nation and empowered Union generals to impose martial law – effectively to rule by military decree – insofar as they judged it necessary. Over the course of the war, the Union army arrested and detained thousands of people without civilian trials, at least some of them for exercising what would today be regarded as basic speech rights (for example, by expressing sympathy for the Confederacy).

World War I brought enactment of the Espionage Act and its enforcement by the Supreme Court in the famous cases under the clear and present danger test, discussed in Chapter One. In the first of those cases, *Schenck v. United States*[24] (1919), Justice Holmes, himself a Civil War veteran, asserted pointedly that "[w]hen a nation is at war many things that might be said in time of peace are such a hindrance to its effort that their utterance will not be endured [or deemed protected under the Constitution] so long as men fight."

During World War II, speech rights generally fared better, but the government pursued its infamous policy of excluding all persons of Japanese descent, citizens as well as noncitizens, from the West Coast of the United States. Writing nearly twenty years later and attempting to draw lessons from the Supreme Court's decision to uphold the exclusion, then-Chief Justice Earl Warren (who had himself played a role in executing the policy while Attorney General of California) wrote that "there are some circumstances in which the Court will, in effect, conclude that it is simply not in a position to reject descriptions by the Executive of the degree of military necessity."[25]

The Supreme Court's decision in *Korematsu v. United States*[26] (1944) may be explainable on that basis, but the potential of wartime fears and emotion to distort judgment should not be denied. Warren's perspective is again revealing. As David Halberstam has written: "The one serious blot on [Warren's] record was [his role as California's Attorney General in the Japanese relocation]. He was playing to the growing fear of sabotage and the country's anger against the Japanese, particularly in California. Later he expressed considerable regret for his actions...: In 1972, when he was interviewed on the subject, he broke down in tears as he spoke of the little children being taken from their homes and schools."[27]

Looking backward at the history of civil liberties in wartime, commentators have reached differing assessments and, perhaps even more strikingly, have drawn sharply different conclusions about how courts ought to behave in the future. Perhaps the most common view maintains that past wars have produced not merely violations, but egregious violations, of constitutional liberties. Those who hold this view tend to argue that current and future courts should scrutinize claims that rights must yield to wartime imperatives with great, great skepticism.[28]

Judge Richard Posner – a brilliant former law professor who has continued to comment provocatively on public issues while serving as a lower court judge – has advanced a challengingly contrary view. "[T]he lesson of history," he argues, is not that governmental officials "habitually exaggerate dangers to the nation's security," but "the opposite": "It is because officials have repeatedly and disastrously underestimated these dangers that our history is as violent as it is," including such events as the terrorist attacks of September 11, 2001.[29] Although there are plain mistakes that have become obvious in hindsight, Posner appears to believe that America's wartime record with civil liberties is actually quite good. He sees no reason to ratchet up the level of judicial scrutiny in cases requiring a balance of individual liberties against national security interests. On the contrary, he appears to believe that it could be a grave, potentially disastrous mistake to do so.

A third group of commentators, prominently including Chief Justice William Rehnquist in a recent book on civil liberties in wartime,[30] emphasize what they take to be the encouraging historical trend: Although wartime has been bad for constitutional liberties, there have tended to be fewer, or less serious, abuses in each war than in those that preceded it. As a factual matter, this claim is hard to judge. There is no adequate metric with which to compare the World War I deprivations of speech rights, for example, with the Japanese relocation during World War II. Nevertheless, it is surely true that the American people and their elected leaders have learned lessons from experience. In the aftermath of the Civil War, no branch of government seriously considered broadly suspending "the privilege of the writ of habeas corpus" in either World War I or World War II.[31] As the Holmes–Brandeis view about freedom of speech won increasing acceptance in the years following World War I, Congress did not reenact an Espionage Act in World War II, though it did later pass laws under which Communists were punished for speech and association during the Cold War.

With respect to the courts, Rehnquist says that they, too, have drawn lessons from wartimes past. One kind of example comes from *Brandenburg v. Ohio* (1969), which was discussed in Chapter One. Reflecting the Court's conclusion that wartime courts were too quick to suppress speech under the clear and present danger test, *Brandenburg* gives more nearly categorical protection to even loosely political speech; until overruled or modified, it recognizes no wartime exception. Rehnquist concludes his book with cautious prophecy and with equally cautious judgments about the role of courts in wartime:

> [Although there] is no reason to think...that future Justices of the Supreme Court will decide questions differently from their predecessors[,]...there is every reason to think that the historic trend against the least justified of the curtailments of civil liberty in wartime will continue in the future. It is neither desirable nor is it remotely likely that civil liberty will occupy as favored a position in wartime as it does in peacetime. But it is both desirable and likely that more careful attention will be paid by the courts to the basis for the government's claims of necessity as a basis for curtailing civil liberty.[32]

The Constitution and the "War" on Terrorism

Following the terrorist attacks of September 11, 2001, the United States embarked on what is recurrently described as a "war on terrorism." Steps taken by the government as part of this "war" are certain to raise questions about the scope of governmental power and about the status of individual rights in war and emergency. It is debatable, of course, whether the war on terrorism is really a war at all, at least in some of its elements. Although military attacks on the governments of Afghanistan and Iraq resemble those of traditional wars, other steps are directed against terrorist organizations rather than against nations or governments. But to try to give a single answer to the question of whether the war on terrorism is a war, and especially to treat it as a threshold question of great importance in all cases, would be a mistake. Emergency circumstances can exist even when war does not. In addition, many constitutional rules have limits or exceptions that do not formally depend on reference to either war or "emergency," but may still serve the government's asserted needs in times of felt crisis. A brief discussion of some of the elements of the war on terrorism, and of the constitutional issues to which they give rise, may therefore help to teach some general lessons about constitutional law.

As of this writing, major steps in the war on terrorism have included the following:

- In the immediate aftermath of September 11, governmental officials rounded up and detained over 1,000 foreign citizens living in the United States. Almost all were of Arab descent. Many were held for relatively long periods without access to courts or lawyers.
- The United States has conducted major military campaigns in Afghanistan and Iraq. Casualties have included an unknown number of civilians as well as armed combatants.
- During and after fights on the battlefields of Afghanistan and Iraq, United States forces captured or arrested a number of suspected war criminals or terrorists. Many of those captured in Afghanistan were subsequently transferred to a United States military installation at Guantanamo Bay, Cuba.
- In November of 2001, President Bush issued an executive order authorizing the trial of alleged terrorists who are not United States citizens before so-called military tribunals, without right to trial by jury, rather than in the civilian courts normally used for criminal trials.[33] A subsequent order by the Defense Department contemplates that these military tribunals can meet in secret and that various procedural rights guaranteed in "ordinary" criminal trials will not apply.
- Apart from trials before military commissions, the Justice Department has taken the position that if the President certifies a person as a terrorist, the government can hold that person in jail for as long as it thinks necessary without providing for any kind of trial at all.
- Congress has enacted legislation easing prior restrictions on domestic spying.
- The federal government has assumed responsibility for the screening of airline passengers. Published reports have indicated that race or national origin may sometimes play a role in the identification of particular passengers for special examination before they can board a plane.

Not all of the constitutional issues arising from these and other developments have yet come sharply into focus. Nor, even if they had, could I provide close analysis of all the questions that the war on terrorism raises. It seems clear, however, that debate about many if not most of the constitutional issues is likely to take one of two interestingly different forms.

In one, disputed questions will be resolved within frameworks already discussed in previous chapters in this book. For example, if the government were to engage in racial profiling in screening passengers in airports, the question would be whether this particular type of race-based decision-making could be justified under ordinary equal protection principles as "necessary to promote a compelling governmental interest." If the government undertook aggressive searches of every person in an area where it feared a suicide bombing, the question within "ordinary" Fourth Amendment doctrine would be whether those searches should be deemed "reasonable" under the circumstances, even though it is usually unreasonable for the government to conduct invasive searches in the absence of individualized suspicion.

Significantly, however, many constitutional issues arising from the war on terrorism seem likely to take a second form and to depend on the applicability of various, more nearly categorical limits on or exceptions to what most Americans would probably regard as "normal" constitutional rules – those defining the rights of American citizens within the United States who have not joined a hostile army to inflict atrocities on their own country. Not all of those categorical exceptions depend expressly on war or emergency, although some of them do.

Some Categorical Limits on Constitutional Rights

The Constitution affords few if any rights that extend outside the territory of the United States to citizens of other countries.[34] When American planes drop bombs in Afghanistan or Iraq, or when American armies cause destruction and death, no victim, no matter how innocent, can claim a violation of constitutional rights. Moral rights the victims may have, but not rights under the American Constitution. For better or for worse, the Constitution is mostly a constitution for the territorial United States of America, not for foreign territories visited or occupied by the American military.

Even within the United States, noncitizens do not always have the same rights as American citizens. The Supreme Court has held that noncitizens residing in the United States cannot be convicted of ordinary crimes and subjected to criminal punishment without being afforded the same rights to fair criminal procedures that Americans enjoy.[35] In some contexts, however, noncitizens, or "aliens," have fewer rights than citizens. Aliens cannot vote. In addition, the Supreme Court has ruled that federal policies discriminating against aliens (in ways other than denying them constitutional guarantees of fair procedures in criminal trials) are presumptively permissible, not "suspect," under applicable equal protection doctrine: Only rational basis review applies.[36]

The starting point for the Court's reasoning is the commonsense notion that Congress must be able to exclude noncitizens from coming to live here. There is thus an obvious distinction between citizens and aliens with respect to who is entitled to enter the United States and to remain within its borders. The Court, however, has taken the further position that "[a]ny policy toward aliens," regardless of whether it directly regulates immigration, "is vitally and intricately interwoven with [federal] policies in regard to the conduct of foreign relations, the war power, and the maintenance of a republican form of government" here in the United States.[37]

It is no accident that many of the government's harshest policies in the war on terrorism have specifically targeted "aliens."[38] In cases of different kinds, the courts will be asked to determine whether, when, and to what extent it is permissible to treat aliens differently from citizens or to deny to noncitizens rights that citizens enjoy.

Although the government needs to follow "ordinary" constitutional rules when prosecuting aliens for "ordinary" crimes, different rules often apply when officials act to enforce the immigration laws. In defense of its actions in rounding up of large numbers of noncitizens and detaining some of them without access to lawyers in the aftermath of September 11, the government cited its special prerogatives in enforcing the immigration laws – or, what comes to the same thing, the very limited rights that noncitizens can assert against enforcement of the immigration laws. For example, the Justice Department has maintained that aliens suspected of immigration violations can be detained while investigations are conducted and can be denied access to lawyers – whereas those arrested for ordinary crimes have nearly immediate rights of access to lawyers and cannot be detained for more than brief periods without a judicial hearing. Even if it is conceded that enforcement of the immigration laws does not trigger the same constitutional safeguards as enforcement of "ordinary" criminal laws, the government's policies in the war against terrorism would seem to raise questions, which currently lack clear answers, about the minimal rights of aliens being investigated and detained for suspected immigration violations.

Constitutional rules that apply in "ordinary" criminal cases do not always apply in cases involving offenses against the "law of war." For at least some purposes, the Constitution recognizes a distinction between ordinary criminal laws, the enforcement of which triggers ordinary constitutional guarantees, and the law of war – a body of international and American law that governs the rights and duties of combatants during wartime. Among other things, it is constitutionally permissible to try at least some alleged violations of the law of war before "military tribunals" or "commissions," consisting of military officers, rather than in ordinary civilian courts with all the guarantees of procedural fairness that ordinary courts provide.[39] Alleged war criminals captured on foreign battlegrounds can clearly be tried before military tribunals.[40] Less clear is when suspected terrorists can be tried by military tribunals within the United States. Among other things, terrorist acts committed in the United States by relatively isolated individuals, not trained abroad as part of a terrorist army, may be hard to characterize as violations of the law of war, rather than as ordinary crimes. Questions about the outer boundaries of the law of war and about the exceptions to ordinary constitutional guarantees permissible in "war crimes" cases thus seem virtually certain to arise as the war on terrorism continues.

Prisoners of war do not have the same constitutional rights as criminal suspects. Normally prosecutors and police must either bring criminal charges and prove those charges in court or release a suspect from detention: The government cannot simply detain those whom it suspects of wrongdoing, or believes likely to engage in future wrong-doing, for indefinite periods.[41] But this ordinary assumption does not apply to enemy combatants captured in wartime, who can be detained as prisoners of war until the conclusion of hostilities.

Insisting that the war on terrorism is indeed a "war," the government has taken the position that it can detain suspected terrorists as prisoners of war, without bringing them to trial in any court, until the war is over.[42] As this book went to press, several such cases were before the Supreme Court, but the Court had not yet announced its decision. From a constitutional perspective, a central issue once again will be whether all terrorist suspects – especially those appre-hended in the United States – can fairly be classed as unlawful com-batants captured and made prisoners of war, rather than being treated as persons accused of crimes, who must be either tried or released.

Conclusion

It is sometimes said that *inter arma leges silent* – in times of war, the laws are silent.[43] This old Latin maxim claims too much. During every war in the history of the United States, the Constitution has re-mained in force. Elections have occurred on schedule. Public servants have continued to perform their constitutional duties. Most ordinary citizens have retained most of their ordinary constitutional rights.

But if the Constitution does not go silent in wartime, it undoubt-edly speaks to some issues in more muted, equivocal tones than it does in time of peace.[44] During the Civil War, after ordering the suspension of the writ of habeas corpus and defying an order by the Chief Justice to release a prisoner, Abraham Lincoln at least tacitly acknowledged that his position could be squared with the Constitution only with difficulty (even though he insisted that it could indeed be squared). In defending his stance, Lincoln emphasized that the constitutional provision that he was alleged to have violated – preserving rights to the writ of habeas corpus – was only one among many and that he, in taking his oath of office, had pledged to preserve, protect, and defend the entire Constitution of the United States. The entire Constitution was at risk, he maintained, unless he could take necessary steps, which he thought included the suspension of habeas corpus, to win the war. Assuming this to be the case, was he obliged to honor the letter of the provision dealing with the writ of habeas corpus? If he preserved and protected what he described as "all the laws, *but one,*"[45] was that not better, constitutionally speaking, than to put the entire constitutional order at risk?

War and emergency sometimes require the compromise of ideals, if not deals with the devil. Unfortunately, not every wartime leader asserting claims to extraordinary power or demanding the sacrifice of constitutional liberties will share the humane spirit of Abraham Lincoln. The challenges of war and emergency require practical wisdom. The Constitution creates a framework within which such wisdom can be exercised but does not, alas, ensure that it will always be furnished. No constitution could.

THIRTEEN

The Reach of the Constitution and Congress's Enforcement Power

[C]ivil rights, such as are guaranteed by the constitution against state aggression, cannot be impaired by the wrongful acts of individuals, unsupported by State authority.
> – *The Civil Rights Cases* (1883)[1]

Congress does not enforce a constitutional right by changing what the right is. It has been given the power "to enforce," not the power to determine what constitutes a constitutional violation.
> – *City of Boerne v. Flores* (1997)[2]

THIS CHAPTER DEALS WITH THREE SEPARATE but related issues concerning the nature and reach of constitutional rights. One involves the applicability of the Constitution: Against whom does the Constitution create rights? Another has to do with the character of the rights that the Constitution creates. Nearly all are rights to be free from one or another kind of hostile governmental action. Few are rights to affirmative governmental assistance. Why? The final topic involves the scope of Congress's power to "enforce" constitutional guarantees. In enforcing the Constitution, to what extent, if any, does Congress share in the power to determine the Constitution's meaning?

State Action Doctrine

A few years ago, a major league baseball pitcher named John Rocker gave a magazine interview in which he denounced New York City, the New York City subways, and gays. He mocked foreigners and referred to a Latino teammate as "a fat monkey." Rocker's comments disturbed a lot of people, including officials of Major League Baseball, a private, for-profit organization of private, for-profit baseball teams. In response, the Commissioner of Baseball – an employee of Major League Baseball, not associated with the government in any way – ordered Rocker to undergo sensitivity training, fined him, and suspended him from a number of games. Many applauded the Commissioner's response to Rocker's outburst. Some complained that the situation called for even harsher discipline.

Others, however, worried about Rocker's constitutional rights. Across the country, sportswriters began to ring the phones of lawyers and constitutional law professors. Hadn't the Commissioner and Major League Baseball violated Rocker's First Amendment right to freedom of expression? Didn't Rocker have a constitutional case?

To the evident surprise of many sportswriters and presumably some nonsportswriters as well, the answer to these questions was simply "No." Almost without exception, constitutional rights exist only against the government, not against private citizens or private businesses or organizations. Neither Congress nor a state legislature could have made Rocker's remarks a crime. Nor would the First Amendment have let the government fine Rocker for what he said. But the First Amendment creates no rights enforceable against Major League Baseball or its Commissioner. In other words, the First Amendment prohibits the government from interfering with freedom of speech, but does not prevent Major League Baseball from doing so.

The general rule that the Constitution creates rights only against the government, and not against private citizens, has one important exception. The Thirteenth Amendment, which abolished slavery, says that "[n]either slavery nor involuntary servitude . . . shall exist within the United States." Private attempts at enslavement violate the Thirteenth Amendment.

The rule that only the government can violate the Constitution (other than the Thirteenth Amendment) is usually referred to as "the state action doctrine," but it would be less confusingly called "the *governmental* action requirement," for the Constitution applies as much to Congress, the President, and other governmental officials as it does to the states. Once this terminological point is understood, the state action doctrine is virtually self-applying in most cases. On the affirmative side, Congress engages in state action whenever it enacts a law, as do state legislatures, city councils, and other governmental bodies. Similarly, governmental officials engage in state action when they enforce the law or otherwise exercise official responsibility. The school officials involved in *Brown v. Board of Education* were state actors, as were the prosecuting attorneys who stood ready to enforce the antiabortion law in *Roe v. Wade*.

On the negative side, private citizens are generally not state actors, for the obvious reason that they are neither the government nor the government's agents. There are a few exceptions, involving special circumstances that occasionally make it appropriate to treat action by private parties as if it were taken by the government itself. One exceptional category includes otherwise private citizens performing what the Supreme Court has characterized as inherently "public functions." For example, the Court has held that operating a prison is an inherently public function. If a state hires a private, for-profit company to incarcerate and supervise those convicted of crimes, the company and its officials are state actors, and prisoners possess constitutional rights against them.[3] By contrast, the Court has held that operating a school is not an inherently public function. Private schools and their employees are therefore not state actors, and they are not subject to constitutional restraints (even though public schools and public school employees are).[4]

The Court has also found that private citizens can be treated as state actors and sued for constitutional violations when state law empowers them to act in the name of the government or control the conduct of governmental officials. For example, in both civil and criminal trials, applicable law authorizes the parties, if they so choose, to exclude a certain number of would-be jurors by exercising "peremptory challenges." Because peremptory challenges direct the court – plainly a governmental actor – to dismiss potential jurors, the Supreme Court has held that the Equal Protection Clause applies to their use. Under the Equal Protection Clause, private parties cannot use their peremptory challenges to exclude jurors on the basis of race.[5]

Again, however, cases such as these are the exception, not the rule. Although the details of the state action doctrine are sometimes tangled, the Supreme Court has generally resisted efforts to characterize private parties as state actors subject to the Constitution – even when they are heavily regulated by the government, or enjoy governmentally conferred monopoly power (as do public utilities), or exercise powers specifically conferred by law (such as a power to seize private property as a remedy for nonpayment of debt). When constitutional rules apply, they operate as constraints. The Court clearly thinks it best to limit the reach of those constraints and thus to preserve a large space for the exercise of private, unconstrained liberty. Major League Baseball should be "free" to suspend John Rocker if he makes comments that alienate fans. John Rocker (who is no more a state actor than Major League Baseball) should be free to make bigoted decisions, not bound by the Equal Protection Clause.

As is probably obvious, protecting the "liberty" of some often entails costs for others. The liberty of Major League Baseball meant that John Rocker had to suffer a fine and suspension. In a case closer to the edge of the state action doctrine, to deem a public utility a private rather than a state actor means that it can cut off service to customers – who have no place else to turn for water, or gas, or electricity – without needing to provide "due process of law" under the Due Process Clause.[6] Without denying that costs exist, the Supreme Court reads the Constitution as relying on the political process, rather than on the courts, to balance the competing interests. Democratically accountable legislatures frequently pass laws restricting the liberty of some in order to protect the interests of others. But the resulting rights and restrictions come from statutes, not the federal Constitution.

The Paucity of "Positive" Fundamental Rights

The reach of the Constitution is also bounded in another way: As construed by the Supreme Court against the backdrop of history, it confers very few "positive" rights. Most recognized rights operate as shields against hostile government action. Few create entitlements to affirmative governmental assistance.[7] Thus, to use obvious examples, the First Amendment protects against governmental interferences with speech, but it does not oblige the government to furnish anyone with a microphone or a printing press. The Fifth and Fourteenth Amendments forbid deprivations of property without due process of law, but they do not confer a positive right to be given property, even for those who otherwise have none.

Positive constitutional rights are surely not impossible. The constitutions of some other countries guarantee rights to education, medical care, shelter, and food. Indeed, the Supreme Court has recognized a few positive rights under the American Constitution. People accused of crimes have a right to a government-appointed lawyer if they are too poor to afford one. Inmates in prisons have an affirmative right to health care and a decent diet.[8] In a broader-reaching example, all citizens have a right to have the streets and sidewalks maintained as a public forum available for speech and expressive activities. But these and a few more examples complete the list.

From time to time, commentators have argued that the Supreme Court should recognize various positive rights as fundamental rights implicit in or presupposed by the Constitution. Their obvious concern has involved the poor. Someone who is hungry, impoverished, homeless, sick, or uneducated may have no practical opportunity to enjoy or exercise express constitutional rights that others take for granted. According to some commentators, when the Constitution confers rights, it must presuppose that people will be able to exercise or enjoy them, and thus it must implicitly create positive rights to such things as education, health care, food, and shelter (without which, again, it may be impossible to take advantage of recognized constitutional rights).[9]

If positive rights such as these were recognized, they might be absolute, in which case the government would have no choice but to honor them. Alternatively, they might be defined as fundamental rights under the Equal Protection Clause. When rights are fundamental under the Equal Protection Clause, the government need not to confer them at all, but if it distributes them to anyone, any inequalities trigger strict judicial scrutiny. To cite just one example, some voting-rights cases follow this model. A town need not allow anyone to vote for members of the school board. It could provide for the school board to be appointed by the mayor or town council. But if a town allows anyone to vote for school board members, then restrictions on who can vote will trigger strict judicial scrutiny, because of the fundamental status of voting rights (once they are conferred).[10] So it might also be with rights to education, welfare, or housing.

In cases decided during the 1950s and 1960s, the Warren Court took some tentative, isolated steps toward the recognition of positive constitutional rights and also of equal protection rights framed in part to protect the poor. The Warren Court recognized the right of indigent criminal suspects to have a lawyer appointed for them. It required the states to waive fees and expenses that made it impossible for the poor to file criminal appeals. The Warren Court also held that because the right to vote is fundamental, a state may not impose a "poll tax" that made it difficult or impossible for the poor to exercise that right.

It will never be known whether the Warren Court, in time, might have recognized positive constitutional rights to welfare, education, and health care, or held that these are fundamental rights such that, once the government furnishes them to anyone, it must provide them equally to others. The Court clearly chose not to do so, but the decisive cases came later, after Earl Warren had retired from the bench and after the 1968 presidential campaign, in which Richard Nixon had pledged if elected to appoint "strict constructionist" conservative Justices. Four Nixon appointees joined the bare 5–4 majority in *San Antonio Independent School District v. Rodriguez*[11] (1973), which held that education is not a fundamental right.

The plaintiffs in *Rodriguez* were the parents of school children who lived in relatively poor Texas communities. In essence, they challenged the constitutionality of the state's overall scheme for funding public education. That scheme relied heavily on local property taxes. In wealthy communities, it was possible to raise lots of money through the property tax, and the schools were generously funded. In poorer communities, the property tax generated much smaller revenues, and the average per-pupil expenditure on public education was as much as sixty percent lower. In light of the accepted constitutional assumption that cities and towns are "arms of the state" for which the state is ultimately responsible, the *Rodriguez* plaintiffs argued that Texas should be forced to adopt a different funding scheme that would more nearly equalize per-pupil expenditures across public school districts. Education, they argued, was a fundamental right under the Equal Protection Clause, which the state of Texas (and by implication other states too) must therefore distribute on a more equal basis. The challengers also argued that Texas's financing system was unconstitutional because it disadvantaged the poor, who should be deemed a "suspect" class.

Nixon appointee Lewis Powell wrote the Court opinion rejecting the constitutional challenges. Education, he ruled, was not a fundamental right, because it was neither explicit nor implicit in the Constitution. Nor, he held, do the poor constitute a suspect class. To support the assertion that fundamental rights cannot be recognized unless they are "implicitly or explicitly guaranteed by the Constitution" – a formulation that is unexceptionable in itself, as it leaves open the question how the Court should identify implicit rights – Powell's opinion cited *Roe v. Wade*,[12] a case decided only months earlier. From one perspective, *Rodriguez*'s invocation of *Roe* was simply bizarre. Many would say that Roe reveals the wide, almost boundless breadth of the Court's authority in identifying fundamental rights. What is more, the argument that education is a fundamental right was in many ways stronger than the parallel argument with respect to abortion. *Brown v. Board of Education*[13] (1954) had strongly suggested that education had become a fundamental right because of its practical importance in modern life. In addition, because education is practically necessary to the enjoyment of other rights, its claim to fundamental status is structurally similar to the accepted argument for recognizing a constitutional right to freedom of association. If freedom of association is constitutionally protected because it facilitates speech, education can be equally crucial in making speech rights meaningful.

Nevertheless, the contrast between *Roe* and *Rodriguez* is revealing. Whereas the abortion right is a "negative" right to be free from governmental interference, the asserted fundamental right to education was a "positive" right, which would have taken affirmative governmental steps to implement. If the Court had characterized education as a fundamental right, distributed by the state, it could quickly have found itself enmeshed in complex disputes about when Texas (and other states) had achieved the equality that the Constitution requires. To escape those disputes, the Court might have adopted a financial measure: The fundamental right to education is distributed equally when per-pupil expenditures on education are roughly equal in every school district. But a ruling to this effect would have forced Texas and many other states to alter their historic reliance on local property taxes to fund local education. As a practical matter, property taxes will not permit relatively poor communities to achieve equality of funding with wealthier communities. To achieve equalized funding at acceptable levels would therefore have required substantial economic redistribution from the better-off to the less well-off in the teeth of loud protests from politically influential middle and upper class communities. (Interestingly, a number of *state* supreme courts have subsequently held that their *state* constitutions require the state legislature to take steps either to equalize educational funding within the state or to ensure every child a minimal level of educational quality. In doing so, however, state supreme courts have generally relied on state constitutional provisions that specifically refer to education. The Constitution of the United States includes no such provision.)

Arguably it is the job of the Supreme Court to mandate economic redistributions – involving such basic goods as education and health care – to guarantee all citizens "the equal protection of the laws." Arguably it is not, in light of historical understandings of the Equal Protection Clause, targeted at economic inequality. To be sure, the Court has departed from original constitutional understandings in many other areas. But when it has done so successfully, it has usually reflected or helped to crystallize broadly shared judgments of fairness, necessity, or propriety. In 1973, there was scant evidence of an emerging national consensus supporting more equal distributions of educational funding (or of funding for health care or welfare either) in order to benefit the poor.

What is perhaps most clear with respect to positive rights is that the Supreme Court will not, and in the long run probably could not, enforce broad-based economic redistributions opposed by the reigning political coalition. For a long and lengthening season, *Rodriguez* has epitomized the view of a conservative Court in a generally conservative political era about both positive rights and economic equality. As construed by the Court, the Constitution is overwhelmingly a charter of negative, not positive, liberties, and the Equal Protection Clause, as currently interpreted, imposes very few affirmative governmental obligations to redress economic inequality.

Congressional Power to "Enforce" the Reconstruction Amendments

The Thirteenth Amendment, which abolishes slavery, the Fourteenth Amendment, which includes the Due Process and Equal Protection Clauses, and the Fifteenth Amendment, which bars race discrimination in state and national elections, all include clauses that authorize Congress to "enforce" their substantive provisions "by appropriate legislation." Because Congress cannot legislate at all in the absence of an affirmative grant of authority to do so (as was discussed more generally in Chapter Seven), the specific terms of the authority granted by the Civil War Amendments assume great importance. What does it mean for Congress to enforce the Constitution? Does it possess a power to determine what counts as a constitutional violation? If so, how would that congressional authority fit with the Supreme Court's power, as recognized in *Marbury v. Madison*[14] (1803), to "say what the law is"?

For many years, the leading case addressing these questions was *Katzenbach v. Morgan*[15] (1966). At issue in *Katzenbach* was a provision of the federal Voting Rights Act, enacted by Congress to enforce the Equal Protection Clause of the Fourteenth Amendment, providing that no one who had completed the sixth grade in a non-English-speaking school in Puerto Rico could be denied the right to vote because of lack of English literacy. New York officials challenged the provision's constitutionality. In an earlier case, *Lassiter v.*

Northampton County Board of Electors[16] (1959), the Court had upheld an English literacy requirement for voters against a constitutional challenge based on the Equal Protection Clause. In light of *Lassiter*, New York election officials argued, legislation barring New York from insisting on English literacy as a voting requirement could not qualify as "appropriate legislation" to "enforce" the Fourteenth Amendment: Rather than "enforc[ing]" the Equal Protection Clause, Congress had attempted to go further than the Fourteenth Amendment required, and no provision of the Constitution authorized it to do so.

The Supreme Court disagreed. Justice William Brennan's opinion for the Court appeared to offer at least three theories on which, despite *Lassiter*, Congress's limited prohibition against literacy tests might count as "appropriate legislation" to "enforce" the Fourteenth Amendment. The first theory was simultaneously remedial and preventative. According to Brennan, Congress could rationally have concluded that unconstitutional discrimination against Puerto Ricans occurred in a variety of settings, not limited to voting but including public schools, welfare administration, and law enforcement. Brennan suggested that Section 5 of the Fourteenth Amendment authorized Congress to provide a remedy for those violations, and a safeguard against their recurrence, by investing Puerto Ricans with an expanded right to vote. The right to vote, he wrote, was "preservative of all rights."[17]

Brennan's second theory postulated that Congress could justify the enactment of legislation to "enforce" the Fourteenth Amendment by invoking its "specially informed" fact-finding abilities. In upholding the particular literacy test that was challenged in *Lassiter*, the Supreme Court had not held that all literacy tests were constitutionally valid. Under well-established principles, literacy tests would be invalid if they were enacted for discriminatory purposes. Judging for itself, the *Lassiter* Court was unwilling to presume that most literacy tests were enacted for discriminatory purposes or that they were not a "necessary or appropriate means" of furthering legitimate state ends.[18] But Congress, Brennan suggested, might know better. If Congress concluded that many or most literacy tests were adopted for discriminatory purposes or were otherwise unnecessary to further legitimate state interests, the Court should defer to these largely factual judgments by Congress and should uphold the challenged prohibition against literacy tests as "appropriate" to "enforce" the Fourteenth Amendment.

Finally, and most controversially, Brennan hinted that when legislating under Section 5 to enforce constitutional rights, Congress could permissibly define those underlying rights at least slightly more broadly than the Supreme Court would otherwise define them. Under this theory, which commentators dubbed the "ratchet theory,"[19] Brennan maintained that Congress had "no power to restrict, abrogate, or dilute" constitutional guarantees,[20] but he suggested that Congress might indeed have power to ratchet up the level of constitutional protection beyond that afforded by the Court.[21]

If accepted, *Katzenbach v. Morgan*'s ratchet theory would dramatically expand the scope of congressional authority and correspondingly diminish the centrality of the judicial role. In effect, it would call for the Supreme Court to share its power to interpret the Constitution. Under the ratchet theory, judicial rulings would establish the minimum content of constitutional guarantees, but not necessarily the maximum. Perhaps troubled by this implication, the Court pointedly failed to embrace the ratchet theory in a couple of subsequent cases, but without expressly renouncing it either. Equivocation ended in *City of Boerne v. Flores*[22] (1997). *City of Boerne* decisively rejects the ratchet theory and sharply limits Congress's enforcement powers under the Thirteenth, Fourteenth, and Fifteenth Amendments.

Specifically at issue in *Boerne* was the constitutionality of the Religious Freedom Restoration Act (RFRA). Congress enacted the RFRA in response to the Supreme Court's decision in *Employment Division v. Smith*[23] (1990), discussed in Chapter Two, which gave a narrow interpretation of the Free Exercise Clause. Previous free exercise decisions had held that statutes could not be enforced against religious practices (such as the sacramental use of peyote) unless the burden on religion was "necessary to promote a compelling state interest." *Smith* substituted a narrower test, under which the Free Exercise Clause usually affords no right to religious exemptions from generally applicable laws. Through the RFRA, Congress tried to restore the pre-*Smith* regime. The RFRA prohibited federal, state, and local governments from "substantially burdening" a person's exercise of religion, even through the enforcement of neutral laws of general applicability, unless the burden on religious practice was necessary to further a compelling governmental interest.

With no Justice dissenting on this point, the Supreme Court held that Congress has no power "to enact legislation that expands the rights contained in Section 1 of the Fourteenth Amendment" (including those, such as free exercise rights, that the Fourteenth Amendment "incorporates").[24] Congress's power is to enforce constitutional rights as defined by the Court, not to define constitutional rights for itself, the Justices ruled.

Having dismissed the ratchet theory, the Court acknowledged that Congress could provide remedies for constitutional rights violations and, under some circumstances, could legislate to prevent them – provided that what counted as a constitutional rights violation was defined by the courts, not Congress. But the Court insisted that preventive and remedial legislation must be "congruen[t] and proportional[]"[25] to an underlying pattern of identified constitutional violations. The Court suggested that the legislation involved in *Katzenbach v. Morgan* met this test: "The provisions restricting and banning literacy tests . . . attacked a particular type of voting qualification . . . with a long history as a 'notorious means to deny and abridge voting rights on racial grounds.'"[26] By contrast, it said, the RFRA was wholly "out of proportion to a supposed remedial or preventive object":[27] Congress was trying to redefine the rights guaranteed by the Free Exercise Clause, not remedy or prevent violations of the narrow right that the Court had identified in *Employment Division v. Smith*.

Subsequent cases have revealed *Boerne's* "congruence and proportionality" test as a stringent one. Before Congress can remedy or prevent unconstitutional state action, it must specifically identify a pattern of conduct that is unconstitutional under judicially established criteria, perhaps by holding fact-finding hearings and compiling evidence. Ordinarily, Congress can legislate on the basis of its general knowledge or reasonable suppositions (as the Court often emphasizes when applying the rational basis test to legislation challenged under the Due Process Clause). The post-*Boerne* cases suggest that the Court will hold Congress to a higher standard when it invokes its powers under Section 5 of the Fourteenth Amendment.[28]

Taken as a package, *Boerne* and its successor cases are not only extremely important, but also extremely revealing about the views and attitudes of the current Supreme Court. Why would the Justices think that Congress should attract unusually searching judicial review when it exercises a specifically delegated constitutional power to enforce constitutional rights? I would speculate that at least three factors may have influenced the Justices' interpretation of the constitutional text and its history.

First, and perhaps least controversially, *Boerne*'s restricted interpretation of Congress's power to enforce the Constitution reflects the current Court's commitment to reinvigorating constitutional federalism. Legislation enacted under Section 5 typically imposes obligations directly on state and local governments. (Because the Constitution generally creates rights only against the government and its officials, legislation to enforce the Reconstruction Amendments will almost invariably apply only to state and local governments and their employees. The RFRA, for example, would have forced state and local governments to exempt persons engaged in religiously motivated conduct from otherwise applicable laws.) By constraining Congress's power to regulate state and local governments, *Boerne* advances the Court's continuing agenda – discussed in Chapter Seven – of promoting federalism by limiting congressional power and expanding state and local governments' freedom of action.

Second, *Boerne* manifests the modern Supreme Court's sense of its own vital role and special capacities. As reflected not only in *Boerne* but also in *Bush v. Gore*[29] and myriad other cases discussed in earlier chapters, the Court believes that it possesses a disinterested wisdom not shared by other institutions of government, especially those that operate in the messy domain of electoral politics. The Court wants to protect its own turf, not simply because it enjoys the exercise of undiluted power, but because it believes that a dominant role for the Supreme Court in constitutional matters serves the nation's best interests. By giving a narrow interpretation of Congress's power to enforce the Civil War Amendments, *Boerne* helped to preserve that dominant judicial role.

A third consideration is more subtle, and in suggesting that it may have influenced the *Boerne* decision I necessarily become more speculative. This consideration involves the Supreme Court's apparent perception of the nature of constitutional interpretation and the Justices' stake in maintaining that perception. In *Boerne*, the Court formulated the issue before it as whether Section 5 of the Fourteenth Amendment authorizes Congress to "expand" constitutional rights. To this question, the answer is surely no. But in answering it, the Court did not pause, as it might have, to consider exactly what constitutional rights are and, in particular, to consider what it does in adjudicating constitutional claims. Without being self-conscious about it, the *Boerne* Court assumed what might be termed a Truth Model of constitutional adjudication and constitutional rights. Under that model there is one truth about what the Free Exercise Clause, for example, protects and does not protect, and the Court's job is to find that single, determinate, nondiscretionary truth. After the Court had performed that job in *Employment Division v. Smith*, for Congress to adopt a broader view of the right to free exercise of religion when it enacted the Religious Freedom Restoration Act necessarily amounted to an attempted expansion of constitutional rights.

Although the Truth Model is alluring in many ways, its central premises are deeply contestable. An alternative model, which might be termed a Reasoned Judgment Model, contemplates that sometimes there may be no single, ultimate truth about constitutional meaning; the reach of a constitutional guarantee can be vague and indeterminate, at least to some extent. Along a spectrum, it may be clear that some formulations would afford too much protection to religious liberty, for example, whereas other formulations would protect too little. Within bounds, however, the Reasoned Judgment Model postulates that the Supreme Court does not attempt so much to identify a timeless truth about constitutional meaning as to exercise reasoned judgment about how best to implement a constitutional provision – such as the Free Exercise Clause, the Due Process Clause, or the Equal Protection Clause – at any particular time. Within the Reasoned Judgment Model, legislation such as the RFRA would not necessarily need to be seen as "expanding" the rights conferred by the Constitution; insofar as a right is vague or indeterminate, there would be some room, within a range, for Congress to substitute its reasoned judgment for that of the Court about how that right would best be implemented. If a Reasoned Judgment Model were adopted, the Court's job in Section 5 cases would be to assess whether Congress moved beyond the vague or indeterminate range and thereby expanded or contracted a constitutional guarantee. Within the indeterminate range, however, Congress could substitute its reasoned judgment for that of the Supreme Court.

In many ways, the Reasoned Judgment Model explains better than the Truth Model the nature of the most difficult and important decisions that the Supreme Court has to make. In at least some of the cases that they decide, the Justices do not seek constitutional truth so much as make practical judgments about how to implement vague constitutional values. History matters to constitutional adjudication, but original understandings do not always bind the Court. The Justices adjudicate in light of moral and political ideals, but sometimes they temper their judgments to accommodate prevailing public sentiments and considerations of prudence and practicality.

In *City of Boerne v. Flores*, however, the Justices implicitly disavowed the Reasoned Judgment Model and embraced the Truth Model. It is easy to see why they would want to do so. The Reasoned Judgment Model may reflect the reality of Supreme Court decision-making, but it also diverges in sharp, even shocking ways from familiar, comforting views that the Court should simply find the law and apply it, without the Justices allowing their own views to come into play. What is more, the Reasoned Judgment Model acknowledges an enormous personal responsibility of the Justices for decisions that they make in the name of the Constitution. The Justices may hesitate to admit even to themselves the burdens of judgment that they bear in implementing the Constitution.

FOURTEEN

Conclusion

[The] constitution [was] intended to endure for ages to come, and consequently, to be adapted to the various crises of human affairs.
　　　　　　　　　　　　　　　　　　　　– Chief Justice John Marshall[1]

I have a dream.
　　　　　　　　　　　　　　　　　　　　– Dr. Martin Luther King, Jr.

IN THE INTRODUCTORY CHAPTER, I emphasized that this would be a book about American constitutional practice – not just about the Constitution as a written text, but about the social, cultural, and political processes through which constitutional law emerges. To a large and possibly excessive extent, the Supreme Court has tended to dominate the book, because the Court stands center stage in the production of constitutional doctrine. But the Court is not the only actor in the drama. In this concluding chapter, I therefore want to step back from the details of constitutional doctrine and offer a few summary theses about the role of the written Constitution and the Supreme Court in our constitutional practice.

Our Constitution is a dynamic document, which draws its meaning partly from evolving thinking and the pressure of events. In the course of this book, I have offered many illustrations of this claim, involving (among others) the historical flow of power to the executive branch, the scope of congressional power under the Commerce Clause, the expansive reach of currently recognized rights to freedom of speech and association, and the interpretation of the Equal Protection Clause. To reiterate just one vivid example, the originally written Constitution imposed no obligation on the *federal* government to accord all citizens "the equal protection of the laws," and no subsequent amendment has added such a requirement. Nevertheless, the Supreme Court has held consistently for a half-century that the Due Process Clause of the Fifth Amendment, which was written and ratified at a time when the Constitution tolerated slavery, subjects the federal government to the same equal protection norms as the states. It has thus invalidated federal legislation that discriminates on the basis of race and gender.

In theory, many of the changes in our constitutional practice might have occurred through constitutional amendments. Generally they have not.[2] The Constitution is difficult to amend. Also, many Americans regard it worshipfully and hesitate either to change it or to think it needful of change. For better or for worse, American constitutional practice thus relies more on flexible, pragmatic practices of constitutional interpretation than on frequent formal amendment.

Despite the dynamism of American constitutional practice, the Constitution is at the center of decision-making and debate. Americans revere their Constitution. In the courts and on the outside, constitutional argument is a reasoned process, in which justifications for governmental action must ultimately trace to the written Constitution. For example, we tend not to say that "it is an emergency, and therefore the Constitution does *not* apply" or that "the Constitution does not control because the situation is one that the framers and ratifiers could never have foreseen." Rather, for better or worse, we tend to echo the famous words of Chief Justice John Marshall, quoted at the beginning of this chapter, that the Constitution was "intended to endure for ages to come, and consequently, to be *adapted* to the various crises in human affairs."[3] In some circumstances, we defend interpretations restricting constitutional guarantees by recalling Justice Robert Jackson's equally famous observation that the Constitution should not be interpreted as "a suicide pact."[4] Always, however, *interpretations* of the Constitution are required. Even in times of crisis, we embrace the Constitution as the ultimate law and adhere to the forms of constitutional argument. In many cases, a restraining force almost surely results, even if the net effect – as discussed in Chapter Twelve – is to encourage an approach to constitutional adjudication that leaves the document highly flexible and that leads to endless debates about whether and how its flexibility ought to be exploited.

Despite the Constitution's flexibility on some points, it is inflexible on others. Although the President's "war powers" are flexible and various rights may be compromised when necessary to promote a compelling government interest, elections for Congress are reliably held every two years and for President every four years. Americans can be confident, largely because of the Constitution, that the head of government next year will be the elected President of the United States, not some other official who may command greater support from the Joint Chiefs of Staff.

It is important to understand, however, that claims such as these depend as much on constitutional practice as do other claims about constitutional law. It takes knowledge of constitutional history and American political culture, not just the constitutional text, to know which elements of the Constitution are likely to be regarded as most flexible and which as most unyielding. If President Abraham Lincoln and the Congress had jointly decided to postpone the 1864 elections on grounds of military necessity, and if their doing so had won approval in the court of public opinion, it would be harder to say with confidence today that whatever else may be subject to compromise, the Constitution flatly demands regular elections. In American constitutional practice, precedent matters.

Actors besides the courts influence the development of constitutional law. As I have emphasized, constitutional questions involving the scope of presidential power in war and foreign affairs have mostly been resolved in informal political struggles between Congress and the President. The courts have generally stood on the sidelines, either because the issues present "political questions" in the formal sense (as discussed in Chapter Nine) or because judges and Justices have recognized that management of issues of war and peace lies beyond their practical competence.

It is also worth recalling that judicial orders are not self-enforcing. The officials to whom the Supreme Court issues its directives are vital players in American constitutional practice. Occasionally they drag their feet. As discussed most fully in Chapter Four, gaps sometimes exist between "the law in practice" and "the law on the books." On at least a few occasions the Supreme Court appears not to have issued rulings that it otherwise would have handed down simply because it knew that those rulings would have met defiance.

In recent years, state legislators in a number of states have recurrently enacted legislation resisting *Roe v. Wade*[5] and prodding the Supreme Court to reconsider that decision. Before the Civil War, abolitionists maintained a drumbeat of pressure to try to force reconsideration of a Supreme Court ruling that upheld harsh legislation involving the return of "fugitive slaves."[6] When the Supreme Court of the same era held that Congress had no authority to limit the spread of slavery into the territories,[7] Abraham Lincoln argued that although the rule of law required obedience to particular judicial decisions (and their declarations of the rights of the immediate parties to a case), a single Supreme Court ruling could not definitively settle the issue of ultimate constitutional principle: "[I]f the policy of the government, upon vital questions, affecting the whole people, is to be irrevocably fixed by decisions of the Supreme Court, the instant they are made, in ordinary litigation . . . , the people will have ceased, to be their own rulers, having, to that extent resigned their government, into the hands of that eminent tribunal."[8]

As so often, Lincoln hit close to the truth. Presumptively the Supreme Court does and should have the last word on constitutional questions within its domain. Among the Court's central functions is to resolve conclusively matters about which reasonable people might otherwise differ. But the lines between constitutional justice and moral right are sometimes blurry and permeable. In the area of overlap, the Court's authority ultimately rests on the respect with which it and its judgments are viewed. That respect can be great, but probably never boundless. As I noted in Chapter Twelve, Lincoln, ranked by many as the greatest of all American Presidents, once defied an order by the Chief Justice of the United States.

Judicial decision-making is inevitably "political" in one sense of that term. Interpreting the Constitution is an inherently practical affair, not a merely intellectual one. As I emphasized at an early point, in trying to draw guidance from the Constitution's text and history and from judicial precedents, judges and Justices must often ask which interpretation would be "best." This is a practical judgment, sometimes with a moral dimension, about what will give us the best law that our Constitution will permit. Judgments of this kind will often be controversial, with liberals and conservatives disagreeing in ways that ultimately trace to their political views.[9]

Nevertheless, judicial decisions are not characteristically political in the same way that decisions by Congress or the President are political. Judicial decisions are both made and expressed in the medium of law, not electoral politics, and the medium of law demands considered attention to the Constitution's text, history, and structure, as well as to judicial precedent. In addition, judges and Justices do not vote just for outcomes, but for rules that will be applied in future cases. They do, or should, care about the integrity of constitutional doctrine – about having sensible and consistent *rules* governing freedom of speech, for example, and not just about deciding whether a particular speaker gets to utter a particular statement. Finally, judicial decisions rarely are (and never should be) partisan in the sense of being designed to favor one or another political party.

The role of politics appropriately triggers concern. In discussing the role of politics in judicial decision-making, I have repeatedly made both a descriptive and a normative claim. The descriptive claim is that moral and political values influence constitutional decision-making. The normative claim is that when there is a choice between one *otherwise plausible* interpretation that would be morally or practically better and another that would be morally or practically worse, judges and Justices are right to take the moral or practical implications into account. For them not to do so would seem to me wrong-headed.

I should emphasize, however, that my normative claim is a limited one, which does not rule out the possibility that Supreme Court Justices may currently give too much weight to their views of moral or practical desirability and thereby make constitutional decision-making *too* political. If the Justices give excessive weight to their own views, in disregard of other factors that also ought to matter in constitutional adjudication (including reasonable fidelity to the text, history, precedent, and interests in consistency and predictability), we lose at least some of the benefits of what John Marshall called "a government of laws, and not of men."[10] In addition, the Justices acquire an excessive and unfair amount of political power, including power to frustrate democratic self-government.

Precisely how much weight should Supreme Court Justices give to their views of what would be morally or practically best? Do they currently tend to give too much weight to those views? These are complex questions, with no short or easy answers. Indeed, the question whether the Justices *generally* let their moral and practical judgments have too much influence in their decision-making may well be misleading. It seems unlikely that there is one "right" formula about the role that moral and practical considerations ought to play in all cases, equally applicable to run-of-the-mill disputes under the Due Process and Equal Protection Clauses (currently governed by a "rational basis" test) and, for example, to *Brown v. Board of Education*.[11] Moreover, as the example of *Brown* may also suggest, we should not let concern with the degree to which the Justices are influenced by moral and practical considerations distract attention from substantive questions, involving which moral values and practical factors the Justices ought to be guided by. Perhaps the most infamous cases in Supreme Court history are those in which the Court arrayed itself on the wrong side of an issue with an irreducibly moral aspect.

The Supreme Court seldom diverges too far from the central values of popular political majorities. This vitally important and possibly obvious point was first stated with respectable precision and documentation by the distinguished political scientist Robert Dahl.[12] (It had been anticipated roughly a half-century earlier by political cartoonist Finley Peter Dunne, whose "Mr. Dooley" offered the pungent observation that "th' supreme coort follows th' iliction returns."[13]) Indeed, only twice in American history does the Court appear to have veered seriously out of line with generally prevailing views: An aged and conservative court notoriously outraged the public by threatening to scuttle the New Deal in one era, and the Warren Court prompted a political demand for "law and order" and "strict constructionist" judges in another.

The factors that tie judicial doctrine to prevailing cultural trends are probably as psychological and sociological as overtly political. In determining what is the fairest, best, or most reasonable interpretation of constitutional language, judges and Justices are likely both to share and to apply the prevalent values of their time. The appointments process is also of vital importance. Supreme Court Justices must be nominated by the President and confirmed by the Senate. Both attend closely to the values and political views of candidates for the bench.

Although the courts have an important role in protecting minority rights, the protection historically afforded to minorities should not be exaggerated. As people of their times, judges and Justices of the Supreme Court have seldom been at the forefront of movements to protect minorities, whether African Americans before *Brown v. Board of Education*, or women before the 1970s, or gays and lesbians before very recently. In addition, judges and Justices are as prone to fear in fearful times as is nearly everyone else. It is therefore no surprise that civil liberties have tended to fare badly in periods of war and emergency.

Once a view about basic fairness has achieved broad acceptance, however, courts can be expected to insist that the shared ideal should be enforced consistently throughout the nation. To take an obvious example, once the ideal of racial equality became widely accepted, the Supreme Court moved determinedly to stamp out pockets of resistance. More recently, the Court invalidated a statute barring homosexual sodomy[14] after, but only after, statutes of this kind had become rare, apparently because of an emerging consensus that the government has no business regulating private sexual conduct among mature adults.

Political movements help to shape constitutional law. Prevailing national norms of fairness, which obviously influence the Supreme Court, do not crystallize spontaneously. The civil rights movement undoubtedly had a profound effect on the Justices of the Supreme Court as well as on public opinion. Many of the Court's decisions of the 1960s and 1970s enforcing civil rights are the legacy of that movement. The Court's steps to protect rights of gender equality, beginning in the 1970s, again show the tendency of politics, in its various manifestations, to influence constitutional law.

It matters who sits on the Supreme Court. To maintain that the Supreme Court seldom strays too far from the political mainstream, as I just did, is not to claim that the Court's rulings make no difference. The Justices can do their job poorly or well. Assessment partly involves technical competence. Constitutional law should be clear, consistent, and predictable. But the job of a Supreme Court Justice also calls for sound practical judgment and moral vision.

When deciding constitutional issues in light of a moral vision, Supreme Court Justices have at least some capacity to shape the political environment in which the Court operates: They have a power to persuade. Under the leadership of Earl Warren, the Court probably helped to forge the national consensus that race-based discrimination was wrong – a remarkably rapid development in light of the long history of the contrary view. The "great dissenters," Justices Oliver Wendell Holmes and Louis Brandeis, helped to persuade first liberal intellectuals and then a wider public that the First Amendment should protect a broad right of people to speak their minds, even when uttering "the thought that we hate."[15]

Further, although the mass public takes a lively interest in some of the issues that come before the Supreme Court, it pays little or no heed to, and indeed probably has no firm views about, others. With respect to these matters, the Court enjoys a relatively open field within which to exercise judgment, for better or for worse.

In view of the important and partly "political" role played by Supreme Court Justices, appointments to the Court call for sensitive judgments, both by the President, who nominates candidates for the bench, and by the Senate, which must confirm or reject the President's selections. When the President and the Senate differ in their judgments, confirmation battles can be messy affairs, which occasionally bring discredit on all involved. Even so, at least some pulling and tugging is invited by the Constitution itself, which assigns important if not coequal roles in the appointments process to separate branches of government.

There are fewer simple truths about constitutional law than most Americans would probably expect. The principal aim of this book has been to assist those who want to understand our constitutional practice in all of its daunting, sometimes maddening, and occasionally inspiring complexity. The life of the law, Holmes once wrote, has not been logic but experience. In the past, constitutional law has taken many turns that would not have been easy to predict. The Constitution's future remains to be shaped.

Appendix: The Constitution of the United States

Preamble

We the People of the United States, in Order to form a more perfect Union, establish Justice, insure domestic Tranquility, provide for the common defence, promote the general Welfare, and secure the Blessings of Liberty to ourselves and our Posterity, do ordain and establish this Constitution for the United States of America.

Article I

Section 1. All legislative Powers herein granted shall be vested in a Congress of the United States, which shall consist of a Senate and House of Representatives.

Section 2. [1] The House of Representatives shall be composed of Members chosen every second Year by the People of the several States, and the Electors in each State shall have the Qualifications requisite for Electors of the most numerous Branch of the State Legislature.

[2] No Person shall be a Representative who shall not have attained to the Age of twenty five Years, and been seven Years a Citizen of the United States, and who shall not, when elected, be an Inhabitant of that State in which he shall be chosen.

[3] Representatives and direct Taxes shall be apportioned among the several States which may be included within this Union, according to their respective Numbers, which shall be determined by adding to the whole Number of free Persons, including those bound to Service for a Term of Years, and excluding Indians not taxed, three fifths of all other Persons. The actual Enumeration shall be made within three Years after the first Meeting of the Congress of the United States, and within every subsequent Term of ten Years, in such Manner as they shall by Law direct. The Number of Representatives shall not exceed one for every thirty Thousand, but each

State shall have at Least one Representative; and until such enumeration shall be made, the State of New Hampshire shall be entitled to chuse three, Massachusetts eight, Rhode Island and Providence Plantations one, Connecticut five, New York six, New Jersey four, Pennsylvania eight, Delaware one, Maryland six, Virginia ten, North Carolina five, South Carolina five, and Georgia three.

[4] When vacancies happen in the Representation from any State, the Executive Authority thereof shall issue Writs of Election to fill such Vacancies.

[5] The House of Representatives shall chuse their Speaker and other Officers; and shall have the sole Power of Impeachment.

Section 3. [1] The Senate of the United States shall be composed of two Senators from each State, chosen by the Legislature thereof, for six Years; and each Senator shall have one Vote.

[2] Immediately after they shall be assembled in Consequence of the first Election, they shall be divided as equally as may be into three Classes. The Seats of the Senators of the first Class shall be vacated at the Expiration of the Second Year, of the second Class at the Expiration of the fourth Year, and of the third Class at the Expiration of the sixth Year, so that one third may be chosen every second Year; and if Vacancies happen by Resignation, or otherwise, during the Recess of the Legislature of any State, the Executive thereof may make temporary Appointments until the next Meeting of the Legislature, which shall then fill such Vacancies.

[3] No Person shall be a Senator who shall not have attained to the Age of thirty Years, and been nine Years a Citizen of the United States, and who shall not, when elected, by an Inhabitant of that State for which he shall be chosen.

[4] The Vice President of the United States shall be President of the Senate, but shall have no Vote, unless they be equally divided.

[5] The Senate shall chuse their other Officers, and also a President pro tempore, in the Absence of the Vice President, or when he shall exercise the Office of President of the United States.

[6] The Senate shall have the sole Power to try all Impeachments. When sitting for that Purpose, they shall be on Oath or Affirmation. When the President of the United States is tried, the Chief Justice shall preside: And no Person shall be convicted without the Concurrence of two thirds of the Members present.

[7] Judgment in Cases of Impeachment shall not extend further than to removal from Office, and disqualification to hold and enjoy any Office

of honor, Trust, or Profit under the United States: but the Party convicted shall nevertheless be liable and subject to Indictment, Trial, Judgment, and Punishment, according to Law.

Section 4. [1] The Times, Places and Manner of holding Elections for Senators and Representatives, shall be prescribed in each State by the Legislature thereof; but the Congress may at any time by Law make or alter such Regulations, except as to the Places of chusing Senators.

[2] The Congress shall assemble at least once in every Year, and such Meeting shall be on the first Monday in December, unless they shall by Law appoint a different Day.

Section 5. [1] Each House shall be the Judge of the Elections, Returns, and Qualifications of its own Members, and a Majority of each shall constitute a Quorum to do Business; but a smaller Number may adjourn from day to day, and may be authorized to compel the Attendance of absent Members, in such Manner, and under such Penalties as each House may provide.

[2] Each House may determine the Rules of its Proceedings, punish its Members for disorderly Behavior, and, with the Concurrence of two thirds, expel a Member.

[3] Each House shall keep a Journal of its Proceedings, and from time to time publish the same, excepting such Parts as may in their Judgment require Secrecy; and the Yeas and Nays of the Members of either House on any question shall, at the Desire of one fifth of those Present, be entered on the Journal.

[4] Neither House, during the Session of Congress, shall without the Consent of the other, adjourn for more than three days, nor to any other Place than that in which the two Houses shall be sitting.

Section 6. [1] The Senators and Representatives shall receive a Compensation for their Services, to be ascertained by Law, and paid out of the Treasury of the United States. They shall in all Cases, except Treason, Felony and Breach of the Peace, be privileged from Arrest during their Attendance at the Session of their respective Houses, and in going to and returning from the same; and for any Speech or Debate in either House, they shall not be questioned in any other Place.

[2] No Senator or Representative shall, during the Time for which he was elected, be appointed to any civil Office under the Authority of the United States, which shall have been created, or the Emoluments whereof shall have been increased during such time; and no Person holding any Office under the United States, shall be a Member of either House during his Continuance in Office.

Section 7. [1] All Bills for raising Revenue shall originate in the House of Representatives; but the Senate may propose or concur with Amendments as on other Bills.

[2] Every Bill which shall have passed the House of Representatives and the Senate, shall, before it become a Law, be presented to the President of the United States; If he approve he shall sign it, but if not he shall return it, with his Objections to the House in which it shall have originated, who shall enter the Objections at large on their Journal, and proceed to reconsider it. If after such Reconsideration two thirds of that House shall agree to pass the Bill, it shall be sent together with the Objections, to the other House, by which it shall likewise be reconsidered, and if approved by two thirds of that House, it shall become a Law. But in all such Cases the Votes of both Houses shall be determined by yeas and Nays, and the Names of the Persons voting for and against the Bill shall be entered on the Journal of each House respectively. If any Bill shall not be returned by the President within ten Days (Sundays excepted) after it shall have been presented to him, the Same shall be a Law, in like Manner as if he had signed it, unless the Congress by their Adjournment prevent its Return in which Case it shall not be a Law.

[3] Every Order, Resolution, or Vote, to Which the Concurrence of the Senate and House of Representatives may be necessary (except on a question of Adjournment) shall be presented to the President of the United States; and before the Same shall take Effect, shall be approved by him, or being disapproved by him, shall be repassed by two thirds of the Senate and House of Representatives, according to the Rules and Limitations prescribed in the Case of a Bill.

Section 8. [1] The Congress shall have Power To lay and collect Taxes, Duties, Imposts and Excises, to pay the Debts and provide for the common Defence and general Welfare of the United States; but all Duties, Imposts and Excises shall be uniform throughout the United States;

[2] To borrow money on the credit of the United States;

[3] To regulate Commerce with foreign Nations, and among the several States, and with the Indian Tribes;

[4] To establish an uniform Rule of Naturalization, and uniform Laws on the subject of Bankruptcies throughout the United States;

[5] To coin Money, regulate the Value thereof, and of foreign Coin, and fix the Standard of Weights and Measures;

[6] To provide for the Punishment of counterfeiting the Securities and current Coin of the United States;

[7] To Establish Post Offices and Post Roads;

[8] To promote the Progress of Science and useful Arts, by securing for limited Times to Authors and Inventors the exclusive Right to their respective Writings and Discoveries;

[9] To constitute Tribunals inferior to the supreme Court;

[10] To define and punish Piracies and Felonies committed on the high Seas, and Offenses against the Law of Nations;

[11] To declare War, grant Letters of Marque and Reprisal, and make Rules concerning Captures on Land and Water;

[12] To raise and support Armies, but no Appropriation of Money to that Use shall be for a longer Term than two Years;

[13] To provide and maintain a Navy;

[14] To make Rules for the Government and Regulation of the land and naval Forces;

[15] To provide for calling forth the Militia to execute the Laws of the Union, suppress Insurrections and repel Invasions;

[16] To provide for organizing, arming, and disciplining the Militia, and for governing such Part of them as may be employed in the Service of the United States, reserving to the States respectively, the Appointment of the Officers, and the Authority of training the Militia according to the discipline prescribed by Congress;

[17] To exercise exclusive Legislation in all Cases whatsoever, over such District (not exceeding ten Miles square) as may, by Cession of particular States, and the Acceptance of Congress, become the Seat of the Government of the United States, and to exercise like Authority over all Places purchased by the Consent of the Legislature of the State in which the Same shall be, for the Erection of Forts, Magazines, Arsenals, dock-Yards, and other needful Buildings; – And

[18] To make all Laws which shall be necessary and proper for carrying into Execution the foregoing Powers, and all other Powers vested by this Constitution in the Government of the United States, or in any Department or Officer thereof.

Section 9. [1] The Migration or Importation of Such Persons as any of the States now existing shall think proper to admit, shall not be prohibited by the Congress prior to the Year one thousand eight hundred and eight, but a Tax or duty may be imposed on such Importation, not exceeding ten dollars for each Person.

[2] The privilege of the Writ of Habeas Corpus shall not be suspended, unless when in Cases of Rebellion or Invasion the public Safety may require it.

[3] No Bill of Attainder or ex post facto Law shall be passed.

[4] No Capitation, or other direct, Tax shall be laid, unless in Proportion to the Census or Enumeration herein before directed to be taken.

[5] No Tax or Duty shall be laid on Articles exported from any State.

[6] No Preference shall be given by any Regulation of Commerce or Revenue to the Ports of one State over those of another: nor shall Vessels bound to, or from, one State be obliged to enter, clear, or pay Duties in another.

[7] No money shall be drawn from the Treasury, but in Consequence of Appropriations made by Law; and a regular Statement and Account of the Receipts and Expenditures of all public Money shall be published from time to time.

[8] No Title of Nobility shall be granted by the United States: And no Person holding any Office of Profit or Trust under them, shall, without the Consent of the Congress, accept of any present, Emolument, Office, or Title, of any kind whatever, from any King, Prince, or foreign State.

Section 10. [1] No State shall enter into any Treaty, Alliance, or Confederation; grant Letters of Marque and Reprisal; coin Money; emit Bills of Credit; make any Thing but gold and silver Coin a Tender in Payment of Debts; pass any Bill of Attainder, ex post facto Law, or Law impairing the Obligation of Contracts, or grant any Title of Nobility.

[2] No State shall, without the Consent of the Congress, lay any Imposts or Duties on Imports or Exports, except what may be absolutely necessary for executing its inspection Laws: and the net Produce of all Duties and Imposts, laid by any State on Imports or Exports, shall be for the Use of the Treasury of the United States; and all such Laws shall be subject to the Revision and Controul of the Congress.

[3] No State shall, without the Consent of Congress, lay any Duty of Tonnage, keep Troops, or Ships of War in time of Peace, enter into any Agreement or Compact with another State, or with a foreign Power, or engage in War, unless actually invaded, or in such imminent Danger as will not admit of delay.

Article II

Section 1. [1] The executive Power shall be vested in a President of the United States of America. He shall hold his Office during the Term of four Years, and, together with the Vice President, chosen for the same Term, be elected, as follows:

[2] Each State shall appoint, in such Manner as the Legislature thereof may direct, a Number of Electors, equal to the whole Number of Senators and Representatives to which the State may be entitled in the Congress; but no Senator or Representative, or Person holding an Office of Trust or Profit under the United States, shall be appointed an Elector.

[3] The Electors shall meet in their respective States, and vote by Ballot for two Persons, of whom one at least shall not be an Inhabitant of the same State with themselves. And they shall make a List of all the Persons voted for, and of the Number of Votes for each; which List they shall sign and certify, and transmit sealed to the Seat of the Government of the United States, directed to the President of the Senate. The President of the Senate shall, in the Presence of the Senate and House of Representatives, open all the Certificates, and the Votes shall then be counted. The Person having the greatest Number of Votes shall be the President, if such Number be a Majority of the whole Number of Electors appointed; and if there be more than one who have such Majority, and have an equal Number of Votes, then the House of Representatives shall immediately chuse by Ballot one of them for President; and if no Person have a Majority, then from the five highest on the List the said House shall in like Manner chuse the President. But in chusing the President, the Votes shall be taken by States the Representation from each State having one Vote; A quorum for this Purpose shall consist of a Member or Members from two thirds of the States, and a Majority of all the States shall be necessary to a Choice. In every Case, after the Choice of the President, the Person having the greater Number of Votes of the Electors shall be the Vice President. But if there should remain two or more who have equal Votes, the Senate shall chuse from them by Ballot the Vice President.

[4] The Congress may determine the Time of chusing the Electors, and the Day on which they shall give their Votes; which Day shall be the same throughout the United States.

[5] No person except a natural born Citizen, or a Citizen of the United States, at the time of the Adoption of this Constitution, shall be eligible to the Office of President; neither shall any Person be eligible to that Office who shall not have attained to the Age of thirty five Years, and been fourteen Years a Resident within the United States.

[6] In case of the removal of the President from Office, or of his Death, Resignation or Inability to discharge the Powers and Duties of the said Office, the Same shall devolve on the Vice President, and the Congress may by Law provide for the Case of Removal, Death, Resignation or Inability, both of the President and Vice President, declaring what Officer shall then

act as President, and such Officer shall act accordingly, until the Disability be removed, or a President shall be elected.

[7] The President shall, at stated Times, receive for his Services, a Compensation, which shall neither be increased nor diminished during the Period for which he shall have been elected, and he shall not receive within that Period any other Emolument from the United States, or any of them.

[8] Before he enter on the Execution of his Office, he shall take the following Oath or Affirmation: "I do solemnly swear (or affirm) that I will faithfully execute the Office of President of the United States, and will to the best of my Ability, preserve, protect and defend the Constitution of the United States."

Section 2. [1] The President shall be Commander in Chief of the Army and Navy of the United States, and of the militia of the several States, when called into the actual Service of the United States; he may require the Opinion, in writing, of the principal Officer in each of the Executive Departments, upon any Subject relating to the Duties of their respective Offices, and he shall have Power to grant Reprieves and Pardons for Offenses against the United States, except in Cases of Impeachment.

[2] He shall have Power, by and with the Advice and Consent of the Senate to make Treaties, provided two thirds of the Senators present concur; and he shall nominate, and by and with the Advice and Consent of the Senate, shall appoint Ambassadors, other public Ministers and Consuls, Judges of the supreme Court, and all other Officers of the United States, whose Appointments are not herein otherwise provided for, and which shall be established by Law; but the Congress may by Law vest the Appointment of such inferior Officers, as they think proper, in the President alone, in the Courts of Law, or in the Heads of Departments.

[3] The President shall have Power to fill up all Vacancies that may happen during the Recess of the Senate, by granting Commissions which shall expire at the End of their next Session.

Section 3. He shall from time to time give to the Congress Information of the State of the Union, and recommend to their Consideration such Measures as he shall judge necessary and expedient; he may, on extraordinary Occasions, convene both Houses, or either of them, and in Case of Disagreement between them, with Respect to the Time of Adjournment, he may adjourn them to such Time as he shall think proper; he shall receive Ambassadors and other public Ministers; he shall take Care that the Laws be faithfully executed, and shall Commission all the Officers of the United States.

Section 4. The President, Vice President and all civil Officers of the United States, shall be removed from Office on Impeachment for, and Conviction of, Treason, Bribery, or other high Crimes and Misdemeanors.

Article III

Section 1. The judicial Power of the United States, shall be vested in one supreme Court, and in such inferior Courts as the Congress may from time to time ordain and establish. The Judges, both of the supreme and inferior Courts, shall hold their Offices during good Behaviour, and shall, at stated Times, receive for their Services a Compensation, which shall not be diminished during their Continuance in Office.

Section 2. [1] The judicial Power shall extend to all Cases, in Law and Equity, arising under this Constitution, the Laws of the United States, and Treaties made, or which shall be made, under their Authority; – to all Cases affecting Ambassadors, other public Ministers and Consuls; – to all Cases of admiralty and maritime Jurisdiction; – to Controversies to which the United States shall be a Party; – to Controversies between two or more States; – between a State and Citizens of another State; – between Citizens of different States; – between Citizens of the same State claiming Lands under the Grants of different States, and between a State, or the Citizens thereof, and foreign States, Citizens or Subjects.

[2] In all Cases affecting Ambassadors, other public Ministers and Consuls, and those in which a State shall be a Party, the supreme Court shall have original Jurisdiction. In all the other Cases before mentioned, the supreme Court shall have appellate Jurisdiction, both as to Law and Fact, with such Exceptions, and under such Regulations as the Congress shall make.

[3] The trial of all Crimes, except in Cases of Impeachment, shall be by Jury; and such Trial shall be held in the State where the said Crimes shall have been committed; but when not committed within any State, the Trial shall be at such Place or Places as the Congress may by Law have directed.

Section 3. [1] Treason against the United States, shall consist only in levying War against them, or, in adhering to their Enemies, giving them Aid and Comfort. No Person shall be convicted of Treason unless on the Testimony of two Witnesses to the same overt Act, or on Confession in open Court.

[2] The Congress shall have Power to declare the Punishment of Treason, but no Attainder of Treason shall work Corruption of Blood, or Forfeiture except during the Life of the Person attainted.

Article IV

Section 1. Full Faith and Credit shall be given in each State to the public Acts, Records, and judicial Proceedings of every other State. And the Congress may by general Laws prescribe the Manner in which such Acts, Records and Proceedings shall be proved, and the Effect thereof.

Section 2. [1] The Citizens of each State shall be entitled to all Privileges and Immunities of Citizens in the several States.

[2] A Person charged in any State with Treason, Felony, or other Crime, who shall flee from Justice, and be found in another State, shall on demand of the executive Authority of the State from which he fled, be delivered up, to be removed to the State having Jurisdiction of the Crime.

[3] No Person held to Service or Labour in one State, under the Laws thereof, escaping into another, shall, in Consequence of any Law or Regulation therein, be discharged from such Service or Labour, but shall be delivered up on Claim of the Party to whom such Service or Labour may be due.

Section 3. [1] New States may be admitted by the Congress into this Union; but no new State shall be formed or erected within the Jurisdiction of any other State; nor any State be formed by the Junction of two or more States, or Parts of States, without the Consent of the Legislatures of the States concerned as well as of the Congress.

[2] The Congress shall have Power to dispose of and make all needful Rules and Regulations respecting the Territory or other Property belonging to the United States; and nothing in this Constitution shall be so construed as to Prejudice any Claims of the United States, or of any particular State.

Section 4. The United States shall guarantee to every State in this Union a Republican Form of Government, and shall protect each of them against Invasion; and on Application of the Legislature, or of the Executive (when the Legislature cannot be convened) against domestic Violence.

Article V

The Congress, whenever two thirds of both Houses shall deem it necessary, shall propose Amendments to this Constitution, or, on the Application of the Legislatures of two thirds of the several States, shall call a Convention for proposing Amendments, which, in either Case, shall be valid to all Intents and Purposes, as part of this Constitution, when ratified by the Legislatures of three fourths of the several States, or by Conventions in three fourths thereof, as the one or the other Mode of Ratification may be proposed by the Congress; Provided that no Amendment which may be made prior to the Year One thousand eight hundred and eight shall in any Manner affect the first and fourth Clauses in the Ninth Section of the first Article; and that no State, without its Consent, shall be deprived of its equal Suffrage in the Senate.

Article VI

All Debts contracted and Engagements entered into, before the Adoption of this Constitution shall be as valid against the United States under this Constitution, as under the Confederation.

This Constitution, and the Laws of the United States which shall be made in Pursuance thereof; and all Treaties made, or which shall be made, under the Authority of the United States, shall be the supreme Law of the Land; and the Judges in every State shall be bound thereby, any Thing in the Constitution or Laws of any State to the Contrary notwithstanding.

The Senators and Representatives before mentioned, and the Members of the several State Legislatures, and all executive and judicial Officers, both of the United States and of the several States, shall be bound by Oath or Affirmation, to support this Constitution; but no religious Test shall ever be required as a Qualification to any Office or public Trust under the United States.

Article VII

The Ratification of the Conventions of nine States shall be sufficient for the Establishment of this Constitution between the States so ratifying the Same.

Amendments of the Constitution of the United States of America, Proposed by Congress and Ratified by the Legislatures of the Several States Pursuant to the Fifth Article of the Original Constitution

Amendment I [1791]

Congress shall make no law respecting an establishment of religion, or prohibiting the free exercise thereof; or abridging the freedom of speech, or of the press; or the right of the people peaceably to assemble, and to petition the Government for a redress of grievances.

Amendment II [1791]

A well regulated Militia, being necessary to the security of a free State, the right of the people to keep and bear Arms, shall not be infringed.

Amendment III [1791]

No Soldier shall, in time of peace be quartered in any house, without the consent of the Owner, nor in time of war, but in a manner to be prescribed by law.

Amendment IV [1791]

The right of the people to be secure in their persons, houses, papers, and effects, against unreasonable searches and seizures, shall not be violated, and no Warrants shall issue, but upon probable cause, supported by Oath or affirmation and particularly describing the place to be searched, and the persons or things to be seized.

Amendment V [1791]

No person shall be held to answer for a capital, or otherwise infamous crime, unless on a presentment or indictment of a Grand Jury, except in cases arising in the land or naval forces, or in the Militia, when in actual service in time of War or public danger; nor shall any person be subject for the same offence to be twice put in jeopardy of life or limb; nor shall be compelled in any criminal case to be a witness against himself, nor be deprived of life, liberty, or property, without due process of law; nor shall private property be taken for public use, without just compensation.

Amendment VI [1791]

In all criminal prosecutions, the accused shall enjoy the right to a speedy and public trial, by an impartial jury of the State and district wherein the crime shall have been committed, which district shall have been previously ascertained by law, and to be informed of the nature and cause of the accusation; to be confronted with the witnesses against him; to have compulsory process for obtaining witnesses in his favor, and to have the Assistance of Counsel for his defence.

Amendment VII [1791]

In Suits at common law, where the value in controversy shall exceed twenty dollars, the right of trial by jury shall be preserved, and no fact tried by jury, shall be otherwise re-examined in any Court of the United States, than according to the rules of the common law.

Amendment VIII [1791]

Excessive bail shall not be required, nor excessive fines imposed, nor cruel and unusual punishments inflicted.

Amendment IX [1791]

The enumeration in the Constitution, of certain rights, shall not be construed to deny or disparage others retained by the people.

Amendment X [1791]

The powers not delegated to the United States by the Constitution, nor prohibited by it to the States, are reserved to the States respectively, or to the people.

Amendment XI [1798]

The Judicial power of the United States shall not be construed to extend to any suit in law or equity, commenced or prosecuted against one of the United States by Citizens of another State, or by Citizens or Subjects of any Foreign State.

Amendment XII [1804]

The Electors shall meet in their respective states and vote by ballot for President and Vice-President, one of whom, at least, shall not be an inhabitant of the same state with themselves; they shall name in their ballots the person voted for as President, and in distinct ballots the person voted for as Vice-President, and they shall make distinct lists of all persons voted for as President, and of all persons voted for as Vice-President, and of the number of votes for each, which lists they shall sign and certify, and transmit sealed to the seat of the government of the United States, directed to the President of the Senate; – The President of the Senate shall, in the presence of the Senate and House of Representatives, open all the certificates and the votes shall then be counted; – The person having the greatest number of votes for President, shall be the President, if such number be a majority of the whole number of Electors appointed; and if no person have such majority, then from the persons having the highest numbers not exceeding three on the list of those voted for as President, the House of Representatives shall choose immediately, by ballot, the President. But in choosing the President, the votes shall be taken by states, the representation from each state having one vote; a quorum for this purpose shall consist of a member or members from two-thirds of the states, and a majority of all the states shall be necessary to a choice. And if the House of Representatives shall not choose a President whenever the right of choice shall devolve upon them before the fourth day of March next following, then the Vice-President shall act as President, as in the case of the death or other constitutional disability of the President. – The person having the greatest number of votes as Vice-President, shall be the Vice-President, if such number be a majority of the whole number of Electors appointed, and if no person have a majority, then from the two highest numbers on the list, the Senate shall choose the Vice-President; a quorum for the purpose shall consist of two-thirds of the whole number of Senators, and a majority of the whole number shall be necessary to a choice. But no person constitutionally ineligible to the office of President shall be eligible to that of Vice-President of the United States.

Amendment XIII [1865]

Section 1. Neither slavery nor involuntary servitude, except as a punishment for crime whereof the party shall have been duly convicted, shall exist within the United States, or any place subject to their jurisdiction.

Section 2. Congress shall have power to enforce this article by appropriate legislation.

Amendment XIV [1868]

Section 1. All persons born or naturalized in the United States, and subject to the jurisdiction thereof, are citizens of the United States and of the State wherein they reside. No State shall make or enforce any law which shall abridge the privileges or immunities of citizens of the United States; nor shall any State deprive any person of life, liberty, or property, without due process of law; nor deny to any person within its jurisdiction the equal protection of the laws.

Section 2. Representatives shall be apportioned among the several States according to their respective numbers, counting the whole number of persons in each State, excluding Indians not taxed. But when the right to vote at any election for the choice of electors for President and Vice President of the United States, Representatives in Congress, the Executive and Judicial officers of a State, or the members of the Legislature thereof, is denied to any of the male inhabitants of such State, being twenty-one years of age, and citizens of the United States, or in any way abridged, except for participation in rebellion, or other crime, the basis of representation therein shall be reduced in the proportion which the number of such male citizens shall bear to the whole number of male citizens twenty-one years of age in such State.

Section 3. No person shall be a Senator or Representative in Congress, or elector of President and Vice President, or hold any office, civil or military, under the United States, or under any State, who having previously taken an oath, as a member of Congress, or as an officer of the United States, or as a member of any State legislature, or as an executive or judicial officer of any State, to support the Constitution of the United States, shall have engaged in insurrection or rebellion against the same, or given aid or comfort to the enemies thereof. But Congress may by a vote of two-thirds of each House, remove such disability.

Section 4. The validity of the public debt of the United States, authorized by law, including debts incurred for payment of pensions and bounties for services in suppressing insurrection or rebellion, shall not be questioned. But neither the United States nor any State shall assume or pay any debt or obligation incurred in aid of insurrection or rebellion against the United States, or any claim for the loss or emancipation of any slave; but all such debts, obligations and claims shall be held illegal and void.

Section 5. The Congress shall have power to enforce, by appropriate legislation, the provisions of this article.

Amendment XV [1870]

Section 1. The right of citizens of the United States to vote shall not be denied or abridged by the United States or by any State on account of race, color, or previous condition of servitude.

Section 2. The Congress shall have power to enforce this article by appropriate legislation.

Amendment XVI [1913]

The Congress shall have power to lay and collect taxes on incomes, from whatever source derived, without apportionment among the several States, and without regard to any census or enumeration.

Amendment XVII [1913]

[1] The Senate of the United States shall be composed of two Senators from each State, elected by the people thereof, for six years; and each Senator shall have one vote. The electors in each State shall have the qualifications requisite for electors of the most numerous branch of the State legislatures.

[2] When vacancies happen in the representation of any State in the Senate, the executive authority of such State shall issue writs of election to fill such vacancies: *Provided*, That the legislature of any State may empower the executive thereof to make temporary appointments until the people fill the vacancies by election as the legislature may direct.

[3] This amendment shall not be so construed as to affect the election or term of any Senator chosen before it becomes valid as part of the Constitution.

Amendment XVIII [1919]

Section 1. After one year from the ratification of this article the manufacture, sale, or transportation of intoxicating liquors within, the importation thereof into, or the exportation thereof from the United States and all territory subject to the jurisdiction thereof for beverage purposes is hereby prohibited.

Section 2. The Congress and the several States shall have concurrent power to enforce this article by appropriate legislation.

Section 3. This article shall be inoperative unless it shall have been ratified as an amendment to the Constitution by the legislatures of the several States, as provided in the Constitution, within seven years from the date of the submission hereof to the States by the Congress.

Amendment XIX [1920]

[1] The right of citizens of the United States to vote shall not be denied or abridged by the United States or by any State on account of sex.

[2] Congress shall have power to enforce this article by appropriate legislation.

Amendment XX [1933]

Section 1. The terms of the President and Vice President shall end at noon on the 20th day of January, and the terms of Senators and Representatives at noon on the 3d day of January, of the years in which such terms would have ended if this article had not been ratified; and the terms of their successors shall then begin.

Section 2. The Congress shall assemble at least once in every year, and such meeting shall begin at noon on the 3d day of January, unless they shall by law appoint a different day.

Section 3. If, at the time fixed for the beginning of the term of the President, the President elect shall have died, the Vice President elect shall become President. If the President shall not have been chosen before the time fixed for the beginning of his term, or if the President elect shall have failed to qualify, then the Vice President elect shall act as President until a President shall have qualified; and the Congress may by law provide for the case wherein neither a President elect nor a Vice President elect shall have qualified, declaring who shall then act as President, or the manner in which one who is to act shall be selected, and such person shall act accordingly until a President or Vice President shall have qualified.

Section 4. The Congress may by law provide for the case of the death of any of the persons from whom the House of Representatives may choose a President whenever the right of choice shall have devolved upon them, and for the case of the death of any of the persons from whom the Senate may choose a Vice President whenever the right of choice shall have devolved upon them.

Section 5. Sections 1 and 2 shall take effect on the 15th day of October following the ratification of this article.

Section 6. This article shall be inoperative unless it shall have been ratified as an amendment to the Constitution by the legislatures of three-fourths of the several States within seven years from the date of its submission.

Amendment XXI [1933]

Section 1. The eighteenth article of amendment to the Constitution of the United States is hereby repealed.

Section 2. The transportation or importation into any State, Territory, or possession of the United States for delivery or use therein of intoxicating liquors, in violation of the laws thereof, is hereby prohibited.

Section 3. This article shall be inoperative unless it shall have been ratified as an amendment to the Constitution by conventions in the several States, as provided in the Constitution, within seven years from the date of the submission hereof to the States by the Congress.

Amendment XXII [1951]

Section 1. No person shall be elected to the office of the President more than twice, and no person who has held the office of President, or acted as President, for more than two years of a term to which some other person was elected President shall be elected to the office of President more than once. But this Article shall not apply to any person holding the office of President when this Article was proposed by the Congress, and shall not prevent any person who may be holding the office of President, or acting as President, during the term within which this Article becomes operative from holding the office of President or acting as President during the remainder of such term.

Section 2. This article shall be inoperative unless it shall have been ratified as an amendment to the Constitution by the legislatures of three-fourths of the several States within seven years from the date of its submission to the States by the Congress.

Amendment XXIII [1961]

Section 1. The District constituting the seat of Government of the United States shall appoint in such manner as the Congress may direct:

A number of electors of President and Vice President equal to the whole number of Senators and Representatives in Congress to which the District would be entitled if it were a State, but in no event more than the least populous state; they shall be in addition to those appointed by the states, but they shall be considered, for the purposes of the election of President and Vice President, to be electors appointed by a state; and they shall meet in the District and perform such duties as provided by the twelfth article of amendment.

Section 2. The Congress shall have power to enforce this article by appropriate legislation.

Amendment XXIV [1964]

Section 1. The right of citizens of the United States to vote in any primary or other election for President or Vice President, for electors for President or Vice President, or for Senator or Representative in Congress, shall not be denied or abridged by the United States or any State by reason of failure to pay any poll tax or other tax.

Section 2. The Congress shall have power to enforce this article by appropriate legislation.

Amendment XXV [1967]

Section 1. In case of the removal of the President from office or of his death or resignation, the Vice President shall become President.

Section 2. Whenever there is a vacancy in the office of the Vice President, the President shall nominate a Vice President who shall take office upon confirmation by a majority vote of both Houses of Congress.

Section 3. Whenever the President transmits to the President pro tempore of the Senate and the Speaker of the House of Representatives his written declaration that he is unable to discharge the powers and duties of his office, and until he transmits to them a written declaration to the contrary, such powers and duties shall be discharged by the Vice President as Acting President.

Section 4. Whenever the Vice President and a majority of either the principal officers of the executive departments or of such other body as Congress may by law provide, transmit to the President pro tempore of the Senate and the Speaker of the House of Representatives their written declaration that the President is unable to discharge the powers and duties of his office, the Vice President shall immediately assume the powers and duties of the office as Acting President.

Thereafter, when the President transmits to the President pro tempore of the Senate and the Speaker of the House of Representatives his written declaration that no inability exists, he shall resume the powers and duties of his office unless the Vice President and a majority of either the principal officers of the executive department or of such other body as Congress may by law provide, transmit within four days to the President pro tempore of the Senate and the Speaker of the House of Representatives their written declaration that the President is unable to discharge the powers and duties of his office. Thereupon Congress shall decide the issue, assembling within forty-eight hours for that purpose if not in session. If the Congress, within twenty-one days after receipt of the latter written declaration, or, if Congress is not in session, within twenty-one days after Congress is required to assemble, determines by two-thirds vote of both Houses that the President is unable to discharge the powers and duties of his office, the Vice President shall continue to discharge the same as Acting President; otherwise, the President shall resume the powers and duties of his office.

Amendment XXVI [1971]

Section 1. The right of citizens of the United States, who are eighteen years of age or older, to vote shall not be denied or abridged by the United States or by any State on account of age.

Section 2. The Congress shall have power to enforce this article by appropriate legislation.

Amendment XXVII [1992]*

No law, varying compensation for the services of Senators and Representatives, shall take effect, until an election of Representatives shall have intervened.

---

* On May 7, 1992, more than 200 years after it was first proposed by James Madison, the Twenty-Seventh Amendment was ratified by a thirty-eighth state (Michigan). Although Congress set no time limit for ratification of this amendment, ten of the *other* amendments proposed at the same time (1789) – now known as the Bill of Rights – were ratified in a little more than two years.

Notes

Among the sources most commonly cited in these Endnotes are judicial decisions and articles published in journals specifically devoted to the publication of legal scholarship, usually referred to as "law reviews." In citing to such sources, I have generally followed a version of the citation practices most commonly observed in judicial opinions and in articles published in law reviews. Citations to cases generally begin with a volume number for the "reporter," or collection of cases, in which the case appears; followed by an abbreviation for the name of the reporter; followed by the page on which the decision of the case begins; followed (in some cases) by the page on which particular cited language appears; followed, in parenthesis, by the year in which the case was decided. Thus, a citation to a famous quotation in the famous case of *Marbury v. Madison* would be 5 U.S. 137, 177 (1803), signifying that the case, which was decided in 1803, appears in volume 5 of a reporter called the United States Reports, beginning on page 137, with the quotation appearing on page 177. Citations to articles appearing in law reviews generally begin with the name of the author, followed by the title of the article, followed by the volume number of the law review in which the article appeared, followed by the name of the law review, followed by the page on which the article began, followed by the page(s) of any specifically cited material, followed – in parenthesis – by the year in which the article was published.

Prologue: *Bush v. Gore*

1. 5 U.S. 137, 177 (1803).
2. 531 U.S. 98 (2000).
3. Ibid. at 106.
4. Justices John Paul Stevens and Ruth Bader Ginsburg wrote opinions finding no equal protection violation, and Justice Steven Breyer "joined" their opinions, thereby saying that he agreed. But Justice Breyer also wrote an opinion of his own, in which he appeared to say that the Equal Protection Clause required clearer guidance to vote counters than the Florida Supreme Court had given. As a result, Breyer's position was equivocal on the equal protection issue, but he made it crystal clear that he thought

the Florida Supreme Court should be given a chance to solve any possible problem by issuing more detailed instructions.

5. See ibid. at 143 (Ginsburg, J., dissenting).
6. *Brown v. Allen,* 344 U.S. 443, 540 (1953) (Jackson, J., concurring in the result).

Introduction: The Dynamic Constitution

1. *Abrams v. United States,* 250 U.S. 616, 630 (1919) (Holmes, J., dissenting).
2. For an especially rich practice-based account of law in general and applied to constitutional law in particular, see Ronald Dworkin, *Law's Empire* (Cambridge/London: The Belknap Press of Harvard University Press, 1986).
3. 5 U.S. 137 (1803).
4. See Bruce Ackerman, *We The People: Foundations* (Cambridge/London: Belknap Press of Harvard University Press, 1991), vol. 1 (considering the relationship between legality and illegality and the theory of political legitimacy reflected in the framing and ratification of the Constitution). Compare Akhil Reed Amar, "Philadelphia Revisited: Amending the Constitution Outside Article V," 55 *University of Chicago Law Review* 1043 (1988) (asserting the availability of legal justifications for the course of action followed at the Convention and thereafter).
5. See Thomas C. Grey, "The Origins of the Unwritten Constitution," 30 *Stanford Law Review* 843 (1978); Suzanna Sherry, "The Founders' Unwritten Constitution: Fundamental Law in American Revolutionary Thought," 54 *University of Chicago Law Review* 1127 (1987).
6. The best recent work on the Convention is Jack N. Rakove, *Original Meanings: Politics and Ideas in the Making of the Constitution* (New York: Knopf, 1997). For an older but still valuable account, see Max Farrand, *The Framing of the Constitution of the United States* (New Haven, CT/London: Yale University Press, 1913).
7. See Article I, Section 2 (basing a state's representation in the House of Representatives on its free population and three-fifths of "all other Persons" within its territory); Article I, Section 9 (barring Congress from abolishing the slave trade before 1808); and Article 4, Section 2 (providing for the return of runaway slaves).
8. One element that was designed with political parties in mind is the Twelfth Amendment, which was ratified in 1804 to accommodate party-based presidential voting.
9. See Richard H. Fallon, Jr., Daniel J. Meltzer, and David L. Shapiro, *Hart & Wechsler's The Federal Courts and the Federal System,* 5th ed. (New York: Foundation Press, 2003), 10–11.
10. See *Barron v. City of Baltimore,* 32 U.S. 243, 247–50 (1832).
11. See Fallon et al., *Hart & Wechsler's The Federal Courts and the Federal System,* 11–12.
12. *The Federalist,* No. 78, at 491–4.

13. See *Cooper v. Telfair*, 4 U.S. 14 (1800); *Ware v. Hylton*, 3 U.S. 199 (1796).
14. On the Federalists' maneuvers during the lame-duck period following the 1800 election, see Richard E. Ellis, *The Jeffersonian Crisis: Courts and Politics in the Young Republic* (New York: Oxford University Press, 1971); James F. Simon, *What Kind of Nation: Thomas Jefferson, John Marshall, and the Epic Struggle to Create a United States* (New York: Simon & Schuster, 2002), 104–90.
15. See Simon, *What Kind of Nation*, 191–219. The Republicans impeached and removed a lower federal court judge and commenced impeachment proceedings against a Supreme Court Justice, although the case against the latter ultimately failed when the Senate, which "tries" impeachment cases, failed to vote a conviction.
16. 5 U.S. 137 (1803).
17. See, for example, Akhil Reed Amar, "Marbury, Section 13, and the Original Jurisdiction of the Supreme Court," 56 *University of Chicago Law Review* 443, 456 (1989). For a rare dissenting argument that Congress actually intended to invest the Supreme Court with a "freestanding" jurisdiction to issue writs of mandamus, see James E. Pfander, "Marbury, Original Jurisdiction, and the Supreme Court's Supervisory Powers," 101 *Columbia Law Review* 1515, 1535 (2001).
18. See U.S. Constitution, Article III, Section 3, Clause 1.
19. See *Marbury*, 5 U.S. at 179.
20. 17 U.S. 316, 407 (1819).
21. Ibid.
22. See Dworkin, *Law's Empire*, 255–6.
23. 60 U.S. 393 (1857).
24. The ruling came in *Ex parte Merryman*, 17 F. Cas. 144 (C.C.D.Md. 1861), a case discussed in Chapter Twelve.
25. *Lochner v. New York*, 198 U.S. 45 (1905).
26. Revisionist works that attribute the "switch in time" less to immediate political pressure than to gradually unfolding changes in constitutional doctrine and prevailing jurisprudential assumptions include Barry Cushman, *Rethinking the New Deal* (New York: Oxford University Press, 1998), and G. Edward White, *The Constitution and the New Deal* (Cambridge, MA: Harvard University Press, 2000).
27. 347 U.S. 483 (1954).
28. See, for example, Jeffrey A. Segal and Harold J. Spaeth, *The Supreme Court and the Attitudinal Model* (New York/Cambridge: Cambridge University Press, 1993).

One. Freedom of Speech

1. *Schenck v. United States*, 249 U.S. 47, 52 (1919).
2. See *Near v. Minnesota*, 283 U.S. 697, 713 (1931).
3. See, for example, David A. Anderson, "The Origins of the Press Clause," 30 *U.C.L.A. Law Review* 455 (1983); William T. Mayton, "Seditious

Libel and the Lost Guarantee of a Freedom of Expression," 84 *Columbia Law Review* 91 (1894).

4. See, for example, Leonard W. Levy, *The Emergence of a Free Press* (New York/Oxford: Oxford University Press, 1985); David Lowenthal, *No Liberty for License: The Forgotten Logic of the First Amendment* (Dallas, TX: Spence Publishing, 1997), 10.

5. See Steven J. Heyman, "Righting the Balance: An Inquiry into the Foundations and Limits of Freedom of Expression," 78 *Boston University Law Review* 1275 (1998).

6. See International Convention on the Elimination of All Forms of Racial Discrimination, Article 4, pledging signatory nations to "declare as an offence punishable by law all dissemination of ideas based on racial superiority or hatred [and] incitement to racial discrimination." See generally Mari J. Matsuda, "Public Response to Racist Speech: Considering the Victim's Story," 87 *Michigan Law Review* 2320 (1989) (discussing practices of other liberal democracies in prohibiting racist speech).

7. *Schenck v. United States*, 249 U.S. 47, 52 (1919).

8. On the earlier history of First Amendment litigation, see David M. Rabban, "The First Amendment in Its Forgotten Years," 90 *Yale Law Journal* 514 (1981).

9. 249 U.S. 47 (1919).

10. Ibid. at 51.

11. Ibid. at 52.

12. 249 U.S. 211 (1919).

13. Ibid. at 214.

14. See *Abrams v. United States*, 250 U.S. 616, 627–28 (1919) (Holmes, J., dissenting).

15. Ibid. at 630 (1919) (Holmes, J., dissenting).

16. 274 U.S. 357 (1927).

17. Ibid. at 375 (Brandeis, J., concurring).

18. Ibid. at 376–77.

19. 341 U.S. 494 (1951).

20. Ibid. at 510.

21. John Hart Ely, *Democracy and Distrust: A Theory of Judicial Review* (Cambridge, MA/London: Harvard University Press, 1980), 109.

22. 395 U.S. 444 (1969) (*per curiam*).

23. Ibid. at 447.

24. See *Hess v. Indiana*, 414 U.S. 105 (1973) (*per curiam*).

25. *United States v. Schwimmer*, 279 U.S. 644, 654–55 (1929) (Holmes, J., dissenting).

26. 391 U.S. 367 (1968).

27. Ibid. at 376.

28. Ibid. at 377.

29. 491 U.S. 397 (1989).

30. 496 U.S. 310 (1990).

31. *O'Brien*, 391 U.S. at 377.
32. See *Clark v. Community for Creative Non-Violence*, 468 U.S. 288 (1984).
33. Among the most influential early commentaries was John Hart Ely, "Flag Desecration: A Case Study in the Roles of Categorization and Balancing in First Amendment Analysis," 88 *Harvard Law Review* 1482 (1975). See also Laurence H. Tribe, *American Constitutional Law*, 2nd ed. (Mineola, NY: Foundation Press, 1988), 789–94.
34. See generally Elena Kagan, "Private Speech, Public Purpose: The Role of Governmental Motive in First Amendment Doctrine," 63 *University of Chicago Law Review* 413 (1996).
35. 403 U.S. 15 (1971).
36. Ibid. at 26.
37. Ibid.
38. See, for example, *Virginia v. Black*, 123 S.Ct. 1536 (2003) (holding that the Constitution would permit the prohibition of cross-burning with the intent to intimidate, but invalidating a Virginia statute that treated all cross-burnings as presumptively intended to intimidate).
39. 315 U.S. 568, 571–72 (1942).
40. Ibid.
41. *Jacobellis v. Ohio*, 378 U.S. 184, 197 (1964) (Stewart, J., concurring).
42. 354 U.S. 476 (1957).
43. *Memoirs v. Massachusetts*, 383 U.S. 413 (1966).
44. 413 U.S. 15, 24 (1973).
45. See *Paris Adult Theater*, I. V. Slatong 413 U.S. 49, 57–58 (1973).
46. See Frederick Schauer, "Causation Theory and the Causes of Sexual Violence," *American Bar Foundation Research Journal* 737 (1987).
47. 458 U.S. 747 (1982).
48. Compare *Ashcroft v. Free Speech Coalition*, 122 S.Ct. 1389 (2002) (holding an anti-child pornography statute unconstitutional insofar as it applied to images that appear to be, but in fact are not, actual minors engaged in actual sexual conduct).
49. See, for example, *Valentine v. Chrestenson*, 316 U.S. 52 (1942).
50. 425 U.S. 748 (1976).
51. Ibid. at 781 (Rehnquist, J., dissenting).
52. 447 U.S. 557 (1980).
53. Ibid. at 566.
54. See generally Ronald H. Coase, "Advertising and Free Speech," 6 *Journal of Legal Studies* 1 (1977).
55. 533 U.S. 525 (2001).
56. Justice Sandra Day O'Connor wrote the Court's opinion, relevant parts of which were joined by Chief Justice Rehnquist and by Justices Scalia, Kennedy, and Thomas.
57. On the history of broadcast regulation, see Lucas A. Powe, Jr., *American Broadcasting and the First Amendment* (Berkeley/Los Angeles/London: University of California Press, 1987).

58. 395 U.S. 367 (1969).
59. 438 U.S. 726 (1978).
60. Quoted in ibid. at 751.
61. See, for example, *Denver Area Educational Telecommunications Consortium, Inc. v. FCC*, 518 U.S. 727 (1996). The Court has suggested, however, that cablecasters can be required to ensure the effective blocking of channels that feature sexually explicit programming when a subscriber specifically so requests.
62. 521 U.S. 844 (1997).
63. The Court also invalidated a statutory provision that barred the knowing transmission of indecent messages to any recipient under 18 years of age on the ground that the term "indecent" was excessively vague and potentially overbroad.
64. 357 U.S. 449 (1958).
65. 468 U.S. 609 (1984).
66. Ibid. at 623.
67. Ibid. at 627–28.
68. 530 U.S. 640 (2000).
69. Ibid. at 657–58.

Two. Freedom of Religion

1. 310 U.S. 296, 303 (1940).
2. See *Clay, aka Ali v. United States*, 403 U.S. 698, 700 (1971).
3. 403 U.S. ibid. at 698 (1971).
4. Obviously troubled by this objection, the Supreme Court, in *Welsh v. United States*, 398 U.S. 333, 344 (1970), interpreted the statutory provision providing exemptions for those opposed to war on religious grounds to encompass "all those whose consciences, spurred by deeply held moral, ethical, or religious beliefs, would give them no rest or peace if they allowed themselves to become a part of an instrument of war." See also *United States v. Seeger*, 380 U.S. 163, 165–66 (1965).
5. See, for example, *Wallace v. Jaffree*, 472 U.S. 38, 98–103 (1985) (Rehnquist, J., dissenting).
6. See, for example, *County of Allegheny v. ACLU*, 492 U.S. 573, 659 (1989) (Kennedy, J., joined by Rehnquist, C. J., and White and Scalia, J. J., concurring in the judgment in part and dissenting in part).
7. See *Bradfield v. Roberts*, 175 U.S. 291 (1899) (upholding federal appropriations to a Catholic hospital in the District of Columbia); *Quick Bear v. Leupp*, 210 U.S. 50 (1908) (upholding disbursement of federal funds held in trust for the Sioux Indians to Catholic schools designated by the Sioux).
8. The watershed case was *Everson v. Board of Education*, 330 U.S. 1 (1947).
9. Indeed, at the time of the Constitution's ratification, a number of states maintained "established" churches, supported out of public tax revenues.

Against this background, one of the apparent purposes of the federal Establishment Clause was to bar Congress from interfering with state establishments of religion. Nonetheless, the Supreme Court has assumed that the Establishment Clause, like most of the rest of the Bill of Rights, was made applicable against the states by the Fourteenth Amendment, adopted in the aftermath of the Civil War. See *Everson*, cited in note 8 of this chapter. Today the Establishment Clause bars state governments, fully as much as the federal government, from making laws "respecting an establishment of religion."

10. See, for example, Michael W. McConnell, "Religious Freedom at a Crossroads," 59 *University of Chicago Law Review* 115 (1992).
11. See *Engel v. Vitale*, 370 U.S. 421 (1962).
12. See ibid. (prayer); *Abington School Dist. v. Schempp*, 374 U.S. 203 (1963) (Bible reading).
13. The test took its name from *Lemon v. Kurtzman*, 403 U.S. 602 (1971).
14. 393 U.S. 97 (1968).
15. Ibid. at 107–08.
16. 449 U.S. 39 (1980).
17. 472 U.S. 38, 40–41 (1985).
18. The dissenting opinions were written by Chief Justice Warren Burger, Justice Byron White, and then-Justice William Rehnquist.
19. See *Good News Club v. Milford Central School*, 533 U.S. 98 (2001).
20. A majority of the Justices appear to have adopted this test, albeit without uniting in a single majority opinion, in *Capitol Square Review and Advisory Board v. Pinette*, 515 U.S. 753 (1995).
21. See *Lynch v. Donnelly*, 465 U.S. 668, 691 (1984) (O'Connor, J., concurring).
22. See *County of Allegheny v. American Civil Liberties Union*, 492 U.S. 573, 626–27 (1989) (O'Connor, J., concurring in part and concurring in the judgment).
23. 505 U.S. 577 (1992).
24. Ibid. at 593. See also *Santa Fe Independent School Dist. v. Doe*, 530 U.S. 290 (2000) (invalidating a school district policy of electing students to deliver a brief invocation or message at high school football games).
25. See *Marsh v. Chambers*, 463 U.S. 783 (1983).
26. 397 U.S. 664 (1970).
27. For an insightful social, political, and legal analysis of the unfolding history of the debate about the constitutionality of public funding for parochial schools, see John C. Jeffries, Jr. and James E. Ryan, "A Political History of the Establishment Clause," 100 *Michigan Law Review* 279 (2001).
28. See Jeffries and Ryan, "A Political History of the Establishment Clause."
29. 530 U.S. 793 (2000).
30. See ibid. at 812–21 (opinion of Thomas, J., joined by Rehnquist, C. J., and Kennedy and Scalia, J. J.).

31. See ibid. at 839 (O'Connor, J., joined by Breyer, J., concurring).
32. 536 U.S. 639 (2002).
33. Ibid. at 649.
34. Justice Souter wrote the principal dissenting opinion, joined by Justices Stevens, Ginsburg, and Breyer. Justice Breyer wrote an additional dissenting opinion, which Justices Stevens and Souter joined.
35. 98 U.S. 145 (1878).
36. Ibid. at 164.
37. *Braunfeld v. Brown*, 366 U.S. 599, 616 (1961) (Stewart, J., dissenting).
38. 406 U.S. 205 (1972).
39. 374 U.S. 398 (1963).
40. Ibid. at 403, 406.
41. See *United States v. Lee*, 455 U.S. 252 (1982).
42. See, for example, Christopher L. Eisgruber and Lawrence G. Sager, "The Vulnerability of Conscience: The Constitutional Basis for Protecting Religious Conduct," 61 *University of Chicago Law Review* 1245 (1994).
43. 494 U.S. 872 (1990).
44. Ibid. at 881.
45. Ibid. at 877.
46. See, for example, Michael W. McConnell, "Free Exercise Revisionism and the Smith Decision," 57 *University of Chicago Law Review* 1109 (1990); Douglas Laycock, "The Remnants of Free Exercise," 1990 *Supreme Court Review* 1.
47. In dissenting opinions in *City of Boerne v. Flores*, 521 U.S. 507 (1997), Justices O'Connor, Souter, and Breyer all took this position.
48. Compare *Corporation of Presiding Bishop of Church of Jesus Christ of Latter-Day Saints v. Amos*, 483 U.S. 327 (1987) (upholding a statutory exemption that benefited religious groups only) with *Texas Monthly, Inc. v. Bullock*, 489 U.S. 1 (1989) (invalidating a state sales tax exemption for religious periodicals).
49. See, for example, *Corporation of Presiding Bishop v. Amos*, cited in note 48 of this chapter; *Texas Monthly, Inc. v. Bullock*, cited in note 48 of this chapter, 489 U.S. at 18, n.8 (plurality opinion).
50. See *Welsh v. United States* and *United States v. Seeger*, cited in note 4 of this chapter.

Three. Protection of Economic Liberties

1. Charles A. Beard, *An Economic Interpretation of the Constitution of the United States* (New York: Macmillan, 1913), 324.
2. *Lochner v. New York*, 198 U.S. 45, 75 (1905) (Holmes, J., dissenting).
3. See *The Federalist*, No. 10 (Madison) (characterizing "[a] rage for paper money, for an abolition of debts" as among the phenomena demonstrating a need for a new constitution).
4. 198 U.S. 45 (1905).

5. 17 U.S. 122 (1819).
6. 10 U.S. 87 (1810).
7. Ibid. at 139.
8. See generally Suzanna Sherry, "The Founders' Unwritten Constitution," cited in note 5 of Introduction.
9. 3 U.S. 386, 388 (1798) (Chase, J.) (*seriatim* opinion).
10. 25 U.S. 213 (1827).
11. For discussion of the legislative history, see Alexander M. Bickel, "The Original Understanding and the Segregation Decision," 69 *Harvard Law Review* 1 (1955).
12. 6 F. Cas. 546 (No. 3230) (C.C.E.D. Pa. 1823).
13. Ibid. at 551.
14. 83 U.S. 36 (1872).
15. Ibid. at 78.
16. Ibid. at 96 (Field, J., dissenting).
17. *Saenz v. Roe*, 526 U.S. 489 (1999), was unusual in relying on the Privileges or Immunities Clause as the constitutional home of a traditionally recognized right to travel, but the Court gave no indication that it intended any broader revitalization of the Clause. See Laurence H. Tribe, "Saenz Sans Prophecy: Does the Privileges or Immunities Revival Portend the Future – Or Reveal the Structure of the Present?," 113 *Harvard Law Review* 110, 197–8 (1999).
18. John Hart Ely, *Democracy and Distrust: A Theory of Judicial Review* (Cambridge, MA/London: Belknap Press of Harvard University Press, 1980), 19–20.
19. 198 U.S. 45 (1905).
20. On the concern of the *Lochner*-era Court concerning class legislation, see Howard Gillman, *The Constitution Besieged* (Durham, NC/London: Duke University Press, 1993), 10, 127.
21. *Lochner*, 198 U.S. at 60.
22. Ibid. at 75 (Holmes, J., dissenting).
23. 300 U.S. 379 (1937).
24. Ibid. at 399.
25. *Ferguson v. Skrupa*, 372 U.S. 726, 729 (1963).
26. Ibid. at 729–31 (internal quotation marks omitted).
27. In *Eastern Enterprises v. Apfel*, 524 U.S. 498 (1998), however, Justice Kennedy's conclusion that an economic regulatory statute violated substantive due process was necessary to the Court's decision that the statute was unconstitutional – a conclusion that four other Justices reached under the Takings Clause.
28. 290 U.S. 398 (1934).
29. 17 U.S. 316 (1819).
30. *Blaisdell*, 290 U.S. at 443 (quoting *McCulloch*, 17 U.S. at 415).
31. Ibid. at 435.
32. See *Allied Structural Steel Co. v. Spannaus*, 438 U.S. 234 (1978).

33. 328 U.S. 256 (1946).
34. Ibid. at 261.
35. 260 U.S. 393 (1922).
36. See, for example, William Michael Treanor, "The Original Understanding of the Takings Clause and the Political Process," 95 *Columbia Law Review* 782 (1995).
37. *Mahon*, 260 U.S. at 415.
38. *Connolly v. Pension Benefit Guaranty Corp.*, 475 U.S. 211, 225 (1986) (internal quotation marks omitted).
39. For a provocative sketch of the conservative path that the Court has so far declined to travel, see Richard A. Epstein, *Takings: Private Property and the Power of Eminent Domain* (Cambridge, MA/London: Harvard University Press, 1985).
40. See, for example, *Lucas v. South Carolina Coastal Council*, 505 U.S. 1003 (1992) (holding that regulations depriving a land owner of all economically beneficial use of land constitute takings); *Nollan v. California Coastal Commission*, 483 U.S. 825 (1987) (finding that the state effected a taking by demanding that a property owner grant a public easement to cross the property as a condition for the award of a building permit).

Four. Rights to Fair Procedures

1. See *Goss v. Lopez*, 419 U.S. 565 (1975).
2. These rights all stem from the Fifth and Sixth Amendments.
3. The series began with *Mapp v. Ohio*, 367 U.S. 643 (1961). The Court adopted the formula that the Fourteenth Amendment incorporated the procedural rights included in the Bill of Rights that were "fundamental to the American scheme of justice" in *Duncan v. Louisiana*, 391 U.S. 145, 149 (1968). Before the 1960s, the Court had held some of the guarantees of the Bill of Rights to be applicable against the states, but only insofar as they were "implicit in the concept of ordered liberty." *Palko v. Connecticut*, 302 U.S. 319, 325 (1937). Under this formula, the demands of due process were "less rigid and more fluid" than the more specific guarantees of the Bill of Rights, and "[t]hat which may, in one setting, constitute a denial of fundamental fairness ... may, in other circumstances and in the light of other considerations, fall short of such denial." *Betts v. Brady*, 316 U.S. 455, 462 (1942).
4. Jerold H. Israel, "Selective Incorporation: Revisited," 71 *Georgetown Law Journal* 253, 281 (1982).
5. Ibid.
6. 304 U.S. 144 (1938).
7. Ibid. at 153, n.4.
8. Ibid. (citations omitted).
9. See John Hart Ely, *Democracy and Distrust: A Theory of Judicial Review* (Cambridge, MA/London: Harvard University Press, 1980), 73–7.

10. *Gideon* itself involved a conviction for a felony, an especially serious crime. Subsequent cases extended the reach of the principle enunciated in *Gideon* to any case in which the defendant receives a jail or prison sentence.

11. 372 U.S. 335 (1963).

12. 384 U.S. 436, 479 (1966).

13. Ibid. at 439.

14. 367 U.S. 643 (1961).

15. See generally John Morton Blum, *Years of Discord: American Politics and Society, 1961–74* (New York/London: Norton, 1991), 207–17, 313–14.

16. See, for example, Joshua Dressler, *Understanding Criminal Procedure*, 3rd ed. (New York LexisNexis, 2002), 20.

17. The principal judicial cutback came in *Teague v. Lane*, 489 U.S. 288 (1989), which held that federal courts could not grant habeas corpus relief based on "new constitutional rules of criminal procedure," the recognition and application of which were "not dictated by precedent existing at the time the defendant's conviction became final." Ibid. at 291, 301. Congress mandated a number of further cutbacks in the Antiterrorism and Effective Death Penalty Act of 1996, Pub. L. No. 104-132, 110 Stat. 1214, codified in scattered sections of the United States Code.

18. See Vincent Blasi (ed.), *The Burger Court: The Counter-Revolution That Wasn't* (New Haven, CT: Yale University Press, 1983).

19. 530 U.S. 428 (2000).

20. See William J. Stuntz, "The Substantive Origins of Criminal Procedure," 105 *Yale Law Journal* 393, 436–9 (1995).

21. See Richard A. Leo, "Inside the Interrogation Room," 86 *Journal of Criminal Law & Criminology* 266, 276 (1996).

22. See ibid. at 280.

23. See Katherine Y. Barnes and Samuel R. Gross, "Road Work: Racial Profiling and Drug Interdiction on the Highway," 101 *Michigan Law Review* 651, 672 (2002).

24. See, for example, Yale Kamisar, "In Defense of the Search and Seizure Exclusionary Rule," 26 *Harvard Journal of Law & Public Policy* 119, 130–1 (2003).

25. See *Santosky v. Kramer*, 455 U.S. 745 (1982).

26. See ibid. at 753, 768.

27. *Addington v. Texas*, 441 U.S. 418, 433 (1979).

28. See, for example, *Bailey v. Richardson*, 182 F. 2d 46 (D.C. Cir. 1950), *aff'd by an equally divided Court*, 341 U.S. 918 (1951) (finding Due Process Clause inapplicable to dismissals from federal civil service employment).

29. 397 U.S. 254 (1970).

30. See ibid. at 262, n.8.

31. See ibid. at 261.

32. See, for example, *Board of Regents of State Colleges v. Roth*, 408 U.S. 564, 577 (1972) (asserting that property interests "are created and . . . defined

by existing rules or understandings that stem from an independent source such as state law").

33. See ibid. at 578.
34. See *Ingraham v. Wright*, 430 U.S. 651 (1977).
35. See, for example, *Mathews v. Eldridge*, 424 U.S. 319 (1976).
36. Ibid. at 334–35.
37. See Jerry L. Mashaw, *Due Process in the Administrative State* (New Haven, CT/London: Yale University Press, 1985), 33–5.

Five. Equal Protection of the Laws

1. 123 S.Ct. 2411 (2003).
2. 347 U.S. 483 (1954).
3. *Bolling v. Sharpe*, 347 U.S. 497, 500 (1954).
4. See Michael J. Klarman, "An Interpretive History of Modern Equal Protection," 90 *Michigan Law Review* 213, 252, n.180 (1991) (citing and discussing authorities). For a rare dissenting view, based largely on unsuccessful congressional efforts to forbid school segregation under the 1875 Civil Rights Act, see Michael W. McConnell, "Originalism and the Desegregation Decisions," 81 *Virginia Law Review* 947 (1995). For a critical response, see Michael J. Klarman, "Brown, Originalism, and Constitutional Theory," 81 *Virginia Law Review* 1881 (1995).
5. See Alexander M. Bickel, "The Original Understanding and the Segregation Decision," 69 *Harvard Law Review* 1, 12-17, 56–8 (1955). See also Klarman, "An Interpretive History of Modern Equal Protection," 235, n.95 (reviewing subsequent debate including the view that most of the Fourteenth Amendment's ratifiers viewed it as protecting only fundamental rights).
6. See, for example, William E. Nelson, *The Fourteenth Amendment: From Political Principle to Judicial Doctrine* (Cambridge, MA/London: Harvard University Press, 1988) (arguing that the framers and ratifiers were mostly concerned with general moral ideals and did not attempt to reach clear understandings with respect to many specific applications); Ronald Dworkin, *Freedom's Law* (Cambridge, MA: Harvard University Press, 1996), 8–10 (arguing that whatever the framers' specific expectations, the Equal Protection Clause embodies a moral principle, which must be interpreted in light of its ultimate moral meaning).
7. 83 U.S. 36 (1872).
8. See, for example, *FCC v. Beach Communications, Inc.*, 508 U.S. 307, 313–14 (1993) (emphasizing that rational basis review "is a paradigm of judicial restraint").
9. See Robert C. Farrell, "Successful Rational Basis Claims in the Supreme Court From the 1971 Term Through Romer v. Evans," 32 *Indiana Law Review* 357, 370 (1999).
10. See ibid. at 357–8.

11. 413 U.S. 528 (1973).
12. Ibid. at 529.
13. Ibid. at 534.
14. 163 U.S. 537, 540 (1896).
15. Ibid. at 544.
16. Ibid. at 551.
17. Charles L. Black, Jr., "The Lawfulness of the Segregation Decisions," 69 *Yale Law Journal* 421, 422, n.8 (1960).
18. *Plessy*, 163 U.S. 562 (Harlan, J., dissenting).
19. Ibid. at 559.
20. Ibid.
21. 323 U.S. 214 (1944).
22. Ibid. at 216.
23. *Korematsu*, 323 U.S. at 245 (Jackson, J., dissenting).
24. Ibid. at 223.
25. See Mark V. Tushnet, The *NAACP's Legal Strategy Against Segregated Education, 1925–50* (Chapel Hill, NC/London: University of North Carolina Press, 1987), 1925–1950.
26. 347 U.S. 483 (1954).
27. Michael Klarman, "An Interpretive History of Modern Equal Protection," 241–2.
28. Phillip Elman and Norman Silber, "The Solicitor General's Office, Justice Frankfurter, and Civil Rights Litigation, 1946–1960: An Oral History," 100 *Harvard Law Review* 817, 840 (1987).
29. *Brown*, 347 U.S. at 492.
30. Ibid. at 493.
31. Ibid. at 493–94.
32. Ibid. at 495.
33. See *Brown v. Board of Education* (II), 349 U.S. 294 (1955).
34. Ibid. at 301.
35. 350 U.S. 891 (1955).
36. See Klarman, "An Interpretive History of Modern Equal Protection," 243.
37. See, for example, *Green v. County School Board*, 391 U.S. 430 (1968).
38. See, for example, *Swann v. Charlotte-Mecklenburg Board of Education*, 402 U.S. 1 (1971).
39. See *Loving v. Virginia*, 388 U.S. 1 (1967).
40. 466 U.S. 429 (1984).
41. Ibid. at 433.
42. Alexander M. Bickel, *The Least Dangerous Branch: The Supreme Court at the Bar of Politics* (Indianapolis, IN/New York: Bobbs-Merrill, 1962), 239.
43. 426 U.S. 229 (1976).
44. Ibid. at 248.
45. Sylvia A. Law, "White Privilege and Affirmative Action," 32 *Akron Law Review* 603, 620 (1999).

46. See, for example, J. Ely, *Democracy and Distrust*, 135–79.
47. 438 U.S. 265 (1978).
48. 488 U.S. 469 (1989).
49. See *Metro Broadcasting, Inc. v. F.C.C.*, 497 U.S. 547 (1990).
50. See *Adarand Constructors, Inc. v. Pena*, 515 U.S. 200 (1995).
51. 123 S.Ct. 2411 (2003).
52. 123 S.Ct. 2325 (2003).
53. Justice Kennedy expressly endorsed Justice Powell's *Bakke* approach in his dissenting opinion, but, unlike the majority, concluded that the Michigan Law School's affirmative action policy should be invalidated under *Bakke*.
54. Ibid. at 2347.
55. Ibid. at 2340.
56. *Bradwell v. Illinois*, 83 U.S. (16 Wall.) 130, 141 (1872).
57. *Goesaert v. Cleary*, 335 U.S. 464, 465 (1948).
58. See *Reed v. Reed*, 404 U.S. 71 (1971).
59. 411 U.S. 677 (1973).
60. 429 U.S. 190, 197 (1976).
61. See *United States v. Virginia*, 518 U.S. 515, 524 (1996).
62. See *Dothard v. Rawlinson*, 433 U.S. 321 (1977).
63. See *Rostker v. Goldberg*, 453 U.S. 57 (1981).
64. 518 U.S. 515 (1996).
65. See ibid. at 533, n.7.
66. Ibid. at 531, 533.
67. 517 U.S. 620 (1996).
68. 478 U.S. 186 (1986), overruled by *Lawrence v. Texas*, 123 S.Ct. 2472 (2003).
69. Ibid. at 633.
70. Ibid. at 634.
71. 123 S.Ct. 2472 (2003).
72. 304 U.S. 144 (1938).
73. See, for example, City of *Cleburne v. Cleburne Living Center*, 473 U.S. 432 (1985); *Heller v. Doe*, 509 U.S. 312 (1993).

Six. Fundamental Rights

1. *Poe v. Ullman*, 367 U.S. 497, 543 (1961) (Harlan, J., dissenting).
2. *Bowers v. Hardwick*, 478 U.S. 186, 194 (1986), overruled by *Lawrence v. Texas*, 123 S.Ct. 2472 (2003).
3. 316 U.S. 535, 536 (1942).
4. Ibid. at 544 (Stone, C.J., concurring).
5. *Skinner*, 316 U.S. at 541.
6. 83 U.S. 36 (1872).
7. 198 U.S. 45 (1905).

8. See Ronald Dworkin, "Unenumerated Rights: Whether and How Roe Should Be Overruled," 59 *University of Chicago Law Review* 381 (1992).
9. 381 U.S. 479 (1965).
10. Ibid. at 481–82.
11. Ibid. at 483, 485.
12. Ibid. at 483.
13. Ibid. at 485.
14. See ibid. at 499 (Harlan, J., concurring in the judgment). Justice Goldberg also wrote a concurring opinion, in which Chief Justice Warren and Justice Brennan joined.
15. Ibid at 486 (Goldberg, J., concurring).
16. 405 U.S. 438 (1972).
17. 410 U.S. 113 (1973).
18. See, for example, Jesse H. Choper, "Consequences of Supreme Court Decisions Upholding Individual Rights," 83 *Michigan Law Review* 1, 185 (1984) (stating that "the risk of death from an illegal abortion is twelve times greater than from a legal one").
19. 505 U.S. 833 (1992).
20. See ibid. at 849–53.
21. See ibid. at 864–69.
22. 60 U.S. 393 (1857).
23. See, for example, Lincoln's speech at Springfield, Illinois, on July 17, 1858, reproduced in Abraham Lincoln, *Speeches and Writings, 1832–1858*, (New York: Library of America, 1989), 460, 472–9.
24. 478 U.S. 186 (1986).
25. Ibid. at 194.
26. Ibid. at 191–920.
27. See ibid. at 188, n.2.
28. See ibid. at 197 (Burger, C. J., concurring).
29. *Bowers*, 478 U.S. at 194.
30. Ibid. at 195–96.
31. Ibid. at 206 (Blackmun, J., dissenting).
32. Ibid. at 199–200.
33. 123 S.Ct. 2472 (2003).
34. Ibid. at 2482.
35. Ibid. at 2496 (Scalia, J., dissenting).
36. 521 U.S. 702 (1997).
37. 521 U.S. 793 (1997).
38. *Glucksberg*, 521 U.S. at 721.
39. See ibid. at 720.
40. Justice O'Connor's concurring opinion, joined by Justices Ginsburg and Breyer, expressly raised and reserved this question. See ibid. at 736–37. Although Justice Stevens was less specific, his concurring opinion suggested that individual liberty interests should outweigh competing state

interests in at least some cases. See ibid. at 741–42, 745. Justice Souter also reserved the question whether individual interests might prevail over state interests in preserving life under some conditions. See ibid. at 782 (Souter, J., concurring in the judgment).

41. Ibid. at 737 (O'Connor, J., concurring).
42. See, for example, *Loving v. Virginia*, 388 U.S. 1 (1967); *Zablocki v. Redhail*, 434 U.S. 374 (1978).
43. See *Jacobson v. Massachusetts*, 197 U.S. 11 (1905).
44. 530 U.S. 57 (2000).
45. *Zablocki v. Redhail*, 434 U.S. at 392 (Stewart, J., concurring in the judgment).
46. Ibid.

Seven. The Powers of Congress

1. 529 U.S. 598 (2000).
2. U.S. Constitution, Article I, Section 8, Clause 3.
3. U.S. Constitution, Article I, Section 8, Clause 1.
4. See Jack N. Rakove, *Original Meanings: Politics and Ideas in the Making of the Constitution* (New York: Knopf, 1996), 177–80 (describing the Convention's efforts to give determinate meaning to a proposal to confer national legislative power "in all cases to which the separate States are incompetent, or in which the harmony of the United States may be interrupted by the exercise of individual Legislation"); Robert L. Stern, "That Commerce Which Concerns More States Than One," 47 *Harvard Law Review* 1335, 1341 (1934); Donald H. Regan, "How to Think About the Federal Commerce Power and Incidentally Rewrite *United States v. Lopez*," 94 *Michigan Law Review* 554, 556 (1995).

   By noting that the framers apparently intended to empower Congress to deal with all genuinely national problems, I do *not* intend to imply that they viewed the Commerce Clause as reaching all such problems. For a range of views, see, for example, William Winslow Crosskey, *Politics and the Constitution in the History of the United States* (Chicago/London: University of Chicago Press, 1953), vol. I, 50–292 (arguing that the Commerce Clause authorized regulation of all gainful activities); Randy E. Barnett, "The Original Meaning of the Commerce Clause," 68 *University of Chicago Law Review* 101 (2001) (arguing that the Commerce Clause authorized only the regulation of the trade of goods and the shipment of goods for trade); Grant S. Nelson and Robert J. Pushaw, Jr., "Rethinking the Commerce Clause: Applying First Principles to Uphold Federal Commercial Regulations but Preserve State Control Over Social Issues," 85 *Iowa Law Review* 1 (1999) (adopting an intermediate view).
5. For a lucid and balanced discussion of constitutional debates about federalism and their underlying stakes, see David L. Shapiro, *Federalism: A Dialogue* (Evanston, IL: Northwestern University Press, 1995).

6. For a reading of the Commerce Clause in light of views such as these, see Richard A. Epstein, "The Proper Scope of the Commerce Power," 73 *Virginia Law Review* 1387 (1987).
7. 188 U.S. 321 (1903).
8. See ibid. at 364–65 (Fuller, C. J., joined by Brewer, Shiras, and Peckham, J. J., dissenting).
9. *Houston, East & West Texas Ry. Co. v. United States*, 234 U.S. 342 (1914).
10. 247 U.S. 251 (1918).
11. The account offered here is a relatively standard one. A recent book by Barry Cushman, *Rethinking the New Deal Court: The Structure of a Constitutional Revolution* (New York: Oxford University Press, 1998), argues that the Court's decisions reflected much greater consistency than other commentators have discerned.
12. See Larry D. Kramer, "We the Court," 115 *Harvard Law Review* 4, 122 (2001).
13. See, for example, *United States v. Darby*, 312 U.S. 100, 115 (1941) (holding that "the prohibition of the shipment interstate of goods produced under... forbidden substandard labor conditions is within the constitutional authority of Congress").
14. See ibid. at 119 (upholding congressional power to regulate "intrastate activities which have a substantial effect" on interstate commerce).
15. See *Wickard v. Filburn*, 317 U.S. 111 (1942).
16. 379 U.S. 294 (1964).
17. See Charles L. Black, Jr., *The People and the Court* (New York: MacMillan, 1960), 59–63 (suggesting that support for the New Deal manifest during the 1936 election would properly provoke doubtful Justices to reconsider their views). For the bolder suggestion that the effect of the 1936 elections, fought over the wisdom and constitutionality of the New Deal, was to enact an informal or unwritten amendment of the Constitution, see Bruce Ackerman, *We The People: Foundations* (Cambridge, MA/London: The Belknap Press of Harvard University Press, 1991), vol. 1.
18. 514 U.S. 549 (1995).
19. 529 U.S. 598 (2000).
20. See *Lopez*, 514 U.S. at 602 (Thomas, J., concurring); *Morrison*, 529 U.S. at 627 (Thomas, J., concurring).
21. See *Maryland v. Wirtz*, 392 U.S. 183 (1968).
22. 426 U.S. 833, 852 (1976).
23. 469 U.S. 528 (1985).
24. Ibid. at 580 (Rehnquist, J., dissenting).
25. See, for example, *Reno v. Condon*, 528 U.S. 141 (2000).
26. See *New York v. United States*, 505 U.S. 144 (1992).
27. 521 U.S. 898 (1997).
28. Foremost in this category is Justice Antonin Scalia, author of "The Rule of Law as a Law of Rules," 56 *University of Chicago Law Review* 1175 (1989).

29. See *United States v. Butler*, 297 U.S. 1, 65 (1936) (describing Madison's view).
30. See ibid. at 65–66.
31. See *Charles C. Steward Machine Co. v. Davis*, 301 U.S. 548 (1937); *Helvering v. Davis*, 301 U.S. 619 (1937).
32. *Helvering*, 301 U.S. at 641.

Eight. Executive Power

1. See generally Theodore J. Lowi, *The Personal President: Power Invested, Promise Unfulfilled* (Ithaca, NY/London: Cornell University Press, 1985).
2. *McCulloch v. Maryland*, 17 U.S. 316, 415 (1819).
3. 343 U.S. 579 (1952).
4. See U.S. Constitution, Article II, Section 2, Clause 1.
5. Article II, Section 3.
6. Article II, Section 1, Clause 1.
7. For discussions of formalism, see, for example, Peter L. Strauss, "The Place of Agencies in Government: Separation of Powers and the Fourth Branch," 84 *Columbia Law Review* 573 (1984); Rebecca L. Brown, "Separated Powers and Ordered Liberty," 139 *University of Pennsylvania Law Review* 1513 (1991).
8. See *Youngstown*, 343 U.S. at 635–38 (Jackson, J., concurring).
9. Ibid. at 637.
10. For a celebrated judicial statement of this view, see *United States v. Curtiss-Wright Export Corp.*, 299 U.S. 304, 319–21 (1936).
11. U.S. Constitution, Article II, Section 2, Clause 2.
12. See *United States v. Belmont*, 301 U.S. 324 (1937), and *United States v. Pink*, 315 U.S. 203 (1942).
13. 453 U.S. 654 (1981).
14. 321 U.S. 414 (1944).
15. Ibid. at 424.
16. 462 U.S. 919 (1983).
17. Ibid. at 959.
18. 524 U.S. 417 (1998).
19. Ibid. at 468.
20. See, for example, Steven G. Calabresi and Kevin H. Rhodes, "The Structural Constitution: Unitary Executive, Plural Judiciary," 105 *Harvard Law Review* 1153 (1992).
21. The leading modern case is *Buckley v. Valeo*, 424 U.S. 1 (1976).
22. See William G. Ross, "The Senate's Constitutional Role in Confirming Cabinet Nominees and Other Executive Officers," 48 *Syracuse Law Review* 1123, 1127 (1998).
23. *Myers v. United States*, 272 U.S. 52 (1926).
24. 295 U.S. 602 (1935).

25. Ibid. at 629.
26. Ibid. at 630.
27. For an especially forceful statement of this point, see Justice Scalia's dissenting opinion in *Morrison v. Olson*, 487 U.S. 654 (1988).

Nine. Judicial Power

1. *Planned Parenthood of Southeastern Pennsylvania v. Casey*, 505 U.S. 833, 996 (1992) (Scalia, J., dissenting).
2. *United States v. Nixon*, 418 U.S. 683 (1974).
3. 5 U.S. 137 (1803).
4. *United States v. Butler*, 297 U.S. 162 (1936).
5. See Henry Paul Monaghan, "Stare Decisis and Constitutional Adjudication," 88 *Columbia Law Review* 723, 744 (1988).
6. See *Legal Tender Cases*, 79 U.S. 457 (1871) (overruling *Hepburn v. Griswold*), 75 U.S. 603 (1870)).
7. The Court first said that "all legal restrictions which curtail the civil rights of a single racial group are immediately suspect" and "that courts must subject them to the most rigid scrutiny" in *Korematsu v. United States*, 323 U.S. 214, 216 (1944).
8. See *Adarand Constructors, Inc. v. Pena*, 515 U.S. 200 (1997), and especially the concurring opinions of Justices Antonin Scalia, ibid. at 239, and Clarence Thomas, ibid. at 240.
9. See Ronald Dworkin, *Law's Empire* (Cambridge, MA/London: The Belknap Press of Harvard University Press, 1986).
10. See, for example, Jeffrey A. Segal and Harold J. Spaeth, *The Supreme Court and the Attitudinal Model* (Cambridge/New York: Cambridge University Press, 1993).
11. I adopt the metaphor of law as a medium from Duncan Kennedy, *A Critique of Adjudication: Fin de Siecle* (Cambridge, MA/London: Harvard University Press, 1997).
12. See generally Richard H. Fallon, Jr., *Implementing the Constitution* (Cambridge, MA/London: Harvard University Press, 2001).
13. 384 U.S. 436 (1966).
14. 410 U.S. 113 (1973).
15. The label traces to Alexander M. Bickel, *The Least Dangerous Branch: The Supreme Court at the Bar of Politics* (Indianapolis, IN/New York: Bobbs-Merrill, 1962), 16.
16. See *United States v. Morrison*, 529 U.S. 598 (2000).
17. See, for example, Antonin Scalia, *Common Law Courts in a Civil-Law System: The Role of United States Federal Courts in Interpreting the Constitution and Laws*, in Amy Guttman *(ed.), A Matter of Interpretation: Federal Courts and the Law* (Princeton, NJ: Princeton University Press, 1997), 3, 38–47; Clarence Thomas, "Judging," 45 *University of Kansas Law Review* 1, 6–7 (1996).

18. See, for example, Paul Brest, "The Misconceived Quest for the Original Understanding," 60 *Boston University Law Review* 204 (1980).
19. Frank Freidel, *Franklin D. Roosevelt: A Rendezvous with Destiny* (Boston/Toronto/London: Little, Brown, 1990), 163.
20. See, for example, Antonin Scalia, Response, in *A Matter of Interpretation*, 138–40; Robert H. Bork, *The Tempting of America: The Political Seduction of the Law* (New York/London: Free Press, 1990), 155–8.
21. The great exemplar of this approach is Ronald Dworkin. See especially Ronald Dworkin, *Freedom's Law: The Moral Reading of the American Constitution* (Cambridge, MA: Harvard University Press, 1996).
22. See James B. Thayer, "The Origin and Scope of the American Doctrine of Constitutional Law," 7 *Harvard Law Review* 129 (1893).
23. See Monaghan, "Stare Decisis and Constitutional Adjudication," 727–39.
24. See John Hart Ely, *Democracy and Distrust: A Theory of Judicial Review* (Cambridge, MA/London: Harvard University Press, 1980), 135–79.
25. See, for example, Harry H. Wellington, *Interpreting the Constitution* (New Haven, CT/London: Yale University Press, 1990); David A. Strauss, "Common Law Constitutional Interpretation," 63 *University of Chicago Law Review* 877 (1996).
26. See Richard H. Fallon, Jr., "Judicial Legitimacy and the Unwritten Constitution: A Comment on *Miranda* and *Dickerson*," 45 *New York Law School Law Review* 119, 133–36 (2001).
27. *Marbury v. Madison*, 5 U.S. 137 (1803).
28. Bickel, *The Least Dangerous Branch*, 239.
29. See Max Farrand (ed.), *The Records of the Federal Convention of 1787* (New Haven, CT/London: Yale University Press, 1911), vol. I 430 (reproducing James Madison's notes of a discussion and vote of August 27, 1787).
30. See, for example, *Allen v. Wright*, 468 U.S. 737 (1984).
31. U.S. Constitution, Article II, Section 4.
32. 506 U.S. 224 (1993).
33. See *Baker v. Carr*, 369 U.S. 186, 210–17 (1962) (reviewing and categorizing grounds on which the Supreme Court had identified political questions not fit for judicial resolution).
34. For general discussion of such doctrines, see Fallon, *Implementing the Constitution*, 87–97.
35. See, for example, *Goldman v. Weinberger*, 475 U.S. 503, 507–08 (1986).
36. These include cases holding that states of the former Confederacy were not subject to suit in federal court for failure to make payments due on state bonds and allowing German saboteurs apprehended in the United States during World War II to be tried before so-called military commissions rather than by regular civilian courts. See Richard H. Fallon, Jr., "*Marbury* and the Constitutional Mind: A Bicentennial Essay on the Wages of Doctrinal Tension," 91 *California Law Review* 1, 29–33 (2003).

37. U.S. Constitution, Article III, Section 1.
38. See Michael J. Gerhardt, *The Federal Appointments Process: A Constitutional and Historical Analysis* (Durham, NC/London: Duke University Press, 2000), 163.
39. See Robert A. Dahl, *A Preface to Democratic Theory* (Chicago/London: University of Chicago Press, 1956), 110 (reporting that there is not a single instance in American history in which a persistent legislative majority has failed to achieve its wishes despite initial Supreme Court resistance).
40. See generally Gerald N. Rosenberg, *The Hollow Hope: Can Courts Bring About Social Change?* (Chicago/London: University of Chicago Press, 1991).

Ten. Elections, Political Democracy, and the Constitution

1. *Kramer v. Union Free School District* No. 15, 395 U.S. 621, 626 (1969).
2. 446 U.S. 55 (1980).
3. 426 U.S. 229 (1976).
4. 377 U.S. 533 (1964).
5. Ibid. at 568.
6. There are, to be sure, some important ambiguities in this formulation. For discussion, see Sanford Levinson, "One Person, One Vote: A Mantra in Need of Meaning," 80 *North Carolina Law Review* 1269 (2002).
7. 478 U.S. 109 (1986) (plurality opinion).
8. See ibid. at 164 (O'Connor, J., joined by Burger, C. J., and Rehnquist, J., concurring in judgment).
9. See ibid. at 164 (Powell, J., joined by Stevens, J., concurring in part and dissenting in part).
10. Ibid. at 132 (plurality opinion).
11. See *Thornburg v. Gingles*, 478 U.S. 30 (1986).
12. 509 U.S. 630, 647 (1993).
13. Ibid. at 679 (Stevens, J., dissenting).
14. 531 U.S. 98 (2000) (footnote and citation omitted).
15. Ibid. at 106.
16. Ibid. at 109.
17. See ibid. at 124, 128 (Stevens, J., joined by Ginsburg and Breyer, J. J., dissenting).
18. *Smith v. Allwright*, 321 U.S. 649, 669 (1944) (Roberts, J., dissenting).
19. For a position of this general kind, see Richard A. Posner, *Breaking the Deadlock: The 2000 Election, the Constitution, and the Courts* (Princeton, NJ/Oxford: Princeton University Press, 2001).
20. *Northern Securities Co. v. United States*, 193 U.S. 197, 400 (1904) (Holmes, J., dissenting).
21. 479 U.S. 189 (1986).
22. 393 U.S. 23 (1968).

23. See, for example, *Smith v. Allwright*, 321 U.S. 649 (1944). Because the Constitution generally does not forbid "private" discrimination, but only discrimination by "state actors," this ruling reflected a judicial determination that political parties are "state actors" insofar as they conduct primary elections, the winners of which are guaranteed access to the ballot in state-run general elections. But the Supreme Court does not treat political parties as state actors for all purposes. The "state action" requirement is further discussed in Chapter Fourteen.
24. 530 U.S. 567 (2000).
25. 424 U.S. 1 (1976).
26. 124 S.Ct. 619 (2003).
27. Ibid. at 666.
28. Ibid. at 695–96.
29. Ibid. at 706.
30. Ibid.

Eleven. Structural Limits on State Power and Resulting Individual Rights

1. *H. P. Hood & Sons, Inc. v. DuMond*, 336 U.S. 525, 537–38 (1949).
2. 73 U.S. 35 (1867).
3. U.S. Constitution, Article I, Section 8, Clause 11.
4. U.S. Constitution, Article I, Section 10, Clause 3.
5. See, for example, *Board of Trustees of the University of Illinois v. United States*, 289 U.S. 48, 56–57 (1933) (holding that congressional power to regulate foreign commerce "may not be limited, qualified, or impeded to any extent by state action").
6. 505 U.S. 504 (1992).
7. 437 U.S. 518 (1978).
8. *Corfield v. Coryell*, No. 6 F. Cas. 546, 3230, 551 (C.C.E.D. Pa. 1823).
9. 436 U.S. 371 (1978).
10. See *United Building & Construction Trades Council v. Mayor and Council of Camden*, 465 U.S. 208 (1984).
11. This situation is highly unusual. Under *Marbury v. Madison*, 5 U.S. 137 (1803), Supreme Court rulings of constitutional invalidity normally bind the other branches of government. To be reconciled with *Marbury*, judicial interpretations of the dormant Commerce Clause should probably be thought of as constitutionally mandated "default" rules, to be applied unless Congress legislates to the contrary. See Laurence H. Tribe, *Constitutional Choices* (Cambridge, MA/London: Harvard University Press, 1985), 29–44.
12. *Wyoming v. Oklahoma*, 502 U.S. 437, 454–55 (1992) (quoting *New Energy Co. of Indiana v. Limbach*, 486 U.S. 269, 273–74 [1988]).
13. 294 U.S. 511, 522 (1935).

14. See *Maine v. Taylor*, 477 U.S. 131 (1986) (upholding a state prohibition against the importation of baitfish likely to contaminate Maine baitfish stocks).

15. See, for example, *Pike v. Bruce Church, Inc.*, 397 U.S. 137, 142 (1970): "Where [a state] statute regulates even-handedly to effectuate a legitimate local public interest, and its effects on interstate commerce are only incidental, it will be upheld unless the burden imposed on such commerce is clearly excessive in relation to the putative local benefits. If a legitimate local purpose is found, then the question [whether the regulation should be invalidated] becomes one of degree. And the extent of the burden that will be tolerated will . . . depend on the nature of the local interest involved, and on whether it could be promoted as well with a lesser impact on interstate activities."

16. See Donald H. Regan, "The Supreme Court and State Protectionism: Making Sense of the Dormant Commerce Clause," 84 *Michigan Law Review* 1091 (1986).

17. 447 U.S. 429 (1980).

18. See *New Energy Co. of Indiana v. Limbach*, 486 U.S. 269, 278 (1988) (observing that the dormant Commerce Clause "does not prohibit all state action designed to give its residents an advantage in the marketplace" and that "[d]irect subsidization of domestic industry does not ordinarily run afoul of [the constitutional] prohibition").

19. See *West Lynn Creamery, Inc. v. Healy*, 512 U.S. 186 (1994) (invalidating a state subsidy scheme that, in effect although not in form, called for the rebate of special taxes imposed to fund the scheme to in-staters but not to out-of-staters). Academic literature reconsidering the traditional line between permitted subsidies and forbidden discriminatory taxes includes Dan T. Coenen, "Business Subsidies and the Dormant Commerce Clause," 107 *Yale Law Journal* 965 (1998), and Peter D. Enrich, "Saving the States from Themselves: Commerce Clause Constraints on State Tax Incentives for Business," 110 *Harvard Law Review* 377 (1996).

Twelve. The Constitution in War and Emergency

1. 372 U.S. 144, 160 (1963).

2. The relevant developments are succinctly summarized in Daniel Farber, *Lincoln's Constitution* (Chicago/London: University of Chicago Press, 2003), Chap. 6.

3. U.S. Constitution, Article I, Section 8, Clause 11.

4. U.S. Constitution, Article I, Section 8, Clauses 12 and 13.

5. Message of Abraham Lincoln to the Senate and House of Representatives, May 26, 1862, reprinted in Abraham Lincoln, *Selected Speeches and Writings 1859–1865*, (New York: The Library of America, 1989), 325–6.

6. U.S. Constitution, Article I, Section 9, Clause 7.

7. U.S. Constitution, Article I, Section 9, Clause 2.

8. I adapt this line of questions from Sanford Levinson, "Was The Emancipation Proclamation Constitutional? Do We/Should We Care What the Answer Is?," 2001 *University of Illinois Law Review* 1135.

9. An excellent recent discussion is Farber, *Lincoln's Constitution*, Chap. 6. See also James G. Randall, *Constitutional Problems Under Lincoln*, rev. ed. (Urbana, IL: University of Illinois Press, 1951; originally published in 1926).

10. "An Act to Increase the Pay of the Privates in the Regular Army and of the Volunteers in the Service of the United States, and for Other Purposes," Chap. 63, Section 3, 12 Stat. 326, 326 (1861).

11. See *The Prize Cases*, 67 U.S. 635 (1863).

12. See *Ex parte Merryman*, 17 F. Cas. 144 (C.C.D.Md. 1861).

13. See Abraham Lincoln, "Message to Congress in Special Session of July 4, 1861," reprinted in Lincoln, *Speeches and Writings 1859–65*, at 252–3.

14. *McCulloch v. Maryland*, 17 U.S. 316, 407 (1819).

15. John E. Nowak and Ronald D. Rotunda, *Constitutional Law* (St. Paul, MN: West Group, 2000), 255.

16. See, for example, John C. Yoo, "The Continuation of Politics by Other Means: The Original Understanding of War Powers," 84 *California Law Review* 167, 242 (1996). The contrary view is that although the President has inherent constitutional authority to repel sudden attacks and to protect lives imminently at risk, Congress possesses exclusive constitutional power to commit the country to war, whether declared or undeclared. See, for example, John Hart Ely, *War and Responsibility: Constitutional Lessons of Vietnam and Its Aftermath* (Princeton, NJ: Princeton University Press, 1993), 3–10, Harold Hongju Koh, *The National Security Constitution: Sharing Power After the Iran-Contra Affair* (New Haven, CT/London: Yale University Press, 1990), 74–7.

17. 87 Stat. 555, Public Law No. 93–148, 93d Cong. (H. J. Res. 542, adopted over presidential veto on Nov. 7, 1973).

18. For discussion of whether the existence of "war" is a political question, see the concurring opinions in *Campbell v. Clinton*, 203 F. 3d 19 (D.C. Cir. 2000).

19. *Youngstown Sheet & Tube Co. v. Sawyer*, 343 U.S. 579 (1952).

20. See *Yakus v. United States*, 321 U.S. 414 (1944).

21. U.S. Constitution, Article I, Section 9, Clause 2.

22. See generally Richard H. Fallon, Jr., "Individual Rights and the Powers of Government," 27 *Georgia Law Review* 343 (1993).

23. See generally Mark E. Neely, Jr., *The Fate of Liberty: Abraham Lincoln and Civil Liberties* (New York/Oxford: Oxford University Press, 1991).

24. 249 U.S. 47, 52 (1919).

25. Earl Warren, "The Bill of Rights and the Military," 37 *New York University Law Review* 181, 192–3 (1962).

26. 323 U.S. 214 (1944).
27. David Halberstam, *The Fifties* (New York: Villard Books, 1993), 417–18.
28. See, for example, David Cole, "The New McCarthyism: Repeating History in the War on Terrorism," 38 *Harvard Civil Rights-Civil Liberties Law Review* 1 (2003).
29. Richard A. Posner, "The Truth about Our Liberties," 13 *The Responsive Community* 4, 5 (2002).
30. William H. Rehnquist, *All The Laws But One: Civil Liberties in Wartime* (New York: Knopf, 1998).
31. The Supreme Court invalidated a declaration of martial law in Hawaii, which was then a territory rather than a state, in *Duncan v. Kahanamoku*, 327 U.S. 304 (1946).
32. Rehnquist, *All The Laws But One*, 224–5.
33. See "Detention, Treatment, and Trial of Certain Non-Citizens in the War Against Terrorism," 66 *Federal Register* 57833 (Nov. 13, 2001).
34. See, for example, *United States v. Verdugo-Urquidez*, 494 U.S. 259 (1990); *Johnson v. Eisentrager*, 339 U.S. 763 (1950).
35. For a survey of the rights of aliens, see Gerald L. Neuman, *Strangers to the Constitution: Immigrants, Borders, and Fundamental Law* (Princeton, NJ: Princeton University Press, 1996).
36. See, for example, *Mathews v. Diaz*, 426 U.S. 67 (1976).
37. Ibid. at 81, n.17 (internal quotation omitted and emphasis added).
38. See generally David Cole, "Enemy Aliens," 54 *Stanford Law Review* 953 (2002).
39. See generally Richard H. Fallon, Jr., Daniel J. Meltzer, and David L. Shapiro, *Hart & Wechsler's The Federal Courts and the Federal System*, 5th ed. (New York: Foundation Press, 2003), 407–16.
40. The United States relied heavily on military courts to maintain law in occupied Germany and Japan in the aftermath of World War II.
41. The prohibition against preventive detention is not absolute. The Supreme Court has upheld the nonpunitive detention of people with mental illness who pose a threat to themselves or others, including, after the expiration of a criminal sentence, "a limited subclass of dangerous persons" who have committed "a sexually violent offense" and who suffer from "a mental abnormality or personality disorder" portending "predatory acts of sexual violence." *Kansas v. Hendricks*, 521 U.S. 346, 357 (1997) (internal quotations omitted). See also *United States v. Salerno*, 481 U.S. 739 (1987) (holding that a person accused of a crime and found to pose a sufficient threat of danger to the community may be denied release on bail pending trial).
42. See *Hamdi v. Rumsfeld*, 316 F. 3d 450 (4th Cir. 2003); *Padilla v. Bush*, 233 F. Supp. 2d 564 (S.D.N.Y. 2002), *remanded*, 352 F. 3d 695 (2d Cir. 2003).
43. For discussion, see Rehnquist, *All The Laws But One*.
44. See ibid.

45. Abraham Lincoln, "Message to Congress in Special Session of July 4, 1861," reprinted in Lincoln, *Speeches and Writings, 1859–65*, at 246.

Thirteen. The Reach of the Constitution and Congress's Enforcement Power

1. 109 U.S. 3, 17 (1883).
2. 521 U.S. 507, 519 (1997).
3. See *Richardson v. McKnight*, 521 U.S. 399 (1997).
4. See *Rendell-Baker v. Kohn*, 457 U.S. 830 (1982).
5. See, for example, *Georgia v. McCollum*, 505 U.S. 42 (1992); *Edmonson v. Leesville Concrete Co., Inc.*, 500 U.S. 614 (1991).
6. See *Jackson v. Metropolitan Edison Co.*, 419 U.S. 345 (1974).
7. See generally David P. Currie, "Positive and Negative Constitutional Rights," 53 *University of Chicago Law Review* 864 (1986).
8. See *Estelle v. Gamble*, 429 U.S. 97 (1976).
9. See, for example, Charles L. Black, Jr., "Further Reflections on the Constitutional Justice of Livelihood," 86 *Columbia Law Review* 1103 (1986); Frank I. Michelman, "On Protecting the Poor Through the Fourteenth Amendment," 83 *Harvard Law Review* 7 (1969).
10. See *Kramer v. Union Free School District* No. 15, 395 U.S. 621 (1969).
11. 411 U.S. 1 (1973).
12. 410 U.S. 113 (1973).
13. 347 U.S. 483 (1954).
14. 5 U.S. 137, 178 (1803).
15. 384 U.S. 641 (1966).
16. 360 U.S. 45 (1959).
17. *Katzenbach v. Morgan*, 384 U.S. at 652 (quoting *Yick Wo v. Hopkins*, 118 U.S. 356, 370 (1886)).
18. Ibid. at 654.
19. See, for example, Douglas Laycock, "RFRA, Congress, and the Ratchet," 56 *Montana Law Review* 145, 155 (1995).
20. *Katzenbach v. Morgan*, 384 U.S. at 651, n.10.
21. On the surface, the ratchet theory might appear inconsistent with *Marbury v. Madison*, 5 U.S. 137 (1803), and especially with its celebrated assertion that "[i] is emphatically the province and duty of the judicial branch to say what the law is." Ibid. at 177. But *Marbury* need not be read to hold anymore than that courts must determine whether legislative enactments comport with the Constitution. If Section 5 of the Fourteenth Amendment gives Congress a limited power to interpret constitutional guarantees, *Marbury* requires only that the Court assess whether legislation enacted under Section 5 comes within the Section 5 grant of congressional power.
22. 521 U.S. 507 (1997).
23. 494 U.S. 872 (1990).

24. *City of Boerne v. Flores,* 521 U.S. at 527–28.
25. Ibid. at 508.
26. Ibid. at 533.
27. Ibid. at 532.
28. See, for example, *Kimel v. Florida Board of Regents,* 528 U.S. 62 (2000). There may be an exception for cases in which Congress legislates to remedy or forestall discrimination (such as race- and gender-based discrimination) that would itself trigger heightened judicial scrutiny. See *Nevada Department of Human Resources v. Hibbs,* 123 S.Ct. 1972 (2003).
29. 531 U.S. 98 (2000).

Fourteen. Conclusion

1. *McCulloch v. Maryland,* 17 U.S. 316, 415 (1819).
2. See generally David A. Strauss, "The Irrelevance of Constitutional Amendments," 114 *Harvard Law Review* 1457 (2001).
3. *McCulloch v. Maryland,* 17 U.S. 316, 415 (1819) (emphasis added).
4. *Terminiello v. Chicago,* 337 U.S. 1, 37 (1949) (Jackson, J., dissenting).
5. 410 U.S. 113 (1973).
6. The decision came in *Prigg v. Pennsylvania,* 41 U.S. 539 (1842).
7. See *Dred Scott v. Sandford,* 60 U.S. 393 (1857).
8. See Abraham Lincoln, "First Inaugural Address," March 4, 1861, reprinted in Abraham Lincoln, *Speeches and Writings, 1859–65* (New York: The Library of America, 1989), 215, 221.
9. See generally Ronald Dworkin, *Law's Empire* (Cambridge, MA/London: The Belknap Press of Harvard University Press, 1986).
10. *Marbury v. Madison,* 5 U.S. 137, 163 (1803).
11. 387 U.S. 483 (1954).
12. See Robert A. Dahl, *A Preface to Democratic Theory* (Chicago/London: University of Chicago Press, 1956), 109–12.
13. Finley Peter Dunne, *Mr. Dooley's Opinions* (New York: Harper & Brothers, 1906), 26.
14. See *Lawrence v. Texas,* 123 S.Ct. 2472 (2003).
15. *United States v. Schwimmer,* 279 U.S. 644, 655 (1929) (Holmes, J., dissenting).

Index

abortion, 144, 195, 197, 201. *See also specific decisions*
Abrams v. United States (1919), 36–37
absolutists, 46
Adams, John Q., 11
advertising, 49, 50, 51
affirmative action, 94, 107, 108, 115, 122, 123. *See also* equal protection; *specific groups*
after-the-fact punishments, 32
aliens, 250. *See also* citizenship
Allegheny County v. ACLU (1989), 304n.6
American Supreme Court, The (McCloskey), xi
antisubordinationist view, 125
Articles of Confederation, 2–4
association, freedom of, 53, 141
autonomy, privacy and, 142

Bailey v. Richardson (1950), 309n.28
Baker v. Carr (1962), 318n.33
Bakke decision. *See Regents of the University of California v. Bakke* (1978),
Baldwin v. Fish and Game Commission (1975), 229
Baldwin v. G.A.F. Seelig, Inc. (1935), 232
Bank of the United States, 17
bankruptcy laws, 77
Barron, David, xiv
Beard, Charles, 75
Betts v. Brady (1942), 308n.3
Bickel, Alexander, 122, 195–196, 200
Bill of Rights, 7–8, 297n. *See specific amendments*
Bipartisan Campaign Act, 222–223

Black, Charles, 116
Black, Hugo, 46–47, 85, 117, 174
Blackmun, Harry, 148
blanket primary law, 220
Board of Regents v. Roth (1972), 309n.32
Boerne, City of, v. Flores (1997), 264, 265, 266, 268
Bowers v. Hardwick (1986), 134, 147
Boyscouts of America v. Dale (2000), 55, 304n.7
Brandeis, Louis, 37–38, 41, 276
Brandenburg v. Ohio (1969), 39–40, 41, 45, 246
Brennan, William, 263, 264
Breyer, Steven, 217, 299n.4
Britain, legislation in, 9
broadcast media, 51, 52
Brown v. Board of Education (1954), 22–23, 108–109, 118, 119, 120, 121, 122, 123–124, 137, 198, 256, 260, 274, 275
Brzonkala case. *See U.S. vs. Morrison*
Buckley v. Valeo (1976), 221, 222
Burger, Warren, 47, 97, 98, 145, 148, 180, 305n.18
Bush, George W., 145
Bush v. Gore (2000), xv, xvii, xviii, 15, 25, 216, 217, 218, 266

cable television, 52–53
Calder v. Bull (1798), 77
California Democratic Party v. Jones (2000), 219
Capitol Square Review and Advisory Board v. Pinette (1995), 305n.20
Cardozo, Benjamin, 171–172

327

Carlin, George, 52
Carolene Products case, 94–95, 124–125, 137
case or controversy requirement, 201
Catholics, 65
censorship, 32, 42
Central Hudson Gas & Electric Corp. v. Public Service Commission (1981), 49
Champion v. Ames (1903), 163
Chaplinsky v. New Hampshire (1942), 45
Chemerinsky, Erwin, xiv
children, 48, 52, 73, 101, 153–154, 160, 164. *See also* education
Chopper, Jesse, xiv, 313n.18
churches. *See* religion
Cippolone v. Liggett Group, Inc (1992), 227
citizenship, 8, 79, 80–81, 250
civil rights, 117, 120, 121–122, 165, 168, 275, 310n.4. *See also specific decisions*, 117, 120, 121–122, 165, 168, 275, 310n.4
Civil War, xx, 8, 19–21, 35, 76, 80–81, 109, 175, 185, 237, 244, 246, 252, 262, 267, 272
classifications, governmental, 112
Clay, aka Ali, v. United States (1971), 57
clear and present danger, 35–36, 37, 40
Clinton, Bill, 132
Clinton v. New York (1998), 182–183
Coase, Ronald, 50
Cohen v. California (1971), 44, 45–46
commerce clause, 84, 158, 159, 165, 166, 167, 169, 171, 192, 193, 232, 233, 269, 314n.4
commercial speech, 48
common law, 199–200
communes, 114
Communist Party, 39
compelling interest, 69, 70, 71
Congress, U.S., 4
    Constitution and, 5, 6, 17, 18, 254
    federal regulations, 170
    historic practices, 1
    House of Representatives, 4
    powers of, 5, 157, 172, 254
    regulation of, 168
    Senate, 4, 276
    spending power, 171

state governments and, 168
Warren court and, 93–94
See also specific topics, decisions,
conservatism, 21, 23–24, 25, 47, 50, 65, 89, 105, 141, 145, 162, 167, 169–170, 195–196, 216, 217, 259, 308n.39
Constitution, U.S.
    amendments to, 6, 7, 288. *See also specific amendments*
    Article I, 5, 192, 283
    Article II, 5–6, 283
    Article III, 6, 10, 200–201, 286
    Article IV, 6, 79, 101, 110, 228, 229, 287
    Article V, 6, 287
    Article VI, 6, 10, 226, 288
    Article VII, 6–7, 288
    Articles of Confederation and, 3–4
    Bill of Rights, 7–8, 297n. *See also specific amendments*
    categorical limits, 249
    citizens and. *See* citizenship
    Congress, 6, 9, 17, 18, 254. *See* Congress, U.S.
    Constitutional Convention, 3–4, 5, 7, 10, 14, 278, 300n.6
    Court and. *See* Supreme Court
    discrimination and. *See* discrimination
    due process and. *See* due process
    as economic document, 75
    equal protection. *See* equal protection
    Executive and. *See* Executive
    government and, 8
    as higher law, 9
    historical, 2
    interpretation of, 1–2, 15, 16–17, 18–19, 193, 200
    judicial review, 9, 14–15, 16, 18–19. *See* judicial review
    limitations of, xix
    meaning of, 193
    politics and, 10, 18–19, 274, 300n.8
    Preamble, 5, 278
    race and. *See* race
    ratification of, 7
    reach of, 254
    rhetoric and, 5
    text of, 278
    women and. *See* women

See also specific issues, topics
Continental Congress, 2, 4
contracts, 76, 77–78, 86
Corfield v. Coryell (1823), 79
Corporation of Presiding Bishop v. Amos
    (1987), 306n.48
countermajoritarianism, 195–196
Craig v. Boren (1976), 130–131, 132
Crandall v. Nevada (1876), 225
criminal procedures, 92, 93, 94–95, 96,
    138, 139, 140

Dahl, Robert, 274
Dames & Moore v. Regan (1981), 178
Davis v. Bandemer (1986), 212, 213
death, right to, 151–152
Debs v. United States (1919), 35–36, 39,
    40
delegated powers, 178
Democrats, 216, 219
Dennis v. United States (1951), 38–39, 40
Denver Area Educational
    Telecommunications Consortium,
    Inc. v. FCC (1996), 304n.61
Dickerson v. United States (2000), 98
discrimination, 6, 8, 108, 114, 121,
    123–125, 130, 133, 204, 228, 230,
    262, 302n.6, 320n.23. *See also* equal
    protection; *specific decisions, topics*
dissent, freedom of, 36, 43
domestic affairs, 178 .
dormant commerce clause, 231, 232,
    234, 321n.18
Douglas, William, 46, 139, 142
draft cards, 42
Dred Scott v. Sanford (1857), 20
drug stores, 48–49
drugs, prescription, 48–49
drunk driving, 131
due process, 21, 76, 81, 85–86, 89, 91,
    100, 195, 257, 262
    administrative proceedings and, 101
    economic legislation, 85–86
    Fifth Amendment, 270
    Fourteenth Amendment, 93
    Lochner era, 76, 112
    privileges and immunities, 81
    property rights and, 85
    substantive due process, 81
Dunne, Finley P., 274

Dworkin, Ronald, 193, 318n.21
dying, rights of, 151

Eastern Enterprises v. Apfel (1998),
    307n.27
economic legislation, 85–86
education, 61, 62, 66–67, 108–109,
    126–127, 157, 167, 260, 305n.24
Effective Death Penalty Act (1996),
    309n.17
Eighteenth Amendment, 293
Eighth Amendment, 7, 139, 290
Eisenstadt v. Baird (1972), 143
elections, xv–xvi, 97, 207, 216, 259
    districting and, 212, 214
    finance regulation, 220
    minor party candidates, 219
    primaries, 219
    speech and, 220
    voting and, 210, 212, 214, 216, 218
    See also Bush v. Gore,
Eleventh Amendment, 290
Ely, John Hart, 39, 199
Emancipation Proclamation, 175
emergency, 237. *See also* war
Emergency Price Control Act, 179
Employment Division v. Smith (1990),
    70, 71, 73, 264, 265, 267
environmental protection statutes, 88
Epperson v. Arkansas (1968), 61
equal protection, xviii, xx, 8, 109, 110,
    123, 124–125, 260, 262, 269
    affirmative action. *See* affirmative
        action
    antisubordinationists and, 125
    classifications and, 112
    conservatives and, 217
    discrimination and. *See* discrimination,
    districting and, 211, 215
    Lochner era, 112
    minorities and, 125
    peremptory challenges, 256
    Plessy and, 115
    positive rights and, 258
    race and. *See* race
Espionage Act (1917), 34, 36–37, 58, 244
establishment clause, 58, 305n.9
    accommodationists, 60
    free exercise clause and, 72
    introduction to, 59

establishment clause, (*cont.*)
  neutrality rationale, 67
  public education and, 62
  separationism, 60, 62
Everson v. Board of Education (1957),
  304n.8
exclusionary rule, 96
Executive, 173, 189
  appointments and, 11, 184
  Article II and, 5–6
  Cabinet and, 186
  delegated powers, 178
  executive privilege, 189
  historic practices, 1
  impeachment, 184, 301n.15
  powers of, 173
  presidential election, xv–xvi
  removals, 184
  unitary executive theory, 184
  veto powers, 5–6, 180
  war powers, 5–6, 237, 240, 241, 271,
    322n.16. *See* war
  *See also specific administrations,
    decisions*
exemptions, religions and, 71, 72–73
express preemption, 226–227
expressive organizations, 42, 54

Fair Labor Standards Act, 168–169
fair procedures, rights to, 91
family, rights and, 152
farmers, 165
FCC v. Pacifica Foundation (1978), 51
Federal Communications Commission
  (FCC), 51
Federal Corrupt Practices Act, 220
Federal Election Campaign Act, 220,
  221, 222
Federal Reserve Board, 187, 188
Federal Trade Commission, 186
federalism, 10, 11, 168, 169, 301n.14
Federalist Papers, 10, 171
Feingold, Russell, 222–223
Fifteenth Amendment, 8, 292
Fifth Amendment, 7, 75, 76, 87, 110,
  262, 270, 289
  due process clause. *See* due process
  takings clause, 76, 87, 88, 89, 90
First Amendment, 7, 34, 36, 37, 46, 58,
  257, 288

absolutists, 46
Court and, 32
Debs and, 36
Espionage Act, 34
establishment clause. *See* establishment
  clause
free exercise clause. *See* free exercise
  clause
free speech. *See* speech, freedom of
literalists and, 46
flag-burning, 42, 43
Fletcher v. Peck (1810), 76–77
Florida Supreme Court, xvi–xvii, xviii,
  216
food stamps, 114
foreign affairs, 177, 186
formalism, 175, 176–177, 182
Fourteenth Amendment, 8, 76, 78, 93,
  110, 115, 262, 263, 265, 291
  due process, 93. *See* due process
  equal protection, 110. *See* equal
    protection, 110
  privileges and immunities, 79. *See*
    privileges and immunities, 79
Fourth Amendment, 7, 289
Frankfurter, Felix, 118, 211
free exercise clause, 58, 67, 264–265,
  267
  exemptions and, 70–71
  Smith and, 71, 73
free speech. *See* speech, freedom of
Frontiero v. Richardson (1973), 130
functionalism, 176–177
fundamental rights, 32, 77, 138, 140,
  149–150, 153

gambling, 163
*Garcia v. San Antonio Metropolitan
  Transit Authority* (1985), 169, 170
gay rights, 55, 147
gender issues, 54, 108, 129, 130, 131,
  204
Gerken, Heather, xiv
gerrymandering, 213
Gideon v. Wainright (1963), 95, 98
Ginsburg, Ruth Bader, xx, 129, 130, 132,
  217, 299n.4
Goldberg v. Kelly (1970), 102, 105
Gore, Al, xv. *See Bush v. Gore*
government contracts, 127

Gratz v. Bollinger (2003), 106, 108, 127–128
Great Depression, 21, 164, 197
Griswold v. Connecticut (1965), 142
Grutter v. Bollinger (2003), 128

habeas corpus, 239, 244
Hamilton, Alexander, 10, 171
Hammer v. Dagenhart (1918), 164
Harlan, John Marshall, 116
Hicklin v. Orbeck (1978), 228, 229, 230
Holmes, Oliver Wendell, 33–34, 35, 83, 218, 276
  free speech and, 34, 36, 37
  Great Dissenter, 36–37
  legal mind of, 38
  Lochner and, 83–84, 90
  marketplace of ideas and, 36–37
  regulatory powers and, 88
  Yankee from Olympus, 38
  See also specific decisions
Home Building and Loan Association v. Blaisdell (1934), 86
homosexuality, 43, 55, 108, 133, 135, 147, 275
housing, 120–121
Humphrey's Executor v. United States (1935), 185, 186, 187

Immigration and Naturalization Service v. Chadha (1983), 180
immigration laws, 180, 251
impeachment, 203
implied preemption, 226–227
individual rights, 21, 225, 229, 243
Internet, 53
Interstate Commerce Commission, 163
Iraq war, 241
Islamic faith, 57

Jackson, Robert, xxi, 174, 175, 242–243, 270
Jefferson, Thomas, 190, 202
Johnson, Andrew, 185
judicial review
  Article III and, 6
  constitutionality of, 9–10, 14–15
  Court and, 6, 10, 13, 14
  foundations of, 10
  history of, 19

Marbury and, 13, 14–15, 16
Marshall and, 14–15, 19–20
state judges, 10
Stone and, 94

Katzenbach v. McClung (1964), 165
Katzenbach v. Morgan (1966), 262, 264, 265
Kennedy, Anthony, 135, 146, 149–150
Kimel v. Florida Board of Regents (2000), 325n.28
King, Martin Luther, Jr., 120
Korematsu v. United States (1944), 117, 122, 245
Ku Klux Klan, 39–40, 41, 54

labor, 84, 174
laissez-faire system, 85, 90
Lassiter v. Northampton County Board of Electors (1959), 262–263
League of Nations, 177
Lee v. Weisman (1992), 63
Legal Services Corp. v. Velazquez (2001)
Lemon test, 64
Levinson, Sandy, xiv
libel, 32, 45–46
liberalism, 50, 161, 162
liberty interests, 103
Lincoln, Abraham, 21, 175, 238, 239, 271, 272
line-item veto, 182, 183
literacy, 263
literalists, 46
Lochner v. New York (1905), 21, 22, 76, 82, 83, 140
  aftermath of, 93
  due process and, 76, 112
  equal protection and, 112
  Holmes and, 83–84, 90
  laissez-faire and, 90
  Lochner era, 84, 111, 118, 139, 140, 142, 146–147, 195
  Warren court and, 22–23
Lorillard Tobacco Co. v. Reilly (2001), 50
lotteries, 163
Lucas v. South Carolina Coastal Council (1992), 308n.40

Madison, James, 11–12, 171, 190, 297n
magazines, 51

majority-minority districts, 214, 216
mandamus, writs of, 301n.17
Mapp v. Ohio (1961), 96, 308n.3
Marbury v. Madison (1803), xv, 2, 10,
   17, 173, 190, 202, 262, 320n.11
  Bush v. Gore and, 15
  Court and, 14
  judicial review and, 13, 14–15, 16
  political factors, 12, 15
market participant exception, 234
marketplace of ideas, 36–37
markets, regulation of, 50
Marshall, John, 11, 16, 17, 86, 162, 173,
   240, 270
  contract rights and, 77, 78
  importance of, 18
  judicial review and, 14–15
  Marbury and. *See Marbury v. Madison*
  state laws and, 77
Mathews v. Eldridge (1976), 104
McCain, John, 222–223
McCarthy, Joseph, 39
McCloskey, Robert, xi
*McConnell v. Federal Election
  Commission* (2003), 223, 224
McCulloch v. Maryland (1819), 17, 19,
  86
Meltzer, Daniel, xiv
*Metropolitan School District v.
  Rodriguez* (1973), 259
Michigan, University of, 107, 113,
  128
military service, 34, 57, 145, 179,
  323n.40
Miller v. California (1973), 47, 48, 52
minimum wage, 84
minorities, 94, 124, 125. *See* equal
  protection; *specific groups*
Minow, Martha, xiv
Miranda v. Arizona (1966), 95, 96,
  97–98, 99, 194
Mitchell v. Helms (2000), 66, 67
Mobile v. Bolden (1980), 207, 209, 210,
  214–215
money, 192, 226, 306n.3
Mormon Church, 67–68
Muhammad Ali, 57
Munro v. Socialist Workers' Party (1986),
  219

Myers v. United States (1926), 185

Naim v. Naim (1955), 119
National Association for the
  Advancement of Colored People, 53,
  117
national bank, 17
National League of Cities v. Usery
  (1976), 169, 170, 171
Native American Church, 71
natural rights, 32, 77
necessary and proper clause, 5
neutrality, 67
New Deal programs, 165, 166, 167, 172,
  191
New York v. Ferber (1982), 48
newspapers, 51
Nineteenth Amendment, 8, 293
Ninth Amendment, 7, 290
Nixon, Richard, 23, 47, 97, 189, 190,
  201, 220, 241, 259
Nixon, Walter, 201
non-delegation doctrine, 179

obscenity, 45, 47, 51
O'Connor, Sandra Day, 62–63, 66, 128,
  129, 146, 152, 223, 303n.56
Ogden v. Saunders (1827), 77, 78, 86
originalists, xii, 196–197, 199–200

pain, rights and, 151–152
Palko v. Connecticut (1937), 308n.3
Palmore v. Sidoti (1984), 120–121
paper currency, 192
parents, children and, 153–154
parliamentary sovereignty, 9
parochial schools, 64, 66
Parsons, Ed, xiv
Pearl Harbor, 117
Pennsylvania Coal Co. v. Mahon (1922),
  87
peremptory challenges, 256
Persian Gulf War, 241
peyote, 71
Pike v. Bruce Church Inc. (1970),
  321n.15
Planned Parenthood v. Casey (1992), 146
Pless v. Ferguson (1896), 115, 116, 118,
  121, 122

political issues, 10, 274, 300n.8
political question doctrine, 242
poll tax, 259
polygamy, 67–68
pornography, 46, 48, 160, 303n.48
Posner, Richard, 245
post-deprivation hearings, 102
positive rights, 128, 138, 257, 258
poverty, 95
Powell, Lewis, 126, 128, 260
precedent, 70
predominant factor test, 215
preemption, statutory, 226–227
Printz v. United States (1997), 171
prior restraint, 32
privacy, 142
privileges and immunities clause, 6, 79,
    81, 110, 227, 229
  citizenship and, 80
  due process and, 81
  Fourteenth Amendment and, 79,
    81
  individual rights and, 229
  rights and, 101
  states and, 79, 80–81, 228, 230
procedural rights, 92, 100. *See also*
    specific decisions
Progressive Era, 82
property rights, 77, 85, 87, 88, 90, 103,
    153
property taxes, 259
protectionism, 232, 233
Protestants, 65
protestors, 43
public schools. *See* education

Quick Bear v. Leupp (1908), 304n.7

race, 94, 108, 115, 116, 122, 123, 275
  affirmative action and. *See* affirmative
    action,
  Constitution and, 114
  discrimination and. *See* discrimination,
  equal protection and. *See* equal
    protection
  gender and, 130
  interracial marriage, 120–121
  minority groups, 107
  quota systems, 126

racism, 41, 45, 53–54, 110
slavery, 20, 110, 255, 262
  voting and, 207
  women and, 157
radio, 51, 52
ratchet theory, 264, 265, 324n.21
rational basis test, 111, 114, 132, 139,
    310n.8
Reagan, Ronald, 62–63, 145
reasoned judgment model, 267, 268
Reconstruction period, 109, 120, 262,
    266
Red Lion Broadcasting Co. v. FCC
    (1969), 51, 52
Reeves, Inc. v. Stake (1980), 234
Regan, Donald, 233
*Regents of the University of California v.
    Bakke* (1978), 125–126, 127–128
regulatory legislation, 88
Rehnquist, William H., 24, 49, 97, 151,
    166, 169–170, 246, 303n.56
religion, 58, 59, 94
  accommodationists, 60
  Amish groups, 69
  conservative coalition, 65
  establishment clause. *See* establishment
    clause
  exemptions, 63–64, 70, 72–73
  free exercise clause, 59
  freedom of, 7, 57
  governmental aid to, 63, 71
  Islamic faith, 57
  minorities and, 73
  public schools and, 61
  states and, 60
  Supreme Court and, 60
Religious Freedom Restoration Act, 71,
    264, 265, 266
Reno v. American Civil Liberties Union
    (1997), 53
Republicans, 10, 11, 219
revisionist works, 301n.26
Revolutionary War (U.S.), 2
Reynolds v. Sims (1964), 210, 211
Reynolds v. United States (1878), 67–68
Richmond v. J.A. Croson Co. (1989),
    127–128
right, vs. privilege, 101, 102
Roberts, Owen, 22, 191

Roberts v. United States Jaycees (1984), 54, 55
Rocker, John, 254, 257
Roe v. Wade (1973), 144, 145, 146, 195, 197, 256, 260, 272
Roman Catholic Church, 64
Romer v. Evans (1996), 134
Roosevelt, Franklin, xii, 21, 22, 84, 85, 164–165, 191, 197
Roth v. United States (1957), 46
Rust v. Sullivan (1991)
Rutledge, John, 203

Sabbatarianism, 69
Saenz v. Roe (1999), 307n.17
Scalia, Antonin, 70, 150, 183, 196, 220, 315n.28
Schauer, Fred, xiv
Schenck v. United States (1919), 34, 35, 36, 39, 40, 244
Schlanger, Margo, xiv
schools. *See* education,
Second Amendment, 7, 289
sedition, 32
separation of powers, 175
separationism, 62
September 11 attacks, 247
Seventeenth Amendment, 293
Seventh Amendment, 7, 290
Shaw v. Reno (1993), 215
Shervert v. Verner (1963), 69
Shreveport Case (1914), 163
Simpson, O. J., 99
Sixteenth Amendment, 8, 293
Sixth Amendment, 7, 289
Skinner v. Oklahoma (1942), 138, 139, 142, 144
Slaughter-House Cases (1872), 79, 80–81, 82, 111, 140
slavery, 20, 110, 255, 262
Smith v. Alright (1944), 320n.23
Social Security, 102, 104, 105, 172
Souter, David, 146, 217, 306n.34
speech, freedom of, 7, 31, 244–245, 246
  Black and, 46–47
  crowded theater argument, 35
  expressive conduct, 42
  First Amendment and, 32
  Holmes and, 34, 36, 37

  markets and, 48, 50
  modern doctrine, 32–33
  obscenity and, 45
  offensive speech, 44
  terrorism and, 31
  war and, 36
states, 8, 164
  appeals from, 10
  citizenship and, 80
  Civil War and. *See* Civil War
  constitutions of, 261
  contracts. *See* contracts
  discriminatory taxes, 321n.19
  individual rights and, 225
  interstate commerce, 163, 232, 233
  judicial review and, 10. *See* judicial review, 10
  limits on, 225
  Marshall and, 77
  out-of-state competitors, 233, 234
  privileges and immunities, 79, 80–81, 228, 230
  regulation of, 168
  religion and, 60
  rights of, 8
  role of, xix, 7
  state action doctrine, 254
  state judges, 10, 261
  subsidies and, 321n.19
statutory preemption, 102, 226–227
Steel Seizure case, 182, 243
Stevens, John Paul, 215, 217, 223, 299n.4
Stewart, Potter, 46, 68, 153–154
Stone, Harlan Fiske, 94, 139
Stone v. Graham (1980)
strict scrutiny test, 69, 121, 153
strikes, 174
Sturges v. Crowinshield (1819), 76, 77
suicide, 151
supremacy clause, 6, 226
Supreme Court, 21, 89, 93, 115
  anti-regulatory stance, 21
  Article III and, 6
  case selection, 194
  conservatism. *See* conservatism
  consistency of, 315n.11
  decision-making in, xiii
  doctrinal innovation, 94–95
  First Amendment and, 32

first women on, 62–63, 132
interpretation and, xii, xx–xxi, 2, 9, 16
judicial review. *See* judicial review
jurisdiction and, 12, 13, 189, 191, 194, 200
liberalism and, 50. *See* liberalism
mandamus and, 13
New Deal and, 164, 165
politics and, xx–xxi, 274
role of, xii–xiii, 122

Taft–Hartley Act, 174, 176
Taft, William Howard, 185
takings clause, 76, 87, 88, 89, 90, 307n.27
Taney, Roger, 239
taxation, 111–112, 226
Teague v. Lane (1989), 309n.17
television, 51, 52
Tenth Amendment, 7, 18, 158, 290
Tenure of Office Act, 185
terrorism, 31, 40–41, 247, 250
Texas v. Johnson (1989), 43
Thanksgiving holiday, 59
Third Amendment, 7, 243, 289
Thirteenth Amendment, 8, 76, 78, 79, 81, 110, 115, 255, 262, 263, 265, 291
Thomas, Clarence, 168, 196
tobacco products, 50
Tocqueville, Alexis de, xix–xx
travel, right to, 141, 165
treason, 16
trial, 91
Troxel v. Gransville (2000), 153
Truman, Harry, 117, 174
truth model, 267
Twelfth Amendment, 290
Twentieth Amendment, 294
Twenty-Fifth Amendment, 296
Twenty-First Amendment, 294
Twenty-Fourth Amendment, 296
Twenty-Second amendment, 8
Twenty-Second Amendment, 8, 295
Twenty-Seventh Amendment, 8, 297
Twenty-Sixth Amendment, 297
Twenty-Third Amendment, 295

United States Department of Agriculture v. Moreno (1973), 113

United States v. Carolene Products (1938), 94, 136
United States v. Causby (1946), 87
United States v. Eichman (1990), 43
United States v. Lopez (1995), 167, 170
United States v. Morrison (2000), 157, 158, 159, 167, 170
United States v. O'Brien (1968), 42, 44
United States v. Virginia (1996), 132, 133

Vacco v. Quill, 151
Versailles, Treaty of, 177
veto powers, 5–6, 180
Vietnam War, 42, 44, 57, 202
Vinson, Fred M., 118
Violence Against Women Act, 157, 158, 196
Virginia Military Institute, 133
Virginia State Board of Pharmacy v. Virginia Citizens Consumer Council (1976), 48–49
voucher programs, 67

wages, 165
Wallace v. Jaffree (1985), 62, 304n.5
Walz v. Tax Commission (1970), 64
war, 38, 237, 240
free speech and, 36
individual rights and, 243
inflation and, 179
laws of, 251
political issues and, 322n.18
terrorism and, 247
war criminals, 251
war powers, 241, 242, 322n.16
Warren, Earl, 22–23, 93–95, 97–98, 105, 118–119, 195, 245, 259, 274, 276
Washington, Bushrod, 79
Washington, George, 59, 79, 203
Washington v. Davis (1976), 122, 123, 208
Washington v. Glucksberg (1997), 151, 152
Weinreb, Lloyd, xiv
welfare, 102, 104
Welsh v. United States (1970), 304n.4
West Coast Hotel Co. v. Parrish (1937), 84, 85

White, Byron, 214
Whitney v. California (1957), 38, 41
Williams v. Rhodes (1968), 219
Wisconsin v. Yoder (1972), 68
women, 5, 84, 129, 130, 144, 157, 158, 204
World War I, 244

World War II, 117, 179, 246

Yakus v. United States (1944), 179
Youngstown Sheet & Tube Co. v. Sawyer (1952), 174, 242–243

Zelman v. Simmons-Harris (2002), 66, 67